SUSPICIOUS LOOKING PACKAGES

THE BOMB SQUAD: A CRIME STORY

GREGORY DELAURENTIS

Copyright © 2024 by Gregory Delaurentis

All rights reserved.

No part of this book may be reproduced in any form or by any electronic or mechanical means, including information storage and retrieval systems, without written permission from the author, except for the use of brief quotations in a book review.

Cover Design by JD Smith

Title Production by The BookWhisperer

ISBN (eBook): 978-0-9891857-9-0
ISBN (Paperback): 979-8-9909240-0-0
ISBN (Hardcover): 979-8-9909240-1-7

Dedicated to all those who supported me in the long making of this book, and a double thanks to the Brooklyn Public Library on-line. You've made information free so that the most important commodity—knowledge—can be distributed freely.

"Not only was the original manuscript good, hectic, and kaleidoscopic, it was also unpublishable. Henry had given free rein to a furious unraveling of passions—erotic scenes and obscene stories that no publisher, neither in France nor elsewhere, would dare to print. Even Anaïs, who recognized the mark of Henry's genius, grumbled about certain passages she found particularly crude. Refusing categorically to edit out these passages, Henry attempted to justify himself. He was trying to write as a man, and to be true to his art he could suppress nothing. Henry and Anaïs would fail to find a publisher."

HENRY MILLER: THE PARIS YEARS,
BRASSAÏ - PAGE 107

I'm not comparing myself to Henry Miller in his writing of Tropic of Cancer...just my chances of publication.

GREGORY DELAURENTIS

"All suspicious-looking packages must be considered by you men to be deadly machines of death, full of dynamite and shrapnel. Remember, you don't have to die to prove your courage. When you are called upon to look at a package, take it to the most secluded spot available. Keep others away. Get away from it yourselves. NOTIFY THE BOMB SQUAD. Remember, you are not running away. You are simply following the instructions of the head of this department. You owe it to yourself, your family and the city."

POLICE COMMISSIONER LEWIS JOSEPH "HONEST COP" VALENTINE, 1940

PREFACE

"The end of the human race will be that it will eventually die of civilization."

RALPH WALDO EMERSON

Primarily, I am a writer of fiction.

One day, while reading a newspaper article, I came across the interesting case of George P. Metesky, the Mad Bomber. I was amazed that New York had experienced a bombing terrorist once before. I knew virtually nothing about the history of indomitable Gotham and had no idea that we'd had a homegrown terrorist long before Timothy McVeigh parked a van in front of a building in Oklahoma City.

But disasters are measured by the yardstick of lifetimes when it comes to their personal impact. I'm certain that my grandfather, who

PREFACE

is long gone, experienced tragedies in his lifetime, but he would never be aware of mine, much less measure them anything against. Yes, I realized that there were disasters in New York's history that were pivotal to their time—events so central to a public consciousness that the heart of the city was forever changed. Conditions that we thought were immutable were instead swept away, and profound emotional seismic shifts occurred.

As I began to research Metesky, I came to realize that terrorist bombings were near commonplace in the formative years of the city, and past catastrophe galvanized her in such a way that she completely reshaped herself. We may never fully know or understand this shapeshifting but I wanted to try.

In my research, I gained an appreciation for the courageous individuals who put their lives on the line in dealing with the "Infernal Machines" that were roughly the Improvised Explosive Devices of their day. This was literally the golden age of bomb disposal—the nail-biting days when explosive devices were dealt with in gabardine suits, firmly knotted ties, and snappy fedoras. Those were the days when devices with the capacity to sweep life clean for a radius of several hundred feet in less time than between heartbeats were carried through unsuspecting crowds or handled without thought or care of the possibility of detonation.

These men lived in an age where no one cared about the effectiveness of their diet, hypertension, cholesterol, or lung cancer. They didn't worry about blowing a .08 on a Breathalyzer before climbing behind the wheel of a car or take sensitivity classes on their jobs when dealing with women or minorities. Who cared back then about social niceties, politically correct conversations, racially insensitive comments, or names?

It was a time when people asked you for a "gasper," looked out for persons with a "Chinese Angle," and where you were safe to "wear iron" or if not, and "droppers" would most definitely fit you for a "wooden kimono" in a New York minute.

PREFACE

The landscape of law enforcement was both more respected and more disreputable; this too has forever changed. There was a more nefarious NYPD, even after the Lexow Committee, after the Reverend Charles H. Parkhurst, and before the Knapp Commission, where the good cops were more crusaders than role-models, and an "Honest Cop" wore his virtue like a warning label, like "High Explosive" on a stick of dynamite. It was a time when most big cities had carefully carved out sections of themselves with names like Satan's Circus, Skid Row, Hell's Kitchen, and the Tenderloin. In these neighborhoods carnality and corruption found a fertile breeding ground. These sections were outlined with blood; booze and babes painted their entrances while pimps, gangsters, chop-squads, and goons moved among the dance hall lights of the glittering streets, with their partners in venality—dirty cops, shyster lawyers, and corrupt politicians in a pas de deux of vice.

In those early days, there weren't seminars, courses, and camps held by the Army, the FBI, or specialized groups in bomb disposal, or criminal profiling. The highway had no road map, the school had no teachers; it was a game without rules.

There was only on-the-job training, and perilous job seniority. There might be a superior in the field if luck made it possible, whose prolonged presence in the squad meant by default that he had an inkling of what he was doing. Either that or he would be buried in a closed casket.

These were simply human beings asked to live extreme lives. They were not glamorized icons, merely mortals with common human frailties and weaknesses, who suffered from strained nerves and symptoms, with chronic stressors assailing their bodies, minds, and lives.

This was a long-ago era, now little more than soft whispers, the graying memories of the aged, or grainy text in old newspapers, books, and monochromatic photos. It was a time of oncoming war when the far-reaching maw of fascism relentlessly swallowed Europe. It was a time of rationing, of blowback against intemperance after Prohibition, and there was a cultural mindset that the world was quite possibly coming to an end.

They were our fathers, brothers, and relatives, but they had become something else right before our eyes, and we never saw it.

Finally, it was a time of great clamor, a Promethean orchestra tuning their instruments before the concert of the end...and a single maestro, a Mozart of his own age in the background performing his final opus to a deafened audience.

I familiarized myself with the events, dates and places that outlined the start of the Bomb Squad. I made a historically resonant fictionalized account of life during this time—from 1940 to 1957. Using true events and some real individuals as 'landmarks,' 'road signs,' and 'highway markers,' I attempted to create a lifelike reality to this long-departed past. Many of my characters did not exist, many did. Most of the dialogue in this time did not happen, some of it did.

I didn't want to make an exact accounting of the Bomb Squad and its fateful meeting with the Mad Bomber, simply because others already have. I used other researchers, news events, and census records as my primary sources, and instead chose to tell another tale, the proverbial other side of the coin, delving into New York City's jazz and bebop scenes, hipsters, blatant corruption, vice, drug and alcohol abuse, rampant racism, sexism, wholesale prostitution, and the all too prevalent debauchery.

My sources included reputable newspapers that often told conflicting stories. I searched for resolution before deciding which story proved most satisfying. I culled information from all directions without overburdening the narrative with tiresome exposition and minutia. I chose instead to build characters that could exist in this remarkable environment where life was hard and brutal for the destitute who lived within such a prosperous Emerald City.

The courageous men you will meet in these pages faced frightening and disturbing conditions as they did what they were called to do.

PREFACE

I would like you—the reader—to relax, grow calm, and allow me to carry you along the stream of time, with a story of people placed in dire situations, who had to deal with death and destruction every day, either creating these horrors or averting them.

Here, let me tell you a story.

THE WAR YEARS

1940-1941

"The world's most dangerous job."

PROLOGUE

"The bitterest tears shed over graves are for words left unsaid and deeds left undone."

HARRIET BEECHER STOWE

IN MEMORIAM

JULY 2${}^{\text{ND}}$, 1940

Susan Clark sat at her chair before the ebony wall of the switchboard. It was quiet, still, the row upon row of lights and sockets were as death-like and dark as the very color of the tall board itself, making it a monotonous figure before her. The silent and lifeless torporific summoned her to slumber. To keep from nodding into the curved mouthpiece of her telephone set, which hooked upwards past her chin from the center of her chest by a lightweight harness around her neck, she would sit up and take a deep breath, open her eyes wide and look about. If she gave way to a good nod of sleep her head would send her lips and nose into the hard plastic, waking her both painfully and suddenly.

To combat the boredom, she absentmindedly flipped through the pages of an old *Look* magazine on the desktop of the switchboard, just below the columns of keys in the off positions. It was the January 30th issue, with Anne Gwynne in a bathing suit on the cover, showing off the top of one of the new designs for 1940. Everything about her clashed, Susan thought, but in a good way. Her dark but shimmering red hair contrasted to her pearl white skin, blood red lips and even whiter bathing suit top. The photo stopped just below her bust, but she could make out the pretty patterns of the...

A light flashed on the switchboard. Now fully alert she reached for a cord, pulling it to free slack from a spool under the desktop, and plugged it into the socket directly above the light.

"Extension please," she said with her practiced, professional voice.

The voice was male, raspy, low, and menacing. "The Pavilion is going to be blown up today. You have been warned. You'd better GET OUT!" To begin so low and measured, the horrible screeching shout at the end of the call made Susan jump, almost losing her headset, her heart pounding so hard that she could feel it in her face.

Thursdays were one of her days at the British Pavilion switchboard. Granted, it was far easier than the busy switchboard of the telephone company, but these prank phone calls were a growing annoyance among the girls, and no doubt to the executives of the Pavilion that had to be notified of each and every bomb threat coming in. June was a busy month of bomb threats at the Pavilion, and to Susan, they were becoming commonplace, but this call irritated her by shouting in her ear. Or maybe it frightened her. She wasn't certain.

Regardless, she wasted no time in closing and tossing the magazine to the floor at her feet, just in case her supervisor was to walk in and find her busy doing something else other than giving her full attention to a black wall of apathy. But after this call, maybe she shouldn't complain. Long stretches of soul-sucking monotony were punctuated with seconds of white-hot fright. Maybe there was some kind of balance in that.

She connected herself to her superiors, who, with the smooth skill of professionals, bounced the information to Cecil N. Pickthall, the Commissioner General of the British exhibit.

The entire Tri-state area and beyond was in a state of jubilant hysteria. The city was whipped into a frenzy over the July 4th weekend. The myriad preparations to celebrate the birthday of the nation held a new impetus for its ferocity. Just beyond the great wall of the North Atlantic Ocean, a conflict was brewing, like a pot of ignored coffee on the stove. Britain and Germany were waging a seesaw-like air war, where during the last twenty-four hours before the celebrations in this country, British planes had bombed a German naval base in the Kiel Canal, badly damaging the 26,000-ton battleship Scharnhorst, and left the base a raging netherworld of flames. In rapid retaliation, Germany made its familiar runs over Britain, bombing its northeastern cities, making the casualty list the largest of any raid upon Britain so far.

The volume on the celebration in New York was so loud that these and other events spelling a frightening countdown were drowned out as simple background noise.

Railroads, airlines, and bus companies shifted into high gear in preparation for the heaviest Fourth of July traffic in their history. Brooklyn as well as other boroughs prepared Independence Day observances with a variety of ceremonies and exercises. Plans were made at seven army posts that at the stroke of noon, 48-gun salutes would be fired 336 times in honor of Independence Day from Fort Hamilton, Fort Totten, Fort Jay, Fort Wadsworth, Mitchel Field, Fort Slocum, and Fort Hancock.

In the morning at Prospect Park in the Music Grove, the Long Island General Assembly, Fourth Degree, Knights of Columbus made ready to conduct a patriotic program, including the reading of the Declaration of Independence.

The New York Central made ready to run an extra 125 trains. Pennsylvania Railroad arranged for 135 extra. The Long Island Railroad braced itself, the likes it had never known, promising to provide shuttle service from Pennsylvania station to the World's Fair if demand merited it. The airlines—Transcontinental, Western Air, American Airlines, United Airlines, TWA—were completely booked and adding additional flights to and from La Guardia Field. A great hurricane was brewing, drawing millions from all directions into the city like a mighty storm. With its immense reach and portending staggering numbers, the celebration's mighty heart roared over Flushing Meadows, in the Borough of Queens.

The New York World's fair central unintentionally ironic theme was "Building the World of Tomorrow." Established upon 1,200 acres, it was indeed an operational and logistical feat and a marvel to experience. It was a fully realized vision, a futuristic construction of a city to come, built by close to sixty nations, thirty-three states and U.S. Territories, and more than a thousand exhibitors, among them some of the largest corporations in the United States. The staggering enormity and sheer complexity of it proved that all countries could work together to build prosperity for all. So large was the city that the World of Tomorrow found itself in, that it could be seen by air from miles around as an enormous splash of white on the otherwise mottled landscape of Queens.

The massive city was comprised of seven zones: Government, Food, Community Interests, Communication and Business, Production and Distribution, Transportation, and Amusement. In this city was the promise of a bright future presented by car companies and other commercial and industrial designers and manufacturers. Westinghouse-featured its "Electro the Moto-Man" a seven-foot-tall robot that spoke and smoked cigarettes. U.S. Steel and General Electric had exhibitions that displayed the staggering advances they would be offering mankind in the many decades ahead. It possessed governments participating in the endeavor including The Court of States, where twenty-three states along with Puerto Rico were represented, the United Kingdom, Iceland, Polish national pavilions, and others, and oddly enough—not a government on its own—the New York City Pavilion, each exhibiting their cultural uniqueness in food, dress, and ceremonies.

It was part amusement park with rides that marveled the imagination, such as a 70-foot high, 3000-foot-long roller coaster bordering the beautiful Fountain Lake. And the centerpiece was two towering and enormous white constructs, the Trylon, a sharp spire, rising into the skies some 700 feet, and next to it, a perfect, massive sphere 200 feet in diameter, the Perisphere. Included in this incredible spectacle was the 61-foot-tall statue of George Washington, standing like Gulliver over the Lilliputians and at the head of a long, wide rectangular pool bordering geyser-like fountains down the center of its entire length.

The World of Tomorrow showed the power and grandeur of what nations could build together, a sweeping vision of a prosperous future. However, outside the door, like an approaching violence, was the turmoil overseas of the methodical and slowly growing might of the Third Reich, heralding World War II. The World's Fair, in a major city as was New York, was just loud and gaudy enough to melt away the uncertainties and doubts of the real world just outside of its park.

And loud and gaudy it was with thousands pouring in from the elevated Independent line.

The day was hot. Clouds slid lazily by the Trylon, which appeared to be able to snag them. There wasn't much of a breeze in the direct sunlight, but there were many ice-cream carts which made being out in the open tolerable.

William Federer had his jacket draped over one arm, an ice-cream cone in the other. Dressed in a shirt and tie, now open and slack, he wished he had left his fedora back at the bullpen because its band felt like a ring of fire around the top of his skull. He raised the ice-cream cone to his mouth, leaving ice-cream in his mustache. He didn't care, it made his upper lip the coolest area on his body.

He stood near the British Pavilion on his right and the Australia Pavilion on his left that became the Presidential Row North, that went past many of the smaller international pavilions, New Zealand, France, Hungary, Italy, and Iraq.

The pathway was filled with pedestrians. Women in long, flowery dresses waving like spinsters on the dock as a navy ship filled with seamen. The men who had started the day in suits, ties, and hats had, like Federer long stripped out of their oppressive jackets and carried their hat in hand. It was just too hot, Federer thought, to be wearing so much. He took a lick of his ice cream as a man passed by with his wife. She looked quite cool in her sleeveless cotton dress that cinched at her narrow waist and fell to her ankles. However, her husband, attired in jacket, hat, and tie, looked miserable. Beads of sweat grew on his bright, sun-shined forehead, his collar was open, his shirt damp and sticking to his chest. The row of flagpoles near the Pavilion, high up in the sky, waved listlessly in the torpid air.

Court Street, in front of him, on his left, Court met the pathway that circled the Lagoon of Nations, punctuated by a row of evenly spaced bollards to keep the many vehicles that roamed the Fair out. Federer turned left looking out towards the lagoon, a huge body of water about four city blocks wide, that served as a centerpiece for the Government sector. Music burst from that direction, a classical song with a name he could not remember. He'd never been exposed to classical music in his youth and was surprised that he vaguely recognized the tune. From this genuine distance, he could still hear the whoosh of the fountains coming to life in the center of the lagoon, creating circles of vertical alabaster geysers, feathery white arches of spraying water leaping from the edge of the Lagoon towards the geysers in the center. Other fountains within the lagoon burst, shooting a tower of water into the air. There had to have been hundreds of fountains in the wide body of water, appearing and disappearing. They came on and went off, this way and that, and with a smile, Federer realized that the sprays of water were dancing to the music pounding the air.

Frederick Morlach appeared beside him, coming from behind. Somewhat startled, Federer stepped away from him, looking behind him as if the walkway hadn't been there all this time.

"Damn, what are you trying to do, give me a heart attack?" Federer asked, his tone neutral. Morlach smiled, dressed similarly in a suit, tie, vest, and a homburg hat. He was taller than Federer, lanky and older. His face had a strange, 'fatherly' appearance due to the strands of gray in his full mustache.

They looked out at Court Street. On the other side of the street was a stretch of lush green grass, like an even-toned green carpet laid out on the shore of the wide inlet to the lagoon, the Old Flushing River, now just called "The River". Although there were ample benches dotting every square foot of the fair, scores of men, women, and children, who had brought blankets had laid them on the grass and stretched out upon them, some even having small picnics. Others soaked up the sun, rubbing suntan lotion into their faces, arms, and shoulders.

The thing that astonished and probably infuriated Federer the most about his partner was that he was never sweating, nor did he look uncomfortable wrapped tightly and neatly in his clothing. Morlach looked Federer up and down with a level of dissatisfaction at his disheveled appearance.

"You should straighten yourself out," he said. "You look like a mess."

With some consternation, Federer watched a drop of ice cream run down his tie. "Shit."

"If Lieutenant Hayes ever checked on us and caught you looking like that, you'd be dead," Morlach warned.

"Hayes has more common sense than to be out here in this heat dressed like we are."

"Bill, we've been on this detail for so long now, and you haven't learned how to dress for it yet?"

"Dress for it? At least there was a nice stiff breeze the last two weeks. Today, it's a dead heat." Federer squinted at the sun, scowled, then felt a cool rivulet of ice cream run down the back of his hand. Like a child he licked it away before it could drip on his black leather shoes. Looking down to admire their polish, he found himself too late, his left shoe blighted with splatters.

Morlach looked at the well-dressed men, women, and children milling about or heading to one exhibit or another. His partner was indeed right. The sun was less punishing back in June, there was a fair amount of cloud cover, and the unseasonably cool wind was a paradise when it came by. But today heralded the first day of a real summer. Who knew that the weather did not care for the timing of calendars? "Find anything?"

Federer shook his head. "What? You mean something looking like a bomb walking about in this heat, holding a balloon? No. Nothing. Nothing out of the ordinary."

"Looks like this call is going to be another dud."

"I have the same feeling. Back and forth with this detail for a month now. It's like whoever is making these calls is doing it just to bust our balls." Federer looked about, absentmindedly licking at his ice-cream, now just a small vanilla mound over his waffle cone. "Hey, let's go back around the British Pavilion to Continental Avenue. I think that there's a park with some shade over there."

"Yeah, but we got this call that just came in."

"So? Didn't you say you thought it would be a dud?"

Morlach made a sour face. "This one just wasn't a bomb threat. The message said that the switchboard operator was told to get out."

"Yeah, you tell her that to make it sound real. What? Were you going to say: 'Take your time, each your lunch, we'll blow you up when we get around to it?'"

"Whatever, I think we'd better check the bushes and compartments on the outside, close against the Pavilion this time. What do you think?"

"Isn't there some kinda huge park just around the corner?" Federer turned his attention to the rows of families across the street on the stretch of grass, eating.

Morlach said sharply but not loudly. "There's an entire row of benches over there. You want to sit down before we beat the bushes?"

He shook his head, then struggled tiredly with a name, snapping his fingers as if the sound could frighten the memory out of the deep recesses of his mind, "Some sort of Gardens on Fountains, or of the Nations or something like that."

"Gardens on Parade."

Federer turned and pointed at him emphatically with his ice cream cone. "Yeah, that's it. That's the one with the paths going all around in there and benches and shade trees. Let's go there."

"I'm telling you, this message from Wood is different this month." Morloch said, speaking of Sidney G. Wood who oversaw the building's private security. He rooted through his pockets. Federer walked completely across the wide road that was Court Street, sloshing through the crisscrossing crowds like a fisherman wearing a chest high wader. He went to the garbage can at the end of their bench to drop in his unfinished cone. From where he stood, at the back end of the benches, he could see across the thick, green carpet of grass to the river languidly trickling by, dark yet sparkling with the afternoon sun.

Morlach came up behind him cautiously. "Hey, if it's getting too hot for you, you can find some shade in the Gardens. I'll beat the bushes."

Federer tore his gaze from the tranquil waters and turned to face his partner. Morlach's mustached features were set with concern. He waved him back to show he was fine. "Let's make a quick run over to the food tents near the gardens and let me get a cold pop. Then I say: we give the entire pavilion a good once over."

"Sure, you look like you could use a little air-conditioning." Morlach smiled, backed away and walked on with Federer.

They trudged into the stream of humanity that sloshed in two directions on Court Street. Federer, a step behind Morlach headed west for the Gardens. Now, the rectangular portion of the British Pavilion loomed large beyond a comfortable courtyard of grass and concrete. Running along the second floor of the building was a row of windows with red and white striped awning. A small, curved restaurant sat at the top of a rise of brick-worked stairs. Round tables with red and white striped umbrellas provided much needed shade. People seethed like angry ants under umbrellas and inside the restaurant itself. They were busy laughing, chatting, and enjoying their day in such an amazing place, where everywhere you looked, something seemed to catch the eye. He turned to look at his mature, graying partner who walked with a certain swagger.

Federer liked Morlach's moxie. Even though they were obviously being sent to search for Easter eggs at Christmastime, the old bastard remained alert and keen not to miss a trick if one happened. With all the patience and care of a searchlight on a rocky promontory, his head swiveled back and forth, studying the oversized and colorful rear end of the woman passing on his left, the rolled-up newspaper under the arm of the man on their right. A summer butterfly, Morlach's detective eyes lighted upon every person in the field, including a very familiar and quite numerous sight, a Patrolman of the Private Police force of the World's Fair.

At a thousand strong, the independent police presence under the supervision of former police inspector Richard Sheridan, was an incredible deterrent to any overt malfeasance that might decide to visit the fair. Coupled with Commissioner Valentine's added police and detective presence, they had security as tight as a fly's asshole, Federer thought. Later, the Queens district attorney would only report two criminal indictments being handed down for the entire season.

At first blanch, the private patrolmen were similar to the Canadian Mounted Police except they wore navy blue trousers with a yellow stripe down the side of each leg. The military-like tunic was bright red with brass buttons, patch pockets, and a Sam Browne black leather belt with shoulder and waist strapping, finally topped off by a wide brimmed western hat.

The Special Patrolman appeared proud of his bright uniform, standing out in the milling crowds, which was no doubt the point. Again, Federer noticed with a level of resigned disdain how even though heavily uniformed, the Patrolman also seemed oblivious to the heat.

"There's another one," Morlach said, pointing with his chin to another passing Special Patrolman.

"You see, Fred. That's what I don't get. They pull legitimate detectives off legitimate cases to come out here in this heat and babysit these cash-a-cops."

"Well, I wouldn't say that we're babysitting anyone."

They made their way down Court Street, the languid British flags finally beginning to flap and snap in a weak breeze.

They stopped at the mouth of the footbridge on the left that carried pedestrians from the Brazilian and French pavilions, and exhibits that he wanted to see around Fireside Row, like American at Home, Gas Wonderland, and not to mention the Schlitz Palm Garden for a few beers.

They stood in the baking sun watching the scores upon scores of men, women and children walking to and from the bridge.

Morlach marched off three paces before he noticed that Federer was no longer at his side. "Aren't you coming?"

Ahead, they approached the Gardens on Parade. From this direction to it, which could only be considered the back of the 'gardens' were a series of connected canvas tents blocking them completely from view save for the south end, which was completely open, and gave a magnificent view of the descending, grassy slope into the river. On the other side of the river, a similar grassy ramp rose to the rooftops of the Town of Tomorrow and the Electrified Farm.

Two cranberry red Special Police bracketed them in less than four steps into the Gardens.

"Can we help you?" one of them asked.

Federer pulled out his shield and held it up for all to see. "Detectives Federer and Morlach from the 110th here to provide logistical support against any clandestine operation."

"You're bomb squad?" the other Special Policeman asked, pointing at them with his chin.

"NYPD Emergency Squad detectives," Morlach said, coming from behind to flank his partner.

"You're the guys that were supposed to come to if we find a bomb, right?"

Federer looked at Morlach who looked back. "Yeah," Morlach said guardedly.

"This guy has been running around asking us if we've seen you. They've found something." One of the Policemen walked off, finding a path, and waving them along with his partner.

"Probably a hoax," Federer mumbled, falling into step behind them. "There goes my cold pop."

"I don't think so, sir," the other officer said over his shoulder. "The guy that found it is an electrician, and he says it's ticking."

Inside the British Pavilion, William Strachan walked into the huge mezzanine. Many people milled around, staring up at the paintings and photographs on the walls, some packing into the pavilions to beat the heat. Women fanned themselves with ornate lace accordion fans, seeking relief. The men did the same with their hats. Strachan stopped short in the middle of the large, pillared chamber, placed space between himself and as much of the crowd as possible and closed his eyes. For some reason he felt that doing so would make his skin more sensitive to the air temperature, but if it did or didn't, he really didn't care. He wore a long-sleeved cotton work shirt somewhat beaten and fraying around the collar and the end of the sleeves, which were rolled up just below his armpits. He didn't need to look at any thermometers in the area to tell for himself that it was warm in the mezzanine.

Strachan headed for the hall, going through one of the corridors into another large viewing room with both a high ceiling and an ornate awning over a dais, leading up to the Magna Carta itself. Two great white pillars held up the rectangular sculptured awning where ensconced and unseen lamps caused the entire ceiling to glow white.

The incredible document itself was in a padded stand encased in bulletproof glass and flanked by two burly security guards. Strachan wondered if they were hot and sweaty underneath their buttoned-up jackets and hats.

A set of black, tubular railings directed the crowds up to the dais, then past the document. Onlookers had to lean over the railing to get a close look at the beautiful and meticulous script. From there, the railing deposited the viewers out in two directions, emptying them at the sides of the dais.

Strachan worked his way through the mass of bodies, cutting through the men, women, and children anxiously waiting to see the exhibit. Here, in a stairwell, he could tell that it was hot in the pavilion because the ceiling was not as high in the Mezzanine and the Hall.

He came out of the stairway on the second floor and went directly for the fan room, skirting the crowds on this floor moving lazily from exhibit to exhibit. He'd have to make this quick because if his superiors could feel the heat in their offices, they'll come out and do exactly as he did, test the heat of the halls. This played in Strachan's favor, giving him time enough to crank up the fans and air conditioning before they could tell it was needed. He needed this job. Jobs were hard to come by.

Up ahead was a room he was familiar with to the minutest detail. The fan room held the controls for the air-conditioning equipment, switches, vents, and electrical junctions. Strachan was an electrician straight from the Bronx. He was still young and strapping, a capable man, his hair slicked back with the hairs at his temple groomed short. He liked this haircut in the hot weather, he smiled to himself.

The first thing that he thought to do was to check the temperature readings in the building to get an accurate reading, and to adjust them if it still seemed too warm in the exhibition halls.

Going to one of the control boards, he checked the readings. They were alright. It wasn't as hot as he thought it was. Strachan rechecked the dials and decided that it was still cool, but with just a few more patrons it could become uncomfortable. He'll come back in another couple of hours to check them again.

The first thing he thought of was a cigarette. Reaching into his pocket he pulled out his pack and checked to see how many he had left. Four. It was going to be a tough week if he ran out of cigarettes so soon. He pulled one free and headed for the door, preparing to smoke outside of the fan room, just in case there were some fumes coming...

On the floor at the back of the swing of the door, against the wall, was a buff-colored canvas bag. A workman's bag. He saw it here yesterday. It sat undisturbed for the entire day. Thinking that its owner would come for it sooner or later Strachan ignored it. But apparently no one came to claim it. He wondered if there was a lost and found in the building and walked over to it, reaching down to pick it up and stopped, his hand hovering directly over its light brown leather handles. He heard ticking.

He stood up, reached for his pocket watch. It was 3:30 in the afternoon. He put the crystal against his ear and could barely hear its ticking. He looked down again. The ticking was coming from the bag.

That's strange, he thought.

Well, it wasn't his problem, whomever lost their bag, it was obviously theirs. However, leaving it here in the fan room might cause him aggravation later down the road, so he decided to take it to his boss' office. Maybe he'd know what to do with it or even who the damn thing belonged to.

Strachan lifted the bag by its two leather straps and walked out of the fan room. The milling crowd surged around him slowly, like muddy waters churning. Children ran around his legs, one colliding into his thigh, smearing some of his ice-cream on his blue jean slacks. With a level of annoyance Strachan wiped at the stain, still moving through the hall to reach the stairway down. Going through the door, he was relieved that it still wasn't all that hot in the tighter quarters of the pavilion. That was good. He cut through the Mezzanine, and into the foyer for the entrance doors on the north end of the building. Here too people were flooding in, giving him the impression of being a salmon fighting upstream. To the right, through the foyer was the office of Cyril Rawlings who oversaw the service staff at the World's Fair.

Cyril Rawlings stood next to his desk, a sheaf of papers in his right hand, reading. He was a skinny man whose clothing hung on his limbs awkwardly as if it was a size slightly larger, and his face was unusually long, which was an optical illusion because his hairline was receding at the temples. He turned to Strachan tiredly as if it was already a long day for him. It was hard to tell by his eyes which were behind a pair of gray colored horn-rimmed glasses, frosted with the glare from the light in the room.

"Yes, Billy, can I help you?" he asked.

"Somebody left their work bag in the fan room." Strachan lifted the bag for Rawlings to see.

"Okay. So, what do you want me to do with it?"

"It's ticking."

Rawlings thought about the statement. Ticking?

"What should I do with it?" Strachan continued.

Rawlings walked up to him, pressed his ear against the bag. After listening for a moment, he stepped away. Lifting his glasses, he squinted at the bag as if he had better vision with them off.

"I don't know what to make of it, Billy." Rawlings returned his glasses to the bridge of his nose and sighed tiredly. "Follow me."

Rawlings led the way, leaving his office with Strachan in his wake. He navigated through the crowds in the west entrance foyer, back through the Mezzanine and into the Magna Carta Hall.

Suddenly, before entering the mass of people waiting at the queue, he turned around to look over his shoulder at Strachan.

"Is it hot in here to you, Billy?" he asked.

"I'll check on that later, Mr. Strachan."

Rawlings went through the crowds, past the stairwell upstairs and into an ensconced office, seemingly hidden from plain sight. He rapped on the door.

"Come in."

The two men entered the office of Sidney G. Wood, Wood was a heavy-set man, in his fifties, potbellied but his suit fitted him better than Rawlings's. His face was a smooth, fleshy oval and he wore a comfortable grin, as if he had just finished a satisfying meal. Wood's chair teetered on its two back legs, his feet on his desk, crossed at the ankles. Rawlings and Strachan reluctantly entered, stopping before the desk.

"I've got something for you, Sid," Rawlings said.

Wood slipped his feet off his desk and sat up in the chair.

"What's that?" He asked.

"Billy here found a bag—and it's ticking."

"It's doing what?"

Rawlings motioned to Strachan to rest the bag on the desk. "Put it there, Billy." To Wood he said, "It's ticking."

Wood leaned forward across his desk and turned his head to press his ear against the canvas bag. He listened for a moment, the corners of his mouth lifting, but he wasn't smiling.

"Yeah, it's a steady ticking," he nodded.

He stood, thought for a moment.

"What should we do?" Rawlings asked.

"Hold on," Wood replied, snatching up the phone receiver from his desk and requested to be connected to Cecil N. Pickthall, Commissioner General of the British Exhibition.

"Cecil," Wood began. "I think you should see something."

It did not take long for Pickthall to walk into Wood's office. As he approached the desk, both Strachan and Rawlings stepped aside, giving him access to the canvas bag.

"What's going on, Sid?" he asked with a great level of authority, stopping before Wood's desk, his arms akimbo. He looked the part—expensive suit, well-groomed hair, handsome features, well in his fifties. He stood imperiously over Wood. Although they were of the same height, it didn't feel like it to Wood under his heated stare. He was the boss's boss; he was the one that made all the 'real' decisions in this idiotic fair. This was one reason why his mantra was "Lord, don't bother me." And here was Wood, the head of personal security for the building...bothering him.

"Billy found a bag—and it's ticking." Wood said with a slight level of reluctance. How would Pickthall take this interruption to his day? Good? Bad?

Pickthall lowered his head to the desk and listened to the bag for a moment, then stood up. His mouth felt as if a cotton ball had wicked away all his saliva.

"I think we've got a really big problem here," Pickthall said, unsure of himself suddenly. He turned to Strachan. "Billy, you know those two detectives out there?"

"Uhhh," Strachan had to think about it for a moment. The unfolding events were scattering his thoughts. What *were* they going to do?

Pickthall could see that Strachan was suddenly pushed into the deep end and was foundering. He looked squarely into the laborer's eyes, honestly searching for any light whatsoever behind those dull windows and found nothing. He said to Strachan in a slow, deliberately pronounced statement, "The two guys in suits that come in here from time to time, walking around. They're probably right outside."

"Yeah, yeah, I remember them now."

"Well, go and get them Billy."

Strachan rushed out of the office.

"My god," Pickthall sighed. "Where did you find *him* from?"

"He's a wizard electrician," Rawlings said. "He's just not good around bombs."

"Neither am I."

Wood cleared his voice. "Me either."

Federer and Morlach marched through the door looking about at the faces as if the men in the room were the bomb makers themselves. Strachan eased in behind them, retiring to a quiet and dark corner of the office.

Federer, in fact, was quite happy to be out of the sun and back into air conditioning. He removed his hat and fanned his face with the chill air coming from the vents.

"What's the matter gentlemen?" Morlach asked, going first in the inquiry, his mature, fatherly features reassuring the men around them that they were in experienced hands. This was their first bomb.

"Sirs," Pickthall began. "I think we have a bomb here." He pointed excitedly to the innocent work bag on the desk. All eyes followed his trembling finger to the item.

"Why do you say that?"

"Because it's ticking."

Morlach frowned and approached the innocent looking bag and bent over to listen.

"Hear anything?" Federer asked.

"Yeah, it's ticking alright."

Morlach stood and turned to Federer who was two paces behind him.

"This is *not* good," Morlach said.

Federer could see the terror growing in the faces of the men in the room rising in panicked degrees. He and Morlach had to take steps quickly but first, he decided to calm everyone down.

"Look people, it can be anything. Nine out of ten times it's something innocent like an alarm clock to remind the guy when his day was over, or lunchtime or something like that, so don't panic," he said.

"Don't panic," Morlach repeated. "But I think we should take it somewhere away from people."

SUSPICIOUS LOOKING PACKAGES

"You," Federer pointed to Wood, who stood behind his desk statue-like, "make a call to the bomb squad and tell them to get over here."

Wood went into action, making the phone call.

"You—" Federer turned behind him, taking a moment to find and point to Strachan. "You go out and get a couple of those special Mounties you have to follow us."

"Where should I tell them to go?" Strachan asked, he was going up and down on the balls of his feet.

Morlach came to life, turning to Pickthall. "Where can we take this thing the furthest away from people?"

Pickthall thought for a moment, but the long-faced Rawlings standing behind Morlach was faster. "There's a service road past the Polish Pavilion. That's a good hundred and fifty feet from anything."

Strachan was gone like the wind.

"Let's do that," Morlach replied.

Federer struck Morlach across the shoulder with his hat. "Fred, we've got to carry this thing through the entire fucking pavilion."

"Yeah, that's right" was Morlach's determined reply. "I'll carry it."

"He's got a point, sir," Pickthall said, raising a finger slightly into the air to get Morlach's attention. "Shouldn't we first clear the Pavilion and then take it out?"

"No, you might cause a panic with people getting trampled over a bag of tools." Morlach went to the desk and looked down upon the simple, slightly dirty canvas bag with Wood standing on the other side doing the same. Morlach continued, "We know it's not motion sensitive, or you guys would have sprung it the instant you tried to bring it here. It's time that's against us now, so we gotta move fast."

And with that, Morlach lifted the bag gingerly from the desk and walked to the door with Federer following. Pickthall, Rawlings, and Wood brought up the rear.

Once again, the suspicious package was carried through the lines waiting in the huge hall to view the Magna Carta, through the corridor into the equally full mezzanine, and out the doors on the west side of the pavilion which opened into the courtyard.

Instantly Federer regretted the decision the moment the heat struck him from the wide-open glass doors. Even Morlach could sense no relief once they left the building. Pressed at the mouth of the opened glass doors was a mass of humanity walking into the building with little steps, like penguins, to keep from plowing into the backs of the waves of people ahead of them.

"Is there another exit?" Federer asked Pickthall.

"We can take the north entrance doors," he replied.

Rawlings's bony hand landed heavily on Federer's other shoulder from Pickthall. His bespectacled features were already sweating without yet stepping outside of the building. "It's going to be just as crowded."

"Where is building security?" Pickthall looked about. "I thought we told that blockhead electrician to go and get security?"

"Well actually," Woods muttered from the back, "The detective told him to get a 'Mountie.'"

"Hold on, let me go and get the building security guards to clear our way," Pickthall said starting to march off but stopped when he heard Morlach.

"We don't have time for that," he said, he pointed to Federer. "Bill, hit the doors."

Like an Arctic icebreaker, Federer plunged into the crowds, cutting a wake through them large enough for Morlach to pass through with Pickthall, Rawlings, and Wood behind them.

The walkway around the courtyard and past the restaurant was filled with people in several columns of lines, waiting patiently to enter the pavilion. Federer went over the low, black, wrought iron railing onto the lush grass, and cut a direct line across the courtyard to the pathway. Like a vaulting race team, the rest of the men went over the railing and fell into a rapid walk with the two detectives out of the Pavilion.

They came out onto a path that Morlach was familiar with but couldn't name. It was the pathway behind the tents of the Garden's on Parade.

"This way!" Rawlings said, heading north toward the Italian Pavilion. He walked faster than Morlach would have wished to and constantly had to stop to wait for the detective to catch up. Morlach was busy swearing under his breath. *What's wrong with this moron? Doesn't he realize that I'm trying to take it slow?*

Rawlings led them past the Italian Pavilion with its towering statues and monuments and onto Continental Avenue. This was a much larger thoroughfare packed full of people coming and going, enjoying the sights, holding up cameras to photograph their surroundings or just standing and eating something, a hot dog, an ice-pop. Everything seemed so normal, so carefree, but Morlach wondered what would happen if they realized that he could be carrying an agent of instantaneous death. Large, angry, vicious—capable to tearing everyone to shreds around him faster than they could inhale the fire and heat of the blast.

Don't be a bomb, Morlach kept repeating to himself.

"This way, this way." Rawlings waved at him to catch up. Somehow Morlach had slowed down. He picked up the pace slightly. Sitting in front of them as if barring their path was the Netherlands Pavilion. They joined the crowds going left, west, with the Polish Pavilion on the right.

Rawlings spun around to say to Morlach, "It right around here."

Morlach turned to his right, coming face to face with a big red balloon. Looking down he found a little girl walking alongside him, her long dark hair in ponytails and ribbons, her little white summer dress and splayed-out petticoat skirt making her look like a little princess. She walked to the canvas bag, her mother next to her, holding the hand that had the balloon tied to her wrist.

Morlach smiled at the thought of the little girl having to have her wondrous balloon tied to her wrist or she would no doubt so innocently lose it. A misfortune that her parents couldn't even get angry at her for if they failed to secure it. If this was a bomb, Morlach thought, she and I would feel no pain.

Federer's thoughts were much farther away as he walked behind his partner. He stared up at the passing statue, high up upon a stone pedestal of King Ladislaus II Jagiello made of metal, riding on a powerful horse. Both hands raised to the sky, a long sharp sword in one of them. Thoughts of King Jagiello rolled through Federer's mind. He had no clue who he was, but he knew the king rode a horse and held swords. That was enough to take his mind off the quiet rage in the bag that Morlach held amid a crowd of hundreds.

They walked around the Polish Pavilion and a Polish Restaurant, turning right, heading north once more. The restaurant was a large, circular building of all windows up on a grassy rise in the earth. In front of it were a score or more tables and chairs with colorful umbrellas to block out the sun for the people gaily enjoying their repasts.

"It's not far," Rawlings panted. "It's right here."

And true to his word, just as true as the pleasant breezes now coming off the path that they walked, it led to a dirt service road some distance from the Polish Pavilion. As they got further from the restaurant, Morlach realized that he'd started breathing again.

"Stop here," he said to Rawlings. "I'll take it from here."

Rawlings halted as if he struck an invisible wall.

A blue uniformed patrolman came up the path from behind them, one hand atop his head to hold onto his six-point hat. He practically dove into the backs of the men before him, wading through Wood, Pickthall, and Rawlings to reach Federer who was standing just in front of them.

"What's going on here," the patrolman asked with great authority, reaching out and taking his shoulder, turning Federer around.

"Who are you?" Federer asked him.

"Patrolman Emil Vyskocil," he replied testily. "Who are you?"

"Detective William Federer, Emergency Squad, one-ten precinct assigned to the fair. Do me a favor, will you? Back these guys up and keep people away from here."

"Why? Is there a bomb?"

"That's right," Federer pointed off to Morlach in the distance. "Right in that bag over there. Now can you back these people up?"

"Sure thing."

Federer turned his attention back to his partner who had reached the service road and rested the bag near a high hurricane fence and a loosely spaced row of twenty-foot maple trees. Morlach turned on his heels and walked briskly back to where everyone was convinced that if the bag did explode, they would be out of its blast splash.

Looking at his partner, Federer shook his head in mute frustration. Morlach was as cool as an opened refrigerator. His tie still knotted, collar buttoned, vest and jacket on. Federer was melting despite the sudden chill making his skin prickly. He was aware that twenty percent of the sweat was no doubt due to the heat, however, a frightening twist in his stomach and the rapid pounding on his heart made it clear that the other eighty percent was due to pure, unadulterated fear.

Patrolman Vyskocil, true to his task, had backed up the men of the British Pavilion who stood watching as if they didn't want to miss the spectacle of the bag's detonation. Coming up from behind and gathering around the group of five pavilion executives, were the two detectives, Joseph J. Lynch and Ferdinand A. Socha, from the Bomb Squad who had worked with Federer and Morlach before on dud and hoax calls.

Lynch was of a regular build, sharp, clean suit that hung on his frame loosely. He was the picture of authority, and his voice instantly clouted Rawlings, Wood, and Pickthall with questions. Standing next to him was Socha, shorter than his partner, portly, his suit tighter, and sleeves slightly higher than fashion dictated. Federer noticed that Socha looked just as uncomfortable as he felt in the heat.

Behind them was John J. Sullivan, Commissioner of the World's Fair police with two of his detectives, Joseph Gallagher and J.

Schuchman. Vyskocil held them back the instant they made way for the detectives. He questioned their identities briefly before stepping away and pointing to Federer, closer to the service road. From there, the three men crowded around Federer and Morlach.

"What's going on Will?" Lynch asked. He was a handsome man with simple features, neatly combed hair, clean white shirt, tie, and hat.

"I think we've got a bomb over there. The bag is ticking," Federer explained.

Socha took a moment to glance into Federer's eyes. There was something electric about them. Socha could see that the man was high off his own adrenaline. He wasn't thinking now, he was reacting. "How long were you around it?" he asked him.

Federer shook his head. The moment of silence had sent him away somewhere, in his own mind. Morlach spoke up: "A couple of minutes. We just got it here."

"So, you moved it?"

"Yes, we did. It was in the British Pavilion."

"Phew," Socha breathed. "Well, at least we know it's not motion sensitive."

"What do we do know?" Federer asked, looking back and forth between Lynch and Socha, an excited puppy between two masters.

Lynch pondered the question for a moment.

"So?" Commissioner Sullivan called out to them. "What happens next? Are you going to dunk it in some water?"

The four detectives turned to his outburst for a moment before returning calmly to their discussion.

"I say we go in," Lynch said boldly.

"I agree," Socha added.

Lynch, now a quarterback in the huddle of men, pointed to Morlach and Federer. "We'll go in and take a look at what we're dealing with before deciding what to do next. You two stay back."

"Fine by us," Federer replied without argument.

All four men nodded. They turned to face the bag in the

distance, each marshaling whatever strength, gathering whatever nerves, or bolstering whatever inner resolve. With Lynch's first step toward the bag, the rest spread out from him, all moving towards the service road, closing the distance. Federer stopped halfway to the bag, his courage finally petering out. Morlach, though, was too interested, too curious. He continued with Socha and Lynch, all three men walking slowly as if they were sneaking up on the bag.

After several more feet, all three men stooped over it, examining it without touching. From this distance from the fair, they could hear whatever it was inside, ticking.

"You brought it out here you say?" Lynch asked Morlach, grimacing.

"Carried it myself."

Far beyond the estimated blast range, detective Joseph Gallagher finally reached the group of men who managed both the pavilion and the fair. Noticing patrolman Vyskocil in NYPD uniform and hat, Gallagher knew he would get definitive answers from him. He pushed his way past the executives to the patrolman.

"What's going on here?" he asked.

"We think we've got a bomb over there," Vyskocil replied, his arms crossed over his chest, standing tall, guarding the space to his left and right. Gallagher was smart enough to stand directly in front of him.

"Who's that behind you?"

Vyskocil glanced over his shoulder briefly to see who Gallagher was talking about, "That's, err, Detective Federer, I think. He's out of the one-ten Emergency Squad."

"Mind if I have a word with him?"

Vyskocil waved him on, holding his hand out to another man who attempted to move forward for a better view of what was transpiring.

Trotting up to Federer in a low crouch, Detective Gallagher whispered, "What are they doing?"

"I have no clue," Federer replied, not taking his eyes off the three men and the bag.

At the service road, the three men ruminated over their course of action.

"Open it?" Socha proposed.

"I don't know about that," Lynch said. "We know we can move it, but that doesn't mean we can open it. It might be booby-trapped. Look, it's a canvas bag, right?"

Socha and Morlach nodded.

Lynch drove his hand into the pocket of his slacks and produced a pocketknife. "I say we stand it on end and cut a slit in the corner and then we can look in and see what we got."

Socha made a face and hunched his shoulders. "Sounds good to me."

Morlach stayed quiet, completely engrossed in what the other two detectives were saying.

With his index and forefinger, Socha carefully pinched one end of the bag and lifted it ever so slowly. When it was nearly on its end, Lynch stuck in his pocketknife at the canvas fabric, haltingly worked it into the fabric, and then made a slit. In a few heart stopping seconds, he had worked a two-inch cut in the fabric.

"That should be enough," he said.

"Go ahead then, you first," Socha said with a smile.

With two fingers of each hand, Lynch parted the cut and peered inside. His head moved this way and that as his eye sought better angles, until he pulled back and calmly said to Socha, "Here, take a look."

Socha lowered his head, peering into the slit still held open by Lynch. After a few moments he looked up, his face red. "Those are sticks of dynamite."

"Yeah, we're playing with a loaded deck now," Lynch assured everyone.

"I'll go tell Sullivan," Morlach said.

Morlach stood, straightened the hat on his head and headed back up the distance to Sullivan, trotting in a low crouch. On attempting to pass Federer and Gallagher, Federer reached out and caught him by his jacket sleeve, yanking him to a stop.

"What's in it?" Federer asked breathlessly.

"Sticks of dynamite. It's a bomb alright," Morlach replied.

Federer's hand sprung open in shock, releasing Morlach, his eyes widening. Morlach continued, approaching Commissioner Sullivan, Detective Schuchman, Patrolman Vyskocil, Rawlings, and Wood. They were a shallow semicircle of concerned faces, everyone staring intently at Morlach's approach. Sullivan could not wait for him to stop before calling out to him the second he was in earshot. "So?" he asked, impatiently.

Morlach kept silent until he was standing before them. "It's the business."

Sullivan sighed in frustrated exasperation. He opened his mouth, but words did not come out. There was a bright flash instead which lifted the group like fall leaves in the wind and sent them scattering. The semi-circle was blown backwards, their hats shooting to the heavens. Morlach was thrown forward, and before they could even hit the ground, there was an otherworldly roar, coming like some unleashed god raging at the sky. Heat and smoke followed.

Face down on the ground, Morlach's ears felt like invisible fingers were pushing in, trying to meet at the center of his skull. This pressure eased, replaced by a loud ringing. He was dizzy, dizzy enough to puke.

Rolling over onto his back he was pelted by clumps of dirt and tarmac, falling like black, heavy snow.

At the Polish Pavilion they saw the flash, felt the weak shock wave. Two windows of the restaurant burst spraying shards of glass inside. The diners, stunned for moment, rushed the remaining windows and the tables outside toward the service road, their attention drawn to the rising black, billowing cloud and the white haze growing in the air. Leaves fell from the heavens like fall under stratospheric high trees.

Morlach finally felt that he could sit up without losing control of his stomach and surveyed the area. A shoe fell to the earth. He looked at it, thinking that it was a high-top men's boot, until he realized that there was actually a foot inside, disarticulated just above the ankle.

Not far from him, closer to the smoldering crater were Federer and Gallagher, their clothing black and tattered. They struggled to their hands and knees, a monumental effort, and attempted to crawl away from the blast crater, almost lost in the haze of smoke.

Morlach looked behind him at the spectators, now a tangle of limbs, still unable to stand. Rising unsteadily on weak legs and buckling knees, Morlach staggered over to the crawling body nearest to him. The clothes were in tatters, every inch of exposed skin was burned black. Morlach fell to his knees and could hardly recognize Federer under the soot, burns and blood. He gingerly rested a hand on his back.

"Willie, lie down. It's all over. The ambulance will be here soon," he said, but he wasn't certain that his partner heard him. He still worked his battered body forward and finally collapsed. Morlach pressed two fingers against his partner's carotid artery. His pulse was weak, but he was still alive.

Patrolman Vyskocil, minus hat, walked like a broken zombie through the low haze to the other battered body. Morlach used his hands to push himself from his knees onto his feet and staggered to the blast crater. Leaves were still falling, faintly now, stragglers in a long-finished race to the ground.

"He's alive!" Vyskocil shouted hoarsely towards Morlach. The best he could do for a reply was wave a limp arm up and down. Not far from Federer, he found a body. He couldn't tell for certain who it was. It was an aggregate of fabric, ash, blood, bone, and organs in a multi-colored stew, loosely shaped like a man. He struggled on, there would be no identifying who that was right now.

Another body slightly closer to the blackened crater could be clearly seen now. Near a gouge in the service road, he could see the second lifeless body, he found it tattered but not as badly as the other, and by the receding hairline of the bloodied head, he could tell that this was Socha.

Across the service road a single maple tree, now totally devoid of leaves, stood stark. The side facing the blast was scorched black. The fence just behind it displayed a gaping hole.

Whatever energy or force that had been driving him forward to check on his companions had exhausted itself. Morlach's legs buckled, and he landed on his knees harshly, and then pitched forward, his face crashing to the blackened earth.

A leaf, as if feeling sympathy for him, landed on his cheek tenderly.

He could hear sirens in the distance.

The people enjoying the exhibitions and pavilions heard the fatal blast.

They looked up.

And thought it was part of the fireworks.

CASUALTY REPORT

On that fateful day...

Detective Joseph J. Lynch - Torn to shreds/Dead.
Detective Ferdinand A. Socha - Lost both feet/Dead.
Detective William J. Federer - Compound fracture of both legs, multiple abrasions, and burns, severe shock/Critical.
Detective Joseph Gallagher - Compound fracture of both legs, burns and contusions/Critical.
Patrolman Emil Vyskocil - Multiple abrasions and contusions/Fair.
Detective Frederick Morlach - Multiple abrasions and burns/Fair.
Detective J. Schuchman - Multiple abrasions and burns/Fair.
Captain John McLaughlin - Treated for cuts on face and leg/Sent home.

ON A FINAL NOTE

Morlach was looked after by nurses on the scene who were able to clean him up. He had felt fine even though they admonished him to get into an ambulance and get checked out at the hospital. He denied transportation, claiming that there were others on the field badly injured. He would go when they were taken care of.

He joined in with the evidence collection crews, walking about the area like strange birds, many standing humped over, rear ends in the sky. Their faces were close to the ground, picking at anything that looked suspicious. He worked with the evidence collection crew carefully picking up anything that looked out of the ordinary.

Morlach worked into the night until the early hours of the morning, until his sight fuzzed over, and his eyes closed. When a nurse handed him a cup of hot coffee and that failed to keep him awake, he decided it was time to leave.

When he reached his home in St. Albans Queens, he took off his jacket and slacks and noticed that there was a dark stain on his back. Darker than the dark color of his suit jacket, and probably completely unnoticeable in the dark of the night. On the top of the stain was a small slit in his jacket. He removed the shirt and looked at the back of it. It too was stained, being a white shirt, he could clearly see that it was blood. It too had a small slit in the back, above the blood, around his rear left shoulder. He reached behind himself to see if he could feel a wound, and when he did it replied with a throb of pain. Since he wasn't even aware that he had sustained a wound, he decided that it wasn't fatal, wrapped it up and fell asleep from exhaustion.

The next afternoon, Morlach reported for work at the precinct and asked to be temporarily relieved from duty. There was no one who was about to deny him anything at this point and let him go. Morlach went directly to Flushing Hospital. He would learn, after seeing the doctor, that he was struck in the left shoulder by a piece of flying metal shard roughly about the size of a penny. The shard was removed, his wound properly bandaged.

He went back to work.

BOMB AND FORGERY SQUADS SEPARATED

"Following the death of Lynch and Socha, the Bomb Squad is detached from the Forgery Unit. This is viewed as the birth of the 'modern' Bomb squad."

BOMB SQUAD PG. 277

ONE
CALLING CARD

"One of the Hardest Men in the city."

FABRIZZIO 'FAB' ACCORSO, BOMB SQUAD DETECTIVE

NOVEMBER 18TH, 1940

The wind whipped a chilly breeze across the top of the icy concrete of the sidewalk. By daylight the reputable people and businesses of the street scraped and salted the ice off the areas in front of their stores or apartments to allow persons safe passage by or into their home or establishment. But once night fell, and the businesses closed, and the apartment dwellers crawled into bed, for some, their day was just starting. It had snowed two nights ago, which became icy slush onto the curb against the sides of parked cars, and buildings. It was safe to walk down the blocks during the day. But late at night, when the snow flurries began to dust the cleared away walks, leaving a frosted, slick icing on the sidewalk, the paths became hazardous.

It was even more so if you found yourself drunk, Accorso thought. He could see himself, spilling end over tea kettle on the ice outside of the watering hole. Its 'entrance' opened up at the side of the establishment in the alleyway. Snow covered garbage cans, boxes. and crates lined the walls of the way. Accorso stopped to light a cigarette from the pack in his coat pocket and turned, like a wobbling nine pin to see Lieutenant Pyke stagger out of the club.

Whack-Assed Willie's was a perfect moonshine club. Open long before prohibition, they operated out of the front of the building. But when the Volstead Act was passed, suddenly a once reputable bar withered like a grape on a vine. The once vibrant bar, 'William's Profile', was filled with jubilant with laughing customers, all working, rough and woolly men. They would stagger out of William's and only made it to the curb, collapsing and wrapping their arms around a pile of trash for a good night's sleep with their brothers.

But once the police started enforcing prohibition, William's Profile shrank backwards, receding like low tide into the sea, the saloon moving into the back half of the building, and a simple drug store opened in the front. The heat came down on William's in the form of cops and agents searching for the illicit sale of alcohol. Drug stores were allowed to sell some forms of alcohol, and this was checked carefully by agents to make certain that William's Pharmacy was not flagrantly breaking any laws.

Of which they were. The owner, Liam Sullivan, paid off the police to overlook his direct sale of moonshine over the counter, wrapped in a brown paper bag and tied with cord. The police made money, Liam made money, and his father William Sullivan could not have been prouder of him. Everyone was pleased in the direction that his saloon went, save for his wife. A consummate shrew, she railed on him daily. Bottles of all types of whiskey was filling the backroom, and soon, no one, not even the police would be able to turn the other way. Liam, she explained, was putting his family at risk. To continue, he'd have to be a jackass.

Liam, instead, had an idea. Within two days, the back of the pharmacy was walled up, its door to the rear vanishing, and the back room, a generous space, was converted into a moonshine club. The loading door on the side of the building, emptying out into the alleyway became the front door, and if you didn't know the knock, you were not getting in.

And Whack-assed Willie's was born. History and women made Prohibition go away just as it had come, but Willie's went nowhere. The front remained a reputable drug store, employing actual pharmacists to dispense over-the-counter drugs, while a few doctors on staff prescribed whatever else someone would need.

However, time marched on. The city changed, women were now a part of the speakeasy culture, with jazz music and flapper girls shaking their tight asses. Speakeasies began warring amongst each other, and Liam didn't want to be a part of the chase. He allowed Whack-assed Willie's to stop, freeze, become an oasis of the past, untouched by the sandstorms of history to where it was just a 'spot' like many once glorious places, now denuded into shadows of themselves. Not even a place any longer, simply a dot on the map.

Whack-assed Willie's was their spot.

Pyke went the wrong way down the alley.

"Where the fuck are you going?" Accorso asked, watching as the lieutenant went around a tin garbage can and bent over violently, puking behind it.

"I told you that you shouldn't drink that shit," Accorso said lighting his cigarette between his lips.

Pyke liked to sneak off to Whack-assed occasionally. He wasn't a regular like Accorso, who was a regular where everyone shouldn't be. Accorso came here on Thursdays and Saturdays when a certain waitress would work. As for the liquor, which was once made in the back woods of Pennsylvania or Kentucky in rusty stills and rotten barrels, was now made in a plant owned by Liam, who stayed as loyal as a

Bassett hound to the recipes. What happened was, with Liam's steadfast adherence to the 'formulas' of impoverished moonshiners in the deep hills and valleys, some potent shit was made. And long after Prohibition, these cobbled together concoctions of God only knew what, were served to some of the hardest men in the city.

Accorso looked at James Pyke, his normally well-combed and slicked hair now hanging before his eyes, his face pale and covered with sweat. Clean shaven with long features, heavy brows and an elongated nose, Pyke was more than a supervisor to Accorso. The man was one of the hardest men in the city.

Pyke's drink of preference was called "Yak Yak Bourbon," a concoction favored in Chicago—an impressive mixture of raw grain alcohol, flavored with burnt sugar and iodine. After a few and you have what was now occurring to Pyke at this moment as he went down for the fourth time.

"How much did you have to eat?" Accorso asked him, backing up to the opposing wall of the alleyway, falling into a stark shadow and nearly vanishing from sight. If not for the warm orange-yellow glow that the cigarette end threw at the center of his features, Accorso would have disappeared altogether.

"I think that was the last one." Pyke mumbled.

"Did you get any of it in the trash can?"

"I didn't take the top off," he stood up, breathing shallow. Looking around, he didn't find what he was searching for, until he looked at his feet. "Aww gawd-damn! My hat fell in the fucking puke!" He bent over to scoop it up.

"DON'T DO THAT!" Accorso stepped out of the shadows dramatically, hand out as if he could grab Pyke by the wrist to stop him. Pyke froze anyway, looking up at him, "Why?"

"Take my word for it. That hat is ruined. You'll never get the smell out of it. Leave it," he waved Pyke up the alley. Pyke, eschewing his hat, wobbled behind Accorso. They reached the sidewalk and Accorso stopped, looking up and down the avenue.

"What's wrong?" Pyke asked. "Whatcha lose?"

"The squad car," he replied. He looked down at the once, well taken care of path to the car was now an ice slick. The still faintly falling snow laying a light powder down underfoot. Accorso walked down the avenue, reaching into his coat pocket for the car keys. "It's a block this way."

Pyke fell into step behind him, seemingly oblivious to his environment. If he was to slip on this sidewalk, right now as slick as oil, Accorso knew that he wouldn't be able to hold it in. Falls were so funny to him, although he hated, with all his heart, to be in one.

They reached the car without mishap. After unlocking the doors, Accorso made himself comfortable behind the wheel while Pyke plopped into the passenger seat. He said something that Accorso could not make out, however he wasn't certain if it was Pyke's busted-up verbal skills, or his own busted-up hearing.

The squad car started and lurched out of the parking space, hitting the light traffic uptown. Accorso stared straight ahead, trying to focus on propelling the car ahead, the streetlight, the stop signs, the other vehicles, they all were becoming a sort of blur to him, passing his senses too early or too late, making for a confusion of...

He skidded the car to a stop at a red light. His screeching halt was so pronounced that all heads on the intersection turned to his vehicle ready to hear the crash coming quickly upon something else equally dense and unmovable. When all eyes found the car safe and still, they continued their way.

Accorso's heart pounded in his chest. He was certain that he hadn't drank that much tonight, but at one of these moonshine clubs, one was never too sure of what they were imbibing. It was not uncommon for Liam's bartenders to switch out the 'top shelf' moonshine, if such a thing was possible, to a cheaper, cost-effective drink made out of dubious chemicals. How could a drunk figure out one octane from another?

Accorso stepped on the gas, slipped into the intersection and suddenly it was upon him. An explosion of sorts shook him to the foundations of his being as it literally sent the car spinning and into the corner of a building. He remembered later that his head was like a mallet striking against the driver's side window, filling his skull with light and sound, a huge fireworks show in his consciousness that went black suddenly.

Accorso's head throbbed once, sharply, pulling him up from the thick, dark mire. He gasped as if he couldn't breathe but found he could with no difficulty. He opened his eyes, as if bursting from a deep pool, gasping and finding himself stretched out on a comfortable, white, hospital bed, in a white hospital ward, with about five other men around him in hospital beds in different states of suffering. As Accorso looked at the beds around his he found Pyke in the bed across the center aisle from him, feet facing feet. Pyke was already sitting up against the headboard, staring across the ward at him. His hair was wildly uncombed, a bandage holding a large gauze pad against his right temple was wrapped several times around his head. His right arm, held to his chest, was in a sling.

"You fucked up the driving, goofy," Pyke said. "And the bad thing was that you weren't even drinking Yak Yak Bourbon." He stopped talking and thought about it. "What giggle juice were you drinking anyway?"

Accorso raised his hand to the side of his head, finding it free of bandages. Except for a few aches here and there he felt fine. He looked at his lieutenant. The right side of his eye was bruised. He looked a little worse for wear to Accorso, "Goat Whiskey."

Pyke made a face. "Goat Whiskey? Why do you drink that shit? Is there real goat in that?"

"No, just like there's no yak in your bourbon."

Shaking his head, Pyke slipped his legs off the side of the bed with a sustained and achy groan.

"Maybe you shouldn't do that, lieutenant." Accorso said, slipping from his bed and crossing the aisle to Pyke's side. "Maybe you should stay in bed. You don't look so good."

Pyke fended off his helpful hands with his own one good left hand. "You were sleeping like black haired Snow White when those useless motherfuckers crowded in here."

"Which useless motherfuckers?"

"The press. For some reason I'm front-page news now that I've been in an accident."

"They were here?"

"Yeah. Asking all kinds of stupid questions. I didn't answer shit."

A heavy-set man, appearing like a huge, white pustule on his barren white bed, had a tray of food on his lap. "Yeah, you missed it. They were crowded all around his bed." He cut at his sunny side up egg with a knife and fork. "The doctors had to run them out."

Accorso looked at the gentleman flatly, then returned to Pyke. "You should seriously consider taking some time. Take a nap or something until the doctors release you."

"Release me?" He slid all the way out of the bed, staggered back into a rolling cabinet against the wall. Accorso reached out to grab him, to keep him from compounding the crash by falling down. Pyke slapped away his hand. "I'm getting outta here," he growled.

"I wouldn't do that if I were you," the heavy-set man said in a sing-song tone to him.

"Shut up!" Pyke barked. To Accorso he said, "Help me over to the clothes cabinet where they got our stuff."

Accorso took him by the left arm, draped it over his shoulders and helped him walk across the ward to one of many tall locker-type cabinets where clothes hung on hangers and folded neatly.

"Help me get into my clothes." Pyke turned around, giving Accorso a chance at the bow ties holding his patient gown together and the one on the back of his right arm, keeping that sleeve together. As it parted, the entire gown fell to the floor.

"Thanks, bud. Get dressed," Pyke ordered.

Accorso noticed that Pyke's cabinet was marked with his bed number. Accorso looked around and found his cabinet. Inside he found his clothes, shoes, and wallet. He dressed quickly and then went to Pyke, helping him back to his bed and then aiding him to dress. As Accorso was draping the lieutenant's shirt over his right arm, two men entered the hospital ward.

The first one strolled in with a grin plastered on his face. His features were handsome, almost too slick looking for his own good. His fedora cocked on the side on his head, he looked rather comical and not one for seriousness.

Following behind him, almost comfortable in the shadow of the first, was a sad face with small lips, soulful eyes, and a short pompadour on his head. He scanned the room carefully before cracking a wan smile, not knowing the temperature of the room.

The first one, Giovanni Pedrotti could care less about the 'temperature' of a room. People were going to behave the way they were going to. He was going to behave the way he was going to. So, to him, there was no foul in a fair trade.

But the man that he was about to visit was his commanding officer, so if common sense was plentiful, he should have enough not to piss off Pyke by walking in like a Jack-o-Lantern. He was in a terrible accident and would no doubt be hard pressed to find the humor in his purposeful greeting.

That was until he found his superior officer getting dressed.

"Where are you going?" Pedrotti asked.

"Did you drive here, Pedrotti?" Pyke asked him.

"Yeah, I got a squad car."

"Good, get us outta here." Pyke leaned on the bed, allowing Accorso access to his feet to help him with his shoes. "I'm already sick of this place."

"How are you feeling, boss?" Basilio Frascone asked around Pedrotti, his sour features turning bright and hopeful.

Pyke shook his head, sighing. "Feeling great Frascone. Can't wait to throw a fastball."

Pedrotti went to Accorso who was rising to his feet after finishing shoeing the lieutenant. "How are you doing?"

He hunched his shoulders. "A little sore, but nothing too tough."

SUSPICIOUS LOOKING PACKAGES

"You look fine," Pedrotti indicated Pyke on the bed with a jerk of his head, "he looks like shit," he whispered.

"He's pretty banged up."

"And you're letting him go?"

Accorso made a face, "*You* stop him."

Pedrotti sighed at him then turned to Pyke. "You should wait. The precinct has no doubt called and picked up your wife by now to bring her here. She'll come and miss you if you leave."

"What better reason to *leave*?" Pyke chuckled painfully.

Pyke jumped off the bed and walked between Pedrotti and Frascone, standing in front of him like goal posts. He went back to his cabinet, draped his jacket and coat over his arm, turned around and said, "Let's dust out."

Pyke and Frascone filed out of the room, leaving Pedrotti and Accorso. Accorso went to his cabinet, taking the rest of his things and turned for the door.

"Is he alright, Fab?" Pedrotti asked, now more concerned, his smile faded away.

"I don't know," Accorso sighed, his shoulders sagging. "You know how he is. He's crazy."

"He wasn't drinking that Yak Yak shit last night, was he?"

"Yeah, you know that's his thing."

"And what? Was it your thing too last night?"

Pyke, walking tall but still limping, returned to the ward, looked around as he stood for a moment in the threshold. He found his two subordinates speaking to each other and crossed the room over to them.

"Where's Petey?" He asked Pedrotti.

"He didn't come. He said he had shit to do. He said…" Pedrotti's voice trailed off.

"He said what?" Pyke angled his head so that he could look him in the eyes. "He said what?"

"Well…"

"Well, WHAT, goddammit, Pedrotti?"

Pedrotti gritted his teeth, "He said to get your lazy bitch ass the fuck up and he'll see you at the restaurant tonight."

Pyke stared at Pedrotti. Pedrotti stared back, visibly afraid. Did he just lose his job? Pyke seriously thought about the comment, turned to Accorso, then back to Pedrotti. "And you *had* to bring *him*?" He jerked his thumb over his shoulder at Frascone somewhere behind him, no doubt lost since Pyke doubled back to the ward.

"Petey said to bring him."

"What? Petey's busting my balls today or something?"

"I think he's afraid for you."

"Afraid for what?"

"It *was* a pretty bad accident, sir."

Pyke thought about it for a moment, as if trying to remember it. However he tried, it would not become clear to his mind. "Help me with this coat and jacket. I look like a fright."

Both men helped his good arm into his jacket and coat, they draped the clothing over his bad shoulder.

"Look at you," Pyke said to Accorso with a scowl. "You look like you've been on a picnic or something." He looked the ward up and down, all over. "I need to get the fuck outta here."

"I wouldn't do that if I was you," the heavyset man called out into the air as Pyke stormed out of the room, taking Pedrotti with him, a paper cup caught in the passing wind.

"Shut up," Pyke called back to the man before vanishing from his life forever.

Accorso walked out of the hospital ward, thinking: "Yeah, he was one of the hardest men in the city."

William McCarthy was still a big, burly man. At fifty-seven he had massive guns that he was very proud of. He loved wearing short sleeves shirts, and he would roll them up to his shoulders so that he could show off his biceps, like solid boulders; his forearms were knotted like cabling. He was still barrel chested. Every day after work he would go into his garage where he had a weight set made of concrete filled plastic and would bench press a hundred and fifty pounds until he could barely push the bar up and catch it on the 'Y' posts. He never counted his repetitions, he just pressed until it hurt. He liked the burn.

He also enjoyed the burn of walking upstairs, which is what he did every day.

A Consolidated Edison employee for more years than he could count, McCarthy was a constantly busy man. Today he had a lot to do on this chilly morning. The second floor was for storage, and he was good with storage. He could put things away up here and find it just as fast, thus he was indispensable. It was also cold up here. There was no heat, or if there was it was turned off. Or maybe—

The window. It yawned open not far away, letting the cold, frost-like air in and what semblance there was of the warm air out. He muttered curses under his breath, then started laughing to himself. There was no one up here to hear him. He was totally alone, being an old fool. But that was why he liked it up here so much. No one to bother him.

He reached the window and stuck his head outside. New York, not far below, was bustling. It was just after lunchtime, and everyone was out to find a local restaurant or deli to engage in their repast. People were walking the sidewalks and cars were cruising the street. There wasn't much snow yet this winter, so the ground was clear. However, the cold and the wind reminded him bitterly that this was wintertime, and soon it would be Christmas.

McCarthy stepped back and drew the window down solidly, and that's when he saw it. A simple wooden toolbox, open top, round handle across it lengthwise. *Hmmm, someone left his tools,* he thought. He peeked in. There was nothing inside of it except a length of pipe about four and a half inches long, capped at both ends and wrapped with paper and secured with a rubber band. For some reason this interested McCarthy who reached in and took out the pipe to examine it closely.

Just a pipe, he concluded.

He pulled the paper away, rested the pipe back in the toolbox, and unrolled the paper like a small scroll. It was two pieces of paper with handwriting on the inside.

He read the first note, which was written in block lettering:

Con Edison crooks, this is for you.

Parker thought about that for a moment. *What?* He pulled away and read the second note. It read:

There is no shortage of powder, boys.

For a moment, McCarthy could not move his legs. It was slowly dawning on him what he was just handling. Either through intuition or some past life he recognized the danger, his survival instincts switching into overdrive. He took a step back, his eyes riveted on the toolbox. Whatever he was doing, he was doing it too fucking slow. His nerves jumped with fright, as if he was struck with volts. With his heart pounding, he whirled around and dashed away from the toolbox, shouting, hitting the door to the stairwell, bounding down the steps several at a time, repeating only two words, repeatedly "PIPE BOMB!"

Fabrizzio "Fabulous" Accorso had years of experience as a detective for the New York City Bomb Squad. At only thirty-one, he was a lean, mean, fighting machine. He liked that idea of himself. He was placed on the earth to deal with explosives. It took time to break the wild fear in his heart when around an explosive device. It didn't come easy. All it took was time around his mentor, his superior, and maybe his friend, Lieutenant Pyke. Accorso wasn't certain.

By spending time with the lieutenant, Accorso became inured to experiencing the same reactions as normal people when it came to a violent end to one's life. He allowed Pyke's dispassion to roll through him like waves on the ocean, washing him clean of fear, calming him as if he was a baby in the arms of its mother. *Besides*, he smirked, *death would be instantaneous.*

SUSPICIOUS LOOKING PACKAGES

He sat in the driver's seat of a flatbed truck rumbling to a stop in front of one of the many buildings in the massive complex of Consolidated Edison on the west side. Its industrial-like piping stuck out like veins and arteries around the buildings, fire escape ladders and railwork, ugly gun gray metal smokestacks, cold and hard building of lifeless granite, were all smudged with dirt and grime. It reeked of mechanical progress and lifeless existence. *Depressing*, Accorso thought, lowering his head to look under the roof of the cab windshield and up at the monolithic buildings towering over them, squat city dwarfs, unlike their skyscraper brothers.

The LaGuardia-Pyke Bomb Carrier lumbered down Amsterdam, puffing, and wheezing as he pressed down on the brakes or stepped on the accelerator. It was a long, protesting, flatbed of a truck moving through traffic like an ox through a flock of sheep.

"Easy Fab."

Giovanni "Beat It" Pedrotti sat in the passenger seat. He was a little younger than Accorso, slim, trim, and equally handsome. He was always told that he had a wise-ass face, and it was hard to tell if it reflected his personality or if his personality reflected his face. Accorso laughed. His guess was that it was probably the face. Many times, his companion was depressed over something, and by looking at him, Accorso mistook his features for someone gloating silently.

"What's so funny?" Pedrotti asked, as he turned from staring out the passenger side window to look at his partner.

Accorso smiled, his features turning younger. His wife, Daria, loved it when he smiled. She said the years dropped off as if by magic and he would quickly resemble a young, mischievous boy. He turned this boyish face to Pedrotti.

"Oh, forget it," Pedrotti waved at him with disgust.

"I was just thinking about something."

"What's that?"

"Nothing."

Sixty-fourth street was coming up, he stomped on the brake. The truck made a declaration of mechanical hardship as it lumbered to a stop. The reason? Welded to the flatbed of the truck was a huge, heavy cage made of woven, flexible steel elevator cables. The construct resembled a steel, wickerwork-like covered wagon from the old westerns. This made the weight bearing down on the back of the truck beyond imagination. The groaning, the difficulty in stopping and starting, the rough handling was all because of the burden of the "cage."

Accorso waited for the oncoming traffic to part, allowing him to make a left onto sixty-fourth and head down the street.

"You know where you're going, Fab?" Pedrotti looked upwards at the hulk of a building towering over them, throwing the street into shadow.

"Yeah, I know." *Why was he worrying*, Accorso thought. He didn't know here he was going. He was just going to stop in the middle of the block, get out, and walk around.

Once in the middle of the block he stopped the truck and shifted into park.

"Let's go," he said.

They jumped out of the cab which was a farther drop to the tarmac than one would expect to clear the huge front tire. Behind them, two Plymouth two-door radio cars in single file came to a stop. Immediately patrolmen jumped from the vehicles. Accorso waved the foremost driver away. The patrolman looked at him quizzically.

"You've got to back up your cars. We'll have to have access to the rear of the carrier," Accorso informed. "And, trust me, you don't want to be anywhere near here."

The patrolman nodded, turned, and marched down the side of his car to the driver of the Plymouth behind his, informing him that they had to back it up. Accorso shook his head. Didn't they see this big assed door in the back of the cage?

The sides and back of the covered wagon of steel mesh had DANGER sprayed on metal plaques in huge black lettering. He wondered what the average driver thought when they came upon this monstrosity on the road. Or did they not even care, because Accorso had to admit, he didn't.

A gust of wind knocked the warm glaze from his body that he picked up from the heater in the cab, cutting through his wool suit like an icy straight razor. Dancing to try to generate body heat he went to the sidewalk, which now had very little foot traffic and found Pedrotti speaking to a man in a suit. He was easily in his late sixties, silver haired and nearly bald. Why he was out here without a hat was beyond Accorso who pulled his fedora nearer to his brows.

As he came upon them, Pedrotti pointed to him for the old man. "This is my partner, Detective Fabrizzio Accorso."

The old man extended his hand. "Thank you for coming so fast. I'm Lawrence Schwab, the building manager."

"Pleased to meet you." Accorso looked him up and down, noting his expensive pinstripe suit and vest. He held a narrow, chewed upon cigar in his hand. His pale face reminded Accorso of a furrowed bloodhound with sunken eyes and loose jowls.

"Here, here, hurry." Schwab was a man in crisis now. He spun on his heels and dashed to an entrance to the left of the middle of the block. *Well, I was close*, Accorso thought, thinking about where he had parked the carrier truck.

As he began to walk off one of the patrolmen stepped in his path. "What do you want us to do?"

More sirens were coming their way, echoing loudly off the high walls of the dead buildings around them.

"Do you hear that?" he asked the patrolman.

"Yeah, incoming."

"Take care of that. Have everyone clear a block and a half away until we get the bomb into the carrier. Those guys are probably the emergency squad. Get them to relax. They're gonna wanna march in. Let them know clearly that they are doing it at the risk of their own lives."

"Yes sir," the patrolman nodded and was off.

Accorso entered the building. A large vestibule of shiny polished granite yawned around him, echoing voices. Pedrotti had joined a group of other men in front of a marble reception desk and receptionist. One was a hulking sort of older man, big arms, barrel chested in a rolled up short-sleeved shirt, trunk-sized thighs in black slacks. Accorso made a mental note not to get on his bad side.

The other was young and clear faced, opposite of the big man. He was gangly, tall, his hair parted down the center, combed to the sides. He appeared very fastidious in his suit, well-pressed and stylish. His features were flat, concerned, his eyes searching and clear. In other words: he was frightened.

Schwab motioned to him. "This is Evan Miller, Labor Supervisor."

Miller nodded to them but remained silent.

Schwab continued, motioning to 'muscles.' "And this is William McCarthy. He found the bomb."

"Yeah, upstairs," McCarthy blurted nervously.

"We called you people last night," Schwab informed, waddling in some insane fashion around from face to face. He too was nervous over the fact that death was somewhere in the building. "You people came over and went through everything."

"And it wasn't here then?" Accorso asked.

"They didn't find anything. Didn't you know?"

"That's the night shift."

Pedrotti clapped his hands and rubbed them together vigorously. "Well, let's get started."

"Sure, sure," was Schwab's anxious reply.

McCarthy led the two detectives and Evan Miller to a doorway with Schwab waddling behind him to an ascending stair and through a second-floor storage area. After a handful of steps from the stairwell door, McCarthy ground to a halt.

"How close can I get?" he asked, his voice trembling.

"Can you point it out to us?" Pedrotti asked.

The muscles in his arm came to life under his skin as he pointed ahead. "It's over there, in a wooden toolbox."

"What did you do when you found the bomb?" Pedrotti asked.

"Well, I didn't know what it was. I just picked it up."

Evan Miller stepped in, tapped Pedrotti on the shoulder and handed him the two notes. "These were wrapped around it."

Pedrotti took the notes and read.

"You handled the device?" Accorso said around Miller's back.

McCarthy nodded, the fear was still on his face, his skin taking on a waxy pallor. "I didn't know what it was."

"Well, fortunately for you it's not motion sensitive, or we'd be cleaning you up with a sponge right now."

"Thank God!" McCarthy breathed.

Pedrotti walked to Accorso and handed him the notes. "Read these."

"So what are you going to do?" Miller asked Pedrotti.

"Well we're going to take a look at it, and then we're going to take it out of here if we can."

"If you can't?"

"Then I won't give a fuck what happens." Pedrotti smiled.

Miller turned away, exasperated. The tension was getting to him.

"Yeah," Accorso said to the three of them. "We need you to leave this area and clear the vestibule."

"Sure, sure," Schwab said. He was close to falling into a panic.

The three civilians scattered, leaving the two detectives alone.

"C'mon," Pedrotti said, striking off toward the window in the distance.

Accorso tucked the notes into his jacket pocket and walked with his partner, making it a point to walk beside him, not behind him. He did not want to hear Pedrotti turn around and ask him was he scared. It was always a stupid question. He never thought about anything when he was in these kinds of situations. All he concentrated on was understanding the task at hand.

They approached the wooden toolbox. Pedrotti pulled his Fedora to the back of his head and they both looked in, and sure enough, it looked like a pipe bomb.

"A Devil Toy." Accorso breathed.

"Yep." Pedrotti nodded. "Let's get the envelope."

They were outside again, at the rear of the carrier. Parked out in the middle of the street was the black Ford E83W van that carried their equipment. They went to the vehicle as Basilio "Big O" Frascone scrambled out of the driver's side door and trotted to the rear to meet them. Frascone was like a happy puppy, anxious to please, grabbing the left side door by the handle and opening it up for Accorso. Accorso opened the right-hand door on his own, staring at his assistant, his tired features attempting to communicate to Frascone to relax.

"So?" Frascone said, "Is it somebody's lunch in a bag?"

"No, it looks like a bomb."

"Shit, really?"

"Yeah. A pipe bomb. Maybe the powder from a couple sticks of dynamite as an explosive force."

Accorso removed their hats, tossing them in the back of the van.

Frascone reached into the van and pulled out a long metal pole and placed it on the street at their feet. Reaching back into the van he dragged out the heavy, woven steel mesh basket, made of the same elevator cabling as the containment truck and folded closed at the top, affectionately known as "The Envelope." Accorso patted Frascone on the shoulder. "Okay Big O, we got it from here. Don't be here when we get back."

Frascone nodded. "Don't worry, I won't."

Pedrotti lifted the metal pole and set it on the loops on the top of the basket, snapping them into metal clasps welded to the pole. With a slight groan he heaved his end of the pole up onto his shoulder. Accorso lifted the other end with a tired sigh, placing it on his shoulder. With the envelope suspended between them on the length of pole they walked back into the building.

Pedrotti stopped at the door to the stairwell gauging dimensions in his mind. "We're not going to be able to get the envelope up there."

Accorso nodded, "Here...... here set it down."

They bent at the knees together, slipped the pole off their shoulders together and rested the envelope on the floor.

"You open it up. I'll go get the 'Toy'." Accorso said, his voice steady, yet beads of sweat were breaking out on his forehead. He blamed it on the exertion of carrying the heavy containment package into the lobby of the building.

"Why should you go?"

"Because I owe a lot of bills this month. If I explode, I can use that as an excuse to skip out on them."

Pedrotti chuckled as he worked on opening the top of the envelope. Accorso marched past him and upstairs. He reached the second floor and against all common sense, against all rhyme, and definitely against all reason, without hesitation, marched over to the toolbox. All the while, tiny voices were screaming in his head. His imagination played a detonation horror story through his body. He could feel the expanding gases, the flames, the shock wave rush through his frame the instant he touched the pipe bomb. Angrily he shrugged the thought out of his mind. That's stupid, he said to himself, death is instantaneous. You don't feel anything. And besides, McCarthy manhandled the thing earlier and lived to talk about it. His chances of death were quite slim in his rational explanation. Although, there wasn't anything rational about walking up to a 'Devil Toy' and carrying it around like an innocent piece of pipe.

But handling it like an innocent piece of pipe is what he did as he simply reached into the toolbox and took up the impeccant length of metal.

Turning he walked nonchalantly back to the stairwell and trotted down the stair seemingly without a care in the world. Pedrotti was waiting for him, the envelope yawning open on the lobby floor. Accorso placed the bomb into the basket and together they closed it.

"So far so good," Pedrotti said smiling back at Accorso.

"Don't jinx us." Accorso replied.

Reattaching the length of pipe through the basket loops, they hoisted the envelope on their shoulders and again marched out of the vestibule and onto the deserted street. In the blocks that followed, closing off a two-block radius to the Con Edison buildings, were squad cars, policemen, and men from the nearest emergency squad. The red turret lights atop their cars flashing light like small flares, filling the street with strobing light. Although concerned and apparently ready to act, the rest of the first responders stayed well away from the front of the building, the containment truck and behind their vehicles.

Upon reaching the rear of the Carrier Accorso and Pedrotti lowered the envelope to the tarmac, allowing Accorso to lift a thick, wide door, similar to the door of a bank vault, at the back of the vehicle. A pulley and cable system inside caused a rectangular box to gently slide out from deep inside the center of the Carrier. This was the trusty Bomb Tank. Twenty-nine inches long, twenty-four inches high, eighteen inches wide and constructed of 26-gauge galvanized iron, it weighed forty-eight pounds. Together Accorso and Pedrotti rested the tank on the ground next to the envelope and transferred the pipe bomb from one to the other. Then they placed the top on the tank and returned it to its carriage protruding from the back of the Carrier. They closed the door, and like a tongue retreating into a mouth, the Tank went in and away, allowing the door to shut and lock.

Carefully, they climbed down from the back of the truck and gathered their equipment amid a raucous round of applause from the people and officers gathered around at a safe spectator's distance.

"Don't look like we're going to die today, buddy." Pedrotti said.

"I'm not going to happy until we dunk this thing."

They returned the length of pipe and the envelope back to the van. Frascone came running to their aid, helping them to push the equipment into the van. An excited extra pair of hands, as his nervous and enthusiastic features went from Accorso's face to Pedrotti's, his passion so high that he threatened to detonate like the thing in the carrier in front of them.

"So far so good, huh?" Frascone asked, both eyes afire.

"You're not going to our funeral, are you?" Pedrotti asked.

Accorso smiled, that boyish grin.

A patrolman walked up to them, clearly reluctant as if they were still handling the 'Toy'. "Is everything safe now?"

"Safe as houses." Accorso replied, donning his hat. "Just give us a chance to get the bomb out of here. We need to have one squad car follow us, the other officers can let those people in the building and surrounding area know that it's all over."

"Alright. Give us a minute."

Accorso, Pedrotti and Frascone walk to the front of the van. Once at the driver's side door, Frascone jumped in, slamming the door shut behind him. Accorso climbed behind the wheel of the carrier once more, with Pedrotti riding shotgun.

They sat for a moment, silently staring ahead out of the windshield.

Accorso turned to his partner. "Brooklyn?"

"Brooklyn."

He leaned forward and started the engine.

The carrier lumbered into Brooklyn, wheezing and puffing, rumbling and roaring. Their destination was an old ash dump off Avenue U and East 76th street. A wide, flat stretch of beaten earth far away from buildings or people. A very lonely, desolate place to die if something went horribly wrong.

Accorso always thought about the finish. With his luck it would happen at the very last moment, the very last instant, when everything seemed fine and done, then boom. He stopped the truck in the middle of nothing. Ahead of them was the sluggish Paerdegat Basin which opened into Jamaica Bay to the south. Here the wind ran cold, straight off the water. The police parked far from the Carrier, whereas Frascone pulled up beside them. Jumping down from the cab of the carrier, they once again went to the rear of the van, this time gathering their coats against the arctic like cold.

"Beat feet, Big O," Pedrotti said, leaning his back against the rear doors of the van.

"You got it." And with a spring in his step, Frascone was off and running.

"One more time." Accorso grinned.

"One more time" Pedrotti nodded.

Once again, they returned to the back of the Carrier. However, this time they carried the tank directly from its carriage by handles at each end and walked it over some distance to a collection of waist high oil drums. Carefully, they rested the tank next to one with a pump spigot.

Accorso lifted the top off the tank and reached in, taking a set of straps attached to the bottom of the inside of the tank and secured the pipe bomb firmly to keep it from floating. Pedrotti took a hose leading from the spigot, stuck it into the tank and started working the hand pump. Thick, black motor oil poured out of the end of the hose and in moments they filled the tank nearly to the rim. When done they returned to the van, closing the doors, and resting back against them, exhausted.

"You know, all of this shit is pretty heavy," Pedrotti said with an awkward smile.

"And it seems like every year it just keeps getting heavier and heavier."

"Or else we're getting weaker and weaker."

Across the distance they could see Frascone break away from the patrolmen and run towards them. The patrolmen retreated into their radio car, backed the vehicle up, turned around, and drove off. Pedrotti reached into his jacket to pull out a pack of cigarettes and stuck one between his lips before handing the pack to Accorso who helped himself to one.

"How long do you think we're going to have to wait?" Pedrotti asked, lighting his cigarette, and handing his partner the matches.

"I don't know. How long do you think it'll take for that motor oil to gum up the works?" Accorso handed him back the matches and pack.

"The usual fifteen minutes?"

"Sounds good."

Frascone stopped before them, his eyes electric like the filament of a light bulb. "All done?"

Accorso and Pedrotti looked at him tiredly. He was young, younger than Pedrotti, skinny with jet black hair combed into a ridiculous pompadour. He reminded Accorso of a child anxious to go outside to play. But there was something about him. Something not quite right. Pyke said that it was bad luck. The young man reeked of it. It hung from his clothing like a heavy cape, dragging behind him black death and destruction. Pyke didn't like or trust him for that feeling. This made it even more difficult for Accorso and Pedrotti to want him around, as if he was the personification of the bombs they carried away, eager to explode, stirred to take a life.

"All done, Big O. You can go home now." Pedrotti sighed.

"Okay, guys. I'll see you back at the precinct."

"Yeah," Accorso said. "You do that."

With a nod, Frascone ran to the front of the van, drove around the carrier, and drove off.

Now standing, the two men watched as the van shrank until it disappeared around the corner of a bank of homes.

"Fuck, it's cold out here." Pedrotti said, now shifting his weight from one leg to the other, gathering the edges of his coat around him.

"Let's get into the cab."

They climbed into the Carrier and relaxed, slouching in the seats.

Out of the clear blue Pedrotti asked: "What were you laughing at earlier?"

"Wha—? Nothing."

"It had to be something."

"What is wrong with you? Beat it?"

"Nothing is wrong with me."

They nod.

"Well maybe one thing," Pedrotti says.

"What's that?"

"I'm getting tired of fucking my wife."

"Really?"

"Really."

"That's not good. You know they say once the sex breaks down the marriage is not that far behind."

"Don't you think I know that?" Pedrotti took a final drag off his cigarette, reducing it down to the butt, cranked down the window and flicked it out of the cab.

"I'd rather sort out my sock drawer, or do housecleaning sometimes more than fuck her," he said, mournfully.

"I've always told you about being a whoremonger. Now you're addicted."

"What are you talking about? You're just as much a whoremonger as I am."

Accorso cranked down his window, tossing out his cigarette butt. "No, I'm not."

"Oh yes you are."

With the window down Accorso could see approaching in the side view mirror, a black Buick Century touring sedan. He cranked up the window. "C'mon."

"What's going on?"

They jumped out of the carrier and marched to the rear of the truck, coming together to face the vehicle that was slowly coming to a stop several yards away. Both doors opened and two dark suited men stood from the car. The passenger approached. Dressed in a three-piece suit and of average build, Peter Edward Hayias strode up to them in a heavy wool coat, silk scarf puffed at the chin, tucked under the lapels of the coat and a snappy fedora, its brim folded down and tilted. His features were smooth and soft, almost like a woman's, sleepy eyes at half-mast, his lips thin, almost non-existent. Under his arm he had a rolled-up newspaper. He looked at the two of them, his eyes darting back and forth as if he was wondering if they could be trusted.

"Accorso, Pedrotti," he said.

"Hayias." Pedrotti replied.

"How long have you been waiting?"

"Almost ten minutes."

"Can I have it now?"

"Sure. Your funeral."

The three men walked to the Tank. With his foot and a little heave ho, Pedrotti kicked the Tank over onto its side, spilling the thick motor oil onto the packed earth, the pipe bomb rolling out with it. Hayias opened the newspaper, stooped low, and wrapped the device up in it.

Accorso called out to him. "Hayias."

"What?"

Accorso reached into his jacket pocket and came away with the two notes, handing them over to him.

"What's this?" Hayias asked.

"They were the notes wrapped around the pipe bomb."

"There was a *note* on the bomb?"

Accorso nodded.

"Thank you, gentlemen." Hayias said, turned and walked back to his car. They watched and he climbed into the passenger side and was driven off.

"Come on," Pedrotti said. "Let's clean this shit up. It's fucking cold out here."

In the late afternoon, Peter Hayias entered his office at 72 Popular Street, Brooklyn where he had left the pipe bomb for safe keeping, walking in, and hanging up his coat, jacket, and hat. Returning to the door, he gently closed it, then looked down at his watch. Six o'clock. He realized that he would be sequestered in his office, probably for the rest of the night. His "office" was a workroom. When entering in, his desk was directly in front of the door, but instead of facing the door, it faced left so that when people peeked in all they could see was his profile. Why was this important? Because he felt more comfortable doing it this way. Everything he did was for his own comfort. It was also very comforting to stay alone, in his office, for hours on end, studying. He liked to read, to learn and strangely enough, the best teachers were those that didn't put their knowledge in books.

He turned off the room light in the office.

In front of his desk, to the right, was a long workbench that traveled the length of the room, divided into four work areas where he could place separate projects. Right now, there was nothing to work on. Nothing on his bench. Nothing until Lieutenant Pyke called him to relate that he had sent two detectives to deal with a pipe bomb. Ahh, at last. Something to do!

Each section of his workbench had its own industrial adjustable goose-neck coil machinist table lamp with the "slim helmet" shade around the bulb. He went to the work area closest to his desk and turned on the light. He looked down at the pool of illumination that shone on the desk and noticed what looked like a thin film of dust. He wasn't certain. With the side of his hand, he brushed lightly at it, sweeping any dust off onto the floor. If that's what it was.

Now growing excited enough to elicit a smile on his otherwise stern features, Hayias turned to his desk and regarded the roll of newspaper from a distance. It already started to present greasy oil spots around it. He went over to and lifted it carefully. Not that he was fearful in any way that it would detonate. No, he was past that. He carried it so gingerly because it was so full of potential. The potential to teach him, to allow him to learn, to learn about its maker.

Every bomb had a signature, a fingerprint that made it unique and if studied enough, the fingerprint could conceivably construct its creator, just as its creator constructed it. It was a heady thought for Peter Hayias. He was a tinkerer. He liked spending long, tireless hours hunched over his workbench, taking apart things. Then, for a real challenge he would put it back together. But even in things, such as a watch movement, or a car engine, you have two completely different signatures. You have two complete purposes. If you ran into the same make of watch, you wouldn't think Ford, you'd think Bulova. The same exact thing with bombs. You can practically tell by the parts used, the order in which they are assembled, even the amount of gun powder or even more exciting—nitroglycerin—who built it.

Hayias smiled at the thought.

There would be little chance of that though. If this bomb contained any amount of nitroglycerin, then it was made to be motion sensitive and Accorso and Pedrotti would not be sitting in a bar drinking booze and smoking cigarettes now, which is what he assumed they would be doing.

No, this was a real interesting device.

He unwrapped it like a Christmas present, laid the badly soiled newspaper flat on the bench and stared down at it. Excitement was building in him as he went to his desk, moved his portable Royal Arrow typewriter from the side to dead center. Then he went through his bottom desk drawer and came away with a pair of rubber gloves, slipping them over his hands. He pulled off his tie, unbuttoned his collar, and got ready to go to work.

Returning to the workbench, he retrieved his rolling chair from the center of the bench and wheeled it over to a stop before the pipe bomb and sat down. In moments, Hayias was struggling with the thing with two sets of pipe wrenches. He stood up to create some form of leverage, pulled one wrench secured to the pipe clockwise while straining to use the other wrench to turn the cap counterclockwise. Success! The cap gave way and started to turn easily around its threads. Putting the wrenches aside he hand screwed the cap off and carefully turned it upside down to shake out its contents, but instead of oil pouring from the opening, its internal components came tumbling out, free of contamination. The oil bath did not penetrate the pipe bomb to render it inert. Surprisingly, it did not detonate.

Hayias cracked a wry smile. He made a mental note, Hayias: one. Bomber: zero. Here, spilling out from the pipe came the usual components such as a flashlight bulb, a battery, a steel spring, and an unwrapped Parke-Davis throat lozenge. Hayias stopped to look at the seemingly random items on his workbench, pushing them around with the end of a pencil.

Well, since the oil did not contaminate the parts...

He stood and went for his fingerprint kit and dusted the bulb for a print and found none. He did the same with the battery, nothing. Another thing—there was no black powder. It wasn't made to detonate. It was built a dud. But like any artist, there is a recipe, and all the components for a good bomb recipe were here. All except one. Hayias reasoned that the message was simple: the creator wanted to prove beyond the shadow of a doubt that he could make a bomb as deadly as he desired, but he chose to make this one a dud. It was a notice, a calling card. And the throat lozenge? Was that his signature, his unique fingerprint? What was that for?

Hayias placed each piece of the pipe bomb apart from each other, in neat rows, one at a time, at perfect right angles along with the two notes. When done he went to his desk, removed his gloves, put a sheet of paper in the Royal, and started typing his report.

Lieutenant Pyke was spending a late night in the office. He had a great many forms to file, fill out, throw out. That's what he liked about working in the Bomb Squad, the paperwork, he thought bitterly. If he handled as many bombs as he did reams of paper, his odds for survival would have dropped to nil in less than a week. Well, at least he had an uneventful day today. A bomb scare, an actual bomb, and the defusing of said bomb without the loss of life. That made it a good day. At least he didn't have to write condolences letters.

His door was open, but someone was rapping their knuckles on the threshold, keeping out of sight from his desk.

"Come in," Pyke said gruffly.

Peter Hayias walked into the room in a long wool coat; dark, three-piece suit; and a fedora. "How's it going?"

"Another fucking night."

"Pikey, I have something for you."

Pyke waved him in tiredly. He looked at his pocket watch. It was pushing 23:30. Before sitting down, Hayias hung his fedora and coat on a nearby coat rack.

"Whaddaya got?" Pyke asked.

"I finished my report for you and the commissioner on the bomb that was deactivated today in the Con Ed building." He leaned forward, handing the file folder over the desk to Pyke. Pyke opened it. A goodly number of pages. He was well aware Hayias did good work, and what's more, he was fast. Very fast. If Pyke didn't know better, he would come to believe that Hayias loved his job. Pyke flipped through pages of the file. Neat, double spaced, no noticeable errors.

"So, Pete, give me the long and short, I'll leave it up to the commissioner to read it." Pyke said.

"Oh, sure." Hayias was somewhat startled. He was a good writer. He received all A's in English and grammar and he thought he did such a remarkable job in simplifying hard topics, why wouldn't anyone want to read his reports? "Well, I went into the device. It had all the components for making a bomb, except for one. Further, I couldn't find any fingerprints on the internal components, meaning that our bomber is very careful, methodical, neat."

"Fingerprints? The internals didn't get gummed up with the motor oil?"

"Airtight job." Hayias cracked a wry smile. Pyke really didn't see the humor, but he still smiled back. "What did you mean about the pipe bomb having all of its components except one?"

"It is my belief that it was intentionally made imperfect and could never detonate, and that it's also some sort of message."

"A message from a nut, that's all we need. Someone get me a soda," Pyke said sarcastically. "How did you draw this conclusion?"

"Firstly, the device had no smoke-less powder needed for a clean detonation."

Pyke sat back in his chair, pondering. "No powder?"

"None."

"Was that all?"

"Not in the least." Hayias's eyes grew wide. "The second reason why I've come to this conclusion is that it had two notes wrapped around the pipe bomb. If the creator's intention was to have it explode, the detonation would have destroyed them. So, it stands to reason that he wanted it found, read, examined, and understood."

"You understand his shit, Pete?" Pyke asked incredulously.

"I think I do."

"Let me ask you a question that needs not leave this room. The only reason why I'm asking you this is because I know the commissioner will be asking me, and I want to be able to do something other than stand before him with my thumb up my ass."

"Sure."

"Is this the work of the World's Fair bomber?"

Hayias frowned. "Absolutely not. First and foremost, those were sticks of dynamite. The residue is unmistakable. This was a pipe bomb. Two completely different signatures."

"Signatures, huh?"

"That's correct."

Pyke fell silent, staring down at the file on his desk, slipping into a daydream. He would indeed have to go to the commissioner over this. Con Ed was an institution, a utility, and someone harassing it had to come to his attention. No sooner would he inform him of such, the first question would be about the only thing still hanging on his mind, like some sort of stubborn symbiont hanging off the side of his head, impossible to remove but feeding silently, stealthily. Pyke could see it easily though everyone else could not. It tormented Commissioner Valentine because not only were two detectives killed cowardly, it was also still an unsolved.

Suddenly Pyke snapped out of it, stood straight up from his desk, and extended his hand to Hayias. "Very good job, Pete. Very good. I'm going to get this file to Commissioner Valentine tonight."

Hayias rose to his feet and shook hands with the lieutenant. "Alright. I'm just glad I got it to you in a timely fashion." He went to the coat rack, snatching away his coat and hat pressing it against his chest. "Going home?"

"I told you...the commissioner."

"After that."

"What's up, Pete? You don't want to go home to Clara?"

"Do you want to go home to Amanda?"

Pyke laughed. "We can do it tomorrow. I don't know how long Valentine is going to keep me at this meeting tonight."

"Are you scheduled to have a meeting with him?"

"No, but as soon as I show up with this report, it'll turn into one."

Hayias nodded, slipped the fedora on his head, "Okay, then. Goodnight." And with that he was out of the office.

Pyke leaned forward on the desk, his hands resting atop it.

"A dud, huh?" He picked up the phone, requested the motor pool. "Hello, it's Pyke. I need a car. Now."

Commissioner Valentine was standing at the window in his office, behind his desk, with a mug of coffee in his hand. He stared down at the cold New York night outside which was indeed one of his most favorite pastimes from his office at 240 Centre Street. He watched dispassionately as cars moved sluggishly down Centre Street towards the intersection at Broome. It was late. He glanced at the grandfather clock across the room which read 24:20 p.m. The lights were off in his office, leaving the desk lamp the only illumination, causing gloomy shadows to stalk the room in lost corners, making his library around him look like flat grins of frightening teeth. Strangely enough, Valentine liked the dark quiet. During the day there was simply too much activity. People walking in and out, phones ringing, document signing, and having to make meeting after meeting and appointment after appointment that seemed to have no end. Nights like these were a godsend. Quiet, coffee, darkness—

There was a knock on the door.

Shit.

Valentine turned around, his mood changing quickly from tranquil to annoyed. "Yes?" he asked testily. It was a male's voice. Alice was long gone by now.

"It's me," Pyke called through the closed door.

Valentine shook his head in mild disgust. He wasn't necessarily angry at Pyke; he was annoyed that Pyke was here with most likely nothing good to tell him. If it was good news, he would have probably waited until the morning.

"Come in."

The door opened slowly, and Pyke stepped into the room, dressed in a brown pin-striped suit, tie, and an open black wool overcoat. Around his neck was a tan scarf wrapped twice. He held his fedora in one hand, a folder in the other.

"Commissioner," he began. "I have a report for you that I thought you'd might like to see."

Pyke's long face was flat, displaying no emotion so as not to give Valentine any impression of what the report contained. Valentine did not answer him directly. He rested his mug down on his desk and pointed to the light switch behind Pyke. "Please turn on the light.

Pyke flicked on the light, filling the room with the bright glow of the wall lamps.

"Firstly, you don't need to be so formal, James. What do you have for me?" Valentine held out his hand.

Pyke crossed the room and handed over the file. "Hayias's report on the pipe bomb found at Con Ed over on the west side."

"Really?" Valentine opened the folder and flipped through the pages. The report was well typed, error-free sheets on clean pages devoid of stains, all the hallmarks of a report written by Peter Hayias, one of his best bomb squad detectives.

"Anything interesting in it?" Valentine took a seat in his chair and motioned to the chair in front of his desk for Pyke to take.

"Well, the bomb was a dud."

"That's interesting." Valentine opened the folder on his desk and flipped through the pages again.

"Hayias thinks that it's a message, a calling card of some kind."

"Does he have any idea what the message is?"

"It's on page three—two notes wrapped around the pipe bomb."

Valentine turned to page three, brought his index finger down on the paper, followed the line of text until he found the notation in the notes. "Hmmm, he doesn't seem to like Con Edison." He wagged a finger, tapped on the paper with it. "'There is no shortage of powder boys'? Sounds like he's promising further attacks."

"Sounds like it."

"But he makes duds."

"That's the interesting thing, sir. Hayias says that the bomb had all the components to operate accordingly. It was just missing one."

"Missing? I don't understand."

Pyke began playing with the brim of his hat in his lap. "The way that Hayias puts it, the bomber wants us to know that he can build an operational device. It's just that this one was a dud, it was instead a message."

"Now that REALLY doesn't sound good." Valentine closed the folder. "Let me ask you your opinion since we are so shy on facts--."

"What's that, Lou?"

"Has this any connection to the World's Fair bombing five months ago?"

"No. Hayias assures me that there is absolutely no connection."

Valentine growled darkly. "Because I want *that* motherfucker that killed my two detectives." He quickly shifted gears, his finger rapping on the folder once more. "I want *this* motherfucker, too, who thinks he's bold enough to send me a fucking message." Then he looked up at Pyke. "Do you get me?"

"I know how you feel. I share it. I want these men myself."

"Do you think you can catch them? Do you think you can catch anyone, James?"

"I hope you're not doubting me, Lou. I can do this." Pyke nodded firmly.

There was a pause. Valentine stared at him, lost in thought. Whatever was churning behind his eyes caused his face to blush. "After the World's Fair, you and I went all in to straighten out the bomb squad. We worked on the construction of the carrier, we made advancements in the technologies that we employ now, like the portable fluoroscope. We dragged every low life we could find through the doors of justice to shake that coward loose. I've appeared in newsreels in movies, I've had placards in movie theater lobbies, and over 30,000 circulars distributed nationwide informing people of the $26,000 in reward for the capture of this motherfucker—do you see what I'm getting at?"

"I do." Pyke nodded.

"I'll bend over backwards for you, James, but I want to be assured that you can do the job. Can you do this job? Can your boys do something other than defuse bombs?"

"We can catch criminals too, Lou. Trust me."

"Well, that's all I can give you, James. My support and my trust. You have them both. Do me a favor, bring these men to justice."

"I can and I will." Rising quickly and planting his fedora on his head, "I will." Pyke turned headed for the door.

"Also, please turn off the light," Valentine called out behind him.

The light in the office went out, the door closed.

Valentine was at peace again. He picked up his mug and returned to his window.

Accorso shifted the Plymouth two-door into park and slipped out of the vehicle. Pedrotti stood from the passenger side and they both walked down the North Service Road to the wide Eastern Parkway, the main arterial going past the Brooklyn Museum, which was directly across the parkway from them, emptying out into the wide Grand Army Plaza, the oval memorial not far away that acted like a beating heart for all the traffic transversing Brooklyn.

Although Eastern Parkway was sluggish from all the rubberneckers easing past the blast area, the North Service Road was jammed to cessation from the scores of police cars, fire trucks, emergency squad trucks, ambulances and other support vehicles not only choking off the road but up on the grassy median and sidewalk. Accorso and Pedrotti waved their shields at intercepting officers, trying to get to the officers in command of the chaos, because they most certainly were looking for them.

Standing near the large emergency squad van were two from their squad, and three uniformed officers. Accorso assumed that these five were calling the shots. As soon as they entered earshot and serendipitously recognized by their fedoras and wool overcoats the two Emergency squad officers pounced.

"Jesus Christ, what took you guys so long?" One of the officers asked.

"Traffic," Accorso replied, "What's going on?"

"We don't really fucking know. We pulled two pieces of toast out of the basement, crying that something exploded."

"Dead? Crying?"

"Very much alive. They left earlier in ambulances."

Pedrotti stepped up. "They said that something just blew up."

"Just about. One of the assholes were smoking, but we don't know if it fits in. The NYPD sent officers to get statements from them to give us some clues. Maybe it was a gas leak?"

"So, what do you need?" Accorso asked, looking around.

"We sent the firemen in to figure out what they could, but they're not happy to be walking around down there not knowing if there's going to be a double header, you know what I mean?"

Accorso nodded. "Which entrance?"

The officer pointed into the distance. "Over there, then downstairs. Follow the firemen."

Accorso and Pedrotti entered the building and if not for the officers hustling the concerned tenants out of the way, it would appear pretty much normal, meaning that the blast was wholly contained in the basement. They took a service flight of stairs down to a winding hall filled with firemen carrying halligans and helmets. They stepped out of their way, walking out, the floor at their feet flooded with water up to the soles of their shoes.

They entered a storeroom where the real carnage was, where the walls, floor and ceiling were seared black, and flammable boxes and crates had gone up in flames. The blast pattern was clear, and they, like the experienced fire fighters, followed it to the center of the blast, where visibly, everything was blown away from.

A weary firefighter, his face streaked with soot, pulled his helmet from his head, and looked Accorso up and down. "You're gonna fuck up that pretty assed coat."

"That's alright," Accorso said, "comes with the territory. Did you figure out what happened?"

"There is a lot of dark room equipment around here, lamps and lights and shit. We think these two meatheads were fucking around with some of the flammable chemicals and lit one up. We're gonna have to talk to them in the hospital. You want to do it, or do you want us to do it?"

"We were late to the party, so we'll take it." Accorso patted the firefighter on the shoulder.

"Thanks buddy. We'll clean up in here."

Accorso looked around for Pedrotti, who had wandered off some distance to the empty window frames high against one wall. He came up behind him.

"See something?" He asked.

"Nothing. What are we doing now? Back to the precinct?"

"To the hospital."

Pedrotti turned to him, frowning. "Why?"

"I told the smoke-eater that we'll interview the victims."

"Why did you do something as stupid as that? We could've taken a break at the nearest watering hole."

"Cakewalk that's why. They've already told us that officers are waiting to take their statements...we'll just take the statements from them."

"Good, cause that's not our job. Once the threat has been made safe, we're done."

"You've gotta tell me my job, Beat It?"

"I'm just sayin'."

Accorso nodded. "Let's get out of here. We're done."

Accorso walked into the bullpen, smoking a cigarette, and already peeling out of his coat, hanging it up on a coat rack next to his desk. Pedrotti walked around to his desk behind Accorso's, doing the same with his coat and hat. Pedrotti, finding the newspaper left for him on his desk, snatched it up and sat down to read.

Accorso, with the police report of the explosion in the Brooklyn basement rolled up in his fist, slid his chair to the side of his desk where he had a smaller, wheeled desk with a black Remington typewriter atop it. He reached into his desk drawer for an incident report form and cranked it into the machine,. Laying the rolled-up police report on his desk as flat as he could muster, Accorso began typing his report of the investigation. He was a slow, laborious typist, not like some that could rattle off a report in minutes. With him, it took two fingers and him hunched over the keyboard banging away one torturous letter at a time.

While he labored, Basilio Frascone strolled up to him with his hands shoved deep into his pockets, leaning back against a pillar to the immediate right of Accorso's wheeled desk. "How did it go with the bomb in Brooklyn? Was it intentional?"

Accorso stopped typing to look up at the man, the only thing commanding his attention was the ridiculous pompadour which was comically too large. Frascone smiled a wavering, nervous grin, his eyes conveying less mirth and more anxiousness. It was his constant nervousness, his ridiculous trembling that made everyone around him just as nervous. It was Pyke's assessment that the young man was just unfortunate—a walking specter of error, a walking poltergeist whose only purpose was to cause mortal men to make errors in judgment. Fatal errors that would cost a detective his life. In other words, to Pyke, Frascone was simply bad fucking luck.

"No, two jamokes were screwing around in a basement filled with photographer's equipment. Apparently, they found a box of photographer's flash powder and threw a match at it." Accorso said, sitting back in his metal chair, causing it to creak and complain as it reclined on its springs.

"Did they know what it was?"

Accorso shook his head, "No. They fucked up trying to figure out what it was."

"What is flash powder?"

"That shit they put in those trays they hold over their heads when they take a picture, and when they pull on a string it ignites it and… BOOM…you get a flash bright enough to illuminate a photograph. I guess too much can just about kill you."

Pedrotti, his back to them at his desk, reading the paper, added, "Or else burn the double fuck outta you," he laughed.

"Did they survive?"

"Yeah, the two idiots are badly burned but the doctor said that they'll pull through."

"That's good to…" Frascone's voice trailed off as he looked over to a growing shadow falling upon them. Pyke came around Accorso's desk, stopping at its corner and with a hand atop it, leaned against it. "Frascone."

"Yes, sir." Frascone lurched off the pillar and stood at instant attention.

"Go get yourself some coffee."

"Yes, sir." Like a puff of smoke, Frascone was gone.

Pyke looked down at Accorso. "That guy's gonna get you killed."

"He's part of my team. What can I do?"

"Don't talk to his goofy ass as much as you do."

"Trade him out?"

"I can't do that. He's yours to deal with."

"That's what I'm doing then." Accorso leaned over his typewriter and began to bang away at the keys once more.

Pyke nodded. "Your funeral." He read the police report, turning around, and sitting against the side of the desk. "You know that dumb-ass that T-boned us two weeks ago?"

"Yeah, Samuel Berdow, right?"

"Yeah, that's him. The crazy fuck is trying to claim that we hit him."

"He hit the side of our car!" Accorso stopped typing, looking up at him.

"Tell me about it. He's claiming we broke the light and shot out in front of him."

"Aww, bullshit."

"Fuck him though. My lawyer said that he's talking out of his hat because the witnesses that saw the accident have him breaking the stoplight and slamming into us, which is exactly what it looks like."

"Well, that's good news, right?"

"Pretty good. The bad news is that my wife wants you and Pedrotti and your wives over to our place for dinner tonight."

Accorso sat back in his chair. Pedrotti, pushing himself away from his desk, rolled across the narrow aisle between them and came to a stop next to Accorso's chair. "What's that?" he asked.

"My wife wants your wives over," Pyke said.

"Who else is going?" Pedrotti asked.

"Pete, you, and Fab." Pyke put the police report back down where he picked it up from and stood from the desk. "But you know Pete, you can't depend on that motherfucker. He'll come up with some stupid excuse, like he has to water the plants or some shit like that."

"You know. I have plants to water too, sir," Accorso said with a broad smile.

"Seven thirty. Don't be late. She's very punctual when she's cooking." Pyke walked off, heading back to his office outside of the bullpen. He had a real office overlooking the pen itself.

Pedrotti moaned. "I've got another night with Sienna."

"Just drag her ass along," Accorso returned to his typing.

"You know how she gets when she's around people that I'm trying to impress."

"So, you're saying she's not trying to impress me?"

Pedrotti scoffed, rolling back to his desk, "You and Dary? Shit. She couldn't give a shit."

Accorso snarled at him before returning to pigeon pecking on his typewriter's keyboard.

Accorso walked down the blocks of uneven sidewalks in Laurelton, Queens. Quiet, tree-lined streets on one side of sidewalks and on the other side, small, well-tended lawns and skillfully pruned shrubbery decorated the simple, A-frame two story homes in the area. Queens was indeed the suburbia of New York City, out in the boondocks, which was at one time pastureland. Now they were carefully constructed neighborhoods, growing in population daily. Laurelton was a little posher than where Accorso lived in Long Island City, but to people from Brooklyn or Manhattan, they were all the same cow paddy.

Walking next to him was his wife, Daria in a close-fitting green dress, with a lime green hat with a white net in front of her face. She held a clutch under her armpit and walked with some difficulty in her high heeled shoes on the uneven, sometimes completely askew slate slabs of sidewalk. Accorso looked her up and down as she struggled but still managed to keep up with his brisk stride.

"What's wrong with my dress?" she asked, pulling at the shoulder straps to raise her moderate neckline to show even less cleavage.

"Nothing. I'm just wondering how you are keeping up with me."

"Is that why you're walking so fast, because you want to see me fall and bust my can?"

"No. We're late."

"It's not our fault the trains were terrible. Why didn't you sign out a car for us this evening?"

"You can't just keep signing out cars on the NYPD's dime."

"You seem to be able to do it whenever you and the boys want to go out drinking."

"Yeah, I know, right?" Accorso smiled. He looked up ahead, pointed with his chin. "That's their place right there."

They walked to the front of the small house, two A framed roofs against the side of a longer A framed roof. The smallest frame had the white front door and gate before it, and a very short flight of red brick stairs leading up to it. A concrete walkway divided the green and well-tended lawn in front of the house in half, and around the house itself was well tended shrubbery of different shapes and sizes. The smallest of the A-frames that housed the front door was made of differing sizes of rough stone of a pale gray color. Accorso knocked roughly on the door and held of his bottle of liquor so that they could see it clearly as they opened the door.

When it did open, Barbara Pyke was standing on the other side. Dressed in a long, white cocktail dress, cinched and bunched at the waist with pleats that fanned the dress outward, its hem stopping just below the knee, Barbara was the model of the suburban wife. Her short, blonde hair in lavish waves. With her natural beauty, large eyes, and full, red lips, she was a rather attractive woman, Accorso noticed, and her smile absolutely beamed from her face.

"Dary, Fab! Welcome!" She called, throwing her arms out and embracing Daria, hugging her tightly before shaking Accorso's hand and taking the bottle in a brown paper bag handed to her.

"What's this? Wine?" she asked, waving them into the home.

"Scotch. I hope you have lots of ice."

"If we don't, we'll get some, Fab." She closed the door behind them and called into the house, "They're here!"

Accorso took Daria's coat and hat, and while he hung them up on a coat rack filled with coats and hats, both Barbara and Daria walked off into the rest of the house, vanishing from view. Accorso, still in the foyer, hung up his coat and hat before walking into the living room.

The house was plainly furnished to the average American's tastes. The Pykes were not extravagant or over the top in their decorating. Everything was functional more than for adornment. Accorso liked it. It reminded him of his home, even down to the paintings of shorelines and crashing waves on the wall.

Sitting on the long living room sofa was Pedrotti and his wife Sienna, by themselves, silent and still, two mute statues next to each other. Sienna fidgeted with a glass of wine in both hands, while Pedrotti did the same with a glass of bourbon.

"How's my two felons?" Accorso said.

Sienna smirked. She had a clear, heart-shaped face, with thin lips and brows, and long flowing auburn hair cascading past her shoulders. Her face was cherubic with the deep, soulful eyes of a child's and a lean build that complemented her modest bust perfectly, Accorso thought.

"I just want to get this over with," she said.

"Why?" Accorso asked honestly. "I thought you liked Barbara?"

"Barbara is Daria's friend. I'm not too keen on her. She's such a gossip."

"Oh, stop with the feminine bullshit please," Pedrotti groaned. "Get up and get Fab a drink."

Sienna rested her drink on the coffee table and stood obediently. "What would you like?" she asked Accorso.

"Three fingers of scotch and one cube of ice."

Sienna nodded and walked off, heading towards the kitchen.

Pedrotti sighed. "I just didn't want to hear her silly-assed shit. I swear, all these women are good for nothing but backbiting and fucking."

"I thought you said you were not fucking her anymore?"

"I'm not. Are you fucking your wife?"

Accorso laughed, shaking his head. "Not much. I save it all up when I'm out with you, kissing on those filthy whores you run with."

"Hey, I've never twisted your arm," Pedrotti leaned over the coffee table to crush his cigarette.

Accorso searched around the living room, peeked around a threshold to where the dining room was and then back to the foyer. "So, where's Pyke?"

Pedrotti slid back into the couch, stretching his arm across the back of it and crossing his legs at the calf. "He's out in his back yard with, Pete."

"Pete's here?"

"Yeah, he's back there."

"Well then, why aren't you back there with them?"

"You go try it."

Sienna returned with his glass of scotch and handed it to Accorso. "Here you go," she said with a disarming smile. She went around the coffee table and took her seat next to her husband, over her glass of wine.

"Why don't you go and hang around with the girls, hun?" He said to her. "We want to talk shop."

"Aright," Sienna took her glass and left.

"You want to talk shop?"

"I want her outta my face. Now's your turn. Why don't you head over to the backyard and see if you can make a conversation with your two superiors."

Accorso hunched his shoulders and walked off, heading past the dining room and the kitchen where the three women clucked like loud hens, drinking, and laughing. The backdoor opened onto a small, fenced-in yard surrounded with a tall, white picket fence. A splash of green oasis sat behind his home. White folding chairs were arranged in a semi-circle around a wide, tin, oval foot basin filled with ice and bottles of beer. In the far corner of the yard, Pyke and Hayias laughed and staggered about each other, roaring over something funny.

Accorso marched up to them and upon doing so, caused them to go stern, stand erect, and hold their beer bottles slightly lower.

"You made it, Fab!" Pyke smiled, regarding Accorso's approach.

"Yeah, sorry I'm late. It was murder on the train," Accorso turned to Hayias who smiled at him, as if he had to drag the lazy edges of his mouth up into a grin. "Accorso," he said.

"Pete," Accorso replied. "Call me Fab."

"Accorso," he repeated.

Accorso nodded and stood with them, waiting for them to return to their raucous conversation, and they stood, waiting for him for something. After a pause so long that all standing found it ridiculous, Pyke said to Accorso, "Pete had a call today in Brooklyn with this guy that owned a shoe store," he turned to Hayias, smiling. "Tell 'em what happened, Pete."

Hayias turned his head, took a large gulp from his bottle of beer, nearly draining it. When done, he returned to Accorso. "This wisenheimer shoe store owner goes to work and finds his store broken into... shit ransacked. Why someone would want to ransack a store for crummy shoes is beyond me. I'd rather rob him for money then pay for shoes, so already something sounds screwy, you know?"

Accorso nodded.

Hayias continued, "So he goes in and starts to straighten out his store and finds a shoebox tied with twine. Now he didn't tie his boxes with twine, so someone brought it into his store and left it there, sitting pretty on his front counter. So, he comes running to the Miller Avenue precinct and got some moron patrolman to go back with him to the fucking store and together they pick up the bomb and walk it two blocks away to a nearby lot. Then they went to a gas station and got them to go to the lot and help them to douse the box in a pail of oil."

"Waitaminute," Accorso interjected, "they just went there and took the bomb all around town, and got other morons to help?"

"That's just about it."

"So what kind of bomb was it?"

"It was a pair of sample shoes that jingle-brain had ordered. He said he forgot what he did."

"You're kidding me? A pair of shoes?"

"A pair of fucking Florsheims!"

Pyke struck Accorso against the shoulder playfully. "Ain't that some shit?"

"That's a funny story," Accorso replied.

"You think a fucking dick-headed cop walking around a potential device is funny?" Hayias asked. "Dumb motherfucker could have killed himself, the storekeeper, the men of the gas station, innocent shitheads walking by on his goofy-ass path to the lot two blocks away. I crawled up his ass the minute that I saw him."

Pyke leaned into Accorso, whispering, "He takes these things seriously."

"Why shouldn't I? People get killed every day from explosives. We don't have to add to the corpses." Hayias finished his beer and stepped off to the nearby trash can.

"What's got his shit all wound up?" Accorso asked.

"You've gotta know Pete to love him." Pyke grinned.

"Then tell me, how do you know him? How did you meet?"

Pyke thought about it for a moment, reached out and tapped the side of his beer bottle to Accorso's glass, and walked off.

They sat around the table, alternating between husband and wife in the seating, Accorso and Pyke at the ends. The women had come out in a flurry of arms and legs, setting up the table and pouring alcohol while, the men gathered around and worked out the seating arrangements. Soon platters of food were being passed around and comments were being made about the deliciousness of the meal.

Accorso reached out and filled Daria's wine glass on the left with Merlot, followed by Sienna's on his right. He pointed to the decanter filled with scotch not far from Daria, who reached over, and brought it to him.

"So," Hayias began as everyone was busy with their plate, "Accorso, I hear you only had one call today?"

"Yeah." Accorso worked on cutting his steak.

"How is that possible when the bullpen picked up seven calls today?"

"We got sidetracked. There was a real detonation, real casualties. Beat It and I had to go to Jewish Hospital to take a statement."

"You mean 'take a statement *from.*' I saw the police report that you wrote yours from," Pyke said.

"Well, no use having both departments bothering the guy. The work was already done. I got the rest from the cops."

"Let me get this right..." Hayias continued.

Pyke interrupted him, "Lets not talk shop at the table."

"I know. There's us girls here too," Clara said to her husband. "You guys can talk about all this tomorrow."

Clara Hayias was a young, vibrant woman. She wore her hair up in tall blonde curls, which made her appear worldly, more cosmopolitan, etched from the same hard rock as New York itself. She wore a loose-fitting white blouse and black, pleated slacks, and carried herself more like a man than a woman. But even though she had definite confidence about her, she obviously took care around her husband, watching for his lead.

She was also a tall woman, like her husband, her height clearly given to her by the length of her long, lanky legs. Because she basically had to look down on nearly everyone, especially women, she seemed to have the personality to also tower above individuals.

Hayias looked down at his plate of food and attacked it with the side of his fork.

"Well," Pyke smiled at Clara, "What kinda girly topic do you want to talk about tonight?"

"Do you think that we're going to be pulled into this war in Europe," she replied.

Everyone at the table stopped eating.

"Oh my gawd!" Daria laughed. "Who do we have here? Secretary of War, Henry Stimson?"

The table laughed.

"Well, I think he's going to drag us into this war over there. It's a very bloody action going on overseas."

France had already fallen to the Nazis and England stood alone against the unflinching heat of the Third Reich.

"We're Americans. We're not going to get dragged anywhere," Lieutenant Pyke said, cocksure of himself. "Adolph just wants the territories to the East of him. Besides, who wants England? Those limeys are gawd-awful ugly anyway."

Everyone at the table chuckled save for Hayias who continued drilling into his plate. Pyke noticed that. "What do you think Pete?"

"Yeah," he said, standing up from the table. "The Brits are an ugly bunch of people." He walked off into the kitchen.

"Where are you going?" Barbara asked.

"To get another beer," he called out behind him.

"Get me one, boy-o!" Pyke leaned back in his chair and shouted out to him.

"Yeah," he called back.

"I'm just concerned," Clara said, more to herself than to anyone else.

"Concerned about what, sweetheart?" Barbara asked.

"They're starting to call in army draftees already. Almost two thousand just two days ago."

"You must have someone close to draft age, huh, Clara?" Daria asked, her voice laced with tremendous concern.

"Yes, my little brother. He's in the lottery."

"Good for him," Pyke said proudly. "A stint in the army never hurt anybody."

"Yeah," Pedrotti laughed, "that's until you get your head blown off."

Pyke turned to him, giving him a flat, lifeless expression. After a moment silently making his point, he returned his attention to the table. "I served in World War I and it made a man outta me."

"What did you do in the war?" Hayias laughingly asked as he returned to the table with three bottles of beer, handing one to Pyke.

Pyke watched him retake his seat, trying to snarl at him but only succeeded in passing a grin. "I was a chauffeur, so what?"

"Run into any dangerous potholes while you were in the war, Pikey?" Hayias replied, laughing.

Accorso turned to Pedrotti, two kids at the table watching their parents start to parry verbally.

"I think it's very dashing he was in the war," Clara said, her eyes glowing as she stared at Pyke.

"Thanks," Pyke replied. "I was serving my country."

"So, I take it that you would rather our country join into the European conflict, huh?" Daria asked.

"I don't think it's our fight. There's always a war going on overseas it seems today." Pike picked up his bottle of beer, staring at it as if it was empty and warm instead of full and cold. "I don't know what to make of the fucking Nazis, but they're pushing their agenda on people who aren't German. There's something wrong in watching that happen."

"Yeah, it's kinda like watching a bully pick on a little kid." Pedrotti said, nodding in agreement with Pyke's statement.

"Something like that."

"So, it's our job to break up the world's petty conflicts?" Clara asked. "Sticking our nose in where it doesn't belong?"

Pyke leaned forward, looking past Clara to her husband. "Where did you find such an informed young woman?" he asked Hayias who waved him off, shaking his head.

"So, it's Sienna, right?" Hayias said to her instead, "What's it like being married to a wise ass like Beat It?"

She laughed. "It has its moments."

"Hey," Pedrotti cried, "what is that supposed to mean?"

"Means to me like he's the same pain in the ass at home as he is on the job," Pyke said.

"Now, don't pick on Sienna," Daria jumped in, waving a fork at Pyke. "She's a quiet person. Don't pry her out of her shell."

Pedrotti dug into his plate, muttering, "Hell with that."

"What?" Daria turned to him across the table. "What was that?"

"Don't get her started," he warned Pyke. "Please god."

"Why? She has valid opinions, doesn't she?" Clara asked.

"Does she?" Barbara backed her up.

Pedrotti, feeling the female attention at the table narrow on him, hunched his shoulders and said nothing as he continued to dig into his plate.

The banter was light, uneventful with the men pulling the conversation to work while the women touched on nearly every subject known to man. After dinner the men retired to the back yard to smoke and talk. The women did the same in the living room.

"You still haven't told us how you got away with the magic of pulling only one call out of seven yesterday, Fab," Hayias said, beer in hand.

Pedrotti elbowed Accorso in the side.

"Like I said," Accorso began, "we had to go to the Jewish Hospital to get statements to better help us understand the explosion."

"But that's not your job. The fire department should have sent someone to get statements if it was an investigation. Your job is to defuse. That's about it."

Accorso hunched his shoulders in dismissal, "I try to go the extra distance."

"The extra distance to the nearest bar?" Hayias turned up his beer to his lips.

"Look Pete," Pyke interjected, "Fab didn't do anything wrong in going to the hospital to get the statements, neither did he do anything wrong by not taking the lion's share of calls yesterday. We have the manpower, and honestly, I'm tired of my best men thinking that they have to handle every single call that comes in. We have other detectives that deserve a chance to meet the *beast* also."

At the mere mention of the word, everyone drew silent, as if giving it a passing moment of respect.

"Two numb skulls met the beast today in a basement in Brooklyn. They probably looked like smoking cartoon characters afterward," Pedrotti said with a broad grin. "Seared black like a nigger right out of Africa, with their hair standing on end and holding a match between their fingers."

Everyone laughed.

"They almost killed themselves," Accorso said. He looked at Hayias who stared back at him, his eyes dark, seemingly outside of the conversation. He turned up his bottle of beer, emptying it. After an unceremonious burp he said, "Pikey, it's getting late. I'm going to call it a night."

"Aright."

"Yeah, I say we should do the same," Accorso said, finishing his drink.

Cigarettes were put out, drinks were finished, and the two parties joined together in the foyer of the Pyke home, the hosts shaking hands and kissing cheeks as everyone filed out of their home and left their property.

"See you tomorrow, guys," Hayias mumbled waving at Accorso and Pedrotti. He and his wife heading up the block in the night. The last two couples drew together to confer.

"I've requisitioned a patrol car for tonight, Fab. Want a lift back to Long Island City?" Pedrotti asked.

"Yeah, that would be great," Fabrizzio gave his famous cherubic smile. His wife smiled too, Daria falling in love over again with his baby face. Or was it the wine in her head?

. . .

"I'm not saying that I hate your dinner parties," Hayias said, fingering a tiny spot on the passenger's side of the Plymouth. "I'm not too keen on the rest of the men of the squad."

"That's your problem, Pete," Pyke replied zipping the vehicle through the white tiled Holland tunnel. Traffic was traveling quickly this late in the evening, 24:15 hours, Friday night. "I want everyone to work like a well-oiled machine. That means that we have to go the extra mile in promoting unity among the ranks, which is the reason for the dinner party."

"But why do I have to be involved?"

Pyke looked sideways at Hayias just as the mouth of the tunnel opened with an amazing whoosh and the night sky greeted them, the moon, a tired eye glowering. They were headed for a long night. "Because, whether you believe it or not, I'm going to ask for you to be promoted to sergeant. Everyone knows that you are my right-hand man and there is no reason why my right-hand guy can't do what I can do."

"I don't want to be sergeant." Hayias turned to his friend.

"Why not? It means more money."

"It means more responsibilities...and fucking dinner parties."

"I don't see what's so fucking hard about you doing a dinner party. Barbara does all the talking. All you do is grunt and give me a hard time."

"I don't give you a hard time," Hayias scoffed, cranking down the window a crack to let air in the car.

"'Run into any killer potholes while you were driving about in the war, Pikey?'" Pyke imitated Hayias bitterly from last night. "That's not busting my balls?"

Hayias laughed. "I didn't say 'killer' I said 'dangerous.'"

Pyke yawned. "Well, we're going into danger again anyway. Run into any *dangerous* packages lately, Pete?"

"Hardly."

Right across the mighty Hudson River was Jersey City, New Jersey where the Jewish Center was located. Pyke navigated the streets and lights until turning a sleepy corner of the city, they entered the usual madness that they were acquainted with every time they were called onto a bomb job. Police and fire vehicles of every stripe parked haphazardly all around the wide avenue, creating a cordon of cars for the purpose of keeping the pedestrians at bay. At the center of the maelstrom was the Center, about two blocks away, standing alone and forlorn in the distance. A hale building of dark red bricks, tan arches, pillars with a high dome on its roof. It sat, imposing, and squat in the moonlight, a backdrop for the flashing strobes of the police cars.

Pyke and Hayias climbed out of their cars, with Hayias heading to the trunk. Pyke, on the other hand walked over to the press of humanity standing by idly, while some struggled to move closer to the front where sawhorses and officers were positioned to keep people away. Pyke, in his wool overcoat and fedora, lit a cigarette and approached the officer in the center of the street waving on traffic.

"Can I help you, sir?" the officer asked as Pyke approached.

Pyke held up his shield. "Bomb Squad...we were called in."

The officer pointed two blocks away where the wide street was starved of civilian cars. Parked in this expanse in the middle of the street, a block away from the Jewish Center was a tight knit of black, unmarked vehicles nestled against an Emergency Squad van. Without words, the formation screamed 'center of operations.' A crowd of men conversed on the side of the van nearest the sidewalk. Many men in suits conversed with uniformed police men with many bars on their chests and worried looking firemen.

As he approached, as if holding a placard reading 'bomb squad,' all heads turned to him, and the earlier, lively conversation fell silent. Pyke held up his sleeve and announced himself. One of the men reached out and shook his hand, "Detective Early," he said, "can I talk to you for a moment." He rested a hand against Pyke's back and walked him away from the clique of men, heading to the rear of the van.

"What's up?" Pyke asked.

SUSPICIOUS LOOKING PACKAGES

"Around 11:30 this evening some crackpot calls the Jersey City Police that there's a bomb on the steps of a synagogue, so of course you know that we have to investigate every call like this."

"Yeah, I know."

"So we've been running up and down every synagogue in Jersey City and finally we found a box on the steps of the Jewish Center over there," he held up his arm, four fingers and a thumb pointing to the building in the distance, "and so since we have shit for a bomb squad, we called you."

"Okay."

"I wanted to pull you aside because we've got too many civilians over there with more questions than answers. There's the management of the center, a few Jewish leaders, other detectives, sergeants, lieutenants, chiefs, and the fucking commissioner of New Jersey clucking like hens in a house. So, I thought that you may want a little heads up before going over there to deal with them."

"Thanks, Early. I'll take it from here," Pyke said both calm and resolute. He walked off, into mass of bodies which quickly formed a semi-circle around him, Early right behind.

"Firstly," one of the uniformed police lieutenants said, "are we far enough from the device if it's a bomb?"

"Probably not." Pyke replied.

Suddenly the mass of men began to boil, turning from a semicircle to a circle, then shrank rapidly like water rushing down a drain. The commissioner, Jewish leaders, management, unnecessary officers and support staff melted away, heading a block away to the sawhorses that the general public was behind.

Early smiled broadly as Pyke was now left with four men. A fireman, a police chief, an Emergency Squad commander, and an adviser to the Commissioner.

"I got the game plan from detective Early. Anyone got anything to add?" Pyke asked.

The four men looked at each other if an answer could be found among them.

"Who's this?" Early asked Pyke. Pyke turned to see who Early was referring to. Behind him came Hayias with two large suitcases. He carried them easily, being that they were more unwieldy than heavy.

"He's with me," Pyke replied.

Hayias rested the cases down in front of his superior and sighed. "What's going on?"

"Bomb, on the steps."

The four men, Hayias, and Early placed Pyke in the center of their circle, looking to him for guidance.

"Is there a vacant lot anywhere nearby?" Pyke asked Early.

Early pointed down the avenue, "About two blocks that way I think there is a large one."

"There is," the Chief said.

"Who are you?"

"Bureau Chief of Transportation, James Conroy," the tall, well pressed uniform replied proudly.

"Okay, can you get your men to open a path on the avenue all the way up to the lot? Get everyone off the sidewalk and have everyone in the buildings on the streets notified to stay away from windows."

"Certainly," Conroy walked off briskly, waving a hand in the air to summon his officers. The rest of the men crowded further on in Pyke.

"I need the rest of you to get as far away from here as you possibly can and prepare everyone you can just in case something bad happens." Pyke said.

"Bad like what?" Early asked fearfully.

"Like dropping his ice cream," Hayias said.

"Why?" Early turned from Hayias back to Pyke. "What are you going to do now?"

Pyke tossed his cigarette to the ground and crushed it with the toe of his shoe. "I'm going out there to get it. Pete, get someone to help you get the barrel to the lot."

SUSPICIOUS LOOKING PACKAGES

Hayias pointed to the Emergency Squad commander dressed in black slacks, sweater, and black cap. "Emergency Squad, right?"

"Yeah," he replied.

"Can I get some of your men to help me?"

"Right away."

Pyke, seeing that the huddle was quickly breaking up, headed towards the synagogue, walking around the front of the van and into the very wide, now desolate street. The night was chilly, working like a can opener to get into his overcoat, the moon shining a ghastly light onto his surroundings. He marched confidently, up a broad flight of stone steps under a beautiful stained-glass window with the Star of David at dead center. Pyke looked at the dark colors of the glass, the moonlight not doing the artwork the justice that it deserved.

He scanned the steps and the two red wrought iron banisters leading up to the door. Resting peacefully against one of the posts of the railing, halfway up the flight of steps was a small, square box about the size of a shoebox.

Pyke approached it, stood over it, examined it carefully. It was constructed out of pine, and he could see the small nail heads fastening it shut. He knelt, lowered his head so that he could rest his ear gingerly upon it and found it to be ticking. He stood up, looked about the streets and sidewalks, making for certain that no one was ignoring sound advice and taking a walk nearby. Finding the area deserted, he reached down and with one smooth motion lifted up the box, finding it considerably heavy. He could almost feel the shudder rock the people in the area once the device came into his possession.

Pyke eased down the steps and made his way across the sidewalk, to the yellow line of the street and then down the avenue in the direction that Early had indicated.

Even though the evening was cold, Pyke began to sweat, feeling the icy rivulets running from under his armpits, down his sides, and dampening his hair. His hands tried to tremble, but he forced them calm, concerned at the weight of the device. There could be a great deal of explosives packed into the tight space. Enough to not only obliterate him, but send cars sliding and bursting into flames, shattering windows, and sending secondary fragmentation flying through homes like bullets from a Tommy gun.

He shut out the entire world and continued his journey, his eyes locked on the box in his hands, held out as far as he could before him as if it that would make any difference if it detonated. But detonation was not on his mind. His thoughts swirled around how much money he had in his savings account, and how long could Barbara live on his pension. And then strangely enough, it whirled around to Hayias sitting in the passenger side of the car, telling him that he didn't want to be a sergeant. For a moment, it infuriated Pyke. He was doing all he could to groom him. In fact, he felt that he'd made a pretty excellent bomb squad detective out of both him and Accorso, and this was the way his partner in crime wanted to pay him back? By declining from service to the work? That ungrateful mother...

Pyke stopped, coming out of his daydream. The vacant lot was on his right. Abandoned, possibly a building was once there, but now there was only weeds, loose dirt, bricks of all types, paper trash lazily moving about, and larger, nonsensical discarded items surrounded by a waist high, chain linked fence.

The Plymouth was already there and in the center of the lot was Hayias standing next to a barrel, , no doubt to aid it in fitting into the trunk of a car. It was made from a corrugated container, appearing like a clothes hamper, painted red with words: 'Danger Bomb Container' stenciled in black around it. The two Emergency Squad officers who helped Hayias use a hand truck to get the container into the center of the lot fled upon seeing Pyke turn towards them. They ran off with a sense of urgency, as if their lives depended on it.

Now, slowing down and passing through a wide opening in the fence, Pyke frowned at Hayias who stood on the other side of the barrel. "Dammit, Pete. You know you're not supposed to be here. This is a one-man job," Pyke growled.

"Throw the fucking thing in," Hayias pointed down at the oil filling the barrel. Upon holding the box above the container, Pyke lowered it gently atop the oil where it sank quickly, trailing large slow bubbles popping on the surface of the inky black liquid. A loud applause rose in the night from all around, like the sound of leaves rustling in the wind.

"Why are they applauding?" Pyke said, turning his back to the mass of people from the direction that he came in, although the same number, if not more, were packed into the intersecting streets in.

"You know why. They see you dunk it, and they think that the thing is inert," Hayias said, turning to kneel over one of the suitcases nearby and producing a stethoscope from it. "Was it ticking?" He asked.

"Yeah, loud and clear."

He donned the earplugs and pressed the stethoscope's chestpiece against the side of the barrel. Muffled, but present, was the sound of ticking. "It's still going."

"It was a well-constructed box. It might take a little time for the oil to get in," Pyke reached into his coat and came away with a pack of cigarettes. "I'm going for a smoke."

He walked off with Hayias, who passed him a cigarette. From the direction of the Emergency Squad van, came the earlier gang of men led by detective Early. In the middle of the avenue they met, Early shaking Pyke's hand. "Very good. Is it over?"

"No."

The smiles and congratulatory glances dropped.

"What do you mean?" Bureau Chief Conroy asked roughly, he was growing frustrated.

"It's still ticking. You have to wait until the oil seeps into the works and gum it up."

"You mean that that thing...can still explode?"

"Exactly."

The four wise men turned to the group of men behind them to advise them of the current danger. Like a receding wave, the mass of men retreated to the distant barricades. Only the four stayed behind.

Conroy asked, "How long is this going to take?"

"As long as it takes," Pyke replied, puffing on his cigarette. "All the excitement is over, sir. There's only danger and injury if you hang around. Call it a night, leave your emergency people, and whenever that thing stops ticking, we'll put the top on the barrel and take it to the police laboratory for examination. There's going to be no more action tonight."

"Yeah, we're just going to go sit in our car," Hayias said. "Smoke a few and talk shit."

The four men turned to each other and after conferring, Conroy said. "I'll keep the traffic cops in place and the barricade detail until you guys take that thing outta here. Have a safe night, gentlemen."

"You too, sir," Pyke replied.

They walked off. Early came to Pyke's side. "I bet they were wondering if there was going to be an opportunity for the press to take pictures of the bomb with the commissioner," he laughed.

"I thought that too."

Hayias asked, with a level of anger, "Why didn't you fluoroscope the damn thing before picking it up?"

"I heard it was ticking. That's all I need to convince me that the damn thing is an instrument of destruction."

"Fluoroscope?" Early asked.

"Hand-held x-ray machine," Hayias explained. "I'm going to take a nap in the car. It's almost two in the morning."

"Yeah, go home and get some rest, Early. We got it from here."

"So, I'm leaving a detachment of my men just in case you might need them."

"That's very generous of you, sir. Good night." Pyke said, and with Hayias headed to their car, parked in the middle of the intersection with a half dozen Jersey City Squad cars.

As the sun rose on 240 Centre Street in Little Italy, the block long and block wide six story building's stone-worked arched and pedimented windows and doors, balustrades, pilasters, and cornices gave the building an official, impressive character. The New York Police Headquarters rose like a pale ghost among the other more colorful brownstones and buildings, a center Corinthian pilaster drum, copper plated dome and soaring lantern on the roof made it unmistakable from a distance. Inside in the over 55 rooms of the building was the NYPD Police Research Laboratory, a bleeding edge analytical marvel of research and exploration. There was no comparable place like it in the country.

The laboratory was instrumental in the examination and identification of such things used by criminals such as tools, instruments, and other paraphernalia. It also examined substances, traces and clues found at crime scenes. There was literally nothing that didn't or couldn't be turned over a million times by the criminal investigative atelier in search of clues to place the unlawful behind bars. Including explosive devices.

Pyke and Hayias, went through the back door of Police Headquarters on Centre Marketplace, rolled the oil barrel in a hand truck up to the laboratory. With a level of great care, they and other technicians fished the now soaked pine box out of the barrel and removed it to one of the worktables, not far from one of the workrooms that Hayias called his.

The detectives and technicians surrounded the box and used sharp scalpels and spudger tools to pry it open. Once done, they had the top of the box removed and the four sides laid flat. Copious amounts of oil puddled on the worktable and at its center, laid open bare were the components of the bomb.

An innocent looking alarm clock, silver, black faced, white numbers and hands; A snake's nest of wires; A copper coil; and a white building brick. They stood back from the table. That was the entire inventory.

"So, what do you think of this shit?" Pyke asked.

Hayias shook his head, thinking, then said, "No explosive, no detonator or battery, and no explosive agent. I have a problem with it though."

Standing across the table was the balding and wrinkled Ross Kelly, an older gentleman wearing comically large glasses. His fleshy nose and tired expression revealed his outright exasperation. "You have a problem with a hoax?" He looked up to Hayias. "It's a hoax, Pete. A hoax."

"It's inert."

"I agree with Ross," Pyke said. "It's a hoax."

"A hoax would have been a box and a brick. That would have been a hoax. This, my friend, is a signature."

"Whose?" Pyke turned to him. "That pipe bomb that you examined from Con Ed?"

Hayias shook his head. "That was a pipe bomb. This 'hoax' as you guys like to call it is someone trying to say something."

"Okay, Pete," Ross sighed, "what's he saying?"

Hayias pointed at the items as he called them out, "Timer; alarm clock. Wire; electrical based. Coil; substitute for a battery. Brick; explosive agent. These are all the parts needed to make a bomb. This is someone saying that they are fully capable of making an infernal machine."

"So, where is this insight taking us?" Pyke asked. "Can your signature intuition connect this to the World's Fair bombing? Or the Con Ed bomb?"

Hayias shook his head. "No. Three distinct signatures. The World's Fair bomber was once like this guy..." he pointed at the material on the worktable, "...or like the Con Ed bomber. He meant deadly business. These guys are claiming to be business. But one day a switch is gonna flick and these two guys are going to be blowing up human lives just like the World's Fair bomber."

"That's not your office," Ross told Hayias, completely ignoring his admonition.

"Shut up," Pyke said angrily.

Hayias turned to two technicians standing at the end of the table. "Wash down the parts, wipe them dry, put them in a box and leave them in my office on one of the clear work areas."

SUSPICIOUS LOOKING PACKAGES

"I keep telling you, Pete," Ross said, "that's not your office."

The Bullpen, a corral of desks and chairs fenced in completely by a waist high wooden railing in the center of the precinct. The commanders' offices were outside of that, surrounding them like herder's quarters. The office that used to belong to Sergeant McGuinness was vacant and had been so for some time. McGuinness had slipped in the tub and struck his head. His wife still brought him around on his birthday to see if he could remember any faces, but he had difficulty even remembering his wife's face at times. He was always cordial though, being introduced to all these new people who were interested in his welfare, but of who he had no clue of, or care for.

Accorso's desk was the 'hot seat' on the other side of the bullpen in front of Lieutenant Pyke's office. All Pyke had to do was step out of his office and across the walkway on the other side of the fence, was Accorso's desk. In plain sight. Accorso didn't care. He was at the point in his career that he knew he was invaluable. He was 'Man Number Three' on the totem pole. Accorso kicked his feet out before him under the desk and crossed them at the ankles. Leaning back on the swivel chair, with newspaper in hand, he glanced at the vacant desk and chair across from him—the station belonging to 'Man number Two', Peter Hayias. Like Pyke, he was a legend, but in other ways. If Hayias was a daisy, Pyke was a rose. The same...but different.

Hayias was never at this desk. Ever. He spent most of his time in his 'office' at 240 Centre Street. Word was that he liked hobnobbing with the bigwigs over there. But Accorso knew the truth better than most. Hayias loved the lab. The Technical Research Laboratory with its toys and science and obviously smarter people. But word was, they were not keen on his nosing around. Like a pestiferous fly, he was tolerated because he was largely ignored. Word was that someone did complain to a supervisor of Hayias's lurking around and loitering in one of the station areas. The supervisor called Pyke, and that was the end of it. That's usually what happened to complaints against Hayias. They would go to Pyke and get sucked up into a black hole of inactivity. Complaints about Hayias went to Pyke to die.

Accorso began to sense the same applied to him. On occasions, when he was certain that he had merited Pyke's wrath nothing happened. But truth be told, even though he knew he could do no wrong in Pyke's eyes, Accorso was still wary to earn his ire. He never knew where the 'line' was and did not know what would happen to the world around him if he did.

Pyke seemed to have the ability to walk on a stormy sea, and Hayias seemed to have the ability to do the same once taking his hand. Accorso was not about to risk taking Pyke's other hand.

Even now, Hayias's roaring laugh bellowed out of Pyke's office. Although the door was open, they could not be seen from within, but they could be heard when they spoke too loudly. One could wonder if there was any real work being done inside. One was even smarter not to investigate if there was.

Pedrotti sat behind Accorso, his desk facing the other way causing them to sit with their backs to each other across a narrow aisle. Pedrotti looked over his shoulder at Accorso. "What are you doing tonight, Fab?"

Accorso lifted the newspaper and gave it a stiff jerk, snapping it. "I don't know. I didn't think about doing anything. Why?"

"Sienna and I are fighting, so…" he let his voice trail off.

"You know the rules, Beat It. You're getting like Big O…"

"YEAH?!" Frascone shouted from the other end of the bullpen, standing up and looking about. "Did someone call me?!"

The detectives between them and Frascone turned to Accorso and Pedrotti. "No." Pedrotti moaned. "No one called you."

"OH, because I thought I heard someone call—"

"No one called you," Accorso shouted to him loudly.

Frascone lowered back into his chair, bent over the paperwork on his desk dejectedly.

SUSPICIOUS LOOKING PACKAGES

Pedrotti turned around in his swivel chair to face Accorso's back. "What are you talking about?"

"You're going to jinx us by talking about doing something after our watch. Don't talk about the end of the tour until after the end of the tour." Accorso shook his head and concentrated on his paper.

"You can't get bad luck from talking," Pedrotti defended bitterly.

The phone rang.

Accorso turned around slowly to look at Pedrotti with 'I told you so' eyes.

Pyke snatched up the phone in his office. "Yeah?"

Hayias had instantly lost his humor, staring at Pyke flatly. A call had come in.

"Yeah, I got it," Pyke said, scribbling on a legal pad next to him. "Yeah. Okay. Right away." He hung up the phone. Looking up, he said to Hayias, "We've got a call."

"I can see that," Hayias laughed. "Where at?"

"The Bronx."

Hayias made a face. "Pass it down."

"Nah, I want this one. I'm getting bored sitting here."

"Then let's go out somewhere. Pass it down."

"Any reason?"

"I wanna do something. A bomb is just going to piss me off."

Pyke nodded. "What do you have in mind?"

"I don't know. Let's go get a drink at Long Brown's."

"That sounds about as boring as sitting here listening to your jokes."

"Yeah?"

"Let's leave the fort to the kids and see who makes a mistake and flies apart tonight." Pyke stood, dusted off his slacks and went to the coat rack to grab his overcoat and hat. Hayias did the same and both walked out of his office. Directly across from them was Accorso at his desk, waiting for orders.

"Fab," Pyke began. "A call has come in. Me and Pete are going out to deal with it. Watch the fort until the end of tour."

"You got it boss," Accorso replied with a smile. "Good luck."

Pyke nodded and walked off. Hayias said, "Luck is for losers," with a grin, and followed the lieutenant.

Accorso watched them go. The two legends of the Bomb Squad. Or just legend, whatever way you wanted to state it.

"See," Pedrotti said. "I told you that just talking about the end of tour doesn't bring bad luck."

"So?"

Pedrotti arched a thumb in the direction of the exit to the precinct. "Let's leave the fort to Big O and get the fuck outta here."

"Did anyone call me!" Frascone shouted aloud.

Accorso and Pedrotti paused to look at each other.

"Big O!" Accorso said loudly. "Get over here!"

Pyke walked into the crowded, noisy bar, filled with men and a few strangely raucous women. He moved to the bar, worked his way between two patrons leaning over the top, drinking, smoking. He waved over the bartender, a portly man, slick hair parted in the middle. He cleaned his hands on his white apron and stopped before Pyke.

"Hey, I'm looking—"

The bartender raised a finger to silence him. "He's in the back."

"How did you know—"

"You look like a cop." The bartender smiled crookedly.

"Just go back there?"

"Just go back there."

Pyke backed from the bar. The two men flanking watching him, filled with curiosity. Pyke ignored them, navigated through the press of people to the back where two men in dark suits stood flanking a doorway. He slowed his approach, the eyes of the men narrowing on him, but they made no effort to stop him as he walked across the threshold and into a large dining room. Many rows and columns of tables filled the pillared space, all empty. Nicotine darkened paintings covered the walls, wood chips carpeted the floor. The beaten wooden tables were bare, a single burning candle at the center of each one.

In the back, where it was darkest, a shadow moved, lifting a mug of beer to its face. The grooved glass surface of the glass altering and twisting the face in the light behind it until the mug lowered again.

Lieutenant Pyke sighed deeply upon seeing Commissioner Valentine sitting in the corner of the dining room at the last table in the back. Pyke, suddenly less fearful, joined him with a smile.

"You like it here?" Pyke asked.

"When I was a patrolman, long before I was brought into the Confidential Squad, my friend and mentor Inspector 'Honest Dan' Costigan used to bring me here. We spent many a night talking about what a police man should be. What he ought to be. What should be expected of him. Honesty. Service. Integrity." Valentine sat back and waved a waiter over. "Order something," he said to Pyke. Pyke ordered a scotch.

"Dinner in fifteen minutes," Valentine said to the waiter, then returned to Pyke. Not missing a beat, he continued, "We'd come here often. Looking back, I never had any idea in my mind that one day I would be commissioner. I was a nose to the grindstone type of cop. I just did my job. I got up in the morning. I reported in, did my arrests, and went home to my four kids. I was a cop."

He paused, looking at Pyke who wondered if he should respond. The reason for Valentine's pause became evident to Pyke when the waiter returned with his drink. The instant he was out of earshot, Valentine continued. "That's what I think you are Pyke. A cop. I respect that."

"Thank you, commissioner."

Valentine laughed. "You know me long enough *not* to call me Commissioner."

"Sorry, Lew."

Valentine stuck his index finger into his beer, brought it out and flicked it several times away from him, flinging the beer from his finger. "That's for the fallen."

Pyke nodded.

"I'm not getting over the bombing at the World's Fair, James. We lost two men from your squad." Valentine cleared his throat. "Lynch and Socha. It's getting to me, stuck between my teeth and gums. It's irritating me that whoever the motherfuckers were that put that bomb in the British Pavilion are still running around, free men. Even more that they are living and breathing. I really want to correct that."

"We've tried everything. At this point, I'm thinking that it's going to take a lucky break to catch 'em," Pyke said. He looked Valentine over, who was fastidiously dressed in a dapper suit and tie. "The Little Flower gave me a mandate…"

Pyke knew who the 'Little Flower' was—Mayor Fiorello LaGuardia. Very few people said it to his face, but many people called him that. Some called him that because Fiorello meant 'Little Flower' in Italian. Others called him that because of his stature, being only five feet, two inches tall. Pyke was certain that Valentine called him that because of the former. He knew that the two men had developed a friendly relationship over the years that was more than professional. It was the same between the two of them.

"…he wanted me to make the NYPD more efficient and to root out corruption. Do you know why he chose me for the job, James?"

"Because of your experience."

"You're damned right." He rapped his sternum with his index finger. "I have over thirty years of experience in investigating police corruption. I started as a patrolman in the forty-ninth precinct, right here in Brooklyn. I made men tremble. Dirty cops gave me a wide berth and called me Lewis 'Honest Cop' Valentine, because that was what I was." His voice was becoming more and more strained, and then halted, wound down and in a more relaxed tone added, "I became this way because I was not only born with it but molded into it by Honest Dan. He made me an efficient cop. Efficient cops make for an efficient NYPD."

SUSPICIOUS LOOKING PACKAGES

The waiter approached. "Are you ready?"

Valentine smiled gently. His pear-shaped head and receding hairline gave him a broad, flat face capable of a range of very fluid features. Now they looked up at the waiter kindly. "I'm sorry, I'm busy talking. He hasn't had a chance to look at the menu."

Pyke shook his head. "No, that's alright. I'll have the special, whatever it is."

"It's seared trout and broccoli with rice," the waiter informed.

"That's fine."

"I'll take the steak and potatoes, rare." Valentine said.

"Very good gentlemen," the waiter replied and walked off.

The table fell silent, with Valentine staring at the wooden tabletop and burning candle on a single brass stand at its center. "Where was I?"

"You were saying something about an efficient NYPD."

Valentine looked up at him, "I was?"

"Yeah."

He dismissed his thoughts with a wave, "Well, I need the public to see the NYPD as honest and reliable. With these bastards running around leaving messages and bombs, we don't look too good in the Bomb Squad."

"I understand."

"James, I want you to do me a favor."

"What's that boss?"

"I know that assigning someone to the Bomb Squad is a two-way street. You have to accept them as much as they have to volunteer. I want you to accept someone that I'm sending to you."

Pyke blinked. "What?"

"I'm sending someone your way. I want you to get your people to accept him, take him into your inner circle, keep an eye on him and keep sending me reports on how he is doing."

"Why?"

"He's a good cop. A good detective. I want you to nurture him, mold him as Honest Dan did for me."

"Sounds like I'm the one doing all the molding and nurturing." Pyke smirked.

"Let's just say that I'm sub-contracting my nurturing through you. I pick 'em, you train 'em."

"And why my squad?"

Valentine nodded, once again returning his thoughts to the candle between them. "I have the utmost respect for the men of the Bomb Squad. There is a mettle that is tempered in you by what you have to do. I want to do the same for this young man. You men deal with a mindless danger. Most cops deal with the opposite. The threat against them is largely sentient, conscious. The threat against you…" Valentine's voice wandered off.

"So, you want me to make this man a Bomb Squad Detective?"

Valentine was suddenly excited. "And for it, I want to give you a rush of new blood. Fresh eyes. I want to kick-start your squad."

"What if my squad doesn't need a kick-start, Lew?"

Holding out both hands, Valentine used them as scales, weighing something in the invisible balance between them. "You give and I give. I'm giving you all these benefits, and you're giving me the chance to be a mentor. No other reason."

Pyke sat back in his chair, raised his drink before his face, but thought for a moment before drinking, emptying the glass.

"What do you think, James? Can you do this for me?"

Pyke looked at him, trying to search out something in his expression. What was Valentine doing? Would he…could he sandbag him? Was he sticking a snake in his midst to catch him doing something untoward? Valentine had been in the Confidential Squad, a point that he left out in his diatribe. When he was a lieutenant, Valentine was fucked over several times by the NYPD, on three occasions he was looked over for promotion. The hurricane-like winds of the department then blew in his favor as he was promoted again and again until he was placed where he was the most feared, the Confidential Squad. He was hell on vice and crime in the city only indirectly because he put the unmerciful screws to precinct commanders and district inspectors instead of unrepentant criminals. Just the mention of the name, Honest Cop, caused teeth to chatter and knees to knock within and without the NYPD.

If anyone's mettle was tested and augmented upon, it was his. He became something more than human, like a dog trained to sniff out truffles, he could find the most entrenched vein of corruption in the department, anytime, anywhere. He was good at improving the NYPD, good, too good. In 1928 when Mayor Jimmy Walker made Grover Whalen Police Commissioner, the roaring mercurial winds of the NYPD turned against Valentine again, harshly. He was painted a tyrant, his squad was disbanded and he was demoted to captain. His truffle-like nose for corruption was sniffing too close to the friends of his bosses, probably of Tammany Hall itself. The cries of outrage went up the ladder of corruption and favoritism in the NYPD and then back down again, right on Valentine's skull.

His fall was so meteoric that the illuminated letters running across the Times Square Electronic News Ticker read: "Valentine, Crown Prince of the Police Department, demoted to captain." But that was not enough for Commissioner Whalen, the Honest Cop was then exiled to a precinct out in Long Island City, banished, in essence, forever. Such a career blow would have felled a mortal man. At his lowest point in the NYPD, the town of Hempstead, Long Island offered him the position of Chief of Police to which he turned down. Good or bad, his full allegiance was to the NYPD.

Pyke looked at a man that he thought he could call friend. Would he try to jam him up, following his truffle-like instincts, or was he the Honest Cop of renown? Was he honestly his friend?

"What?" Valentine asked, smiling at Pyke's blank stare. "Can you?"

Pyke decided that the Honest Cop was his friend. "Yeah, Lew. I'll do it for you."

. . .

The twin wooden doors to the precinct were always hooked open so that the officers and detectives had easy egress and ingress to the building. Ateer stood on the other side of the sidewalk from the doors, leaning against the rear end of a reverse angle parked Plymouth squad car. As it was the custom, many precincts had their vehicles park in such a manner to make for easier take-offs from the building to locales distant and urgent.

Ateer finished smoking his cigarette and tossed it to the side, under the wheel of a car parked beside him. He trotted up the short flight of stairs into the precinct with many other men. Walking down the corridor he stripped out of his overcoat and fedora and headed for a stairway filled with detectives. It was a busy Monday morning between shifts, with detectives going and coming by the score. The ones leaving moving faster than the ones arriving. He navigated through corridors like a salmon swimming upstream and reached the second-floor bullpen. A large and noisy hub of activity. A battery of desks arranged in the center of a large room. Saying a greeting to those at their desks in passing he went to his at the center of the bullpen. Next to it stood a coat rack upon which Ateer hung up his coat, scarf, and hat.

Ateer went through his routine: he hung his jacket behind his chair and put his Smith and Wesson 38 caliber Victory Model into his desk drawer.

Ever since he was a patrolman walking a beat, it had been a constant dream to transfer to the P.M. Squad. He could remember the 'hairbags' in his old precinct warning him that Public Morals was a revolving door. This was so because there was only disillusionment to be found there. Even the name 'Public Morals' meant the highest integrity, the loftiest standards for the men involved. Very few men could then stomach the river of corruption that they brushed against once there. Just being near it caused the revolving door to turn. Rookies to the squad was in this month and out the next.

Cops took bribes, everyone knew. They turned a blind eye to petty crime, everyone knew that. But once in the P.M. Squad, although not fully revealed, the feel of the fabric was coarse, not right. There was something systematic about it, like a machine it turned many gears and levers. Such a mechanism was not to be employed here. This holy of holies was the bring down the mechanism outside. They were to stop the vice in the Public Morals Squad. Once a detective had 'that strange feeling,' he was gone.

The gossip was never good concerning the Bureau, and although they received the highest commendations for clean busts of pool halls, prostitution houses, and unlicensed bars there was a stink that would not go away. Some said that the stench was because they had to operate right up against the immoral sewers of the city. But rumor had it that it was something else. Something unspoken. Something that everyone chose to be blind to.

Still, once upon a time standing on a street corner, watching people walk by, Ateer could remember dreaming of being right here, in the chair that he found himself in, in the heart of the Public Morals squad. At thirty-one, that's exactly how he felt, as if he could take to flight. He was young, free, and loved life, and was finally loving the life he was living.

On the Public Morals Squad for five years, he was clean. Not just clean, sparkling. No marks on his record, not one, and scores of collars when given the go. New York did not have any shortage of bad guys trying to rook society. And when they came past him, he was faster than a Venus Fly trap. In five years, he learned all the hookers, money launderers, gambling joints and clubs that were selling alcohol without licenses. He knew them all, and the Public Morals Squad was busy closing them down with stunning regularity. He was proud of that fact.

Commissioner Valentine was hard on the force, fought hard for honest cops. It wasn't acting like a traitor if you didn't turn a blind eye to a fellow cop with his hand behind his back. That's how his partner phrased it. A cop that walked into an illegal establishment, looked around, turned to face the door, and held a hand out behind his back, waiting for his palm to be greased. Otherwise known as: "On the take."

He smiled. Good squad, good partner, good life.

"What are you smiling about?" someone said.

Ateer glanced over his shoulder to see Sean McGrath standing behind him. Another handsome Irishman, his hair slicked so heavily it looked shellacked to his skull, a pencil thin mustache and a cleft chin. "Mac! Where the fuck were you?"

"Outside, smoking a cigarette." Ateer opened his top drawer, rummaged around in it, and then held out his hand to his partner. "Stiffy, let me use your comb."

"Where's yours? I don't want any cooties."

"Fuck you, Stiffy. Let me use your comb." He felt the length of plastic land in his palm. He checked it for an overabundance of hair oil before he ran it back through his wavy, dark hair, oiled, but not plastered.

When McGrath sat down behind his desk, which abutted Ateer's so that they faced each other, he leaned forward to whisper over the din of the room, "I had a crazy night last night, Mac."

"Why was that?"

"We went to that place we raided last week, Club Carousel on 52nd street."

"Yeah?" Ateer leaned forward, handing him back his comb over the desks.

"Well, they were back at it again, serving alcohol without a license."

"And didya call it in?"

"No way. We drank up. And guess who was with us?"

"Who?"

McGrath leaned forward. "Brennan."

Ateer frowned. "Why'd you take Brennan?"

Flailing out his arms and singing in an ever-rising tone, McGrath said, "Because he wanted to go!"

"I don't think he should've gone."

"You're telling me. I just saw him in the locker room. He said he's transferring out."

"Really? What happened?"

"Well, it was me, the Kraut, Kaz, and Brennan drinking...well, Brennan decided not to drink but the rest of us did. So, as I was saying, we were all there drinking when 'Queenie' came over."

"Queenie? Wasn't she the madam of the whorehouse that we hit two months ago?"

"Yeah, yeah, let me go on with the story. So, Queenie came over and offered to have her girls give the entire table a 'bob-on-the-knob'."

Ateer lowered his head, shook it mournfully, "Oh, no. With Brennan?"

"Yeah, he went off the track," McGrath looked around. No one was at the desks surrounding them. He continued, "He jumped up and started condemning us, he said he was going to report us, and then he just walked out. I thought that was it, until this morning. Can you believe it?"

"It's Brennan, of course I believe it."

McGrath opened his desk drawer, arranged things inside of it quickly, dropped in his comb, then closed it. "I didn't think anything of it last night, but he's transferring. I guess he felt that he would have a harder time reporting us and staying in the squad than just leaving."

Isn't that why you took him with the 'gang'? Ateer thought. To give him his first class on how many are on your side.

"I thought you guys were church minister's sons stuck together." McGrath waved his hand at him.

"I told you; my father wasn't a minister. My mother just instilled certain values in us children."

"Stupid values."

Ateer shook his head. "My mother was very straitlaced."

"Yeah, and she laced them around your cock." McGrath laughed.

"I'm not like you, Stiffy. You should appreciate that." Ateer stood, took his empty coffee mug from his desk. "I'm like Brennan in the sense that I wouldn't put myself in positions that might compromise my ability to do my job. How can you bust Queenie on Thursday and get sexual favors on Friday?"

"That's the way things work. You should know this by now, Mac. You've been here for five years. It's a big wheel that feeds on itself. It goes round and round and, in the end, everyone is happy."

"You're going through this again?"

"Yes, because you need to understand where you are in the big cog that they call the NYPD. You're a gear tooth."

"Yeah, yeah, yeah," Ateer said tiredly, walking off.

McGrath jumped out of his chair to follow him, "You're a gear tooth, Mac. You go round and round, and your fellow officers are toothed into your tooth and our COs and inspectors and chiefs and deputy commissioners and even the commissioner, all the way up, the teeth are all together and all connected and all turning and turning around."

Ateer walked into the break room and went to the coffee pot, lifting it and finding it empty. With a curse under his breath, he began to make another pot.

"And believe it or not," McGrath said at his back. "The teeth and the wheels go all the way down, down, down to Queenie, Jackson, Willis, the corner drug den, pool hall, faro game, whore house and turns them too. We're all connected."

Ateer paused from his labor, "And where does the law fit in with all of this?"

Nodding and pointing, McGrath said, "That's right. Now have you ever heard of the 'spirit' of the law and the 'letter' of the law?"

"Yeah,"

McGrath opened his mouth to reply but Lieutenant Hogan's voice came out of it instead.

"Ateer, gotta talk to you for a moment."

Both men turned to see Lieutenant Commander Liam Hogan in the threshold of the break room. A tall and thin Irishman, he had symmetrical features with sunken eyes, a rich, full head of rigid hair combed backwards like the quills of a porcupine, and a pronounced handlebar mustache. He stood before them in a white shirt, with the collar open and tie slack.

"Who the fuck did you piss off, Ateer?" he said. There was no smile on his face. Ateer started to worry. Hogan had never spoken to him like that in his entire five years on the squad.

"What do you mean?" he asked reluctantly.

"I just got a call. Your presence is being requested at the Gold Dome," Hogan said. After he spoke, he stared intently into Ateer's eyes for some reaction. Ateer couldn't give him one. He was stunned, his blood chilled.

"Did they say why?"

"You know how they talk all that hoity-toity shit at the Dome. But I can translate Dome-lish. They said: Put down everything and get your pale, Donkey ass in here, now!" Hogan's brows rose. "Did you just fuck up?"

"I don't know what it's about." Ateer's world started spinning very slowly.

"Well, snap the fuck out of it and get over there, Ateer. Don't keep them people waiting." Hogan snarled and walked off to his office. It was obvious that the lieutenant was in a nasty mood, but then again, what else was new? Did he enjoy anything in his entire life? If Ateer went home every day to listen to his radio, Hogan must attend funerals.

"Shit, Mac," McGrath breathed. "What the fuck did you do?"

"I don't know."

"I knew you were too clean. You're as corrupt as hell, and it's finally caught up to you, you Mick motherfucker." McGrath wagged a 'told-you-so' finger at him. They walked back to their desks.

Ateer pulled his pistol from his drawer and shoved it into his belt holster. "I have no idea what they could want with me." He slipped into his suit jacket.

"Well, Hogan will know any second. They'll give him the news the minute you walk through the door at 240 Centre."

"They do that?"

"Yeah."

"I wonder who's requesting me?"

McGrath smirked, hunched his shoulders. "You are a regular ol' detective. What the fuck do the big heads that live in the shadow of the Commissioner want you for? Unless it is for some shit you've pulled," he shook his head. "I should have known. For five years you have been shining me on."

Ateer took his scarf, threw it around his neck, draped his coat over his arm and planted his hat on his head.

"I swear I don't know—"

"Get out of here, Mac, and see what those vultures want."

"Yeah."

Ateer dashed to the main corridor.

TWO
RECRUITMENT

"There is a saying that every nice piece of work needs the right person in the right place at the right time."

BENOIT MANDELBROT

---

2 40 Centre Street, NYPD headquarters, otherwise known as 'The Gold Dome' received its moniker because of its bright copper cupola topping the center tower of the block long and wide building. To Ateer it was frightfully huge and imposing. The word that worked best for him was 'intimidating.' Its pediment and columns over the entrance were massive, with a rugged stone worked and intricate facade, made Ateer small the moment he stepped onto the block. He paused in the street before the three arches that served as the entrance into the building and let the cold bite at him momentarily to steel his nerves.

A group of patrolmen passed by on the block, their heads turning, watching him as they moved on. They made him self-conscious. Ateer had to admit, he was frightened. He wasn't afraid of physical harm; he was afraid of all the ghosts and shadows that lie in between reports and memorandum that were filed by misinformed supervisors and witnesses that led to termination. Many cops have lost their jobs for less. He loved being a detective. There was nothing else that he wanted more. For the life of him he had no rational idea why the powers that be were calling him to the carpet, if that was what they were indeed doing.

He marched up the flight of stairs and into the warmer interior of the building. The foyer was spacious, the walls sculptured and polished stone to a bright shine, ornate ceilings, crystal chandeliers, and lavish marble columns.

The lobby was filled with people in suits and dresses, talking in cliques, going here and there. It was a nest of busy activity like looking down into a frantic beehive buzzing with motion.

A uniformed and polished patrolman walked up to him, and it was then that Ateer realized that he was gawking at his surroundings with his mouth agape.

"Can I help you?" the patrolman asked, stepping directly in front of his path.

"I have been called in for an appointment," he said.

"Follow me."

He walked off across the brightly polished floor to an equally polished marble reception desk. A woman officer sitting behind it looked up alertly. "You have an appointment?"

"Yes, I do."

"Name?"

"Dylan Ateer."

She looked down, flipping the pages of an appointment book. "Yes." She looked up at the patrolman. "Please take him to Alice."

With a nod, the stoic patrolman walked off, heading for a wide flight of marble stairs. Ateer struck off with him. He was amazed at the range of faces, from mature men to anxious young women, all intent on urgency. After several flights of stairs and crowded corridors he reached a large set of stained oak doors that led Ateer into another area with couches and chairs and a dark teak desk in the corner of the room. Behind the desk was a pretty blonde in a simple print dress watching silently as they walked in.

The patrolman pointed to a couch. "You can sit there."

Ateer motioned to the couch, but the blonde jumped up, holding out a hand. "Oh, no. You can go right in, Mr. Ateer. I have it from here now, Arthur."

The patrolman nodded and walked out.

"Please follow me." The blonde walked to another set of large dark oak doors on the other side of the room, knocking on them lightly, then she cracked one open, sticking her head in. Ateer stood in the center of the waiting room, lost, as if he was in the middle of the deep blue sea, bobbing like a cork. He was confused with himself. Was his entire feeling of lost detachment because of the ornateness of his surroundings, or the creeping dread that was overwhelming him. The huge painting of a fox hunt nearly covered the entire wall, plush leather padded sofas of blood red were against both walls, the rich wood furnishings with elegant etchings and carvings, and the paisley carpeted floor all read wealth and power.

"He'll see you now, Mr. Ateer," the blonde opened the door for him.

For a moment there was a fright, as if a golden-haired demon opened the maw of hell before him. What in God's name was he doing here? What could he have done to be called here? When he stepped into the room, he realized that it was much worse.

Ateer had only seen the man in the papers. His eyes were cold like a pair of distant stars in the heavens which gave off much less light than all the darkness around them.

Lewis Joseph "Honest Cop" Valentine, police Commissioner of the NYPD was a blank monolith of a man.

"Detective Dylan Ateer, have a seat," he said icebox cold.

Alarms were going off in Ateer's head. He took off his coat and hung it on the back of the chair and then took a seat. As if it was an omen, the muzzle of his gun jabbed him in the thigh. It was as if some higher power was reminding him that he was armed for his protection.

"Ateer, I've been looking through your files." Valentine reached over to a stack of paperwork, lifted a file, and opened it on the desk before him. "You have been a cop for five years, and now a detective for five, and all this time, not one mark on your record. How did you achieve that?"

"I did the best job that I could, sir."

Valentine stared into Ateer's eyes for a long minute before nodding slightly, just a tiny bob of his chin. "How is the Public Morals Squad treating you?"

"I love the Squad, sir."

"You do, do you?" Valentine looked down at the files, flipped a page.

As Valentine read through something in the paperwork, Ateer took a second to scan the large room. Every wall was a bookshelf filled with books. Did Valentine read all of these?

When he turned back to Valentine, those dark eyes were focused on him once again. It made Ateer jump out of his skin for a hot second.

"Looking at your folder, Ateer, you are a blank page. There's nothing in here, so I can't read you." Valentine admitted. "There's no personality, no life...no *you*! If you were a hothead there would be reprimands, if you were courageous there would be commendations, if you were lazy there would be assignment shifts to more adverse jobs. Instead, you are a blank page. A clean slate." He licked dry lips. "But I was never good at reading folders." He fell silent and closed the folder. Valentine was patient, taking his time, stringing Ateer along. But it didn't make the young detective angry, it made him uneasy.

"I used to be the commanding officer over the Confidential Squad for years. The police commissioner at the time, George McLaughlin promoted me to deputy inspector when he gave me the mandate to clean up the city and the NYPD. I was the only one doing that job. The only one. And can I tell you something, Ateer?"

Ateer sat statue still. He was a mouse cornered by a big cat. Valentine remained quiet as if he was waiting for something, and Ateer would be the first to say, he wasn't about to get anything out of him. Not a peep.

Valentine continued, "I lost that job because I did it too well. I did it so well that I pissed off a later Commissioner Grover Whalen. How funny is that Ateer? You are promoted because they needed someone to do a good job, and then you are demoted because you did."

This time Ateer choked out, "I don't think that's funny at all, sir."

Valentine sat back. "Let me tell you why I'm relating this story to you. The NYPD can be capricious and brutal. But there are reasons for this, even if we don't understand them at the time. Not only was I demoted to Captain, I was also transferred to a more adverse precinct. I would have rather been transferred to the moon; it would have been closer."

Valentine stood from the desk and went to the window, his hands clasped behind his back, one fist wringing the other. "I was depressed. I wanted to quit. The NYPD is insane. And then I got a job offer from Hempstead Long Island to be its chief of police. I thought about it."

Valentine turned around so that Ateer could see his stern features. "But I stuck with it, I stuck with the NYPD, and look where I am now. If I gave up on this job, I would never have gotten here. You may not like your assignments, but they build character that you don't realize you're lacking in. Do you understand me, detective?"

"I do, sir."

"Good. Ateer you're an honest cop, do you know how I know that?"

"No, sir."

"You work for the P.M. Squad and still you dress in cheap suits. Let me ask you, how much did you pay for the one you are wearing now."

"Sixteen dollars at Woolworth's, sir."

"That's what I thought." Valentine returned to his chair, lowering into it slowly. "I'm not saying this to insult you, but if you were on the take, you would have on a better suit, or at the very least, better shoes."

Ateer stared back, dumbfounded.

"I know this. I spent years busting corrupt vice cops. I'm good at it. I can smell a crooked cop. I don't need to look through file folders." He tossed the folder before him to the side. "You're young, honest and ambitious, Ateer. I want that. That's why I'm taking you out of the Public Morals Squad."

Ateer's heart fell to the floor. Why? He thought, what did I do?

"I want you to request for a transfer into the Bomb Squad."

Ateer frowned. "The Bomb Squad?"

"That's right. If I could transfer you there I would. But you have to volunteer to get in, and you have to be accepted by them to stay in."

Valentine watched Ateer breathe. He puffed, like an old train, building up a head of steam, although he was probably not conscious of it. "Did I do anything wrong, sir?" Ateer croaked.

"Nothing. Did you understand anything that I just said to you? When you do a good job, you get demoted, or transferred. I'm asking you to re-assign yourself because you are a good, honest cop and I need you. I want someone loyal in the Bomb Squad. Someone loyal to me...and only me."

"Okay, sir."

"Let me explain myself to you, which is more than I got when I was demoted." Valentine leaned forward, clasping his hands together.

"I have a predicament, young man, that you are an ideal solution for. Lieutenant James Pyke is the Commanding officer of the Bomb Squad, and I think that he's becoming...inefficient. We've had an enormous tragedy in the World's Fair bombing last July, and as of today he has absolutely nothing on that case. Nothing. I want to know why. Now we have mad men out there leaving pipe bombs and pine boxes as messages, and it appears there will be more. I greatly fear that these are going to slip through Pyke's fingers too. If he can't perform, then I'll have to let him go discretely. But if you look at the reports that he turns in, they're all glowing." Valentine was suddenly lost in thought, staring down at the top of his desk.

His pause made Ateer even more nervous. He wondered if the pause was for him to inject a comment but what comment that would be, he did not know. When the pause became unbearable, Ateer opened his mouth to speak, but as if it was his cue, Valentine continued: "But why should he report that he's lacking effectiveness to me, huh? So, since I can't depend on him telling me that he's not up to the job, and since I don't want to remove him on my own maybe paranoid suspicions, I'll use you." Valentine paused again. "Pyke might be taking on too much. Their caseload is beyond belief. Their stress, unimaginable. Pyke might not be up to his fighter's weight in getting the job done. Understand this Ateer, Pyke is a living legend. A man *before* his time." Valentine leaned forward, over this desk, between two stacks of folders. "But I fear that there's too much on his plate. I fear that I'm burning out my most precious resource. I depend on Pyke. I fear without him I might not have a bomb squad, but if he has lost his way, if he has lost the line...if he's not delegating, taking too many risks, making bad choices, I need to know."

"May I ask a question, sir?"

"Yes?"

"Why not just ask one of his men to report on Pyke for you?"

A slow smile crept across Valentine's face. "A man like Pyke, you'll see him do some miraculous things. With that, he's a leader of men. He builds in a man the sort of loyalty that only a man like Jesus could. You're going to rub shoulders with the twelve disciples. Just make certain that you do not fall under that spell."

Ateer swallowed, hard. "Yes, sir."

"Now let me ask you a question: how do you feel that I'm asking you to basically report on your fellow officers?"

"Frankly, I'm stunned that you are asking me to do anything for you, sir."

"Good answer." For the first time, one corner of Valentine's mouth had a tic. Was that his version of a smile, Ateer thought? "There are no stool pigeons in the NYPD, just good cops and bad fucking cops, and I do not suffer bad-fucking-cops."

"Do you think this Lieutenant Pyke is a bad cop?"

"I don't know, Ateer. That's why I would like you to volunteer and go in there. You're going to be my eyes on the inside. If Pyke is doing a bang-up job, I don't want to disturb him and end up screwing myself in the process."

"But I'll be an outsider. How am I going to get close enough to spy on him?"

"Don't use the word 'spy.'" Valentine pointed at him.

Ateer's eyes widened, "Uh, yes sir."

"Now I've worked you being an outsider out for you." Valentine reached for another stack of files and opened the folder before him. "Do you know a detective named Fabrizzio Accorso?"

Ateer let the name roll over in his memory until the gears caught. "That sounds like someone I knew in high school."

"You should. Your records reveal that you both went to Cooper Union High the same year. My guess was that if you didn't know each other, you at least shared the same teachers, other school mates, classes—something. When I was going through the files and saw that you two went to the same school, and your record was so clean, that was the germ for this idea of mine."

Ateer nodded. "I understand, sir."

"I want you to use this Accorso guy, get next to him like a tick on a dog and use him to get as close to Pyke as possible. Can you do that?"

"I can do that, sir."

"And then when I'm satisfied with the information you've given me, I'll put you in any department you'd like with a promotion and a raise. How does that sound to you?"

"It sounds good, sir. How will I get the information to you?"

"Don't worry about that. I'll handle it. All you need to do is sink your teeth into Accorso and become an 'insider'."

"When do I start?"

"We put in your paperwork already, backdated it a month. When you go outside, you'll sign them, then go to your precinct, get your things and go on to the Bomb Squad."

"Yes sir."

"And Ateer."

"Yes?"

"Act like you want to be there. I don't care if the pure, white-hot fear of the thought makes you shit your pants. The men of the Bomb Squad will look into your soul. You'll look into theirs. That's the nature to where you're going."

"I don't understand, sir."

"A lot of what I'm doing you won't, son. But don't concern yourself with that. Just *do* the Job, and *trust* the Job."

Ateer walked into the Public Morals Squad bullpen and slowly stripped out of his coat, hat, and scarf like a man sleepwalking. Whatever happened at the Dome changed him deeply. McGrath was sitting at his desk, watching his partner closely as if the answers that he was seeking to his questions would be on his person once he stripped out of his winter clothing. When it became apparent that his partner was not about to speak, McGrath said: "Well, goddammit, what happened?"

Ateer walked off, leaving the bullpen. McGrath frowned. Was it that bad? What the hell happened?

McGrath knew Ateer's number. He was a boring, straitlaced slice of white bread. He was the kind of cautious person who avoided problems. He gave vice a large berth. After work, Ateer took the train home where he was free of corruption. He wallowed in it during the day but avoided it at night. He was so fearful of corruption he avoided clubs and casinos unless he was there with a squad of detectives and officers to bust the joint. McGrath was even surprised that he would go through the door on a prostitution bust. Ateer wouldn't even talk to one, much less have sex with one. McGrath's thoughts hit a speed bump. Did Ateer ever even in his entire life *see* a pussy?

And then the answer why Ateer was called into the Dome came to McGrath like a blow to the head. One vice he knew Ateer had. The vice of all normal men—the bottle. Maybe the reason why he was called to the big house was due to his relationship with alcohol? Maybe he wasn't just going home at night. Maybe he was heading to a bar every night, where he drowned his liver?

"I'm being trans—" He stopped himself. "I'm transferring."

"Which one is it?"

"I'm transferring to the bomb squad."

"What?" McGrath was stunned, "when did you cook this up? Last week?"

"Something like that."

"And why didn't you say anything?"

Ateer stared down at him but there was nothing behind his eyes, no emotion at all, as if he was struck dumb earlier. He turned and left the bullpen. The gate doors of the fence swung back and forth to a stop behind him. McGrath wondered if he looked in a mirror at this moment would his face look like Ateer's? They were talking about Brennan's transfer earlier this morning. That was the opportune time to tell McGrath of his own. Why didn't he?

McGrath was a detective, not some skunk rookie patrolman walking a beat. He didn't act on what he saw, he acted on what he didn't see, and he didn't see any explanations coming from Ateer, largely because there wasn't any. Ateer's transfer, volunteered or not, came to him today, at 240 Centre Street.

Ateer appeared again, coming through the gate of the bullpen carrying a large box. He placed the box in his chair and began opening his desk drawers and pulling out his personal effects one by one and placing them in.

"Okay, so let's say you're volunteering to go to the Bomb Squad...why?"

Ateer, halfway placing a book into the box, froze. His thoughts so penetrating that it froze his gears stuck. He thought about the question, and obviously could not answer it.

"Okay, if that was too hard of a question, how about this one? Who the fuck did you piss off at 240 that wants you dead?"

"What are you talking about?" Ateer returned to placing items in his box.

"Do you know what they do in the Bomb Squad? They fuck around with *bombs*."

"I know that."

"B-O-M-B, BOMBS."

Then McGrath hit the brakes. Their desks were in the middle of the bullpen. Around them many of the detectives who were sitting at their desks were slowing down, slower, and slower at what they were doing, listening harder and harder until they became stone still. McGrath concluded that maybe if they had a little privacy Ateer would open up. McGrath stood and reached out, leaning over both desks, and grabbed Ateer's wrist.

"Mac, stop," he commanded.

Ateer froze.

"Listen, Mac. Let's take a break. C'mon, go with me to McAnn's Bar."

Ateer considered the request. McGrath could see that Ateer was treading deep water, maybe even drowning. He just needed a little more coaxing to get him where McGrath could do him the most good.

"C'mon buddy, get your coat. Take five. They won't be expecting you until tomorrow to start your tour anyway, so take a quick break from packing and let's have a few."

Ateer regarded McGrath's hand clutching his wrist, nodded. "Sounds like a good idea. I'm already finished up here."

They went to the coat rack, took their cold weather attire, and headed for the door.

They headed to McAnn's Bar two blocks down away. This early in the morning one would think that the dark teak wood bar and restaurant, with its ornate gas lamp wall fixtures, now converted to electric bulbs, would be practically empty. Instead, it was practically full.

The range of the New York demographic was broader than most realized until they came upon a circumstance like these two men did when entering an establishment filled with patrons. Irish men with their newsboy caps packed the bar, loud and boisterous. A crew of Italians filled the large circular tables, deep in angry discussion. Other nationalities of unknown languages kept to themselves.

And then there was the German American Bund. Just like having a slice of Germany in the bar, they packed in a large corner of the establishment, dressed in casual Nazi regalia, the dull green matching shirt and baggy slacks of a uniform, nearly knee-high leather jack boots, polished to a mirror shine, and finished with a tightly cinched Sam Browne belt, bottles and glasses of Liebfraumilch covered their table along with plates of sauerbraten and winer schnitzel.

With all the racial tension going on in Germany now, the Nazi Party in New York were largely overlooked and just another racial group. But there was a sinisterness in having a military among civilians, people who openly lauded their nationality before others who had their own cultures to take pride in, just not so extravagantly.

The hostess was gone for more than two minutes either searching or waiting for a table or booth. McGrath was hoping for a booth more than a table to give them greater privacy, because he was preparing to talk a level of shop with Ateer that he never had before, or at a level that might become incriminating. He nodded with a smile when the hostess returned to tell them that all she had was a booth in the corner of the dining area.

"We'll take it." McGrath said.

She led them through a winding path through tables in the middle of the restaurant, through the packed, square shaped bar with the opening in the middle for the bartenders to move about, and then to another seating area to the right, smaller than the first, darker than the first, filled with booths around the walls. She led them to a corner booth, tucked away by healthy seat padding from the rest. As soon as they sat, Ateer shook a cigarette from a pack in his jacket pocket. Placing it between his lips he held the pack out to McGrath. "Want one?"

"Yeah." McGrath pinched one out. After the waitress came with their drink order, McGrath thought it was time to begin. "So? What happened?"

Ateer made a face. "I went to the Dome and met with personnel."

"Yeah, why?"

Ateer picked up his drink, deep in thought, "I had put in for a transfer to the Bomb Squad..." he stopped, thinking, "...about a month ago. They just got back to me to give me the ropes."

"The ropes?"

"I don't know if you know it, but I didn't," he paused. The waitress cleared the table, took the order for a second round and left menus. They put the menus aside. Ateer continued, "But to get in the Bomb Squad, it's a give and take. You must ask for it..."

"And you did." McGrath interjected.

"...and they have to accept you."

"That goes for any squad, though."

"Well, you can't be assigned to the Squad, and they don't have to take you."

McGrath hunched his shoulders, "So what? What feather up your ass moved you to jump out of the P.M.?"

While Ateer took a long pause to pretend to think about the question, the waitress arrived, sitting drinks down before them. Ateer ordered another round before she left.

"The P.M. put me in too close proximity to grime and vice. Much of what I'm exposed to is a corrupting influence. I need to change that before it corrupts me."

"Oh, I forgot. You're high and mighty attitude toward what we do in the P.M. You want to maintain your holier than thou status."

"I don't like where I'm at, Stiffy."

McGrath could feel a warm fire build on the back of his neck, "What are you saying, Mac? I've done my part in regards *you*. I took care of you."

"You did what?"

"Believe it or not, I shielded you from a lot of the shit that's going on in the P.M."

"Why?"

"Because you're my partner."

"And why not Brennan?"

"Because he's *not* my partner."

"So, what have you shielded me from, Stiffy?"

"Stuff that would have made you transfer out faster than Brennan."

"And you stay in it?"

McGrath hunched his shoulders. "Somebody's got to. I'm the garbage man. I take out the trash."

"Oh, I see."

Stubbing out of his cigarette butt in the nearby ashtray, McGrath exhaled smoke, "You should. So, what are you trying to do now? Make penance?"

"What do you mean?"

"Are you trying to purge your record in heaven by becoming a martyr? Because you're in the shit now."

"Exactly how?"

"You know what they do in the Bomb Squad, don't you?"

"They diffuse bombs."

McGrath shook his head angrily. "No. They fuck with bombs."

"Calm down."

"No. Listen. Those motherfucking wops over there carry around UN-exploded bombs in their pants. Didn't you read the news about all those people that got blasted at the World's Fair last July 4th?"

"Who didn't?"

"And you want to be there. Why do you think that they put only guineas in that squad?"

"Why?"

"Because they're as disposable as a cigarette butt, Mac. The only Irishmen that are there are the ones that want to end it all. Are you like that? Do you want to end it all because of kicking in a few doors to whorehouses and gambling halls?"

"Of course not."

"Then you tell me, since you must know: what Irishman in his right mind volunteers for a squad like that? The normal ones usually quit after training because," McGrath rapped his temple with his index finger, "they have common sense. Who wants to be blown to bits?"

"It's not *that* dangerous."

"Tell that to those guys that got blown up at the World's Fair. Do you think they'll tell you that the job wasn't all that dangerous?"

Ateer had no reply. He looked at the cigarette between his fingers. It had burned all the way down to the tipped filter. He dropped the butt into the ashtray, shook another out of the pack. "Want another one?" he asked McGrath.

McGrath ignored him, "And those wops in that squad all have death wishes."

"Why do you keep calling them wops?"

"Because they are! Don't you know the Bomb Squad used to be called: "The *Italian* Squad?"

"It did?"

"Those crazy meatballs were going nuts in their neighborhood, throwing sticks of dynamite all around at each other until they made their own squad to handle them."

"They?"

"The NYPD, stoop! They made a squad native to the neighborhood, just like Mick cops in Irish neighborhoods."

"Mick cops are in all neighborhoods."

McGrath sipped his scotch. "You're going to be surrounded by a bunch of guineas who are bored with the idea of tomorrow."

"That's just your opinion, Stiffy."

"That's a fact, Mac."

Ateer swallowed down his drink, slid the large rocks glass to the edge of the table where the waitress would appear. "Hey," he said, "you said that you were shielding me from the shit in the P.M. What kinda shit was that exactly?"

"I didn't bring people like Queenie and Nico around you. I kept you from all that."

"I met them and others."

"In the professional sense. Not the," he searched for the right word, "the personal sense."

"You're personal with these people, Stiffy?" Ateer's voice was measured and cautious.

He held a hand in the air, splayed the fingers, curving them somewhat, creating the likeness of a gear in which he turned left and right. "I told you earlier, gears within gears, going all the way up to the commissioners and judges and senators and the vice president and president all the way down to the whores, alcoholics, gamblers," he paused, leaning forward over the table, "even the rapists, murderers, thieves, and con men. Everything is connected in this world, and do you know what is the grease that keeps this big assed machine turning?"

"Crime?"

"Money." He held out his hand. "Give me one of those gaspers."

Ateer handed him the pack and matches. "So, you were shielding me from the bad guys?"

"I shielded you from enough. I protected your," he hunched his shoulders, "what do you call it? Your purity?"

"So how did you come to the conclusion that I had some kinda purity that I had to protect?"

"Because you act like it. You never go out with us to clubs or play at our poker games or even go out drinking with the gang. Other than me, you keep to yourself. Why is that?"

"My mother was very strict."

"Is your mother still alive?"

"Yes, she is."

"Is she here?" McGrath tapped the table with a fingertip.

"Of course not."

"So, if you don't mind my asking: what the fuck is going on in your Mick mind?"

Ateer brooded.

"Look buddy," McGrath calmed down, lowered his tone. "I don't mean to shit in your lunch, I just wanted you to know that the P.M. Squad may have its quirks, but you won't die in a ball of fire."

"Nobody is dying in a ball of fire." Ateer knocked back his second drink in one shot.

"Those meatballs in the Bomb Squad die in balls of fire every single, solitary day." McGrath lifted his empty glass at the distant waitress to signal her to bring another round.

"Well, I got it to do," Ateer said with a level of resignation.

"Why? That was my question? Why are you doing this?"

Ateer thought about it. He thought about everything that his partner was saying. The Bomb Squad must have been dangerous. Even Commissioner Valentine alluded to a white-hot fear being associated with it. Stiffy was a friend of his. Well, he was kind of a friend. Why not just come out and tell him the truth that the commissioner told him to volunteer? What harm could it do?

"Huh?" MacGrath pressed. "Why? Or don't you know yourself?"

Ateer looked at his watch, reached into his jacket and produced his wallet. "I've gotta get going. I've gotta go back to the precinct and get my stuff and get to the Bomb Squad."

Ateer pulled dollars out of his wallet and threw them on the table. The waitress arrived with their next round of drinks.

"It's not going to be the same without you, Mac." McGrath finished his drink.

"Same here. I have roots in this squad."

McGrath slid the pack of cigarettes and matches back to Ateer. "Hey, do you remember the time when—"

"Don't start that shit, Stiffy." Ateer finished his last drink. "I'm not going to do the memory lane stuff with you."

McGrath sat back in the booth. "You know, you've been in this squad for five years and I hardly know you. And here you are telling me you have roots in the P.M."

"I do." Ateer stood, scooped up his cigarettes.

"The hell you do," he made a sour face. "I don't really know anything about you, other than you do your job, have a good insight about people, and tell funny jokes when you can remember them. Other than that, I don't know much about you."

"Same with you, Stiffy. I don't know everything about you either. Maybe that's how we should do things, right?"

McGrath sat, staring up at him.

"Are you coming?" Ateer finally asked.

Raising his hand to signal the waitress, McGrath said: "Nah, I'm going to have a few more and then book off for the afternoon. I've got shit to do."

"You do, huh?" Ateer smiled, stood next to his friend, and patted him on the shoulder. "Don't sit here all afternoon sucking down these drinks."

"Why not? Unlike you, I have no purity."

"You're a good man, Stiff."

He smiled. "And you're a crazy man, Mac."

With a slight chuckle, stifled somewhat because what was said smarted, Ateer had to admit, something was wrong. Commissioner Valentine was concerned about Pyke, but why choose him? Was it all because of his casual contact with this Detective Accorso? Was it because his record was so squeaky clean? Was it because he could tell by his suit that he was an honest cop? Was it because of some uncanny ability that he honed during his years leading the Confidential Squad?

Ateer pushed those questions out of his head as he walked off, heading towards the exit of McAnn's, shouldering past the numerous patrons milling around the bar and through the revolving doors.

Ateer seared two things onto his brain, like a branding iron against the side of a steer: He had to *do* the job...and *trust* the job.

There was a knock on the door. Pyke, reading a report from one of his detectives, finished the sentence, which was poorly constructed, before looking up at who had stepped in. Standing tall in the doorway was Chief Inspector John J. O'Connell. He was stout and slim in his uniform, his gold badged cap tucked under his arm along with a stack of folders, the lapels of his white shirt displaying his three gold stars. Pyke jumped to his feet and saluted rigidly.

"Relax Jim," O'Connell said, stepping into the office and hanging his hat on the standing coat rack in front of the door against the wall, then he came down to the chair in front of Pyke's desk, taking a seat. He was mature, tired-looking with snow white hair and thick mustache that seemed to prove that he had the weight of the world on his shoulders. He sighed as if it took great stamina to come to a rest in the chair. Either that or it was an extremely long day for him.

"How you doin'?" He asked.

Pyke lowered like a hot air balloon into his seat. "I'm fine. You, on the other hand..."

"I'm alright. Nothing that a couple of beers can't fix."

"Is that why you're here? You want to go out to the bar?"

"Is Peter around?"

"No, he's out on a call."

"Maybe later then. This is official."

"Oh, it is?"

"Yeah, I just got it from 'on high' that you're getting four new volunteers."

"Four?"

"That's right." O'Connell leaned forward and passed the stack of files over to him.

Pyke rested them on the desktop but did not open them. "Yeah, we're short some guys."

"You've been short a sergeant for some months now. What is that about?" O'Connell sat back, crossed his legs.

Pyke shook his head, "You know Peter. He's a hard head. He doesn't want to be sergeant. He's got his heart over there at the Technical Laboratory. He has a thing for examining bombs."

"You do too, last I heard."

Pyke hooked a thumb over his shoulder. "You know, I've got my work area in the garage. I diddle with shit in there, but I'm still here, with the squad. Peter 'visits' on occasion."

"Or he's out on a call, I suppose?"

"Or he's out on a call."

O'Connell stood. "I wish you better luck with these four."

"It's not luck, John."

O'Connell could only smile at the comment, turned, and walked to the coat rack to snatch away his cap and then left the office. Pyke watched him leave, then looked down at the stack of files on his desk and flipped through them until he found the name of the volunteer that Valentine had asked him to watch over…Dylan Ateer.

In two hours, McGrath returned to the bullpen, still walking steady and sat behind his desk, not saying a word to Ateer as he bent over his paperwork. As for Ateer, as word got around many of the detectives of the squad patted him on the back in passing, wishing him luck in the Bomb Squad. As Ateer and McGrath sat silent as two statues facing themselves in a park someone shouted.

"Ateer!"

Ateer turned to Lieutenant Hogan's office, finding him standing in the threshold.

"Ateer, come into my office," he said, then disappeared inside.

McGrath leaned closer to Ateer and whispered: "I bet he knows who and what's behind this."

"I don't think so, buddy." Ateer walked off, entering Hogan's spartan office.

"Close the door," he said.

Ateer complied. Turning back around, he said: "Sir?"

"Why the transfer, Ateer? What in the fuck did you do?"

"Nothing, sir. I've done nothing."

"This is the NYPD, detective; it doesn't blow a fart for no reason. When you went down to the Dome, they transferred you and explained exactly why they did it. What was the reason?"

Ateer felt cornered. Hogan seemed to know what he was talking about, but even if he did, Ateer knew that he couldn't divulge his meeting with Valentine. "They didn't tell me. They just said I was transferred."

Hogan looked up at him. His handlebar mustache twitched. He simply sat in his chair, looking up at Ateer, counting the seconds, waiting.

"I'm serious, lieutenant. They didn't say anything to me."

"Okay," Hogan finally said. "You're lying to me, so you don't want to say. I'm wracking my brains here trying to figure out what the fuck you've done. You're the straightest laced, uptight, boring son-of-a-bitch I know. When we brought down that whorehouse at Pennsylvania Station, you stayed outside to manage the sidewalk. What were you afraid of, that you might see some pussy?"

"I thought the danger would come from someone outside, not from some women on the inside."

"Ateer you can't rise above the city by excluding yourself from it.

You can't. This is the NYPD. We are part of New York if not New York itself. Your austere lifestyle did not help you, did it? Since you didn't ride the horse, it kicked you in the head. Whatever you've done, you're getting what you deserve. And if you don't want to tell me, I can understand."

Hogan opened his bottom desk drawer and produced a rocks glass and a pint of scotch. He poured some into the glass and as he screwed the bottle tight, he said bitterly: "Now get your fucking leprechaun ass out of my office, and don't get yourself blown up."

Ateer walked into his apartment, closing his door with a bump from his rear end. He rested his box on the small kitchen table and went to the kitchen window to open it. He stuck his head out to see the backs of all the brownstones around his, creating a courtyard of sorts where noisy kids chased each other four stories below. Crisscrossing the air over head and below, like an intricate series of pale spiderwebs were clothing lines, engineered with pulleys so that each apartment had a single system where they could hang their laundry out their kitchen window, reel it out into the middle of the courtyard to hang, and when dry, reel the laundry back in again.

There also were a few, bare London Plane trees, with their stark boughs and branches reaching up to snare the clotheslines and may one day succeed.

He returned to his box where he dropped his mail after taking it from his mailbox in the vestibule. And went through only two pieces of mail. One was a notice from the landlord for the rent. Ateer was a little late because of working on a case, he had spent too many hours in the precinct. He would straighten that out today since he was off work early.

Then there was the other piece of mail. It was from the U.S. Government with its official stamp. He tore it open with a finger and pulled out the folded sheet of paper. It was from Military Entrance Processing. He was to report immediately to the New York City

SUSPICIOUS LOOKING PACKAGES

Recruiting Battalion, Fort Hamilton, New York. He had been drafted.

Both sides of the street were rich with Maple trees, their overarching boughs reaching up and over towards each other as if yearning, creating a large, leafy canopy, nearly choking out the sun in the cloudless skies. The houses, simple, two to three story A frames checkered like teeth with large gaps in between, like the expansive smile of a grinning suburbia.

The Plymouth eased down the street with no real hurry, Accorso at the steering wheel, watching the numbers on the left side of the street ascend, Pedrotti did the same on the right. The usual banter was missing from the car all the way from New York to Jersey City, Pedrotti being unusually quiet.

"Why so silent?" Accorso asked. "Sienna again?"

Pedrotti did not turn around to respond to him. "Yeah. You know, bumpy waters."

"Choppy waters," Accorso corrected.

"Yeah, that too."

"Don't worry about it. Everything smooths over in time."

"Fifty-eight!" Pedrotti exclaimed lightly, pointing to a house that they passed.

Accorso slowed down. He didn't need Pedrotti's warning. Up ahead was a Jersey City squad car and a black Buick double parked in the street, leaving the slimmest of spaces between them and the parked cars on the other side. Accorso pulled over, double parking behind the Buick. They climbed out and looked at the house at 63 Sherman Place, near to them. Pulling up behind his vehicle was Frascone's E83W. Accorso waited for him to climb out and approach.

"Bring out the can," Accorso instructed him.

Frascone turned and walked off.

"Nice little house." Pedrotti said next to Accorso, his hands stuffed deep into his pockets, his hat cocked slyly to the side.

Accorso struck off towards the 'nice little house,' another A frame, just like all the others on the block with an extension attached on its side. They approached and climbed up a stair at the end of a short walkway and reached a quiet porch with chairs and plants both hanging off the pillars and potted in the corners. Pedrotti reached out to knock on the glass and wood doors, curtained for privacy on the other side, but before he could knock it opened. Two lantern-jawed men in dark suits, ties and hats stepped out and smiled.

"Special Agent Walsh, FBI," the foremost man said, nodding to Pedrotti and then continuing to the porch stair. "Good luck."

The second agent, in passing patted Pedrotti on the shoulder in sympathy and left with Walsh.

The Bomb Squad detectives watched as they left, and then a bright, cymbal-like crash of a voice called their attention. "Are you men from the Bomb Squad?"

"Yes, ma'am," Pedrotti said to the short, squat woman in a print, pleated dress. She was mature, matronly, with a full mane of gray, curly hair and oddly large breasts that sat like a shelf on her chest.

"It's in here," she said, stepping aside and opening her door. Pedrotti walked in, nodded, and removed his hat. Accorso did the same. They walked into a small foyer with a thick, paisley runner on the floor leading to a flight of ascending stairs.

"It's in the parlor," the woman closed the front door and walked past them, making a left into the living room of the house. They filed in behind her, examining the early American decor and the short coffee table in the center of the room, in front of the couch under the bay windows to the left. On the table was a box about one foot high, by one foot wide. They paused, standing over it.

The box sat like an innocent accused of a crime, waiting for the law.

And the law was present. Two uniformed Jersey City officers stood in the far corner of the living room, waiting on the detectives. They stood sagging in gratefulness the moment the two men from New York walked into the room.

"Bomb Squad?" One of the officers asked.

"Yeah," Accorso said.

"Good," they replied. Moving quickly, they passed by the woman, saying goodbye.

"We'll be waiting outside," the other officer said.

They shuffled swiftly out of the room and the home, leaving them alone.

"How did it get in here, Mrs...?" Accorso asked, his voice trailing off for her to fill in the blank.

"Brauer," she replied. "Eva Brauer. The mailman left it at my front door, but I didn't ask for it. I don't even recognize the return address. So, I picked it up and brought it in and left it there. Before I opened it, I thought about the bomb that I heard went off and I thought that this could be one of those."

"Good thinking," Pedrotti said. He walked up to the box, tilted it slightly, looking down at the return address. There was no name, just the street, city and state. Fordham Road, Bronx, New York. "Well, we know it's not motion sensitive, because the gorilla handling that it would have received at the post office would have set it off. So that's a good sign."

"That's if the post office left it out there, Beat it." Accorso pointed out.

A chill rushed through Pedrotti's body.

Accorso stood over the old woman. "Mrs. Brauer, can you please go outside and tell the officers to take you far away from your home. We'll take it from here."

"Okay," she nodded and then waddled off out the front door.

Accorso looked over the home, the comfortable fireplace where the officers were once standing, the pictures on the bureaus, bookcases, and tables. And then it all changed. The room was scrubbed clean and scorched black, bricks missing from the fireplace as if unfinished, a pile of rubble, broken wood, shards of glass, crumpled metal piled up like a snow drift against it. The rafters above were either sagging or had split and lolled downward.

To the left, where there was a huge bay window was now missing the entire wall. The rest of the living room, from furniture to porcelain were scattered on the front yard on the other side of a gaping maw, burning in small pockets of flame. Accorso blinked his eyes to make the vision go away and then looked at Pedrotti.

"I'll take it out." Pedrotti said with a smile.

Accorso thought about it for a moment. "No. You wait outside."

"Why?"

"I've got a bad feeling."

"About this box?"

"Yeah."

Pedrotti nodded, "Well, that's all the more so I should take it out."

He turned to pick up the box, but Accorso reached out for his shoulder. "Hold on. Sienna would never forgive me if you got your ass killed."

"And your wife would?"

"My wife would probably pin a medal on ya."

"Stand back." Pedrotti would hear no more. He handed Accorso his hat, bent over the box, trapping it between both hands, and lifted it gingerly from the table. "You had to bring up the point that the mailman might not have brought this damn thing to her door."

"It's true. That was a bad assumption."

Pedrotti carefully turned on a dime and headed for the front door. Accorso held back, watching as he walked through the open door and onto the porch with steps like a man on a high wire. Waiting for him, in the middle of the walkway through Ms. Brauer's front yard was Frascone with the red painted oil barrel carried by a hand truck, its top removed.

"Did you use a stethoscope on it?" Frascone asked as Pedrotti slowly came nearer.

"We could have heard it ticking if it was, now back away."

Frascone ran off, out past the metal fence and to his truck, now double parked in front of the home. The Buick, parked there earlier, now gone. No doubt being the car that brought the two FBI agents.

SUSPICIOUS LOOKING PACKAGES

Now alone, Pedrotti drew near to the barrel, his eyes locked on the dark, viscous fluid inside looking like a black empty void. He rested the box on top and released it, watching as it floated on top of the slick for a few moments before one end dipped lower than the other. Pedrotti reached out and with a finger, forced the other end into the liquid. The entire box bobbed and then sank, vanishing from sight.

Pedrotti sighed with relief and Accorso's hand resting on his shoulder startled him, "Good job."

"Fuck!" Pedrotti gasped. "Don't do that," he said, accepting his hat back from Accorso.

Accorso looked at his watch. "Let's give it forty-five minutes and then we'll go in."

They walked down the path to the sidewalk, stopping in front of Frascone.

"Bomb?" Frascone asked.

"If it is, it's not one anymore." Pedrotti said.

Coming down the block towards them were the two police officers, Ms. Brauer and several of her neighbors, all inching slowly to them, patiently approaching in the event that the Bomb Squad men told them to stop. Accorso strode over to them, waving to the officers to stop the nearing and growing crowd where they were. They were not out of danger yet.

Mrs. Brauer was the only one allowed to continue to meet Accorso halfway between them and the house. "Is everything alright?"

"It's not safe yet, Mrs. Brauer. Do you have a neighbor that you can go stay with until we make the bomb safe?" he asked her with a calm, soothing voice.

"Yes, I can stay with Pam Maluski over there," she pointed behind her.

"Okay, go stay with her and in forty-five minutes, come back."

She nodded, "Thank you Mr. Bomb Squad," she said and then walked off.

Accorso followed behind her, stopping at the police men and the crowd when she entered them.

"What's going on?" One of the officers asked.

"We've gotta soak the bomb in oil for a while. You might want to disperse the crowd. There's nothing more to be seen here."

The officer nodded and left to deal with the gawkers. The other officer doing the same, sending them off like a clowder of cats. Accorso returned to Frascone's van, finding it empty, and then found both he and Pedrotti further down the block in their car. He slid into the back seats, Frascone sitting shotgun and Pedrotti behind the wheel. They sat in utter silence for a few moments until Accorso took off his hat, rested it against his chest, and nodded off into sleep. His time asleep drew him into a dream of nights with his wife, Daria where they sat in silence before the floor standing Zenith 12-S-374 radio with its circular glass face above center and its polished wooden frame. They sat in their living room with their daughter stretched out on the floor and listened to the evening news without a sound from each other. When the night was over, they retired to their bedrooms without saying much of a good night, although they both would put Leora to bed and bid her sweet dreams.

The silence in the car had reminded him of his dream of silence at home.

"Fab, it's time," Pedrotti shook him awake.

Accorso sat up, stepped out of the opened rear door of the car and planted his hat back upon his head as Pedrotti stepped away. "It's forty-five minutes," he said.

Nodding and rubbing sleep from his eyes with two fingers, Accorso made his way to the Brauer home, meeting with the two cops at the front gate, everyone focused on the barrel in the distance. Accorso turned to Frascone who came running up behind him.

"Get the hook," he told him, and he was off.

"I'll hook it," Pedrotti said.

"You've done enough. I'll handle this." Accorso replied. He turned to accept the long broomstick with a hook and sinker at its end. He then made his way up the walk and stopped over the drum. Placing the long handle in hook first, he worked it around, against the side of the box, angled it until the hook was under the box and with a simple jerk, snagged the softened cardboard and hauled it up like a fish out of the water. He pulled it to the side, resting it on the concrete walk and knelt over it and with a penknife from his jacket, gingerly cut it open at a corner, going down, height-wise; towards him, lengthwise; then across him, across-wise until he could peel the box open like the petals of a rose from its corner.

He peered inside, then reached inside, producing a can of Del Monte vegetables. Its label covered with the nearly opaque ooze until he wiped it away. First, a can of corn, then a can of green peas. Several more cans were neatly placed inside.

"The package is safe!" Accorso called out.

The police, Mrs. Brauer, Pedrotti and Frascone approached quickly, anxious to see what Accorso was lining on the walkway in small cans. Accorso stood, regarded, Ms. Brauer, "It looks like a sample box of canned vegetables, Ma'am," he said to her.

"*Oh*, my goodness," she clapped her cheeks with her hands. "I think I ordered those."

"I wonder why it didn't have the name of the product on the box?" Pedrotti asked.

"Maybe packaged by a distributor?" One of the officers said.

"Well, we're done here," Accorso replied. To Mrs. Brauer he said, "You might wanna hose these down before you bring them inside."

"Thank you, Mr. Bomb Squad," she replied in her high, somewhat annoying voice. Accorso wondered what it would be like to listen to her for nights on end. He also wondered if she was still married, or did she put her husband into his grave with that voice?

"You're welcome, ma'am." Accorso doffed his hat and headed off with Pedrotti behind him. "Since you carried the box out, you get to write it up."

"No problem," Pedrotti said.

"Are we going to take a break?" Frascone asked, keeping up behind them.

Accorso waved to the officers in passing. "I don't care." He said over his shoulder to Frascone.

Frascone climbed into his van.

"Where're we goin'?" Pedrotti asked.

Accorso hunched his shoulders. "Maybe get a hot-dog or something."

They climbed into their car, Accorso once again behind the wheel.

Upon returning to the bullpen later in the evening Frascone ran to his desk for some unknown reason; Pedrotti went to his typewriter, loading paper; and Accorso rested his head on his desk, closing his eyes. Before he could drift off a hand rested on his shoulder. He looked up to see the soft, fatherly features of Peter Hayias, staring down at him.

"James was looking for you," he said.

"He was?"

"How was the call? Did you get blown up?" Hayias smiled, patted him on the shoulder. "You might wish you did."

He walked off. Accorso watched him leave, then turned to Pedrotti who was already looking at him, his eyebrows up, stunned at Hayias's warning.

"Whaddaya think he wants?" He asked.

Accorso hunched his shoulders.

"You do some shit behind his back?" Pedrotti ventured.

"I never do shit behind his back," Accorso replied, "lately." He stood, pushed his chair in and walked out of the bullpen gate and around to Pyke's office. The door was opened, and he reached in to knock against it.

"Come in."

The way Pyke's office was laid out, it went immediately to the left, against the left wall. Pyke's desk was at the end of an office with no windows. Pyke worked on paperwork; his head bowed as usual. Accorso had walked into his office many times, watching him sign off on many reports from his detectives, almost overwhelmed by them. He wondered how his superior even got the chance to get out and run a call on his own with all the reports coming in during the day.

Accorso walked up to his dark wood desk and pointed to the chair in front of it.

"Yeah," Pyke glanced up for a moment, "take a seat."

Sitting down slowly, Accorso waited for the Lieutenant to scribble on a typed report, then, after putting it aside he sat back in his chair, making it creak. "I don't know how these guys work, but they can't seem to file a report without a ton of errors and omissions."

Accorso nodded.

"You do pretty good, Fab. I don't find myself correcting the hell out of you, but that Dempsey...good god."

Accorso smiled.

"Fab, we're getting four new volunteers transferring in."

"Four?"

"Yeah, I'm gonna move Dempsey over to head unit two. It's been a long time since Sergeant McGuinness retired."

"Dempsey's getting a promotion to detective first grade?"

Pyke shook his head. "Not yet."

Accorso knew better. Hayias was number two on the pole. With Dempsey taking Sergeant McGuinness's position, the sergeant's slot was wide open, and eyes would turn in the gold dome to see why it was taking so long to fill it. The clear bet that if anyone was going to make sergeant, it would be Hayias. If he would only take it. "Is Hayias going to be made sergeant?"

Pyke snarled. "Don't worry about Pete."

Accorso smiled uncomfortably. "So Beakey stays supervisor over unit three, Dempsey is over two, what about me over one? Moving me?"

"Nah, handing you a special addition."

"Special addition?"

Pyke opened his desk drawer and produced a file folder. He handed it across the desk to Accorso. "I want that back."

Opening the file, Accorso started to scan within. "Dylan Ateer?"

"Yeah, he'll be a detective third grade, under you, and Beat it."

"So then, what makes him so special?"

"We've got to keep a close eye on him, so you've got to keep him as close as possible."

"Why?"

"Because."

"Who says?"

"*He* does."

"Who's *he*?"

Pyke put another piece of paper before him and started reading.

Whoever *he* was, he was not about to be mentioned. Accorso closed the folder, "When do you want this back?"

"Tomorrow, because that's when he's coming in."

Accorso nodded and stood up from the chair, "What do you mean about keeping him close?"

"Let him see how we operate, and don't do shit in front of him."

"Is he in the Confidential Squad or something?"

"Stop pissing in your pants, Fab. The Confidential Squad is long gone. Remember, he's not keeping an eye on us, we're keeping an eye on him." Returning to his paperwork, he said, "Dismissed."

Accorso nodded, slipped the folder under his arm, and walked out of Pyke's office.

Accorso opened the front door to his home. With the folder under his arm, he hung his hat and coat up at the coat rack in the foyer and walked upstairs to the bedroom. He tossed the file folder on the made-up bed, stripped out of his suit, draped it across a padded chair in the room and walked into the bathroom to take a shower.

After a hot shower and a shave, he dressed in his pajamas and robe. Snatching up the folder he came downstairs in his slippers and peeked into his living room. As expected, his wife and daughter were present. Daria reclining across the couch in her nightgown and robe, Leora sitting crossed legged on the floor in her pink, floral print pajamas. Daria had a bottle of red wine on the coffee table, a goblet of wine in her hand. Neither looked up at him as they listened intently to the radio broadcast of the news.

He took the long hallway that ran the length of the house to the back which opened into the kitchen. He found a plate of food in the oven and brought it and a bottle of scotch into the dining room, along with the folder. He flipped it open and began to read the file carefully. There was also a monochrome photograph of Ateer in his uniform and cap.

"You brought your work home?"

Accorso recognized his wife's sultry voice immediately. He looked up at Daria, her taller than normal height for a woman still did not bring her to the stature of a man, but the woman she was inside was definitely towering in ability than anyone around her. If her narrow, feminine frame could transform into an animal, it would be an ox.

"Yeah," he replied.

"Is this something new?" She crossed the kitchen to the sink where he had laid his dirty dishes and ran water on them, scrubbing them down.

"For tonight."

She stacked the dishes into the dish rack, dried her hands with a hand towel and walked out of the kitchen with her long-legged stride. Accorso had to admit that the bitch was a towering testament to female locomotion, and she still aroused him. What he couldn't deal with, which would dampen his ardor like a damp clump of feces thrown on his gonads, was her attitude. By simply opening her mouth, she could fuck up a wet dream.

He returned to the folder, finishing it. When he finally looked up, he found the lights in the living room off, the radio quiet. He took the long hall back to the front door and tested it, making certain that it was locked. From there he climbed the stairs and entered the bedroom. It was dark and silent too. He felt his way along the wall, dropped his file on the bureau. He smoothly dropped his robe, slipped out of his slippers, and climbed in, turning his back to Daria, and closing his eyes.

She did not speak to him, nor would she. He could feel the chill of her presence like an ice floe resting with its back against him. He scowled. Nothing in his life indicated that at this time of his life, he would end up in this hole, this abyss. He did not want to be here, but divorce was such an ugly word, and the courts would hand over his entire paycheck.

Accorso didn't hate his wife, per se, he just wanted her gone. Just disappear like a ghost suddenly finding the light at the end of the tunnel. He would have groused over his marriage to Daria more if sleep didn't choose that very same moment to overtake him.

THREE
COMPRESSED LIFE

"Life changes fast. Life changes in the instant. You sit down to dinner and life as you know it ends."

JOAN DIDION

It was another cold morning, with fall beginning to creep into the city, but not as windy as yesterday, so he didn't fear for his fedora to take to flight. Ateer made his way down the sidewalk, his arms wrapped around his box of effects, when a car horn beeped. Stopping, he looked around. The horn beeped again. How he didn't see it immediately escaped him, but parked next to the curb, among a row of parked cars in front of his apartment, was a beautiful, new black Buick Century with its distinctive curved lines, bright chrome detailing, large bulbous fenders, and dual wheel covers for the spare tires on the front side panels.

Ateer frowned, ducked his head to see through the passenger window who was behind the wheel. It was an unfamiliar male. Slowly approaching the car, he focused on the face in the semi-dark of the interior. He was a much older man, in his late fifties, with a fleshy, jowled face, plump nose and elephant-like ears. His dark fedora was pulled forward, close to his brow, throwing his eyes into shadow. Ateer stuck his head into the car.

"Yeah? Can I help you?" he asked.

"Put your shit in the back seat and get in," the stranger growled.

"Who are you?"

"Commissioner Valentine sent me."

The name caused Ateer to start with such impact that his head almost collided with the top of the opened window. His heart galloped and he looked up and down the block, noticing men and women going about their business, oblivious to his consternation. With some effort, due to the box in his arms, he opened the suicide door at the rear of the vehicle and rested the box in the back car seat before climbing into the passenger seat of the car.

The driver pulled away from the curb and entered the modest traffic.

With one hand on the wheel, he extended the other. "Waclaw Orlowski, homicide."

"Dylan At—"

"I know who you are," Orlowski cut him off. "You can call me Walter."

Ateer shook his hand briefly. "Okay Walter, what's up? Where are we going?"

"To your station house."

"So that makes you, my driver?"

"I'm your handler."

Ateer turned to look out the windshield, digesting the statement.

"In the future, this is how we'll meet. I'll be parked out in front of your house at times, and you just let me know what you've found out. You'll also hand me any paperwork that you decide is important enough for the commissioner to see. You will not go to see the commissioner unless it's of dire importance. Understood?"

"Understood."

Orlowski stopped at the light, the purring engine the only sound heard. While they sat, Orlowski reached into his jacket pocket and handed over a clean, white envelope. "Oh, this is for you."

Ateer took it, tore it open. It was a letter addressed to him from Military Entrance Processing. As the car moved on, Ateer scanned it briefly. He was requested not to come to the New York City Recruiting Battalion at Fort Hamilton. He was deemed an Exemption by the Mayor of New York, the Honorable Fiorello La Guardia.

He turned to Orlowski. "What is this?"

"It's Uncle Sam telling you that you are not going to be picked for the draft. It means Valentine wants you."

"I'm not going to Fort Hamilton?"

"No. You have been marked as 'indispensable' to the draft board."

Ateer returned to the letter, stunned.

Orlowski continued. "You are indispensable and so is your playmate, Accorso. He's not going and you're not going, because your job is to crawl up Accorso's asshole and bring out some shit."

"Don't you mean Pyke?"

"No. Pyke would see you clearly as a plant. But if Accorso goes to Pyke and you're up *his* asshole, Pyke will never see it coming. Don't you fucking get what you're supposed to do?"

"I get it." Ateer put the letter in his jacket.

"Shadow Accorso so close that he'll think you're his shadow's shadow. Get it?"

"I told you I got it." Ateer turned to the passenger window, staring at the passing streets, pedestrians, cars, and buildings of the city. "Didn't Mayor LaGuardia say that he would not support a draft exemption for policemen?"

To Orlowski it sounded like a mumble. He turned to Ateer testily, "What?"

Ateer turned to him and repeated himself.

"Notice that firemen are exempted."

"Yeah."

"The mayor, as well as the commissioner can exempt whoever the hell they please. You, my friend, just happen to be one of very few police officers getting the 'treatment.' The entire fucking Bomb Squad is getting a pass just in case the fucking anarchists start leaving bombs all around the city. There ain't enough dumb son-of-a-bitches in the entire force to go and defuse the damn things. You've been exempted, so drop it."

Ateer returned to the passenger window, looking at the careful, spiderweb like cabling; sturdy, grim iron girders; and hale and imposing brickwork of the Brooklyn Bridge rushing by along with other automobiles as they slipped from the largest borough in the world to enter Manhattan. In time, after passing through the maze of streets in lower Manhattan, under fourteenth street, Orlowski turned the car into a space two blocks from Ateer's new precinct.

"Good luck." Orlowski said, shifting into park, not taking his eyes from the windshield. "And another thing: watch your back. There may be something here, and then maybe not. Don't learn the hard way."

Ateer nodded to the side of Orlowski's head and left the vehicle, taking his box from the back. He walked down the blocks to his station house, his overcoat shielding him from most of the cold wind. Why couldn't Orlowski drop him off closer to the precinct? Was he so recognizable that he had to keep his distance? It was a little too cold to walk so far, Ateer groused. But he must have had his reasons.

Upon reaching the precinct, he stopped several paces from a group of men standing with boxes in their arms, another unlabored detective standing next to them.

"Dylan Ateer?" the detective asked.

Ateer stopped before them. "Yes sir."

The detective, in a wool suit and tie, stretched out his hand. He was stern in appearance, his features severe, clean shaven with a pair of circular wire rimmed glasses over his straight nose. "Detective first grade, Charles Beakey. I'm here to break you into the Bomb Squad."

"It requires breaking?" Ateer said with a smile.

Beakey cracked a weak, but honest grin. "Let me introduce you to the rest of the new volunteers." Beakey stood to the side and with a slow sweep of his hand, introduced the three other detectives, "Detective first grade, Reginald Hardy; detective second grade, Christopher Nicols; and detective third grade Peter Dale."

Ateer followed behind the introductions with handshakes.

"Gentlemen, this is detective third grade, Dylan Ateer."

Everyone nodded.

"Good, now that that's done away with, let's get you guys your lockers," Beakey said, walking off and up the two steps into the precinct with a single, peppy leap. The four detectives followed behind, grateful for the warm interior which embraced them. Their first stop was the locker room where they were appointed lockers. Some began to empty their boxes into them. After a turn, they were led to personnel where they were processed in. Penultimately they were acquainted with the bathrooms and showers before the filed into the busy bullpen.

Beakey went to the desks, assigning one to each of them before walking off.

Ateer was shown his and carefully began filling the drawers and setting a small picture frame on the desk. He struck a key on his Royal typewriter at the side of his desk and smiled at its sharp report.

"Hey."

Ateer looked across his desk at the man sitting behind the desk abutting his. A youthful looking man with easy, handsome features. He grinned like a mischievous child, knowing a prank was coming, but not wanting to reveal its approach. He had a rich head of carefree dark hair and searching eyes. He sat without a jacket, no doubt hanging on the coat rack near him, and a tightly knotted tie.

He stood, reached out with an arm uncovered by his rolled-up sleeves. "Fabrizzio Accorso, detective first grade."

Ateer shook his hand, "Dylan Ateer, detective third grade."

"I know. You're in my unit. Unit one."

"Oh, okay."

"You smoke?"

"Sometimes."

"You *will*, all the time." Accorso lowered back into his seat. "Call me, Fab."

"Okay, Fab."

"What do they call you?"

"Mac."

"Mac."

"Yes, Mac."

"Why is that?"

"Well, my grandmother, on my mother's side, was named MacAteer, but she dropped the Mac to sound more American. So as to not forget where I came from, I picked up the Mac as a nickname."

"Makes sense," Accorso nodded. "You're from Public Morals, huh?"

"Yeah, five years."

"How was that?"

"It was a unique experience." Ateer smiled.

A voice boomed out in the bullpen from the direction of Pyke's office. He stood in the door frame, breathing in before bellowing again, "I want to see the new volunteers in my office." He pointed inside his office, then stepped inside.

"Good luck," Accorso said, giving a jaunty salute.

"Should I carry my gun?" Ateer touched the heavy hardware hanging from his shoulder rig.

"You'd better take it. You never know."

Both men laughed. Ateer walked off, falling into the line that had formed, filing out of the gate of the bullpen and into Pyke's office.

Inside, it was neat and clean. Somewhat spacious with the desk to the left of the room. The four detectives stood before the chair in front of Pyke's desk and stood at attention.

Pyke had a long, even face, with an equally long nose. His dark hair was rakishly styled, his focused eyes dark under heavy brows. The muscles in his jaw moved, clenching, and unclenching gravely, giving the impression of a man that smiled little, and didn't find much humorous. In seconds Ateer could feel the cold, steel beads of sweat running like a rapier down his spine.

"Gentlemen, you aren't rookies," Pyke began, sitting back in his chair and interlacing his fingers on his stomach. "I don't need to hold your hands. You know what units you are in, and your training officers. You will learn your duties and do as they say. You are not to do whatever you please because initiative can get you killed."

Pyke sat up and shuffled some files on his desk. "This is the Bomb Squad. When a regular cop goes out on a call, he *may* be putting his life in danger. When a member of the Bomb Squad goes out, you *are* putting your life in danger. Consider the fact that a patrolman will face off with an armed man faster than he would walk up to an explosive and hold it in his hand." He paused, becoming a kettle on the stove, rattling from the boiling inside. "And remember, a screw-up can kill not only you, but a score of individuals around you. Don't fuck around." He stood, hands on the desktop. "This was your briefing. Get to work."

They nodded and cleared out of the office quickly. Ateer returned to his desk and finally exhaled.

"He's tough, right?"

"He seems that way."

"He's got bite, if you turn your ass to him. So, the trick is not to turn your ass to him."

"Sounds logical."

"Did he give you the ol' 'don't fuck around because a lotta people can get killed' speech?" Accorso sat back, stretched his legs out under his desk, crossing them at the ankles.

"Yes, he did."

"He does that because of the World's Fair."

"The officers that were killed?"

"And those wounded. A bomb is indiscriminate. The *beast* will chase everyone down."

"The beast?"

"The bomb splash. If you're close enough, you'll regret it."

"Okay."

"You're not to do anything in the beginning other than watch. Good?"

"Good."

Accorso frowned, peering at Ateer through squinting eyes. "I think I know you."

"Yeah?"

"Yeah," he wagged a finger. "I know you."

"Yeah?"

"You went to Cooper Union High School, didn't you?"

"Yeah, I did."

"You were in the same graduating class as I was."

"I might have been."

Accorso, with a grin, stared at Ateer, nodding as if the wheels of his mind were spinning madly. He leaned back, glancing at Pedrotti's desk behind him. "Come here Beat It, I want to introduce you to someone."

Pedrotti stood, slick, smooth, exuding an air of breezy confidence. He smiled, but only on one side of his face, making him look dangerously playful. He was simply dressed in a pinstripe gabardine suit and tie, which was clearly not expensive, something purchased from a bargain store. The words of Commissioner Valentine rung back in his memory. Ateer stood to greet him.

Accorso continued, "Say hello to Dylan 'Mac' Ateer."

Pedrotti reached out for Ateer, shaking his hand. "Hey Mac, just call me 'Beat it'."

"Okay." Ateer shook his hand vigorously.

Abruptly a young, thin man with a pompadour, slicked back and heavy brows literally leaped into Ateer's space. Dressed in a shirt and tie, unbuttoned at the collar, and rolled up at the sleeves. He seemed anxious, out of breath, rocking slightly from side to side with wide eyes staring Ateer up and down. He reached out with his hand. "And I'm Basilo Frascone—"

"Go back to your desk Big O," Accorso said with embarrassingly visible exasperation.

Frascone looked at him, his face contorted in disappointment, and then walked off dejectedly.

Accorso leaned over to Ateer, whispering, "You'll come to realize that there are two people in this place. Those that eat steak, and those that suck from the tit. Big O sucks tit."

Ateer nodded dumbly. He understood what the imagery meant; he was just unclear what was the reality.

As if he had a sixth sense, Accorso turned to Pyke's office entrance on the other side of the bullpen and found him standing there. He stood alone, his eyes searching the bullpen as if in search of someone. Accorso knew exactly who he was searching for, Peter Hayias.

Pike walked up to the bullpen balustrade, standing over Accorso's and Ateer's desks.

"Can you two stand each other?" he asked them.

"I'm not certain, sir." Accorso said to him.

"Good." Pyke regarded the still standing Ateer. "You do know that Accorso is your T.O.?"

"I kinda thought that. I wasn't introduced to a sergeant yet."

"We don't have a sergeant," Accorso stated flatly.

Everyone turned to him as if he was spouting an invective. After a tense moment, Pyke returned to Ateer, "We do not have a sergeant as of yet. But we will have one soon."

Now, in a sad tone, as if he was a child who did not receive a gift at Christmas, Pedrotti said, "But what about me? If Fab is going to be training the new guy, who's gonna be my partner?"

"Me, you wop idiot. I'm just training this guy," Accorso replied.

"Oh." Pedrotti laughed, more to himself. "I thought he was splitting us up."

"No. He's giving us a third wheel."

"Oh."

"Sit the fuck down, Beat It."

Pedrotti snarled, pushed Accorso at the shoulder and then left the bullpen. Pyke, Accorso, and Ateer watched him leave, passing through the corral gate and vanishing into the main corridor.

"Okay, let me leave you two to it," Pyke rubbed his hands together, nodded to both, then vanished into his office.

Accorso looked up at Ateer. "How do you feel about bombs?"

"What do you mean?" Ateer asked, a confused look on his face.

"It's a question. If I put a bomb on your desk right now. How would you feel about it?"

"I guess I wouldn't like it."

"Well, there are only two types of bomb squad detectives. The living and the ones that look like maple syrup. If you don't *like* bombs, then you need to ask for another transfer." Accorso stood from his desk and walked around it so that he could lean his hip against it. "We play with Devil Toys here. Do you know what that is?"

"A bomb?"

"That's right. A bomb, or what they really are, 'Death looking for a victim.' But the good news here is that a Devil Toy only searches out a careless motherfucker, and every one of his friends nearby."

"I see."

"No, you don't. But when I'm through with you, you're going to see. I'm not going to die because you have your mind on some pussy one day. A Devil Toy wants to eat up life. All life. You'll get my point as I train you. Trust me. You'll learn to like, and respect them, because if you don't, you won't be around for long."

Ateer nodded.

The phone rang. Accorso walked back around his desk to snatch it up.

"Detective Accorso," he said. Listened, then hung up. He looked at Ateer. "That was Pyke. You've got your first assignment."

. . .

The young female Con Edison clerks dressed in their knee-length skirts and loose white blouses, were young and attractive. When one would saunter into the room Accorso would smile, leaping from his chair and rushing to their side to aid them with carrying the file boxes that they carefully stacked on the table, or against the wall. The conference room somewhere in the bowels of the Con Edison building was lit with drab yellow bulbs, giving everything a jaundiced hue, not that Accorso could tell. The most depressing aspect of this so-called conference room was that it lacked any natural light. There we no windows to be found on any wall. Just a door, chairs, and a table. Against one wall was a mounted blackboard with streaky eraser strokes across it, wiping out chalk markings.

The file boxes that were being carried in were the covered type. Ateer went to one and lifted its top. He catered a brief hope that the box was only half filled with files, but as the yellowish light struck the inside, he could clearly see that it was filled to bursting with the tiresome sheets of paper. Fingering through them, Ateer stopped as three more clerks brought in three more boxes held against their bosoms.

Accorso, returning to his chair at the table, asked: "How many are there?"

A young brunette, with rosy cheeks and even rosier lips, rested her box down, "hundreds."

"Hundreds?" Ateer gasped, his body sagged against the heavy wooden table.

A tall, leggy blonde clerk rested her box next to the brunette's, and gasped up through an exhausted frame, "thousands."

"There's a lot of files in each box, Fab," Ateer complained. He searched his T.O.'s eyes for some common sense. "We'll be here for years."

Accorso told the first brunette clerk, "Just bring us twenty boxes."

She nodded, also sighing from fatigue and left the room, carrying the other two young women in her wake.

"What was Pyke thinking sending us here?" Ateer asked, almost as irritated as he was tired. He pulled out a sheaf of files and sat down on a chair next to the box.

"He was thinking that it's better to have us sitting here, doing this shit, than sitting in the bullpen doing nothing." Accorso pulled his tie slack and unbuttoned his collar. He took the top off a box and flipped thorough the files therein. "Besides, for right now, it's safer than having you running out on calls for your first day."

"What about the other new guys?"

Accorso hunched his shoulders. "What about them?"

"Why aren't they here?"

Accorso opened one of the folders, slamming its cover against the table as if it was the weight of a steel door. "How the fuck should I know, Mac?" He growled, his irritation had risen to a flash boil. "You were standing right in front of me when I got the call. Did it look like I knew what the other washouts were up to?"

After a pause to wait for some smart-assed response, Accorso continued. "Thank you. So, if you feel like you are being unjustly punished for something, just think how I feel being sent to hell with you."

Ateer thought about the comment as he pulled out a handful of fat folders filled with paperwork, stripped out of his jacket, and hung it on the back of the chair next to Accorso before sitting down.

"So let me ask you Fab, what are we looking for?" Ateer asked, pulling his tie slack, and unbuttoning his collar.

"We're looking for disgruntled correspondence in their personnel files. This person most definitely has a problem with Con Ed, so maybe he bitched a lot in writing. I know it's painful, just keep your brain in gear. If something is wrong, you'll know it when you see it."

The women entered in with more boxes. Ateer looked at them tiredly. "How many people have complaints about Con Edison?" He asked them.

"More than you can count on a daily basis," the brunette said in passing. They lined the boxes on the other side of the table on top of another row of boxes. They eyed the men, smiling faintly, their eyes coyly looking away when met. They rushed from the room and began giggling amongst themselves the moment they left the room.

"I think they got a thing for one of us," Ateer said, flipping papers, his elbow on the tabletop, his hand propping up his head.

Accorso was surveying the carnage surrounding them. They were only up to nine boxes. He groaned mightily, "Jesus, this shit is going to take thirty-three-and-a-third eternities."

"Maybe we need to call for more reinforcements," Ateer said.

"I think I'll do just that," Accorso stood and left the room. Ateer watched him go, then opened and flipped through the pages of a file.

Accorso and Ateer carefully, slowly, and completely fatigued flipped through pages within files. Ateer was numb in his forefinger and thumb, and the back of his neck already. The end of the day was the only thing on his mind. But that didn't deter the dragging of time, which seemed to travel at a different pace from what they left outside of the conference room. Every tick of the clock was so eternal that it became no longer beneficial to watch because it wasn't progressing.

The bright yellowish glare of the hanging dome lights above were beginning to hurt Ateer's eyes and there was a tiny throbbing beginning to creep into the rear of his skull. He prayed that it didn't move forward, growing with greater force. He turned wearily to Accorso, whose head was bowed over a folder on the desk. For a hot second it looked as if he found something interesting until Ateer realized that his eyes were closed, fast asleep. Ateer balled his fist to give him a shot against his arm when the door opened, awakening Accorso with a start.

One of the brunette clerks assigned to help them swept into the room, her dark dress cinched at the waist, giving her a pair of killer hips. "Sir, your men are here."

Accorso nodded, then shook his head to clear the thick fog. Standing, he rounded the table and left with her into the hall. At the building entrance, was Brock Dempsey, Barney Copeland, and

Christopher Nichols from the bomb squad detectives and Charley Barnett and Eric Parker from support. They stood, smoking, a few with their hands in their pockets, coats and jackets splayed open. Dempsey with his fedora cocked to the back of his head. They looked like a bunch of thugs loitering for a hit. When one of the young clerks would walk by, they would stare, whistle, and make a lecherous comment on the sly. Upon seeing Accorso, they were conflicted. They didn't know whether to snap to attention, in front of a supervisor that looked like he crawled over ten miles of open road, or fear that they would soon be undergoing the same ordeal.

Accorso was completely disheveled, completely different from the man that they saw daily in the bullpen, neatly pressed and smartly attired. He was now all rolled up sleeves, missing tie, and hat, opened shirt and hair out of place.

"Four? Just four of you?" Accorso groaned. "I told Pyke that there's more files here than a platoon of men can deal with."

"He just told *us* to come," Copeland replied, almost apologetically. He dropped his cigarette and crushed it under the toe of his shoe.

"Where's Pedrotti?" Accorso looked over their shoulders for him.

"He's not here," Nicols said. "He's heading the squad in your absence."

"Fuck!" Accorso snorted. "I'm out here in fucking Palooka-ville, and he's got his feet up on a desk, reading a newspaper." Accorso snarled, then after a deep breath, calmed down. "Alright then, we'll work with what we've got." Accorso turned to the brunette next to him. "What is your name again?"

She giggled, "Jeanie."

"Oh, okay, Jeanie. Where are the rest of the boxes?"

She smiled, her eyes twinkling, happy to be surrounded by no doubt available men. "We have the most current files in a cabinet room."

"Where?"

She sashayed off. Accorso waved his fellow detectives to follow and were led to an enormous rectangular room. Against both walls, on the right and left, were tall metal cabinets, shoulder to shoulder, down the length of the wall. Ahead of them, in the center of the file room were two rows of cabinets, back-to-back, running to the end of the room. Accorso, walking reluctantly into the room behind her, blinked. He was so stunned that his mind refused to accept the magnitude of was he was facing. He turned to Jeanie.

"What in the world is this?" He asked her.

"These are the current files from 1930 to 40," she replied sweetly.

"And that's all you have as far back to, is 1930?"

"Here in this building, yes," she said with a smile. "We have earlier years in the warehouse." Her sparkling eyes darted to the men at the door, and then back to Accorso.

"Okay, thank you," he said to her, with a sweep of his hand motioning to the door. "I'll call you if we need you."

She smiled, nodded, and scurried off. The detectives moved in on Accorso, waiting for detailed orders.

"You're looking through the personnel files for any mention of a disgruntled employee, or correspondence from said employee. Take your time and don't miss a thing."

Dark, wavy haired detective Parker, with his thin moustache, stopped to raise his hand, "What do you mean by 'disgruntled,' sir?"

"Somebody is angry with Con Ed. This somebody might have written letters to the company expressing his displeasure. The company would have filed said letter in their personnel files. If you find such a letter in such a file, separate it from the rest and we'll review them. Understood?"

The group said: "Understood, sir."

The men broke apart in separate directions, stripped out of their coats and jackets, removed their hats, and rolled up their sleeves. Accorso left them to it, returning to Ateer in the conference room. Ateer, somehow stuck in time, continued to flip papers in the windowless room. The only sound, other than the rustling of paper, was the mechanical hum of the air conditioner coming from the ceiling vents.

"Can you believe that they use this room for conferences?" Accorso asked.

Ateer looked up tiredly. "Kill me."

"Don't worry, Mac. Purgatory is for couples." Accorso retook his seat and began flipping through his file.

The hands on the clock moved so slowly they seemed to be dragging themselves over sand, which was quite close to what the two detectives felt like they were doing. When seven o'clock crawled around, both Ateer and Accorso were asleep in a face full of paperwork. Ateer used his forearm as a pillow, Accorso's head rested on the side of his face.

When the door opened and another female clerk walked in, the two men snapped awake, eyes wide. Accorso had a page stuck to his cheek.

"Sirs, it's time for the night shift. Do you want anything to eat?"

"What time is it?" Accorso looked at his watch, the paper against his head rustling. Suddenly noticing it, he snatched it away.

"It's seven o'clock, sir."

Ateer was dumbstruck, closing the folder before him. "Seven o'clock?"

Accorso stood and buttoned his collar. "Where are the rest of the detectives?"

"They left hours ago sir."

"Hours ago?" Ateer stood, buttoned his collar, and tightened his tie.

"Yes, around five o'clock."

"Shit, Mac," Accorso said. "When did you fall asleep?"

"I don't know, but it was *after* you!" He took his jacket from the back of the chair and swept into it.

"Would you gentlemen like some coffee or something?" The clerk asked.

SUSPICIOUS LOOKING PACKAGES

Accorso held up a hand. "Oh no. We're done for today. We'll see you again tomorrow."

"Okay, sir," the clerk nodded and turned on her high heels, exiting the room.

"Tomorrow?" Ateer said to Accorso.

"Well, when hell freezes over tomorrow," Accorso said, slipping into his overcoat, "we'll deal with this shit again. But tonight, I'm going to my favorite dive in Greenwich Village. Wanna come?"

The first response that came to Ateer's mind was that he wanted to go home and forget about his first day in the Bomb Squad. He wanted to forget about everything, including the Bomb Squad. But then Valentine's voice floated in the air, as if the stern disciplinarian was standing right beside him. *Get next to this man!*

"Sure." Ateer smiled. "Sounds like a great idea."

"Let's get the fuck out of here, Mackie."

They left the hulking building that spanned the entire block with its cold, hard granite-work behind. They walked out into the street and hailed a cab in the streetlamp lit gloom. Snow was beginning to fall in the night, twinkling like low flying stars falling to the Earth. They slipped into an arriving taxi. The driver zoomed though open streets and struggled when he encountered traffic the last third of the way to the Village, until they pulled up before the place. A series of brownstones ran the length of the block end to end. Their first floors were stores, with huge ceiling to floor display windows hawking everything from clothing to sporting goods.

Patrons were coming out, opening umbrellas against the falling snow. The sidewalk was surging with people rustling past. Ateer batted aside several umbrellas whose edges were heading for his face. "Where is this place at? Up here?" he asked Accorso.

"No, down there," he took a flight of stairs down into a basement under a brownstone and entered a comfortably warm space. Ateer walked in behind him, removing his fedora, and brushed the front of this coat with it. Then he took in his surroundings. A bar ran down the length of the establishment with no stools. Two bartenders with white shirts and black vests and bow ties stood waiting for them, polishing glasses with white hand cloths.

To the left, the establishment continued. Circular tables were covered with white cloths and chairs were filled with chatting, noisy guests, men, and women both enjoying each other's company.

While Ateer studied the room one of the bartenders marched down to the end of the bar, a heavy-set, serious man with a thin mustache and salt and pepper hair. "Whatdaya having?"

Accorso went to the bar, leaning over it, smiling. "Scotch on the rocks," he gestured to Ateer slowly siding up to the bar beside him. "And my buddy here will be having..."

"Vodka tonic," he said.

The bartender nodded. "I'll have it sent to your table," he said.

Accorso and Ateer navigated through the haphazardly spaced tables until they found an empty one. A coat rack was close enough to hang their coats and hats. They sat down at the table and waited.

"Can you buy food here?" Ateer asked.

"You can, but I wouldn't eat it." Accorso chuckled.

"You know, Fab, everyone was telling me how dangerous the Bomb Squad is, but I didn't know that the danger was in bleeding to death from a million paper cuts."

"Don't be a smart ass, Mackie. Trust me, when you have to deal with a Devil Toy, you'll appreciate days like this when the worse that can happen to you is a fucking paper cut."

"Sorry. I just thought that I would be receiving all this training and experience in defusing bombs, not going through files. Don't you have women that can do this?"

"No. And Con Ed doesn't seem to want us to use any of theirs either so it's on us."

"I'd rather deal with bombs."

"Oh really?" Accorso smiled as if he had a bad taste in his mouth.

A slim, young woman, probably fourteen, walked up with their drinks, resting them on their table.

"Thank you," Accorso said to her. She beamed tiredly before

walking off across the beaten and sand dashed parquet floor. Ateer reached into his jacket and produced a pack of cigarettes. Shaking one out, he stuck it between his lips and lit it with the candle in the center of the table, encased in a crystal wind shield.

After a few puffs he asked Accorso, "Do you want one?"

"That's alright, I have a deck of my own." Accorso replied.

They took a pause to quaff their drinks. Ateer looked around at the chattering faces. At the table next to them two men were drinking and smoking with an equally engaged woman. He wondered if she was a dirty chippy reeling in two men who thought they were setting her up for the kill. That was what Ateer was trained to look for in the Public Morals squad, but he wouldn't be interested in rousting her unless it was a sweep of whores. He would be after the bigger game, the pimp who should have been sitting at a table nearby. Ateer looked for him but couldn't spot anyone that would fit the description.

"So, how long have you been in the Bomb Squad?" Ateer turned to Accorso who was also scanning the room for his own particular reasons.

"Nine and a half years. Almost a fucking decade," Accorso lit a cigarette. "I guess it's only fitting because my father was part of the Black Hand."

"The Black Hand?"

Accorso moved his forefinger around in the air as if he was scrawling a doodle, "You know, they used to drive around town, throwing dynamite into stores and other establishments."

"Like for the mob?"

"Yeah, like for the mob."

"Wow, really?"

"He supported ten children and a wife by doing that."

"He was a criminal."

Accorso nodded. "He took care of his family the best way he knew how." He hooked a finger behind his tie and pulled it slack. "He may have been a bad man, but I can't hate him. He was good to me."

"I understand." Ateer nodded. "But then that brings up a prickly question."

"What's that?"

"How did the son of a bomb terrorist grow up to be a detective chasing bomb terrorists?"

Accorso sat back and smiled. "I know, it sounds like the craziest shit you've ever heard, right?"

"I've heard crazier."

Accorso took a sip of his drink. "Maurizio, that's my dad god rest his soul, was doing a drive by bombing with dynamite and the thrower, in the back seat, lit the fuse and in the throw, dropped it in the car as they drove by their target building. It exploded, killing the both of them."

"How did you find that out?"

"It was all over the papers, and my uncle—who is not really my uncle—told my mother who eventually told us when we were old enough."

"I see," Ateer nodded.

"He was a good man. He was. I hated the Black Hand for using him though, and by extension, killing him, but I was always fascinated with bombs afterward. It felt as if a great beast came and absconded with my father's life, and I guess, from then on, I've been chasing it."

"So, you joined the Bomb Squad?"

"Why not? I wanted to meet the dreaded beast up close. I wanted to understand the last moments of my father's life."

"And how did that work out for you?"

"Well, years later, in the bomb squad, I faced a detonation. Have you ever done that? Stand just outside of a blast, but well within the shock wave?"

"I don't understand that."

"Well, when a bomb explodes several things come out of it."

"Several?"

"Yeah, and the closest that you are to it, the more of these *'several'* things will kill your ass."

"Really?"

"Yeah, I'll outline it for you. Consider this the beginning to the training that you so desperately desire."

"Okay."

Accorso stubbed out his cigarette in the crystal ashtray on the table. Ateer did the same.

"First is the blast wave. Far enough and it'll mess up your hair, close and it'll knock you down, closer and you're in trouble before you know it."

"Blast wave."

"And with that the shockwave. This is the wave that will pass through you and cause the most damage. It's true chaos, happening in the length of a second. Everything in your body will rupture, your lungs, your stomach, your ears, your blood vessels, your balls...yeah, even your balls will go pop."

"I wouldn't like that."

"I wouldn't either." Accorso smiled heartily. For Ateer, he couldn't find the humor. The server girl returned with their drinks in both hands. As she set them down, Accorso reached out and pinched her cheek, turning it a rosy red. "You're a sweet little thing, aren't you?"

Her body went rigid as she grimaced against the pinch. When he let her go, she darted off.

"I can see that these will be our last drinks," Ateer said, finishing the one before him before going after the second one.

"What are you talking about?"

"When you pinched her cheek, she looked like she shit herself. She'd be scared to death to come back here now."

"Are you kidding me, that lil' waif hasn't eaten for days. She'll be back for the quarter tip, just you wait."

"How can you tell?"

Accorso leaned back in his chair, pointing at Ateer. "You need to look at her cheeks. They're fallen in. She hasn't eaten in a while and the owner is working the shit out of her."

"Really?"

"I'm really surprised you didn't notice it."

"What? Do you think that being on the P.M. makes me god?"

"Not god, just interested in motherfuckers."

"I think you're interested in more than that little girl's cheeks."

Accorso broke out laughing. "You've gotta be kidding me, Mackie. I'm a married man."

Ateer didn't know how to answer Accorso. He simply sat in his chair, shook the liquor in this glass.

"You look uncomfortable," Accorso squinted at him, his laughter fading.

"I don't usually frequent bars."

"Why? Did you have to be a boy scout when you were in the P.M. squad?"

"My mother was a temperate woman, she raised us to be the same way."

"Really? She was very religious?"

Ateer thought to answer truthfully, then untruthfully, then not at all. "It's a long story."

"Okay, another long story then. Where was I in the explanation of an explosion?"

"Shockwave."

"Right. Shockwave." Accorso sat up, looked around for the little girl. "Then comes the fragmentation wave. Far enough and it'll still kill you. All kinds of bits of shit, rocks, melted metal, nails, bolts, are traveling within that wave at supersonic speeds. They'll put daylight through you like bullets."

At the thought of bullets ripping through a human body, Ateer's image of it was strikingly clear, with tiny plumes of blood bursting from the other side, ripping and tearing through human tissue. He was certain that his newfound clarity of imagination came from the alcohol now tainting his bloodstream.

"Then there is the heatwave and fire that will set off secondary fires. Far enough and you'll feel like you've placed your face in an oven. Close enough and it'll scorch your clothes and skin, closer and it'll make you a Thanksgiving turkey."

"Really?"

"It'll boil the contents of your stomach, that's if your stomach stays together after the shockwave." Accorso leaned over to the side, reached out and snagged the arm of the little girl still running around the tables. He pulled her close. "Can we have another round?"

"Yes, mister," she said.

As she scurried off, Accorso returned to Ateer. "The beast, at this time, has stood up, but our world is not for her, Mackie. She leaves, and when she opens the door to hell in departing, she sucks everything in behind her. The blast wind rips backwards, carrying debris, again, like fiery projectiles, this is her parting gift. You survived her blast wave, so she'll give you a second chance to get hot pieces of shit in your ass."

Ateer thought about what he had said, stared at him, then sipped his drink. "You call it a beast."

"She is. She is *the beast*. She is a monster, like the ones that you feared were under your bed when you were a child. She has no shape or form, but she's walked across the earth many times and people have described her."

"What was her description?"

"Hell, with the lid off."

Ateer finished his drink. "Have you been close to a blast?"

"Yeah, and you will be too before long. Try not to hurl your cookies."

"I will? Why?"

"Because I'll put you directly in front of one." Accorso laughed, stating an obvious fact to him. Ateer wondered what the mechanism was in this man that caused him to view the most callous and vulgar things humorous. They both returned to their drinks with Ateer looking around over the top of his glass at the "L" shaped room. Its walls were rustic, some paintings, some mirrors. A couple worked their way through the closely packed tables, heading in their direction. Ateer watched them approach, then turned away when they were about to pass by, but they didn't. The male of the two rested a hand on Accorso's shoulder. He was tall, broad shouldered, his face was squared like a brick, heavy eyebrows and jet-black hair combed back with a part on the side.

"Fabulous! What's shaking man!" The stranger rounded the table and pulled out a chair. "It's so crowded in this scene tonight. Did you bring all these people in here with you?"

"It was empty when we got here. It must be you." Accorso grumbled.

The woman with the stranger pulled up a chair on the other side of the table from him. She was slim, petite, with long, curly dark hair and deep, soulful eyes. Ateer jumped to his feet, motioning to pull out her chair for her as she sat down. "Please excuse my lack of manners, ma'am," he blurted.

"She's not a ma'am." Accorso waved at him, grinning. "Sit down, sit down."

The stranger stretched out a hand to Ateer. "The name is Vaughn Davidson, and this is my lady friend, Naomi Brooks."

Ateer shook his hand and then shook Naomi's as he eased back into his seat. "I'm so sorry. I don't know where my manners went."

"That's not a problem." Her coarse, sultry voice came at him like a hot wind carrying grit. Her eyes seemed to stare through him, measuring him up and down, a new living thing for her to feast upon. Her skin was creamy and smooth, like fresh milk, flawless and even. Finally, her lips, like the petals of a red rose, drew his attention when she spoke.

The teen waitress returned with their drinks, resting them down on the table.

"Yeah, she's not a lady," Vaughn said also smiling. "She's a dame."

"Aww, why don't you just button your flap," she replied.

"Hey Vaughn, do you have any on you?" Accorso asked, dropping his voice in volume.

"Sure. Right here." Vaughn reached into his jacket and fetched a silver cigarette holder. Snapping it open, he pinched out a reefer, neatly rolled and twisted at the ends. He handed it over to Accorso with a smile and a flourish.

"Excellent, I owe you one." Accorso stuck the marijuana cigarette between his lips and leaned in the other direction to light it.

"So, you defuse any bombs today, Fab?" Vaughn asked.

"Not today. I only defused paperwork."

"How about you?" Vaughn turned his attention to Ateer. "You work in the bomb squad?"

"Yeah, just started." Ateer replied.

"You like it?"

"What's there to like?"

Accorso took another puff, leaned over the table, and stretched out his hand, handing the joint over to Ateer. Ateer looked at it for a moment, reluctantly. Accorso shook his hand, waving the cigarette at him. The motion awoke Ateer from his daze. He reached out and took it.

"Ever smoked marijuana before?" Vaughn asked him. "By the way, what's your name bud?"

"Dylan, but my friends call me, Mac." Ateer stared at the joint.

Accorso snapped his fingers to get Ateer's attention, "Don't let it burn down, smoke it!"

Ateer put the end of the joint to his lips and drew smoothly. His lungs filled with the smoke, swirling, then burning. An itch in the center of his throat turned into fire and before he knew it, he was coughing violently. Accorso stood up, over the table and reached out for the joint between Ateer's fingers. Snatching it away, he sat back down, sticking it into his mouth.

"You're going to waste it," Accorso snarled.

"Looks like they're going up, baby." Vaughn said to Naomi over the loud coughing of Ateer. They both turned to a small stage at the right of where they sat and an emcee mounted it, waving his hands at the audience.

"Hello, and it's fine to see you here at the Poetry Place. If you would like to read, please put your name on the list. Now, let's get onto the show," the emcee said. He introduced the first poet, an older woman, who mounted the stage insouciantly and spouted a stream of staccato rhymes.

"Shit, listen to that riff, man," Vaughn said between poems.

Accorso ignored him, burning down the joint.

"I'd better go and put my name on the list," Naomi said, standing and walking off.

Ateer sat, lightheaded. That single puff of the marijuana left him floating, swirling, or was it from the lack of air due to his violent coughing. His throat still burned like an inhuman fire, making swallowing difficult. Snatching up his drink, he took several gulps to ease the pain, but it only seemed to add to it. The room moved with a certain sluggishness as he looked about. What the fuck?

"That Hitler is one hung up cat, Fab. He's got issues," Vaughn said.

Accorso handed him the joint. "Fuck Hitler."

"We're going over there to make a scene, man. They've got our boys already protecting British supply ships. We're going over there because he has Germany goofy." Vaughn puffed on the joint.

Another poet, a male one, took the stage, reading from a sheet of paper.

The joint was passed to Ateer. It was small now, barely larger than the pinch between his fingertips. He looked down at it.

"Come on man, it's just a roach," Vaughn said with a level of irritation. "It can't hurt you."

"My throat still burns," Ateer replied sheepishly.

"That's why you've gotta smoke some more on top of it. You have to toughen up your throat if you're going to smoke it." He shook it at him. "Here!"

Ateer reluctantly reached out for the roach, put it to his lips, and inhaled again. Even with the little puff left in the marijuana, immediately the burning sensation, itching, and tickling returned. Both cheeks swelled, the coughs jolted through his chest, but he held back the cough from escaping his mouth loudly. He passed the roach to Accorso who looked at it for a moment, puffed on it to see if the embers were still alive in it, and crushed it out in the ashtray.

"What do you think, Mac?" Vaughn turned to him. "Are we going into Europe?"

"I've never smoked Marijuana before," Ateer said with a gasp, his eyes moving like they were suspended in thick syrup. To him, the world was slipping into a slow-moving sorghum. The most incredible thing about what was happening to him though was his experience with the poems. He turned his head to the stage and could hear every word spoken with a comprehensibility that he found unique and astounding. Suddenly the words coming from the stage had meaning and were moving. With rapt attention, he focused on the poets appearing and disappearing.

Vaughn laughed. "I'm not getting any fucking conversation from you two tonight, am I?"

"I'm talking." Accorso turned up his drink.

"You're about to blow your gig." Vaughn said to him, leaning over towards him to look into his eyes.

"I'm fine, man."

Ateer pointed to the stage. "Your girlfriend."

Accorso and Vaughn turned to the stage to see Naomi climb atop and position herself in front of the audience. After a meaningful pause to ready the shadows all around her, she began to belt away a poem, strong, masculine, harsh, sexually charged, and quite angry. Her sultry voice gave it a deep, grotto-like sound, like wheels rolling over gravel. Her topic—sodomy—was descriptive, down to the feelings and sensations of anal sex. She balled a fist at the audience, marching around the stage, first growling, but now shouting. Her tirade went on for a while. As the three men watched her, one of the bartenders came to the table, lowered his head until it was level with the rest, wringing his hands out on a white cloth.

"Is she with you??" He asked.

Vaughn looked at him. "Yes, she is, in fact."

"We don't appreciate poetry like that here. If she can't stay within the bounds of propriety, we do not want her here."

"You have bounds here?" Vaughn's eyes opened.

"Yes, we do sir, and I would have to say that you are drunk," he looked at Accorso and Ateer, "or on something else. Either way, you can all leave this establishment now."

"We're not ready to blow this scene, man," Vaughn objected.

"Well, blow this scene you must. I'm asking you quite politely to leave."

Vaughn turned to Accorso. "Is your 'short' outside, man."

"My car?"

"Yeah."

"Yeah."

"Okay, this place is a drag. You got eyes to split? Let's make it." Vaughn stood. Accorso, a heartbeat later, stood unsteadily to his feet with him. "Yeah," he said. "Let's get into the wind."

Although not an accomplished drinker, Ateer was used to having one or two belts in his bloodstream, but now he was strangely outside of his body, looking in. This odd perspective made him clumsy, like trying to move a marionette about by strings attached to the wrong arms and legs. The three men staggered from the bar after taking their coats and hats from the rack. Leaving the bar and walking upstairs to the sidewalk, they stood outside in the cold and the dark, looking about.

"So? Where are your wheels?" Vaughn asked, pulling the brim down lower on his head as a cold wind rushed by.

Accorso looked around. He had obviously misplaced it. Ateer looked at him, confused at first as to what he was doing, then asked: "Are you looking for the car?"

"Yeah," Accorso replied. "The patrol car that I drove us here in."

"We took a cab." Ateer pointed out.

"We did?"

"Shit," Vaughn said. "It's time for you guys to go home." He stopped upon noticing Naomi walking upstairs from the bar, donning her long woolen coat with Scotland plaids, the shoulders adorned with lynx-dyed white fox, and wide brimmed hat, with lace netting that covered her face. The instant she was with them Vaughn gathered her up in an arm and held her close. "We're hitting the streets. You guys' better call it a night."

Vaughn and Naomi walked to the curb. Accorso scowled, turned to Ateer. "I think he's right. We've got to get up early tomorrow and be at Con Ed to go through those files."

"We're doing that?" Ateer groaned.

"We'd better, unless you think you'd enjoy Pyke sticking a grenade up your ass and pulling the pin." Accorso laughed. They walked to the subway through the crunching snow underfoot.

Ateer dreamed about explosions. The odd mushroom, or cauliflower shaped structures growing quickly, composed of smoke, fire, and clumps of dirt. They grew in front of him, and he recognized the beast. It stood up, angry to be in this dimension, swelling with might and fury, searching for life and turning it to death. However, her effects, all the waves that Accorso explained, were not present. Nothing touched him as he watched a broccoli shaped explosion rise ahead, towering over him, it's smoke roiling with the yellow glowing of fueled flames. The conflagration bore eyes for a moment, yellowy glowing things scanning the earth seconds before the smoke started to dissipate and the fires died. The falling rain of dirt and debris fell around Ateer, not touching him. A dark haze rolled in, filling the air, obscuring his surroundings and through the murk came a form, a shadowy figure, walking on unsure legs, lurching towards him, a hand raised, clutching. As the specter broke from the smoke, Ateer could clearly make out an armless Accorso staggering towards him, his flesh hanging on him in tatters. Half of his head was gone as well as the eye on that side. He was covered with black soot, his clothes exhausted on his frame, his bones appearing where gaps in his flesh were apparent.

Accorso came close, the side of his face torn away, his cheek on the left side nothing but grinning teeth and mandible. He spoke, his voice a gargle, the throat filled with blood and gore.

"Mac. It's all on you now," the almost unintelligible voice foamed.

Ateer's eyes opened. Not with fright, or fear, just opened. He was done sleeping and rolled out of bed, walking into the bathroom.

After dressing in one of his older suits, he left his apartment, and upon reaching the sidewalk he noticed the black Buick Century parked in front of his home. Reflexively, he scanned the block. The tree lines sidewalk was light with foot traffic. Otherwise, the average street with its row of brownstones receding shoulder to shoulder held nothing suspicious. He crossed the sidewalk, opened the door of the vehicle, and slipped in. Orlowski started the engine and pulled off.

"So, how's it going, Ateer?" He asked.

"Good. No complaints."

"How was your first day? Are you fitting in? Has Accorso taken the bait?"

"Yes, he's training me, and he took me out to a poetry club last night where he smoked marijuana."

"Was that it?"

"Yes. That and alcohol."

"Did he confide in you about any investigations? About his feelings about Pyke?"

"No."

Orlowski hunched his shoulders. "Well, it's way too soon for that anyway. It'll be months before you get into the meat and potatoes. Just stick with this guy. Stay on him. Don't give him any reason to distrust you. He may try you. He smokes dope, you smoke dope. He drinks a beer, you drink a beer. Get me?"

"I'm not used to this, Walter. I'm not a bar drinking, marijuana smoking type of person. I never spend time in those kinda places."

"Sure, you have. You were in the P.M. Squad."

"I raided those places; I never frequented them."

"You never been to a club before?"

"Yeah, once or twice."

"How about a whorehouse? You ever been in a whorehouse?"

Ateer shook his head. "Only when raiding them."

Walter glanced at him in disbelief before returning to the traffic. "Lew really picked a peach with you, didn't he?"

"What do you mean?"

"He picked a sheep to catch wolves. You're gonna fuck this up, I can feel it."

"I can do this job."

"Without being a pussy about it? Because believe me, I don't have the patience for you to be climbing in my car and crying about how you had your dick sucked or snorted nose-candy."

"That won't happen."

"Make sure it doesn't. We've got a job to do here. You were picked to cakewalk through this shit because you had seen it all in the Public Morals Squad. Now you're crying that you're a rube?"

"I'm not saying that. I'm just saying that I was raised differently from Accorso."

"So? Who the fuck cares? You, me and a can of pork and beans, that's who. Just do the fucking job you signed on for."

"Okay," Ateer resigned himself angrily. "I will."

"Stop crying like a baby. As for me, you won't be seeing me for a little while. I've got other things to do. Besides it's going to take you awhile to get anywhere. Just watch out and don't get your ass blown up in the process."

"There's little chance off that. Yesterday, all we did was go through files at Con Ed."

"Is this about the latest bomb found in their building?"

"Yeah. A bomb, they assume, was left by some disgruntled

employee of Con Ed. We're searching through records to see if the bomber had previously sent irate letters to the utility company."

"That's a start."

"Not a good one. Can you imagine all the people that Con Ed hires, and how many are pissed off at them?"

"A lot?"

"First of all, the number of employees over the years is staggering. Second, finding irate employees is like finding a needle in the haystack on one hand, and stopping a flood on the other. There are a lot of lawsuits against Con Ed."

"Your bomber could be writing nasty letters or be involved in a lost court case?"

"That's right. From now to a million years ago."

"Sounds like you've got your work cut out for you."

"In aces and spades."

Orlowski pulled the car over two blocks from the precinct. "Have a good day, Ateer."

"Thanks," Ateer opened the car door and stuck one foot out. He turned to Orlowski. "And call me Mac."

"That's alright, Ateer. Let's not get too friendly. That way I can be nasty to you when you screw this up."

Ateer nodded resolutely. He didn't have a friend here. Slipping out of the car, he marched down the wintry block, pulling the edges of his coat around him and folding up his collar. He pinched the brim in the front of his fedora and pulled it down just over his brow. The wind, although angry at times, was not constant, which was a good thing. And his walk to the station house, although long, was no real inconvenience.

Standing in front of the precinct, talking to two uniformed officers was Accorso, smoking a cigarette, his fedora cocked to the side, his overcoat buttoned up tight to his collar. He laughed, backing up, bending over, and staggering about in loud guffaws as Ateer approached. Upon noticing his subordinate's arrival, Accorso patted the two patrolmen on the shoulders and walked off, heading towards Ateer.

"Hey, partner. How you feeling?" he asked.

"Pretty good."

"No hangover?"

"None. But then again, I'm no stranger to alcohol."

Accorso nodded. "Good. I cranked at Pyke today so they gave us an unmarked that we can get around in faster. It's in the motor pool."

"Sure."

The two men walked off together.

"So, what did you think about smoking dope?"

"It was interesting. It was different from the high I've experienced with liquor."

"That's right, because it unlocks the brain's potential. Your mind opens and you experience things differently."

"I noticed."

"Those poet motherfuckers swear by it. It makes reading poetry an experience all its own."

They turned into a parking lot closed off from the street by a high hurricane fence. Its gate was open. They walked through it and down the length of a fleet of Plymouth two doors parked down both sides of the lot.

"Which one is ours?" Ateer asked.

"The fifth."

They surrounded the car. Accorso driving, Ateer riding shotgun. The car pulled out of the parking space and left the lot, making a right onto the street, its rear tires spinning in the slush of the curb, and took off on its way to Con Ed.

Herbert Schrank looked like a greasy, dishonest used car salesman. Tall, with jet black hair, bushy eyebrows, and small rat-like eyes, he rubbed his hands together anxiously. His expensive cotton suit was well pressed, along with his tie, knotted in a four-in-hand, and a crisp, white shirt with a collar bar holding them at bay pronouncing the tie.

He stood in the reception area of the office, waiting as Accorso and Ateer walked in, removing their hats, and unbuttoning their overcoats.

"Gentlemen, I'm Herbert Schrank, Con Ed Task Force Supervisor. I'm here to help you to find what it is that you are looking for," he said with a smarmy smile.

Accorso and Ateer shook his hand in turn.

"We need more firepower," Accorso said. "We need some of your staff to help us out."

"You can't bring any more of your detectives? You have four of them in the file room now." Schrank gestured in the general direction of the room.

"We need even more."

Schrank sighed, shoved his hands in his pockets. "Damn, detective. We have work to do here too. You want me to pull my staff because some crackpot put something that looked like a bomb in our headquarters?"

"It was a bomb. I handled it myself."

"But it didn't go off."

"That was the aim, my friend."

Schrank sighed again, as if he was having a hard time breathing. "Alright, how many of my people do you want?"

"As many as you can spare."

Schrank nodded, finished and defeated. "Alright, I'll get back to you."

In the conference room, surrounded by boxes, Accorso and Ateer flipped through files tiredly. Seven young women were doing the same, around the long conference table. It was a quiet endeavor with no one talking, just the rustle of papers as they went through file after file, page after page, hour after hour. Another group of young women took reviewed files in boxes out and brought new boxes in. An endless parade of pain that seemed to arrive with trumpets and leave with sighs. Ateer felt as if he was staggering through a desert of papers, blowing, sweeping with each gust of wind. Far ahead, on the horizon, like cloud covered mountains were stacks of boxes rising heavenward. He continued to flip through papers, as if they were made of heavy iron sheets. His mind grew numb, weighed down by the gravity of their labor. They were working uphill every step of the way, a Sisyphean effort that he felt would have the same fruitless outcome.

Another box of files.

With red eyes and tired senses, they reached five o'clock without anything bleeding through the gray haze of black text melting together with white paper. There was no clue, nothing outstanding, nothing that looked odd, no vituperation that looked overly suspicious.

Schrank walked into the stark conference room and excused the girls, sending them home for the night.

"Are you guys going to stay?" Schrank asked.

"Fuck no." Accorso closed the file before him and stood up, buttoning his collar, and straightening his tie. "We're getting the hell out of here."

Ateer stood up and fixed his attire also. He walked to the coat rack and donned his overcoat and hat.

"Well then, I'll see you gentlemen tomorrow," Schrank said.

Shrank left as Accorso donned his winter gear.

"Got anything planned?" Ateer asked.

"Yeah, I gotta get home. The wife has the neighbors over tonight. That translates to a long and boring life."

They made their way to the exit of the building with the rest of the female clerks wrapping themselves in their overcoats and donning headdresses.

"Oh, and another thing," Accorso said, stopping just before the glass and metal double doors of the exit. "How do you feel about dinner parties?"

"I feel nothing, why?"

"My wife wants my new partner over for dinner sometime to meet the family. You available for something like that?"

"Yeah, sure. I'll be there."

Accorso brought the Buick to a stop across the street from Ateer's apartment and said goodnight before driving off into the rainy night. Ateer waited for a break in the traffic before trotting across the shiny, slick asphalt. He ran up and into the brownstone, stopping in the small foyer to shake the rain from his coat and fedora. Standing at the foot of the stairs was Sean McGrath dressed in his overcoat and hat. His dapper ex-partner had his hand shoved deep into his coat pocket, the other holding a black umbrella, and his scarf wound around his chin.

"What are you up to tonight?" he asked when Ateer stopped in the building.

"Nothing. What do you have in mind?"

"Let's take a walk to Liam's Tavern and hoist a few."

"Sure. Why not? I could use a break."

Liam's Tavern was not far.

They walked briskly, close together under the umbrella, listening to the falling rain patting upon the fabric overhead and dancing around the large puddles beginning to form in depressions in the sidewalk. They were soon sweeping into the tavern shaking the rain from their overcoats and hats and hanging everything up on a coat rack. On the left of the establishment was a bar, which held a few customers sitting on chrome and metal stools bent over drinks. On the right was a row of booths. McGrath walked to the back of the tavern and sat in the last booth, facing the door. Ateer sat opposite him, an uncomfortable position for someone used to scanning a room and watching who would walk in and out of an establishment. However, he and McGrath had a long understanding that when presented with situations where one had to sit with his back to the door, that one would be Ateer due to his lack of seniority.

"What's going on?" Ateer asked, holding up his hand to signal the waitress.

"What's going on with you?" McGrath lit a cigarette and tossed the match into an ashtray. "You're the one with the new assignment. You liking it?"

"It's alright," Ateer said, but was looking up at the waitress as she stopped before their table. They ordered drinks before he returned to the conversation. "It's insanely boring to be honest with you. All I've been doing is going though files looking for pissed off people that worked for Con Ed."

"That has something to do with bombs?"

"Yeah, it's a lead, but I don't think there was much thought put into it because the amount of paperwork is enormous. We have literal teams working on this now."

"Seems a little like what we do in our downtime." McGrath smiled, the edges of his well-groomed mustache turning upward.

"Trust me, you wouldn't believe the stacks of shit we go though in a single day. I kinda hate going in tomorrow because that's all I'll be doing. I thought I would be getting bomb training and all that stuff, but no. I'm digging through files."

"I'm sorry to hear that. Well, at least your head is still connected to the rest of you. Who knows what would happen if you were defusing a bomb, this could all be another story."

"Look Stiffy, I know you didn't come here to ask me about the Bomb Squad. You're up to something, what is it?"

"I'm just here to tell you that I'm dropping all of our vice cases. I know I told you that I'll keep working them, but guess what?"

"What?"

"I've been drafted."

The waitress returned with their drinks, resting them down on the tabletop before sauntering off. McGrath stared at her posterior as she walked away, leaning to see over Ateer's shoulder.

"Drafted? Really?"

"Yeah, I'm off to war if we have one. I'm supposed to show up at Fort Hamilton at the end of the week."

"Really? Wow. How do you feel about that one?"

McGrath hunched his shoulders nonchalantly. "I don't know. Hitler's raising hell out there. Personally, I don't know if we should be sticking our nose in other people's shit. When we had the revolutionary war who butted in for us?"

"I don't know if this is the same."

"Well, I know, if two men have a disagreement you lock 'em in a room and let them hash it out. That's what I think we should do, let the Germans and the French and the English hash all this shit out amongst themselves."

"That may be what you think, but you've been drafted."

"It's my country, Mac. Where Uncle Sam wants me, there I am."

They fell silent.

"Good luck to you then, buddy. I wish you the best. I really do."

"Hell, I'm going to need it. I'm a cop and I haven't had to fire my weapon once in the line of duty. I wonder what good I'll be as a soldier."

"Well, you're a pretty good cop, Stiffy."

"Yeah." McGrath stubbed out his cigarette and took a sip of his drink. "I asked Hogan if he could get an exception for me, but he said no. LaGuardia said he wasn't going to grant any to officers. But then he turns around and grants them for firemen."

"I know, right. That little bullshitter. He thinks the city will burn down before crime runs rampant, huh?"

"That's right. Now I would be wrong to say that when he sends all the cops away that God-forbid someone breaks into his mansion and gives his wife some asshole loving against her will without some spit to lubricate his cock and leaves a note that says: 'Nah, nah, nah-nah-nah, you can't catch me.'"

SUSPICIOUS LOOKING PACKAGES

"You know, Stiffy, you can be a bit harsh in your dispensation of justice."

McGrath didn't care. "What? I think ass-rape is better than regular rape. At least with ass-rape you don't have to worry about the bitch getting pregnant."

"You've been in Public Morals too long. It's starting to take its toll on your thinking."

"I think like everyone in Public Morals, and I happen to say whatever is on my mind." McGrath waved at the waitress.

"I know, I've been your partner for five years, but sometimes you should just keep what's inside, inside."

"You bottle all that shit up in you, and you'll bust an artery. All the alcohol, clubs, drugs, whores that we're awash in, you've got to let it out somehow. I've developed a potty mouth. What do you do when you run home every night, Mac? Masturbate with sandpaper?"

Ateer made a painful face. The waitress came and took their next drink order.

"I wonder how your new squad is going to handle your running home every night after your trick. Those guys are a bunch of who-ha wop thugs. Those motherfuckers are so mean that they bit off their mamma's nipples when they were sucking on the tit." He chuckled.

"You are too much."

"Hey, I'm just calling them as I see them."

"You *see* too much then."

They both laughed. Strangely, as if for the first time, Ateer looked his friend over, mainly because of how the lamp-light overhead glinted off his left cufflink. His attention for an instant riveted on the piece of jewelry. He had seen McGrath in fancy clothes and jewelry before, but today they somehow took on a new meaning to him. Yes, the gold tie clip, silk tie, and expensive suit. Where was he getting the money for that? Ateer was in awe that he asked himself that question. It amazed him how just a few minutes with Commissioner Valentine had changed his once lethargic and ingenuous thinking.

"Something wrong?"

Ateer shook his head, finished his cigarette. "No, nothing. I was just thinking about something."

"What's that?"

"Just that we had a pretty good team in Public Morals."

"Yeah, with you playing a fucking nun."

"Oh, c'mon."

"No, I'm serious. You were never really one of us, Mac. You kept to yourself, stayed out of the way. You never really took the time to know anyone. You did your trick, and you were out the door. What the fuck was that?"

"Minding my own business."

"Yeah, and you did that well. You're a good cop, but no one would have had your back. If you got dirty, we wouldn't have known it."

"First you claim that I was a nun. Now you're telling me that I entered a cesspool that we constantly drained nearly every night."

"A dirty cop looks like a good cop; didn't you know that? We watched each other, buddy. That's the only way to stay honest, unless Valentine brings back the spies again and starts up another Confidential Squad."

"No, I don't think they'll ever do that again. The old one didn't work as well as us watching ourselves."

"That's right. We're fully capable of policing ourselves. But that's only if we know each other. We only knew you as another detective."

"That's what I was."

McGrath leaned forward, elbows on the table, interlacing his fingers, "Level with me, buddy. I'm leaving and might never come back, so you can be honest. Are you a Daisy or something?"

"A Daisy?"

"Yeah, Mac. We've never seen you with a woman, unless you were shoving her out of a whorehouse. You don't do anything because as you say, 'your mother raised you better.' Yeah."

"She did."

"So what, you still listen to your mother. It's alright if you're a fairy. It doesn't bother me."

"I'm not a fairy. I like to think that I'm a disciplined man."

The waitress returned. Ateer reached for his wallet, but McGrath waved him down. "Hey, hey, I got this."

"You got it the last time."

"I got this, I said." He had his wallet out and fished out a few coins for the young lady. He dropped some on the tabletop. "You be good, Mac. You were a strange one, but you're a good cop."

"Thank you."

"What are you going to do now? Run home?"

"More like walk home." Ateer stood from the booth, reached down to finish his drink from the table.

"For some reason, I knew you weren't running out to fuck a Pro-Skirt," McGrath said, patting him on the shoulder.

Ateer smiled warmly. McGrath was right, they were never really friends. He had largely kept to himself in the Public Morals Squad, but there was something within him that knew he would earnestly miss his ex-partner.

They headed for the coat rack.

"Listen buddy, I wish you the best of luck in the service. And if they send you to war, keep your head down." Ateer wrapped a brotherly arm across McGrath's shoulders.

"Tell me about it. You just watch your back here in the city. This is New York. It'll hand you one of your balls in a Tiffany box and the other wrapped in newspaper just to make you cry. Watch your back."

"Where do you get your remarks from?"

"I work for the P.M. Squad, buddy," he smiled broadly.

For a moment they stared at each other, not really wanting to go their separate ways. Any other night and they would see each other in the morning for their tour, but not tonight. After tonight they might never see each other again. They were aware of it. They passionately felt it. McGrath took him by both shoulders, shook him as if mute, struggling to speak, snatched his umbrella from his wrist and walked out of the door.

Ateer, frozen in his shoes, watched him leave into the rain, snapping up his umbrella and walking off.

Walking through the rain, staying close to the buildings, Ateer thought about what was happening to his moral stand since leaving the Public Morals Squad. It seemed to be under assault both from within and without. He had strong emotions against certain things immoral, but he had to admit that it was provided to him by his mother. His mother's admonitions were like this falling rain around him, constant, steady. But because or her fear of her husband's grandmother's horrid morals she had set off to crush it in her children. Her husband, being raised by his prostitute mother, was no better of a human being. Whatever bad morals ruled the father would not rule her son. This apple would not fall close to the father's tree, and neither would his sister.

The bullpen buzzed at its usual tempo, with officers and detectives going to their assignments or their desks. For some reason it seemed as if more people than the ten men that Ateer was introduced to a few days ago, milled about the inside of the corral. Among them, standing at the joining of his and Accorso's desk was Lieutenant Pyke. Without a jacket, he stood with his hands in his pockets, rocking back and forth from heel to toe, conversing with Accorso who was seated before his desk and looking up at him. Ateer stopped before passing through the gate from some involuntary reason. Could they be talking about him? Would he be interrupting something? His hesitation seemed to be a flare for their attention, as both men turned to regard him.

"C'mon Ateer," Pyke said, waving him over, "get over here."

Ateer pushed the gate door aside and walked into the corral, passing desks and other detectives until he reached his. Standing behind his chair, he said cautiously, "Yes, sir?"

SUSPICIOUS LOOKING PACKAGES

"Mac," Accorso said, "I just got off the phone with Mr. Schrank and you know what he told me?"

"What's that?" Bad news, Ateer thought. The girls wouldn't be there to help them today.

"That they have on file in their main office only current files back to the 1930s. They have files going further back than that scattered in different vaults and storehouses all over New York City."

"Are you kidding me?" Ateer replied with dismay.

"Yeah, and I'm trying to tell the lieutenant here that we're just wasting our time with this lead. It'll never amount to anything because it's like searching for a needle in a hay field."

Lieutenant Pyke stood there, towering above Ateer, his dark eyes locked on him under his heavy eyebrows. His face was set in stern lines as if he was trying to gouge the truth from Ateer should he lie. "What's your assessment, Ateer?"

"I'm in agreement, sir. It's a mess over there and after ten hours of going through page after page of letters, memorandum, and reports, they all begin to look the same. I know maybe someone thought that this would be a relatively easy clue to run down, but it's shaping up to be a real nightmare," Ateer replied, slipping off his hat and overcoat, dropping the hat on the desk and draping the coat over his chair. "We're not going to get anything in this direction."

Pyke nodded, turned to Accorso. "I see. Maybe we can hunt down another lead. Recall our men from Con Ed if they're there already and let Schrank know that we're pulling our teams out. If he still wants his people to go through the records, he can."

"Yes, sir." Accorso slid his chair back and walked off, heading to the locker rooms to look for the other detectives helping them with the Con Ed job.

Pyke left to his office without another word.

Ateer stood there for a moment, staring at Pedrotti's desk behind Accorso's. He sat with his back to Ateer, reading a newspaper. Is if by some intuition he folded up the paper, laid it on his desk, and swiveled his chair around. His handsome face broke into a crooked smile that could be taken the wrong way, Ateer was certain, as if there was something malicious behind the fleer.

"Mac," he said, acknowledging his stare.

"How are you doing?"

Pedrotti barked a laugh like a cough. "So, you're not going to your little hell hole today?"

Ateer took up his hat and coat and hung them up on the standing coat rack, "I guess not. Common sense prevailed."

"Well, since you guys aren't going to Con Ed today, let's go out and hit a bar."

"You do that?"

"We can do whatever we want until we get a bomb call."

"What about Pyke?"

"What about him?" Pedrotti stood and went to his coat rack. "Hey, I'm heading out for a smoke. If you and Fab would like to come along, be downstairs in no more than ten."

Snatching his coat and hat, he left the bullpen.

Ateer sat down. In time, Accorso returned and sat in his chair across from him, going through his desk drawers. Ateer glanced at Pyke's office, looking for him to be standing there, but when he wasn't. He leaned over the desk towards Accorso.

"Fab, Beat it said he's going to the bar and wanted to know if we wanted to go."

Accorso sat up, looked over his shoulder behind himself to see that Pedrotti's desk was empty, his faithful newspaper on his desk.

"That bastard went without us?" Accorso said, turning back around.

"No, he's downstairs waiting."

"Well, let's get out of here before Pyke comes with something shittier to do." Accorso got up and walked two desks over to Charles Beakey's desk. Beakey, laboring over paperwork, sensed Accorso's approach and looked up. Beakey wore wire-rimmed, circular glasses before his oval face. His hair was well oiled, parted directly down the middle of his head and slicked down both sides. It looked perfect as if he spent hours before a mirror.

"Beakey, do us a favor. Could..."

Beakey interrupted him. "Could I come and get you from Harbor-view Docks if we get a call."

"No, no, no, Beakey, you owe me an entire trick. Take as many calls as you can before coming to get us."

"Are you kidding me, Fab? You'll only get about two hours when the calls come rolling in."

"So? Come get us when you've had enough."

Beakey returned to his paperwork, "I've had enough of you already, Fab," he groaned.

"Good, good. I'll see you later," Accorso skipped away to the coat rack and snatched his heavy clothing, "Mac, let's go!"

They went to the Harbor-view Docks, a dark bar around the corner from the precinct. The three detectives sat over drinks and two ashtrays, waiting to be filled with cigarette butts. Ateer looked around at the narrow establishment. Inside, all the customers were men, some in their blue NYPD uniforms, some in suits—the place noisy with conversation.

"So how does this work?" Ateer asked.

Accorso pulled a Benzedrine inhaler from his jacket pocket, stuck it up into his right nostril and inhaled deeply, "Well, you know that the Bomb Squad has two shifts, right?"

Ateer nodded, watching as Accorso's eyes jiggled in his skull "Day one."

"Well, the day *trick* has all the fun. We get to pick up the suspicious package calls. A lot of people see bombs in many things. A box, a can, a crate a jar, a pipe...bombs fucking everywhere. But they're most likely harmless because either they are hoaxes or the shit in people's imagination."

"Okay."

"Then there's the night *trick* which is just the everyday disabling of war souvenirs."

"War souvenirs?"

"Yeah, you know, some soldiers after World War I wanted things to remember the war by, so they brought home trinkets. You know, European pistols, uniforms, hats…"

"That's a problem?"

"Shit no. It's the jingle-brained G.I. Joe who brings an artillery shell home to keep on his mantel piece or send to his nephew in Sheboygan. Some people think that they're inert. I mean, what dumb son-of-a-bitch would send live ammo to their grandmother, right? For some reason some come to the realization that these things are dangerous, and they call us to haul that shit down to firing ranges or dump sites in Big Bertha and later, at night while people are trying to get a good night's rest, we blow them up."

"You kidding," Ateer smiled.

"He's serious," Pedrotti said, crushing his cigarette out in an ashtray. "When these fucking rubes realize that these souvenirs are dangerous, they shit themselves and jump to their phones. Ring-a-ding-ding."

Accorso laughed. "Beakey just got moved over to head Unit 2, which is good for him because he's a go-getter. He wants Pyke's job; he can taste it. So, I throw him a bone everyone once in a while. The first trick gets the bulk of these calls, so he gets to run around and look good in front of Pyke. It's probably this lion's share mentality that he believes got him this move, and a promotion shortly afterward if Peter doesn't take it."

"Peter doesn't want that shit. He wants to transfer over to the Technical Research Lab to be around bomb disassembly and study. He's never going to reach out for sergeant."

"Whose Peter?" Ateer looked back and forth at both men.

"Oh, that's right." Accorso said. "You haven't met him yet. Detective First Grade Peter Hayias, Pyke's shadow. The Greek, buggering bastard should be sergeant by now. Shit, Sergeant McGuinness cracked his skull open over two years ago, and his position hasn't been filled since because Peter doesn't want the responsibility."

"Why not?"

"Because he has it good. If Pyke is the king, Hayias is his crown prince. Life is good for him. He gets to do what he wants and gets away with it." Accorso sounded almost bitter in his explanation of Hayias.

"What are you talking about, Fab. Look at us," Pedrotti said.

Ateer turned to Accorso. "Look at you, how?"

Pedrotti's reply pulled Ateer's attention back to him. "Fucking Fab does what the fuck he pleases, like taking a day off with his unit and sit in a bar all day. Beakey may be ambitious, but he knows, even if he is overwhelmed because we are taking a day off, it's useless going to Pyke because he'll do nothing. If Hayias is the crowned prince, Fab is his golden-boy."

Ateer regarded Accorso. "Is this so?"

"I don't know why you keep looking at him, Mac," Pedrotti continued. "He'll never admit it. But get this, Beakey's picking up the slack isn't because of some day and night trick deal. Beakey fucked up zeppelin big on an important report to Deputy Chief Inspector Durtayne. Shit went all sideways. The heat came down on Pyke and Pyke went to Beakey, handing him his ass. Fab jumped up and told Pyke that *he* fucked it up by giving Beakey the wrong information. He didn't have shit to do with it, but as soon as Pyke heard that Fab was behind it, he went into his office and that was the end of that."

"So, Beakey feels indebted to me," Accorso said.

"So, when you want to take a break, Beakey covers for you?" Ateer said.

"That's right."

Ateer thought about the Bomb Squad dynamic. Was this what Valentine wanted him to report on? "So, what do you have on Pyke, Fab?" Ateer came right out and asked.

"Absolutely nothing. I just did my job and he moved me to

Detective First Grade. The truth of the matter is that everyone faces the Beast in his own way. Some love it, some are terrified of it and drop out. That's why this position is completely volunteer. When your nerve breaks, you're better off leaving than screwing up and killing people."

"And Fab loves the Beast," Pedrotti cheered. "Pyke sees that in him, and so he draws him close."

"That's about it, Mac," Accorso said. "And that's what we're gonna learn about you, how you face *her*."

"Her?"

"The Beast."

"And that is?"

Accorso smiled, shook another cigarette from his pack and lit it. Seeing that he was not about to be answered, Ateer turned to Pedrotti, "What is the Beast, Beat It?"

"You'll find out soon enough." The uneven grin, humor, and ugliness blended effortlessly.

They fell silent. Ateer thought about the quick lesson that he learned today and was writing it indelibly in his memory to repeat it chapter and verse.

"Have you guys been donating to the metal drive?" Pedrotti said, dismissing the uncomfortable silence. "I gave my extra pots and pans, a metal toolbox that was pretty good, and a bunch of tin spoons and forks.

"My wife is handling all that shit, brother," Accorso said, raising his hand for the waitress. "I start throwing out things from the kitchen and she'll give birth. I gave a lawn mower a rake and shovel that I could spare."

Aluminum was needed for the war effort to build more battleships and bombers a year after congress had budgeted their construction. Metal companies did not have the reserve to ramp up demand, so a call went throughout the country for anything metal that Americans could spare. People went through their homes, attics, garages for any metal object that they could do without for the war effort.

New York, not to be overlooked, entered the drive when the showgirls from the Broadway musical 'Hellzapoppin' went to the famed Algonquin Hotel and collected all their discarded cooking pots from their kitchen. Then using a firetruck, they banged away on their improvised drums and cymbals, riding to the Hotel Astor, raiding their kitchens. In no time, with all the New York housewives, restaurants, and hotels following suit, Times Square and City Hall were greeted with mountains of tin, metal, and aluminum.

Ateer was ashamed to admit that he did nothing. His silence revealed his guilt.

The arriving waitress ended another uncomfortable pause, taking their orders.

Ateer asked, "I got a question. With Italy on the wrong side of the war, what are you going to do if you are called in by the lottery? Are you going to fight against your fellow Pisans?"

They think about the question. "Yeah, why not?" Accorso said.

Pedrotti hunched his shoulders. "I don't really give a fuck. If anyone points a gun at me, they're gonna get shot. Pisan or no Pisan."

"Yeah," Accorso nodded. "I don't care. Fuck it. The lottery is churning up men, and we're not excluded so you can expect us Italians to be called into this mess if there's a war."

"I think the mayor will get in the way of that shit," Pedrotti said. "Pyke is not going to have his squad staffed by a bunch of old men trying to diffuse bombs."

"You haven't really been defusing bombs lately to be honest with you," Ateer said. Both men turned to him, stunned.

Pedrotti said, "If there's a war, there'll be tons of bombs to deal with. And if there is just *one*, ol' 'Little Flower' will be shitting in his pants that he let us all go off to Europe to fight the Nazis."

Accorso laughed. "Then it'll be too fucking late."

"That's right." Pedrotti shook a finger at Ateer. "You tend to forget that LaGuardia is an Italian American too."

"What are you going to do if they call you to the war?" Accorso asked Ateer.

"I'll fight."

Pedrotti laughed. "But at least you don't have to worry about shooting your fellow Micks out there. I don't think you guys even have a fucking submarine." He turned to Accorso. "Do they have a fucking submarine?"

"I don't think they have a rifle among them." Accorso chuckled.

"That's very funny," Ateer replied bitterly.

The waitress returned with their drinks, and they began to imbibe.

"Let me get some of that." Pedrotti held out his hand for Accorso's inhaler.

He passed it on to him and for him to inhale its end deeply.

"Let me ask you another question, Fab," Ateer asked.

"What's that?"

"How did Giovanni get the nick name, 'Beat It'?"

"Oh, we don't have to go through this now, do we?" Pedrotti said, pointing to Accorso who was already laughing aloud.

"It's a fucking good story," Accorso said.

"It's a stupid story. I hate it when people tell it."

Accorso lit another cigarette, took a heavy draw and a puff before starting, "When Giovanni's balls dropped in the Bomb Squad, we were called out to check a device that may or may not have been a 'Devil Toy'."

"What's a 'Devil Toy' again?" Ateer frowned.

"A bomb you dumb Irish fuck," Pedrotti snorted.

"Yeah, okay." Accorso waved Pedrotti silent. "So, we get called in to check out this bomb, right? When we get there, in this building, there is a pipe bomb on a desk, or it looks like one. You know, a little shorter than a forearm, capped on both ends. We went up and got a good look at it and while we were giving it a good look, genius here bumps into the desk and it comes rolling to the edge at us and drops right to the floor at my feet. It moved, like in slow motion, and all I could do was stare at it. I'll be honest with you; I was scared shit-less.

Meanwhile Beat It shot off like a bullet to the barrier that held back the bystanders. He must have been a couple of yards before the fucking pipe hit the floor." Accorso paused for a moment to start laughing again, reeling back in his chair.

"Yeah, yeah, yeah, funny story." Pedrotti scowled.

Accorso patted Ateer heavily on the shoulder, attempting to share his glee. "Obviously the pipe bomb was a dud. Later, under examination it didn't even have all the component parts to explode. Some moron probably built it as part of his learning curve. But ever since then everyone in the Squad called this guy, 'Beat It'."

Ateer started to chuckle. Pedrotti pointed to him as a warning. "Wait until you have your first time up at bat. You won't find shit like that funny. I'll tell you now, Fabulous here has a death wish."

"Shut up, Beat It," Accorso said, putting unnecessary emphasis on the nickname. "You have the same wish as I do, and that's to defuse the motherfucker before people get hurt. Who wishes to die?"

"But it takes time to get there." Pedrotti turned to Ateer to explain himself. "For the first couple of times, all you can think about is yourself, Mac. Every nerve in your body doesn't even want to go near the fucking thing. But when you accept that it's part of your job, and you have it to do, then you start to think about the people that can get hurt or killed if the beast gets out."

"Yeah, the job is to get it where it can come out and not hurt anyone," Accorso added. "That's the job."

Pedrotti said, "It takes a measure of a fatalistic attitude. Like a soldier running into a hail of bullets to take a position. You can't think about yourself, only the job at hand."

Accorso pointed to Ateer sternly. "Listen. If you're close enough when one of these things blow, nine times out of ten, you won't know anything at all. You'll just cease to exist. If you aren't far enough, you'll get wounded badly. Maybe even lose a limb or two if you're lucky. And even if you're further back than that, you'll probably suffer hearing loss, vertigo, bleeding from the ears and mouth, gastrointestinal damage, blast lung, and a dozen other physical traumas. Now, let me ask you, if you had a choice, would you want to be up there where the action is, or cowering behind and maimed for the rest of your life?"

"That's kind of a crazy assed question," Ateer said. "Is this some kind of guinea logic?"

"It sounds crazy now because you are thinking like a civilian. But just wait until you're face to face with one of these fucking things. Your entire thinking process changes," Accorso assured.

Pedrotti, once again with his odd smile. "Wait until your asshole puckers up to where it makes a whistling noise from all the suction fear is applying to it, and your legs tremble and your knees knock while you're standing face to face with a pipe-bomb and I guarantee you, everything you see and experience, from the taste of food, to fucking a woman, will be completely different than what you remembered. You'll experience life a whole lot differently than you are now. Trust me, Mac. You're still not one of us. Whenever you lose your cherry, we'll have this conversation again."

"Beat It," Accorso said, "do you have a joint on you?"

"No. I'm out. I haven't seen Vaughn in a while."

"Last time I did, I only took one."

Ateer waved down the waitress and ordered another round for the table. The conversation had gone off the rails for a moment, each lost in thought.

"Do you think that Pyke is up to the job?" Ateer asked bluntly.

"What?" Pedrotti asked, shocked.

"What do you mean?" Accorso followed.

"I mean, what kind of boss is Lieutenant Pyke?"

"You know what he's like," Pedrotti said. "If you ever saw this guy at work, you'd swear the motherfucker walks on water. The man has absolutely no fear of a bomb. It's as if God Almighty himself had promised him that he'll never get killed by the beast."

"The man is the closest thing that you're going to get to a fucking legend," Accorso added.

"And if shit goes ass up, he'll back you to the end."

Accorso chuckled. "The good thing about that is that if shit goes ass up, there's usually no one left to blame things on to bring before your superiors without a ladle."

"That's right." Pedrotti slammed his hand down on the tabletop, causing the glasses, ashtray, and candle to dance about. "Pyke knows what he's doing. That guy, with LaGuardia, made 'Big Bertha', scribbling her out on a piece of paper."

"Big Bertha?" Ateer raised an eyebrow.

"The bomb carrier. It's called the LaGuardia-*Pyke* Carrier."

"Oh, really?"

"He knows a helluva lot about bombs and how they work, how they think. He and Hayias can sit down and talk all day about bombs. That's what they like to do." Pedrotti lit another cigarette, pointed it at Ateer. "Just stay out of that cocksucker's way. If he even smells fear in you, he'll chew you up and spit your ass out."

"In what way?"

"What, do you think being chewed up and spat out is a good thing?"

Accorso reached into this jacket and pulled out his wallet, throwing change on the tabletop. "Look, we need to head back to put in some time in the bullpen before disappearing for the rest of the day."

"To do what?" Pedrotti asked. "Go wild whore hunting?"

"That's *your* occupation," Accorso replied.

Pedrotti turned to Ateer, smiling and nodding. "He's going to fuck a whore somewhere before going home, I betcha."

"Why do you say things like that to the kid, Beat It? He'll start to believe you."

"He should. You are."

Accorso waved in dismissal at Pedrotti angrily, rose and went to the coat rack for his coat and hat and was gone.

Ateer watched him leave.

"You're joking, right?" Ateer asked Pedrotti who finished his drink and raised his hand for the waitress.

"No."

"But he's married."

"So?"

When the waitress arrived Pedrotti asked for another round. When she was out of earshot, he turned to Ateer, "Listen, you virgin. Nothing drives home the fact that life is too fucking short than standing in front of an active engine of destruction. Simple as that. It's both life affirming and life changing. Trust me. You'll be made new in the man that you are once we break your ass in."

"So, you're not faithful husbands?"

"We're not even good employees," Pedrotti laughed heartily. "All we do is make explosives safe. First, last, always. That we do so well that the higher ups don't really give a fuck what else we are or do as long as they can count on us to do that."

When the waitress brought their drinks, Pedrotti knocked his back in one shot, threw money on the table and stood. "I'm gonna go out and find some loco weed. You wanna come?"

"No thanks. I'm going to think about what you said about my thinking." Ateer grinned.

Pedrotti walked over to the coat rack but pointed at Ateer all the way. "Don't be a smart-ass. I'm the only smart-ass in this squad. Just mark my words. You've got a long road before you're Bomb Squad, that's if you live long enough, to even think like us. So, try not to be a hard-headed Irish donkey and learn something before it passes you by."

"I will. Thanks."

With a flourish of his overcoat, Pedrotti was gone.

Once he found himself alone, for some unexplainable reason, Ateer felt the cold clutch of fear around his heart. What were they talking about, 'changing him'? He was already being changed being with them for Valentine's sake. Even the thought of banging off work to sit in a bar and drink before your 'trick' was inconceivable to him.

Maybe it was how they functioned? How they got through the day walking headlong into death. Ateer's heart sped up several beats simply thinking about what the two detectives were trying to impart to him.

For the first time, he thought seriously about failing at this assignment.

FOUR
DYING IN THE MORNING

"Let us not pray to be sheltered from dangers but to be fearless when facing them."

RABINDRANATH TAGORE

For some reason it was a slow day. Every time the phone rang, Accorso passed the job down the line to the other two units. Beakey was all too grateful to work off his debt to Accorso, however the newly transferred Detective First Grade Brock Dempsey chaffed at being passed over for the job. Dempsey was tall, broad, and underneath his shirt his barrel-like chest and brawny arms struggled against the fabric. He was a mature man, his face beginning to change from youthful to distinguished, clean shaven and immaculately groomed. He took up a position next to Accorso's desk, towering over him, listening to the particulars of the job at hand.

SUSPICIOUS LOOKING PACKAGES

When Accorso finished outlining the job and expecting Dempsey to move on, he didn't.

"What's the problem?" Accorso asked him tiredly.

"You've been passing jobs all day. When are you going to do a pickup?"

Accorso pushed his chair away from him, banging the side of it against the balustrade of the corral. "Are you questioning an order, detective?"

"No, I'm about to do the job. I was just asking you if you're ever going to do a pickup today," Dempsey pressed, undaunted.

"Look," Accorso stopped to remember his first name which was not coming to him. And then it did, Brock. "Look Pebbles, you have been unit commander for less than a week, and you need the experience you're getting today. Trust me, just because you've been here as a detective second grade for a couple of years, you don't know shit from Shinola when it comes to leading a team. I'm giving you the obvious hoaxes, because you haven't even been trained on how to wipe your ass in the precinct men's room when it comes to making the Bomb Squad look good. You must deal with frightened men who are looking to you for strength when one of these damn things rears their ugly heads. So, take this job, the next job and the next until I think you are seasoned enough to *be* a detective first grade. Can you follow me?"

Dempsey opened his mouth to reply but Accorso held up a finger to shut him up. "I don't care if you can follow me or not. Shove in your clutch and get the fuck outta here. And don't kill yourself, your team, or innocent bystanders or I'll beat the shit out of your remains."

Dempsey nodded, turned on his heels and scurried off, which appeared strange for a man as big and imposing as he was.

Ateer leaned forward over his desk, whispering, "Why aren't we 'picking up' any calls?"

Accorso slid his chair back under his desk and whispered back, "Because exactly what I said to Dempsey. I told you about Beakey. Not only is he working off his debt, Dempsy also loves to churn jobs out because he's bucking for the sergeant's position. Besides, we busted our asses for two days straight over Con Ed's paperwork. Don't think that these motherfuckers weren't laughing at us dealing with all that shit."

Ateer nodded. Sitting back, he said at a normal volume, "So when am I gonna get training?"

"Hey, what are you in a rush for? You've got a train to catch?"

He had no reply.

"Just cool your heels and wait until your time comes. It will. Trust me, it will." Accorso kicked at the floor, sending his chair rolling back to bump against the back of Pedrotti's chair. Accorso reached over his shoulder. "Can I see today's paper, Beat It?"

Picking up the paper—folded neatly at the corner of his desk—Pedrotti handed it over his shoulder to Accorso who rolled his chair back under his desk.

"So, what am I supposed to do?" Ateer asked.

Accorso hunched his shoulders. "Do you have any reports to file?"

"I just got here."

"Then beat your meat, go and sort out your locker, run laps around the block. I don't give a fuck."

Nodding resolutely at his dismissal, Ateer stood and went to the break room, pouring himself a cup of coffee.

"So, you're the new one in our unit?"

Ateer stopped the edge of his cup before it met his lips and turned around. Behind him, entering the room was a nebbish looking man with an infectious smile. He seemed sincerely happy to be alive, or else it was over something else in his life. He exuded perkiness. He was clean shaven with a dark, rich pompadour on his head. He rubbed his hand on the side of his pants leg before extending it to Ateer.

"Basilio Frascone, everyone around her calls me 'Big O.' I'm your support for unit one." Frascone said.

Ateer, after a pause, shook his hand, wondering what he was

wiping off it. Frascone, noticing that he was thinking about it, smiled and gave a carefree chuckle taking his hand back, "I'm sorry. My hands, they sweat a lot."

With a level of relief, Ateer smiled back. "No problem."

"So, what do you think?" Frascone asked.

"About what? The coffee?"

"No, the Bomb Squad."

"I haven't had the opportunity to do anything yet, so I really don't know."

"You'll like it here. I do," he touched a hand to his chest, "although I don't make bombs safe."

"So, what do you do?"

"Everything else." Frascone smiled and nodded, then for a brief and fleeting moment, Ateer saw pain in his eyes, but just as quickly as it arrived, it left.

"Well, you sound very important."

"I am, but these guys wouldn't admit it. So? Where are you from?"

"New York. I was born and raised in Manhattan. I live out in Brooklyn now."

"Brooklyn is very nice. They have the Navy Yard out there."

"Big O, do you mind if I asked you what you think about the Bomb Squad?"

"The number one exciting fucking job on Earth!" He broke out in a wide smile, standing up on his toes for a second in exclamation.

Smiling, even though he couldn't help it, Ateer said, "So you like it here. Is it usually as slow as this today?"

"Oh no, we get dozens of calls, but sometimes Accorso doesn't feel up to it and passes them on for an hour or two."

Ateer glanced at his watch. "It's been more than two hours."

"It's not an exact science."

Ateer nodded. "Well, hope to see more of you, Big O."

"Hey!" He was suddenly hit with an idea which caused his entire face to glow. "Do you want to go out to dinner tonight?"

There was something in Frascone's eagerness that warned him of impending doom. "Oh, I'm so sorry...Big O. I've got plans."

"Oh, okay. Maybe some other time."

"Yeah, some other time. Take care." Ateer steered around him and headed back for his desk. In departing from the break room he glanced over his shoulder, for no reason, although he had to admit to himself that he had done so to make certain that he wasn't being followed back to his desk. Frascone just stood in the doorway of the break room. When their eyes met briefly, he waved goodbye.

Ateer sat in his chair, somewhat uncomfortable and rested his coffee down. After a moment he leaned forward and whispered to Accorso who was behind his newspaper, "Tell me about Big O."

Accorso closed the paper, folded it in half, then in quarters, and put it to the side. He leaned forward urgently and hissed under his breath, "Leave him alone, he's one goofy motherfucker, *and* he's bad luck."

"Really?"

Accorso nodded, eyes wide. "People get blown up fucking with him. And if they don't, they'll have to deal with his crazy ass."

"What do you mean by bad luck? Did he ever get someone killed?"

Accorso thought about it, he looked to the side, regarding nothing, the tiny wheels spinning in his brain not engaging. "Not that I can think of, but Pyke thinks so. He says he drags along bad luck like a snake's tail. But don't say that to his face."

"Who's? Pyke's?"

"No, you fucking stupid leprechaun!" He grumbled under his breath, "Big O, goddammit."

Ateer understood, he nodded.

"When Pyke put him with our unit, we took him out for dinner. You know, nothing fancy. And through the entire dinner all he does is sit there, with this stupid fucking grin on his dumb wop face not saying a motherfucking word. Can you believe that? He sat there like some panting dog, tail wagging, looking from face to face, excited as hell. Beat It wondered if he was pulling on his cock all the while under the table."

"No kidding."

Accorso shook his head. "All of his chairs aren't pushed under the table, if you know what I mean?"

"I getcha."

"He's a coupla sandwiches short of a picnic."

Ateer nodded.

"His elevator doesn't go all the way to the top."

Ateer sat back, grinning. He could tell that Accorso was having fun with him suddenly. Was this what it would be like working with Accorso, Pedrotti, and Frascone, easy humor? Was this easy humor a mechanical response to facing horror daily? Was it a coping mechanism?

"Stay the hell away from him."

"I will, I will, but why did Pyke assign him to your unit if he's so unlucky?"

"He can't fire the crazy son-of-a-bitch, so he does the next, best thing. Put him on his strongest, most trusted unit—Unit One."

"And Pyke trusts you enough that if something was to go tits up, you'd be able to handle it."

"With the least loss of life. Think about our brothers at the World's Fair earlier this year. They gave their lives for scores or maybe even hundreds of others. You have to trust your men to do that, to put everything—and I do mean every fucking thing—on the line to save others. Can you do that?"

"I think I can."

Soft and slow, Accorso said, "Boom."

Ateer stared at him, dumbfounded.

"You're already dead," Accorso continued. "That's all the time you'll ever have, an instant. You hesitate, you and others die. You better *know* you can, or you're not gonna last long in this squad." Accorso sat back, not taking his eyes off Ateer, reached to the side to snatch up his paper and unfurled it before his face, blocking their view of each other.

Ateer sat back. Thought about going to talk to someone else in the bullpen other than Frascone but found it vacant except for Unit One.

The phone rang.

Accorso reached for it, but it stopped almost as quickly as it began. He went back to his paper. Ateer sat there, waiting, then, realizing that he had a paper before him, focused on the articles from the distance across the desks. He squinted. The U.S. was expanding its aid to Britain as it struggled against German aggression. The Germans were applying pressure to the island in the North by destroying supply vessels bound for its shores. Roosevelt was pushing for a record busting budget increase for defense spending.

"Accorso!"

Accorso, Pedrotti, and Ateer turned to the threshold to Lieutenant Pyke's office. "I have a call for your team. Walk like angels, understood?"

Accorso threw the paper down on his desk and stood up. "Understood."

Pyke walked up and handed him a sheet of paper over the railing, then returned to his office.

Accorso read it quickly. "Alright Unit One," he said aloud. "Let's go."

Accorso was behind the wheel of the squad car. Pedrotti in the Passenger seat, Ateer in the back. Behind their Plymouth was Frascone in the department support van, the trusty Ford E83W, a narrow turtle-looking vehicle with headlights on the fenders, like a pair of frog's eyes. Accorso hated the rusty smelling vehicle. Everything seemed to be thrown into the back, but Frascone had a way of reaching in at a moment's cause and coming out with exactly what was needed.

SUSPICIOUS LOOKING PACKAGES

They worked their way down Seventh Avenue traffic which started to build at 35th street due to patrolmen on foot waving and halting traffic at the intersections to Pennsylvania Station which was normal since the terminal was a major pivot point for travelers arriving, passing through, or leaving the city.

The second reason why it was normal was the sheer size of the terminal. Pennsylvania Station was modeled after the Gare d'Orsay in Paris, and yet dwarfed such an enormous building, twice over. The station, which was constructed over 500 demolished brownstones of the Tenderloin District, was set back from the avenue by a promenade at its front, so the massive facade of the station could not be seen from around the row of brownstones lining the avenue.

Pedrotti, like some excited dog in the passenger seat, stuck his head out the window, staring at the brilliance of the marble bathed in the light of the dying sun.

Accorso slowed down and turned into the carriage way, passing between two of the four pillars in front of its entrance which was fashioned after the Brandenburg Gate in Germany, another massive construction that Pennsylvania Station also dwarfed. The carriageway dropped via a ramp, entering the building. Massive rectangular apertures on the right let in the fading light upon the partially dim driveway where police squad cars with their overhead lights flickering, two ambulances and dozens of patrolmen with hand-held flashlights gathered. The vehicle group only creating the smallest of space between the parked vehicles for others to pass through. A uniformed patrolman walked up in front of the Plymouth, hand out for it to stop. Accorso rolled down his window and stuck his head out. "Detective First Grade Accorso, bomb squad and support."

The officer nodded, stepped out of the way of the car, and waved him on, pointing to a clique of vehicles under an overhead bridge allowing commuters access to the terminal from street level above them. On this bridge, underneath the vaulting roof of the causeway were spectators, stopping to look over its edge, curious as the large gathering of police.

Accorso pulled over onto the sidewalk of the roadway, not far from a group of men gathered at the clique of vehicles. As the four men approached, they caught the attention of the men, several in suits and ties, others in the uniforms of officers and medics. It was suddenly evident why the coterie had collected in that spot, the entrance into the terminal was nearby.

"Detective Edward Miller, West 30th street station," a dark suited gentleman broke from the group and approached Accorso with his hand extended.

Accorso shook it, introduced himself and Pedrotti. Ateer was standing behind them, partially out of sight.

"So, what's going on?" Accorso looked about. The flashing lights, vehicle headlights on, the entire underground area looked hectic and confused. No wonder spectators were gathering by the score on the span of the bridge above.

"We've got a bomb in the station."

"What kind of bomb?"

Detective Miller, dark haired, square chinned, and clean shaven, turned to call a group of uniformed officers over who were crowding around a security guard. "Bring him over here!" He waved at them.

With the security guard leading the way, the cluster of men entered earshot.

"Tell him what you got," Miller instructed the guard.

The portly guard first pulled up on his mostly empty belt and attempted to stick his chest out over his stomach. "I was in the Long Island Railroad waiting room of the station when I found this old-fashioned suitcase, tied together with a rope under a bench. I looked around for someone who looked like they belonged to it but couldn't find anyone nearby. I went to take it to the lost and found, but since it didn't have an owner, someone must have left it there, maybe intentionally, right?"

"Why do you think it's a bomb?" Pedrotti asked.

"It's ticking."

"Take me to it."

Immediately, the security guard moved more briskly than he appeared to be capable and led them through the massively glass arched 31st street entrance to the wide, stairs down into the Main Waiting Room area. This was the second time Ateer had ever been in the godlike structure. The first time he had entered the gigantic building he was only a strapping fifteen-year-old who Mr. Lewis brought with him to aid in carrying the luggage of one of his friends and his wife. Ateer was strong enough to carry two bags but walked like a penguin as he did. Although the bags were heavy, Ateer could not feel strain from them, for his eyes were locked on the enormousness of his surroundings. Then, like now, as the urgency of the situation blossomed, with a wave of detectives, and police officers led by a single security guard poured down the wide marble stairs, Ateer was blinded by the sheer size of the building around him. Literally breathtaking, the vaulted ceiling, decorated with indented pentagons carved into the marble gave it a honeycombed look from arch to arch, upheld by immense and mighty columns heaving the roof into the heavens. Ateer swallowed hard as he stared up, only using the footfalls of the men around him as a guide to his path behind the guard.

The guard ran through the waiting room, one hand on his cap, the other on his baton attached to his belt, with the surge of police trotting behind him. Commuters and travelers, burdened down with their luggage and bags, leapt or ran from their path, but only going far enough out of the way to avoid being an obstacle, but close enough to become spectators.

The guard veered off to the right in the impressive chamber, heading towards a great windowed archway towering high overhead, letting in a powerful orange light even now as the sun was setting. At the base of the window arch were glass doors. Patrons, seeing the rush of police officers, appearing to be in pursuit of a single security guard, scrammed from their path as if offering them the doors into the Grand Concourse of the station.

And grand it was. As they rushed through the glass doors they entered another expansive space. Not as high as the waiting room behind them, but fantastic because of its intricate latticework of metal support beams, rising and breaking apart like metal palm fronds. For a moment, everyone save the security guard slowed and trotted into this space, the rooftop nothing but glass windows in arch after arch, beam after beam, strut after strut, making the ceiling appear as a greenhouse roof high overhead. Pigeons leapt from perch to perch, their wings flapping and somehow echoing over the loudspeakers announcing arriving and departing trains.

This space rushed in on Ateer, bringing back his childhood memories of Pennsylvania Station, both a nightmare and a dream. His eyes never left any of the two ceilings, grinding to a halt at the entranceway. So did the officers and detectives because before them was an impossible press of humanity. Hundreds upon hundreds of commuters boiling in a million directions. A dark ocean of bodies into which the security guard dove in, wading on.

After their stunned response to the area, the police and detectives gathered their wits and moved on, taking on a V shape behind the guard, moving people out of the way as they swept through the concourse level nearly two city blocks square, only dwarfed by the godlike waiting room two blocks long behind them.

It took time to slice through the stubborn mass of men, women and children from all walks of life, all nationalities and ethnic makeups.

Tall gates and fences held back the populace from the long floating stairs descending to the track level.

Two uniformed security guards stood flanking one of the gates, and upon seeing their comrade being followed by the police, pulled the gate aside allowing them access to the brass railing, descending staircase that seemed to 'float' above the tracks below. After taking several landings down of the black painted stairs they reached the train platform, which was above the track beds on both sides. Several platforms going in both directions.

Half of the length of the platform was lit by the vaulting class ceiling far above, and the portion of the track that went under the concourse above was lit by the glass bricks of its floor letting the natural light coming in from the ceiling through the floor to the tracks below.

Ateer was dizzy with adrenalin both from the seriousness of the task ahead, the mind-boggling size of Pennsylvania Station, and the unimaginable number of people on the Concourse level above. An explosion anywhere here would mean an unbelievable and tragic loss of life and property.

Almost as if they struck a sheet of glass, the detectives and the police officers halted the second their feet left the last step. At first Ateer wasn't even aware that they had faded away, so overwhelmed by a mass of emotions. The world rushed upon him as soon as, up ahead, Accorso grabbed the security guard by the shoulder, bringing him to a stop.

"Hold on." Accorso said.

The guard turned around facing him, "What's wrong?"

"Where's the bomb."

Up ahead were a series of empty seats, back-to-back in a line down the center of the platform for waiting passengers.

"Where is everybody?" Pedrotti asked, looking around at the vacant platform from end to end. On the two immediate platforms on both sides of them were scores of commuters standing on their edges, watching as if a play, the men of the bomb squad between them across the tracks. Pedrotti looked at them, shaking his head, then turning to Accorso.

"Fab, the people are in the blast zone," he said.

Accorso looked around then went back to the security guard. "Look, all of these people are in mortal danger. Go back to the police and tell them to clear those platforms now. We can't do anything until they're gone."

The security guard, his round face and doubled chin glistening with nervous sweat, nodded in mute terror and rushed off back the way they had come.

"How about this guy?" Pedrotti asked, hooking his thumb at Ateer.

Accorso looked Ateer up and down. He looked lost, pale, his eyes fogging over but incredibly he was still present in the moment.

"Mackie, you stay here. Come no closer, and if you see us running, you run faster than Beat It."

"Yes, sir," Ateer replied, nodding his head as if it was trembling.

"You too, Beat It," he said to him. "Only one detective at a bomb."

"Shit up a pole, Fab. I don't care about regulations. I'm going with you," Pedrotti stated.

They looked at each other.

"Besides," he continued, "it's not like we might survive whatever charge that's in there when it explodes." He turned to Ateer. "He's doing you no favors. If the beast gets out, you'll probably get maimed."

"Stop scaring the guy," Accorso grunted. He looked across the track as police officers started at the end of the platform ushering the commuters to the stairs leading back up to the Concourse.

Accorso nodded, turned to Ateer. "Mackie, look up."

"I've been looking up all night," he said.

"What do you see?"

"A huge motherfucking skylight."

"If that bomb detonates and it's large enough it's going to bring that glass roof down like rain, which'll shower everyone in this goddamn station like sharp, razors. So, if you want to survive this explosion—*if* it happens—leave the entire Concourse and track level," he turned to Pedrotti, "there. Are you happy?"

"The platforms are empty. Let's look at this bomb." Pedrotti marched down the track, leaving the two men alone.

"This is your chance rookie," Accorso said to Ateer and walked off.

Accorso casually followed Pedrotti to the long row of seats, and under it was the described battered suitcase wrapped with rope. Immediately he started calculating in his head how many sticks of dynamite it could hold. He didn't have to count any more after ten to know that the answer was too many.

Pedrotti dropped to his hands and knees and lowered his head to the case. "Fuck! I was hoping that that son-of-a-bitch was hallucinating, but this shit is ticking."

"That means there's a clock in it."

"Clock means timer."

"Timer means we gotta get this shit outta here."

"Let's get the fluoroscope." Pedrotti jumped to his feet and knocked the dust off the knees of his pants. They returned to Ateer."

"Mackie," Accorso said. "Go back to Big O and get the fluoroscope."

"Is it ticking?"

"Yeah."

"Do we have enough time?"

Accorso hunched his shoulders. Ateer looked at Pedrotti, "Don't ask me. I don't have a clue," he said.

"Get the equipment," Accorso ordered softly.

Ateer went to the ascending stairs, with Accorso and Pedrotti in tow. Seated on the steps were Detective Miller with two other detectives. Upon seeing them approach they stood up, beating the dust off the seats of their slacks. Ateer went through them and ran up the stairs. Accorso went to Miller, "if it's a bomb, we're gonna have to get it out of here. We need you to make a path...a very, very wide path straight back to our van. Do you have enough men?"

Miller smirked. "You give me enough time; I'll get an army in here."

"You do that."

Miller and his detectives were gone.

Ateer moved briskly through the terminal and to the van still parked in the causeway.

"Big O, they want the fluoroscope."

Frascone's eyes went wide, as if he had just pissed pants. "Is it a bomb?"

"Yeah, it's ticking."

"Holy shit!" Frascone ran to the back of the van, reached in with both hands and came away with the Model F "Suitcase Portable" X-ray unit from the General Electric Company and a stethoscope. He hung the stethoscope around Ateer's neck and handed him the case. "Good luck."

Ateer nodded and returned to Accorso and Pedrotti, handing them the equipment, with which they returned to the scuffed and marked case under the seats. Pedrotti showed Accorso the stethoscope as if he hadn't seen it earlier. "Why the fuck did that numbskull give Mac this? Did you say anything to Mac about a stethoscope."

"It's Big O, Beat It." Accorso sighed. "Let's get to this."

They opened the fluoroscope's case and set the stethoscope on a seat. Pedrotti took the small emitter where the x-ray generator was, and hand-held power control which had the power dials and went to one side of the seats, paying out cable behind it, Accorso took the fluorescent screen and laid on his stomach. Pedrotti, on the other side, did the same.

The fluorescent screen of treated cardboard was inside of the wide end of the hood, the narrow end fitted over the eyes, enshrouding them in darkness making the device look like a big, square set of binoculars. The wide end was pointed to the object in question.

When Accorso had the receiver end of the scope against his eyes, Pedrotti turned on the power to the emitter, starting at a low setting. He watched the tiny gages above the dials rise partially on its semicircular course, wavering on a lower indicator on its scale.

Staring at the fluorescent screen just inches from his eyes the X-ray radiation caused the screen to glow. A black and white image focused into view, becoming sharper and sharper, clearer and clearer until Accorso could see what was inside of the suitcase.

It had two compartments. One was three quarters of the case, which was just white against a black background, meaning that he couldn't discern what it was, and in the corner, in what looked like a compartment that he could see through, was the outline of what looked like an alarm clock.

"Bingo," Accorso said. "I don't know what else is in there, but there is definitely something that looks and sounds like an alarm clock."

They both knew that alarm clocks were sometimes used as timers for detonators in an explosive device. Everything now turned red for the two men. This suitcase was 'unsafe,' meaning loss of life and property would be in the balance if it went off. They quickly stood and repacked the fluoroscope in its case and Accorso snatched up the stethoscope and hung it around Pedrotti's neck.

"What did you roll today?" Accorso asked.

"An Easy Eight."

"That's good then because it's your turn to carry shit."

"Sure. You wanna get out of the building just in case it's motion sensitive?"

"Fuck no. I'm Bomb Squad, Beat It. You know better than that. Besides, if it goes off, and the hundreds of people over us are chopped into hamburger by falling glass, I don't think Pyke would want to see me walk into the bullpen without a scratch."

Pedrotti turned, bent to the platform, and carefully pulled out the suitcase. They walked to Ateer standing at the foot of the floating staircase. Accorso passed the Fluoroscope to Ateer upon facing him. "Here, you give this to Big O," he said.

The three of them walked into the expansive concourse, which appeared too difficult to completely empty. Miller had a wide avenue cut through the crowds by two score number of officers, while commuters and travelers, drawn to the odd commotion, pressed against the invisible walls of their directions like the waters of the Red Sea, struggling against Moses and the power of his God.

In moments, they were outside. The squad cars and ambulances were gone. The few police left stood watching from a considerable distance. Waiting for them outside, with the trunk of the Plymouth open and its engine running, was Frascone. He ran up to them, almost hopping up and down like a puppy with excitement upon seeing the unsafe suitcase.

"What do you got for us, Big O?" Accorso asked, opening the car door.

"Well, we can take it out to the ash heap in Brooklyn," he said.

"I don't think we have that kinda time."

All three men watched as Pedrotti put the suitcase in the trunk of the car, "Do your magic, Big O."

"I found a nearly vacant parking lot several blocks up on 33rd Street."

"You earned your pay this evening O," Accorso said, slipping behind the steering wheel and shutting the door. Pedrotti ran around to the other side of the vehicle. Ateer handed Frascone the equipment. Everyone entered their vehicles and took off, easing though two of the narrow four pillars on the 8th Avenue end of the station and turned onto 33rd street.

Pedrotti looked up at the pillars as they passed. "No, I don't think we could get Big Bertha between those."

"Yeah, they were made for horse drawn carriages, not trucks." Accorso stepped on the accelerator, weaving in and out through the night traffic and soon the vacant parking lot opened on the right. He drove into it and roughly at its center, as he had said, was where Frascone left the barrel of oil. Accorso pulled up next to it.

Accorso passed the keys to Pedrotti and climbed out of the car. Ateer climbed out behind him, looking at the red painted barrel with the words, "Danger Bomb Container" stenciled around it. Pedrotti opened the trunk, took out the suitcase paced to the barrel and gently dropped it into the viscous black fluid within. It bobbed for a moment or two before filling up and slipping under the surface. The three men stood over it for a moments, returned to the car, and drove out of the lot, parking behind Frascone's E83W.

They rolled down their windows and started smoking cigarettes. Frascone stayed in the van.

"How did you feel about your first call today, Mackie?" Accorso asked, turning his head slightly to be heard in the back seats.

"Frightening," Ateer pressed his fist against his chest. "My heart is still pounding."

"Good, sometimes you shit yourself," Accorso said.

Pedrotti burst out laughing, almost losing his cigarette.

"Don't drop that in the car you dumb wop, you'll burn the seat cushions." Pedrotti couldn't stifle his guffaw, although he tried. His struggle first made Ateer crack a smile that he struggled against.

"You laugh," Accorso said bitterly. "This is serious. My first time, I shit myself a little."

Like holding down whooping cough, Ateer sat on his laughter, slouching down in the back seats so as not to be seen in the rear-view mirror. Over time, the laughter subsided.

"Why do you think Pyke gave us this fucking case," Pedrotti asked Accorso.

"Hell if I know. Maybe because of Mackie?"

"You think? Or is it because you were slacking all day."

"I don't slack. I take strategic breaks."

"Do you know what I want to know?"

"No, I don't know what you want to know."

Pedrotti turned in his seat, directing his attention to Ateer. "What do you do to let off steam, Mac?"

"Me?" Ateer asked.

"No, the other guy back there."

Ateer smiled. "Listen to the radio. Read books. Go to the movies once in a while."

There was a pause. Accorso and Pedrotti waited for more. After the pause was long enough, Pedrotti asked, "That's it?"

"Why, what else do I need to do?"

"Mac, I'm beginning to think that you are some kinda retard or something," he smiled broadly.

Accorso looked at his watch. "Must be nearly a half an hour or something by now."

"Twenty minutes," Pedrotti said.

"Well, who gives a shit. Twenty minutes is long enough for that Devil Toy," he opened the door and left.

Pedrotti looked at Ateer."Showtime!"

The three men trudged back to the innocent looking barrel. As they drew closer Ateer's entire body seemed to sense the danger, his heart began to thud against his ribcage. A fluttering pigeon trying to break free.

"Stay here," Accorso said to him.

The two seasoned detectives continued on to the barrel. Pedrotti first put the earpieces of the stethoscope into his ears, grabbed the edge of the barrel with one hand, and used the chest-piece against the side of the barrel. He stayed there in the night, crouched.

"Well?" Accorso asked.

"The son-of-a-bitch is still ticking."

"No, please, no," he begged.

Standing, Pedrotti nodded his head. "Sorry to say."

They turned to the beeping of a car horn in the dark. Looking around, they could tell the familiar beep of the W83E. Frascone was beating on the horn.

"I wonder what the fuck that's about?" Accorso asked.

"From Big O, it could be anything," Pedrotti replied.

As they walked back to the vehicles, they could hear the sirens approaching from the distance, and a great light began to glow upon 33rd street. Police RMPs rolled up to the lot, taking positions, blocking off 33rd from traffic and surrounding the lot on the corner of the street on two sides. Detectives and officers burst from the vehicles and converged into a tight knot, receiving orders.

"Head to the car, Mac," Accorso said when they passed him in the lot. Ateer went on.

Accorso and Pedrotti approached the huddle, finding Detective Miller in the center of it.

"Goddamn boys!" He exclaimed. "It took us awhile to find you. You couldn't have talked to someone before you left?"

SUSPICIOUS LOOKING PACKAGES

"Detective Miller," Accorso replied. "We were carrying a suspicious package through the public. We're not gonna stop to hold your hand. We're gonna deal with this bomb and then we can chew the fat."

Miller turned his back to Accorso and started shouting orders to the men around them to remove pedestrians and onlookers to a safe distance, halt traffic and wait in their vehicles for further instructions. Turning back around, Miller asked, "Are my cordon of squad cars far enough?"

"I don't know."

"What do you mean you don't know?"

"I mean. *I don't know.*" He pointed to the red barrel off in the distance in the growing dark. "If there is explosive in that case it is still unknown. We can think of the worst case, which would be that it's filled to bursting with dynamite. If so, your squad cars will most likely go up in flames right where they are."

"Didn't you put your doohickey on it earlier in the station?"

"Yeah. It didn't look like explosives, but the clock looked like a clock."

"All this for an alarm clock?"

"Bomb makers normally use alarm clocks as timing mechanisms."

"Really?"

"Yes, really."

"They don't like being around when the thing goes boom," Pedrotti said with a smile.

"So, what now?" Miller asked.

"The bitch is still ticking. There's no need to have everyone out here waiting for the oil to gum up the works. Leave a small squad of your men to keep people away from the barrel, send the rest home."

"And what about you?"

"I'm going home too."

Miller blinked. "You're going home?"

"Oil is not one-hundred percent effective. All it really does is stop the clock mechanism, but if when opening it you touch two stripped wires to a battery it goes boom. I say go home. Let it soak overnight and tomorrow, early in the morning, we take a look at this thing and see if it's still ticking."

Miller churned the admonition over in his head before replying. "Alright. Sounds like a good idea. See you tomorrow morning."

"Tomorrow morning."

Miller returned to a patrol car, speaking to a uniformed officer standing nearby it. Accorso turned to Pedrotti, "Go tell Big O to go home. I'm going out tonight. You coming?"

"Are you kidding?" Pedrotti left for the van.

Accorso felt old and worn as he walked back to the patrol car, taking a glance to the barrel barely noticeable in the inky darkness of the lot. Already, around the lot, police were taking up positions, standing with backs straight, arms crossed over their chests.

Sliding into the vehicle, Accorso turned around to look at Ateer in the back seat. "We're going out tonight. Wanna come?"

Ateer thought about the offer.

To say that Ateer had a crisis of conscience was putting it mildly. It was as if the two halves of his being were going to war. One half was an obedient son, following the urgings of his mother to be temperate in habits, moderate in deeds. She admonished him to stay away from the filth of the city. His grandmother on his father's side was tempted by the lures of New York to make quick money. A lot of quick money which sucked her down into whoring and drinking as if it was as dangerous as quicksand. The truth of the matter was that he couldn't even call himself Ateer because his whoring grandmother's husband was long dead before she became pregnant. His father, Brendan, was not born from Rebecca's husband, Patrick Mac-Ateer but instead from one of hundreds of filthy men. Dylan and his sister Emma could call themselves whatever they wanted because they were not Mac-Ateers. Dylan's mother, Shannon, did not care, she was a McLoughlin and only took on the Ateer name because Brendan kept

SUSPICIOUS LOOKING PACKAGES

it. Later, after he vanished, she found it harder to lose the name than to keep it.

However, not to his biological father, Brendan Ateer, but to Commissioner Lewis Valentine, whom he respected, and could also go as far to say, admired. He was a lowly pawn picked from the ranks of bishops, rooks, knights, and other pawns to become something instrumental. To become something more than just a Public Morals detective, kicking down doors and hauling degenerates out, male, and female alike, and tossing their sorry asses into rows of paddy wagons.

He was cleaning up the city, rooting out vermin from within and yet his surrogate father figure, believing that his ideal son was already knee deep in the mud, sent him in as a sheep before wolves. But why did Valentine feel that way? Accorso and Pedrotti never did anything really wrong, other than drink excessively and snort Benzedrine, an over-the-counter weight loss aid that drug addicts used to get stoned. The only questionable thing that meant jail-time if caught was their open use of marijuana. However, they used it in the plain sight of the public who couldn't care less. Did they have some kind of protection against arrest that allowed them to be so flagrant in their illicit drug use? And more importantly, would he, could he, wreck his career by being in the company of these two borderline criminal detectives? Like Stiffy McGrath had said, they watched each other in the Public Morals squad to keep them from falling into the trap of vice. Who was watching the Bomb Squad?

Was it him? Had Valentine moved his pawn into the fray?

He was sent in, which meant that Valentine trusted him to do his job. And he would spy on Pyke to see if he was losing his edge. The fringe objective, to get close to Pyke, was to get close to Accorso and Pedrotti.

This is why he found himself in a strange bar in the Bowery called Whack-Assed Willie.

Upon walking in, it was obvious that the proprietor did not believe in the comfort of his patrons. A roughly sanded and varnished wooden bar was dead ahead of the entrance to the establishment.

The door was only accessible down a long, dimly lit alley. When Accorso and Pedrotti strode unafraid onto the path, taking a quick right from the sidewalk, Ateer stopped. What in the world could be down an alleyway with trash cans, and crates piled up on both sides?

Did these two men already discern that he was 'planted' in their midst and were leading him to his death? Once far enough into the alley would they turn on him with knives? With shoes as heavy as lead, Ateer worked his way down the center of the alley, rubbing his right arm against his coat, feeling the reassurance of his gun some distance under his armpit, secure in its rig.

However, knives were quicker and faster than a man drawing a gun. He was completely at their—

Halfway down the alley they took a right and went through a metal door with ocher rusted hinges, painted battleship gray, it's paint chipping and peeling in areas. He followed behind them, walking into a structure that was simple, offering no pretenses. A bar, tables and wood chip covered floors greeted him. Overhead blackened brass chandeliers lit the space. The smoke was heavy in the air and the smell of sweat and mold accompanied it.

"Let's get a table," Accorso said.

They found a beaten circular wooden table that looked as if it was nearly broken apart. There was no sheet over it to hide this fact, and no candle in the center to create an aura of coziness. Their table was dimly lit, their features etched with the weak light of the overhead bulbs.

"What is this place?" Ateer looked around at the patrons, male and female. The men were in three-piece wool suits and hats as beaten as their tables. Some jackets had holes growing at the elbows, others had disturbing stains on their backs. Hats were misshapen, straw hats frayed. Shoes were separated from their soles as one foot was planted on the bar railing below.

The women wore dusty dresses, their hair made up although itinerant strands gave them little shape. Make-up was plastered on faces to cover the numerous cracks of age, the tops of their dresses gone, allowing breasts to rise like pale melons, some showing the pinkish pie halves of their areolas.

"What in the hell kinda place is this?" Ateer asked, leaning over the table at Accorso and Pedrotti the instant he took his seat.

"It's a moonshine joint," Accorso replied, pulling his chair up closer to the table and looking about.

"Why here? Aren't there other bars that we could have gone to that are more...reputable?"

"What are you saying about *our* bar?" Pedrotti asked, aggrieved.

"You own it?"

"We frequent it."

Ateer wanted to dust off the table with his hand but feared receiving a splinter. "Again, why here?"

"You need to toughen up, Mackie," Accorso explained. "You're about as soft as a baby's ass."

"He doesn't mean it like that," Pedrotti interjected. "We're a little rugged...rough around the edges. We look at this job a little differently than many of the detectives in the Bomb Squad. On top of that, we face The Beast. It changes you, Mac."

"In what way?"

"You'll see." Accorso held up a hand, calling for a waitress. "For tonight, it's just your first step upon a new path," he smiled.

"Yeah," Pedrotti said, "This is your first step on a new path."

Accorso turned to him. "Didn't I just say that?"

Pedrotti waved at him.

"Uh, what path?" Ateer asked.

A waitress came to their table. She was a long, narrow teenager in a blouse and printed skirt. Cleaner than the patrons, her clothing was still worn and exhausted upon her. Her short-sleeved blouse was fraying at the ends, as was the hem of her skirt. She was a brunette with dark eyes and cherry cheeks devoid of makeup giving her a youthful beauty lacking in the older women of the saloon.

"I'm sorry," Accorso said, looking up at her. "I don't mean anything by this, but can you get Deidre to serve us?"

The waitress, exuding an air of indifference, her eyes at half-mast, hunched her shoulders and walked off.

"Who's Deidre?" Ateer asked him with a smile.

"That's his favorite waitress," Pedrotti chuckled. "What? Do you think he comes here for the liquor?"

Accorso shook his head. "Mackie, I come here for the liquor."

"Watch when she comes," Pedrotti informed Ateer.

She came. Deidre was a bright, shining, golden blonde wearing a white blouse and a short, pleated skirt, showing off her lean, muscular calves and thighs. She was a stunning beauty, a flower growing on the edge of a city dump. Her blue eyes found the table with the men she recognized and smiled, her cheeks quickly turning pink. She walked up to them, excited, eyes wide. Taking up a position next to Accorso she looked around at the men. "Fab, Beat It, who's the new guy?"

"He's our new partner, Dylan Ateer, but you can call him Mac." Accorso said.

"Hello Mac," she said to him, her voice soft.

"Hello Deidre," Ateer smiled dumbly. He addressed women many times, but most of the time they were whores. He had little interaction with what he considered normal women and never with women as striking as Deidre. He noticed her blouse, short threads where buttons once were, making it a plunging decollete well below her perky breasts, her nipples hard and noticeable against the fabric. Ateer sat back without thinking, staring into her blouse, seeing the soft outlines of her bust.

"What's your poison boys?" She asked.

"You know what I want," Accorso said slyly.

"I'm sorry, Fab. We're all out of Goat Whiskey."

"What would you have that tastes close to it?"

Ateer frowned. How would she know? Unless—

"Well, I would say the closest to Goat is Kickapoo, but it has a bitter aftertaste. If you want a step up, then Jump Steady is for you."

"Alright sugar tits, I'll take that."

She smiled, looked at Pedrotti. "How about you, Beat it?"

"Pop Skull" he replied.

"And you Mac?" She asked.

"I have no idea," he replied. "Can you suggest something?"

She grinned, showing her teeth which were yellowing from cigarette smoking and coffee drinking. "You look like a man that's just starting with moonshine, is that true?"

"Yes ma'am."

"You don't have to call her ma'am," Accorso said, laughing. He reared back and slapped her sharply against her buttock, making her jump to her tiptoes, and her eyes go wide. Quickly gathering her composure, she used her thumb to take strands of blonde hair that fell before her face and tucked them behind her ear smiling at Ateer. "You'd like a shot of 'Happy Sally'."

"Is it strong?"

"Strong enough."

"He'll take it," Accorso said to her.

"Okay, I'll be right back."

She sauntered away, everyone at the table looking at her posterior, but very little revealed itself through the pleated skirt, leaving everything to the imagination except the gentle, pleasurable sway of her narrow hips.

"Goddamn, her ass was as hard as slapping the side of Grant's Tomb." Accorso said proudly.

"She's pretty." Ateer pointed out. "Hey, can I ask you a question?"

"Sure."

"How does she know so much about moonshine?"

"She drinks everything in here. She's a barfly working at the most correct place for her. Get her drunk enough she'll take you out into the alley and do things to you that your mother would slap the shit out of you for." Smiling Accorso turned to Pedrotti. "Tell him about the time we found her in the garbage."

Pedrotti laughed. "That's a story for another time." He had opted out of the story when he noticed her returning with three old fashioned glasses. She set them on table and slid the appropriate glasses to each of them. As she bent over, Ateer could not help but peer into her blouse at her bare dangling right breast. Something stirred in him, or rather in his slacks. Ateer would have never considered himself a prude, but he was ever vigilant against masturbation, so the erection struggling in his pants caused him to blush. He wasn't a religious person although his mother was. He didn't cater to the concept of sin and hellfire, but he roared with a level of excitement and shame as he stared upon her bare breast and nipples that jutted out as if angry at the men at the table.

When she stood up, she smiled at Ateer, then said to Accorso, "Would you like me to keep slidin'?"

"Yeah, keep 'em coming until one of us passes out on the table, sweetheart."

When she walked off Ateer raised his glass to his nose and was slightly frightened to find it practically odorless. What little he could smell was like sniffing a car engine. "What's in this?"

Pedrotti said, "You should have asked her before she left."

"I'll ask her when she returns."

"Then it'll be too late."

"Why?"

"Because she's not coming back until you finish it."

"Stop being a baby, Mac," Accorso ordered. "Don't have us make a man outta you."

Ateer held the glass up to his eyes, finding small particles floating within the clear liquid. Both Accorso and Pedrotti stared at him, waiting. Pedrotti smiled his crooked grin, looking frightening sinister in the weak light of the bar.

"Well?" Accorso asked. He turned up his glass to his lips and drained it.

Upon seeing him do it, Pedrotti did the same.

They stopped and stared once again at Ateer, this time expectedly.

Ateer counted down silently from three, turned up the glass and filled his mouth with the fluid, then giving it one quick, stubborn swallow. The fire of the drink seared his esophagus in its fall to his stomach where it lit up like a light bulb. Ateer and Accorso laughed heartily, banging their hands loudly on the table.

Ateer breathed out or more like gave a long gasp. The burn slowly started to warm him, blushing his cheeks and chin. "Wow."

"How was it?" Accorso asked.

"Strong but the tail end is pretty comfortable," he smiled back.

Deidre appeared at the table with three more glasses.

His stomach kept rolling over like a little capsizing toy ship. Ateer found that by resting his face down on his desk, from his forehead to his nose and mouth, the churning barely bothered him. He wanted to drag the wastepaper basket closer to him just in case he got too sick and emptied his stomach, but the thought of doing it made it more real. He pushed the thoughts from his mind and others rushed in to take their place. Memories of last night crowded out the racket of the bullpen around him, mostly memories of Deidre's breasts. They were absolutely splendorous. Young, hard, defying gravity. As the night wore on, he became more and more unabashed in staring at them, and the more he did, the more she tempted him. He remembered that her torn buttons were as far down as the blouse was open, however, nearly every time she returned with drinks more and more buttons seemed to come undone to where only the waistline of her short skirt kept the open blouse from flying completely apart. It was as if she was serving him up more than drinks.

Further, he had decided that since he could not trust Happy Sally, he definitely was going to stop at two, respectfully excuse himself, and ride the train back into Brooklyn. But he never met a woman like Happy Sally before. The first time he emptied a glass of it, it burned. By the third time he was having too much fun listening to Accorso and Pedrotti's war stories. Not so strange was that after the third drink he had lost count and Deidre's hard nipples started to demand his rapt attention.

He wasn't a man to babble but he found himself explaining why he didn't chum around with the detectives of Public Morals. He made plain how much he cared for his mother. She was a hardworking woman in a factory at night, and as a maid for the Lewis family during the day. The Great Depression had hit hard, and there were many nights that she could only make potato soup for them, but he never went hungry. He and his sister always had decent clothing to wear, and in time they moved in with the Lewis family, so his home was a large, beautiful house with many floors. At that point, life became substantially easier.

It was in these halcyon days that his mother's admonitions found their fertile ground in his heart. She only wished to protect him. She only desired to give her son instruction enough to succeed in life after she could watch him no more. Because of her sacrifice, because of her struggle, he was indebted to her. Like a ball thrown through the air, his life followed the trajectory that she put him upon, without thinking, without debate. He simply did what he was told, and by not having any real exposure to vice he gravitated to the Public Morals squad, in an attempt to clean his city of the same scourge that he himself avoided. He was good at his job, ready for the call, and the first through the door. So quick was he that he could find the cue of women struggling to crawl out of the furthest window from the entrance, giving them time to flee. But like a hound, he would rush directly there, sweeping them all up like wheat before the sickle. But after the dust settled, the whores, gamblers, bookmakers and illegal bar keeps were behind bars, when all the correct forms were filed, and when it was time to let off a little 'steam,' he would politely excuse himself. He would find his way home, to his radio, his reading, his bed.

His barroom confession made Accorso's, Pedrotti's and even Deidre's face glow as they crowded around him, listening intently. Later, after what was a blurry, woozy ride in the back of the squad car to Brooklyn, he could remember taking minutes trying to put his key into the keyhole.

In the morning, he woke up with a fiery hangover from hell. He couldn't eat, could barely deal with the rickety, rocking train ride to the precinct. He had arrived early for his tour and like a car barreling over a ravine, he lost control of his motor skills and careened into his desk and chair where he bowed his head, a wilted flower, and gnashed his teeth.

When Accorso breezed into the bullpen he struck Ateer behind the head with his folded-up newspaper and hung up his coat and hat. "Hey buddy, are you going to come out of that hat and coat?" he asked, going to his chair, and taking a seat.

"I died this morning," Ateer groaned into his desk. "This is just where my soul came to alight."

"Feeling bad, huh? How are you going to get to work this morning?"

"I'm going to call in sick."

"You can do that. Or you can use my instant cure."

Ateer lifted his head from his arms crossed on the desk as a pillow. His fedora was cocked back, and his eyes seemed on the verge of sleep. "I can't do this."

"Sure, you can, Mackie. You're Bomb Squad. You can do anything."

Frowning, Ateer opened his eyes. "What is this cure?"

Without explanation he opened his bottom desk drawer and produced a silver flask. "Here, take a big swig of this." He quickly unscrewed the top and passed it low to the desk over to him. Ateer took it and sniffed its opening. This time it had the strong smell of something dark with a sharp edge, threatening.

"What is it?"

"Goat Whiskey," Accorso whispered.

"I thought she was out of it."

"At the *bar* you dumb assed leprechaun. This was in my desk."

"Why this?"

"It'll cut the edge off."

Ateer stopped to think. The thought of taking a sip from what he inhaled did not disturb his stomach like the simple thought of eggs and toast this morning. He looked around to make certain that no one had taken note, and then flung his head back, putting the mouth of the flask to his, and poured a good swallow of the drink.

Immediately, his heart burned to a cinder, and when he lowered the flask, he breathed fire. His eyes were awash with tears, his nose ran. His lungs fought against the blast of heat, coughing uncontrollably. In the throes of his barking, he passed the flask back which Accorso quickly returned to his drawer.

Pedrotti walked by them, looking down at Ateer struggling to gain his composure.

"Hangover?" he asked Accorso.

"Yeah." Accorso handed him the newspaper.

"Hair of the dog?"

"Yeah."

"How is that gonna work?" Ateer breathed tiredly, beaten down by his ordeal.

"Put your head back down."

As Ateer returned to his arms on the desk, Accorso stood and took away his hat, hanging it on the coat rack.

Pedrotti spun around in his chair to face them. "Donkey can't hold his liquor."

"I remember you were the same way." Accorso walked off into the break room and poured some black coffee. He reached into his jacket and came away with his Benzedrine inhaler. Screwing the cap off he held it in the palm of his hand and struck it against the corner of the counter-top, snapping it in half. Separating it, he pulled out the strip soaked in Benzedrine, rolled it up into a little ball with his thumb and forefinger and dropped it into the coffee.

When he returned Ateer was sitting up, still feeble looking, his eyes at half-mast. Accorso rested the cup down in front of him, "here, drink this quick."

SUSPICIOUS LOOKING PACKAGES

Ateer stared down at the cup, but it didn't seem to register.

Heavy guffaws came from Pyke's office. Inside, Hayias had told a joke he had heard in the locker room about a dog, two cats, and a man with a little penis. Pyke was still chuckling, wiping tears from his eyes as an officer came to a quick halt from running to his door. Hayias, seeing concern cross Pyke's face, uncrossed and retracted his legs and turned around.

"Sir," the officer said, still panting from his run.

"Yes."

"Mayor La Guardia and his staff are just entering the building. The minute he stepped into the precinct he asked the front desk about a bomb in Pennsylvania Station last night."

Both Pyke and Hayias rushed to their feet and scrambled out of the office. They went directly across the office door to the balustrade next to Accorso and Ateer's desk.

"Accorso, what happened in Penn Station last night," Pyke asked.

"There was a bomb in the waiting area of the of the Long Island Rail Railroad. Accorso did not rise from his seat.

Pyke looked at Ateer who looked visibly sick and exhausted in his overcoat, sipping from a cup of coffee. "What's wrong with him?" Pyke asked Accorso.

"Wack-Assed Willie's."

Both Pyke and Hayias laughed and walked back into the office, dismissing the officer the second a wave of suits and uniforms poured onto the floor. Leading this broad line of authority was a short, portly man with a round, soft face and thinning hair oiled and combed to the side. He was a dapper dresser in a suit, vest, and tie, an overcoat flowing behind him. He stopped short, leaning his head back to say something to a suit standing taller behind him. The suit leaned down to whisper in his ear, pointing at Pyke's office entrance.

Once again, shifting into gear, La Guardia struck off, walking into the office, and stopping for a moment at its center to take in his surroundings. As he looked at the empty walls, neat desk, guest chair before the desk, Pyke jumped to his feet.

Hayias already stood behind Pyke on his right flank at attention. La Guardia's entourage filed into the room, taking up positions against the wall. Deputy Police Commissioners, the Chief Inspector, Deputy Chief inspector, and LaGuardia's protection detail stood silently and at attention.

"Sir?" Pyke said.

"Lieutenant Pyke, what's this that I heard about a bomb in Pennsylvania Station?" La Guardia asked. His voice seemed to fit his short, pudgy stature in some way. It was a nasal voice, pinched and squeezed with a New Yorker twang.

"Yes, sir. We had a call late yesterday and I sent my best people out to take care of it."

"And what happened to it?"

"We took care of it."

"What did you do?"

"Well…" Pyke looked lost for a moment where he couldn't think up what to say in reply. Suddenly, he shifted gears into drive. "Excuse me, sir…."

La Guardia nodded curtly, his eyes on Pyke's.

"DETECTIVE ACCORSO! FRONT AND CENTER!" Pyke bellowed.

In moments, Accorso stepped into the office. La Guardia turned around to look him up and down. All eyes turned to Accorso.

"Front and center, detective," Pyke said.

Accorso approached the desk.

"Tell the Mayor what happened last night."

Accorso turned around to face the Mayor, his lips going dry. La Guardia looked at him ready to hear his report.

"Well, we had a call in to Penn Station and found a device in the LIRR waiting area. We haven't discerned yet exactly what it is, so for right now, it's still just a suspicious package." Accorso said flatly, as if this job had sucked the humanity out of him.

"What does that mean? Where is it?" La Guardia was losing his patience.

"Something is inside the package and it's ticking. We dunked it in motor oil overnight, under police guard, and we were just about to drive out there to check if the ticking had stopped."

"It's still active?"

Accorso shook his head. "We can't call it 'safe' yet, sir."

"Well, why aren't we there now making certain that it is safe?" He turned to look around at his Deputy Mayors and Inspectors, then to Pyke.

"We were just about to leave until we found out that you were entering the precinct," Accorso said.

"Well?" LaGuardia held up his hands and looked heavenward as if pleading with God. "Let's go!"

"Accorso, requisition two cars for us," Pyke ordered.

Accorso left the office.

"You can follow us in, Mr. Mayor," Pyke said to him. "We'll be leaving in five minutes.

In moments, with Accorso taking the lead of the makeshift motorcade, Pedrotti and Ateer in his car, Pyke, and the Deputy Chief Inspector Durtayne in the following squad car. Durtayne grilled Pyke about the standard operating procedure, and was it followed last night at Pennsylvania Station. Two green and white Radio Motor Patrol cars followed them with eight uniformed police. A limousine, carrying La Guardia, some of his Deputy Mayors, and in the last car, more of his Deputy Mayors and Inspectors.

"Fucking, Mayor La Guardia," Pedrotti said in the passenger seat, his voice edgy and anxious. "What the fuck is he doing here?"

"Do you need someone to spell it out for you?" Accorso replied, taking a turn ahead. "Two words: Worlds, Fair."

"You think?"

"If you think that La Guardia doesn't want to show everyone that he's tough on us, you've got another thing comin'."

"Well, La Guardia and his *gavonnes* are the ones that pulled the Bomb Squad off the World's Fair Bombing full time to get back to bomb calls."

"Do you remember who was running bomb calls while we were working with the detective division?"

"Yeah, who?"

"No one you greasy, grease-ball. Calls were coming in and no one was going out. When they realized how many fucking calls come in in a given day, they shat themselves. They pulled us off the bombing case so fast the human eye couldn't follow it."

Ateer leaned forward, sticking his head between them, "They're still keeping it an open case?"

"There's no statute of limitation on murder, Mackie. And when it comes to our brothers in blue it's never gonna stop. The resources devoted to the case are much, much less than they were in the beginning. The NYPD couldn't keep all hands-on deck forever, but it's still being investigated. The thing is that as long as people remember the bombing, La Guardia is in the hot-seat, and as long as he is, we are."

"Then we're fucked," Pedrotti said, his tone like someone who just realized he lost a big hand in poker. "We walked away from a potential Infernal Machine last night before it was rendered safe. We'll never hear the ending of that."

"What are you talking about?" Accorso gave him a quick, puzzled glance. Taking his eyes off the road for a brief second. "What standard procedure did you break?"

"I don't know. It's what we do, isn't it?"

"Who's to tell us how we're supposed to do things? The *Bomb Squad*?"

The relief in Pedrotti's body could be measured rising from his skin. "Yeah, you're right. We know how best to handle things like these and no one else."

"And therefore, why do you think we are Unit 1? The elite of the elite? Because Pyke knows, if something is as important, and could cause the damage that that bomb could have done to life and limb last night, he can either do it himself, or the next best thing, call on us."

"Really?" Ateer gasped.

"You're damned right. We are the *big* guns of the bomb squad, baby." Accorso struck the steering wheel sharply with the heel of his palm.

"Isn't it a right turn up ahead?" Pedrotti pointed out his side of the windows.

Accorso made the turn.

As if it was the entrance to a ballgame, scores of spectators from old man to young girl had gathered at the very periphery of the police line. A literal crowd of people struggling frantically to peer over the shoulders of the person ahead of them to view a single oil barrel in the middle of a near vacant lot. As they closed in on the backs of the mobs on 33rd Street, a party of uniformed officers' dove into it, and parted the people like a pair of flesh and blood gates affording the motor procession the opportunity to pass through and make its way to the lot less than a half a block away.

"I'd better pull over here," Accorso said, doing so.

Pedrotti climbed out of the squad car and pulled the seat forward for Ateer to climb out. They waited in front of their car until, coming from both sides were, the Deputy Chief Inspector Durtayne, several uniformed officers and several members of the mayor's entourage on the right: Pyke, La Guardia, several members of his entourage and another group of uniformed officers on the left. Pyke, with La Guardia next to him, cocking his fists against his overcoat, stopped in front of Accorso and his unit. "Where to now, detective?" La Guardia asked.

Accorso, Pedrotti and Ateer, without actually being able to help it, looked at the big, felt, black hat on the mayor's head, with a stunned silence. No doubt he had donned the head covering to block the slanting morning sun from his eyes. "Up ahead and around that building," Accorso pointed, "there is a lot. The suitcase with the ticking sound is in a barrel of oil in the center of that lot."

"Accorso, with me," Pyke said, "the rest of you stay here." With a wave he walked off, "Let's go."

Accorso walked off with the lieutenant. Ateer and Pedrotti stayed behind. As if not understanding that the term 'the rest of you' included him, Mayor La Guardia marched off behind them, dragging his entourage, like a strong current.

It only took a few steps before Pyke realized this. Turning around he addressed the Mayor. "Sir, may I ask, what are you doing?"

"I'm going with you." He turned to his attendants. "You go back. This is dangerous."

Pyke and Accorso looked at each other: who was *he* talking to? They thought to themselves.

La Guardia's big felt hat returned to them, his eyes directly under the brim, looking up at them. "Let's go."

"Sir, this is going to be dangerous. If that thing goes off…"

La Guardia started brushing them away with his hands, shooing them off. "Let's go, let's go, let's go."

Not believing what was going on, Pyke and Accorso turned around woodenly and marched on with La Guardia in tow. They walked past the last building of the block and there, on the left, standing like a pugilist waiting at the other corner of the ring, was the red barrel. Pyke stopped and regarded La Guardia, his face read: *This is your last chance*. La Guardia looked back at him; his face read: *let's get this shit over with.*

With a tired sigh, Pyke turned and marched on, the three closing the distance between themselves and the barrel. Pyke stopped again, this time a mere ten paces away from waiting death. Pyke, irrespective of if he would lose his job or not, ordered the mayor, "I cannot let you go any farther. If this is a bomb and if it should explode, you are already well within the blast splash of this Infernal Device. The blast wave will rip you asunder. There won't be anything left of any of us. If you don't want to go back, you have to stop here."

Accorso, silent as a statue, could see the blood slowly draining from La Guardia's face, beads of sweat gathering on his forehead. He reached up for his hat with a trembling hand, taking it from his head and holding it against his breast with both hands. "Go on then."

Pyke, stripping off his jacket, handed it and his hat over to Accorso, "You stay here with the mayor."

SUSPICIOUS LOOKING PACKAGES

Accorso knew better than to argue. Knew better than to tell Pyke that he forgot the stethoscope. How was he to tell if the clock inside had stopped ticking? Oil didn't *always* work. But this was how Pyke did things. Insanely.

Pyke marched on, rolling up his sleeves to just under his armpits, walked around the barrel, looked at the surface for slowly popping air bubble in the oil. None were present. Without another pause, he reached in with one hand, felt around for a few moments and found the handle of the case. He hauled the heavy piece of luggage from the barrel and balanced it on the edge of the can. The crowd watched breathlessly as he produced a pocketknife from his pocket, broke the clasps and cut the cord around it. Slowly he lifted the top just a crack, turned the case around so that the morning light could get in and stopped.

Mayor La Guardia, Accorso, the crowds around them, everyone froze, as if time screeched to a halt. Then Pyke turned the case on its side and at first, out poured oil, followed by a yellow rain slicker, clothing, chef's knives, and a cigar box. When it struck the asphalt out popped the small alarm clock.

A mighty shout roared from the crowds around them as they jumped and raised their hands. La Guardia, caught up in the jubilation, whipped the air over his head with his felt hat, suddenly stirring the excitement of the crowd to madness. Then applause came, calming down the masses.

Pyke, flapping his arm to throw off the heavy oil, returned to Accorso and La Guardia who bore a grin so large that his entire mouth opened like a jack-o-lantern. "Oh my god!" He gasped. "I have never felt so much tension and then relief in my life! It was exhilarating!"

"Unless you have a bad day," Pyke grumbled, taking his jacket and hat from Accorso, and draping it over his clean arm.

"Come on," La Guardia said. "Let's go back." Taking up a position between the two men, La Guardia pressed a hand against the backs of both and walked with them, presenting the two heroes to his entourage and what looked like the Press gathering behind the police line a little farther on. "*This*, my friends," he shouted out loudly for such a short man, "is the New York Bomb Squad!"

Cheers rose again. La Guardia shook Pyke's hand and then Accorso's. Under his breath he said to Pyke, "I can see why Valentine puts so much faith in you. You are beyond belief."

"Thank you, sir."

He clapped Pyke twice on the shoulder and then walked off, heading to his group of sycophants and his protection detail. Pyke walked over to Ateer and Pedrotti. "Do any of you have a handkerchief?"

Accorso and Pedrotti pulled out one and handed them over to Pyke so that he could wipe the remaining oil from his arm. "You three take the rest of the day off. You deserve it. I think that's the last time we'll see the 'Little Flower' give us a personal visit." He waved the barrel off behind him. "I'll get 'Bad-Luck-O' to come out here and clean all of this shit up and turn in the case to Property." Pyke walked off, heading to the cars.

"What was all that about?" Ateer asked.

"Politics my boy. It's not what you do, it's who you do what in front of." Accorso said, "In the eyes of New York City, and Mayor La Guardia, we still do the impossible."

"Yeah, and he does the media, coming out smelling like a rose," Pedrotti said.

"You going home, Mackie?" Accorso said to him.

Ateer thought for a moment. He had to admit that that belt of Accorso's Goat Whiskey had settled his stomach and stopped the dizziness, but now he was loopy. It felt good, but he was both out of it and strangely alert. "I wanna go with you guys."

"Good, we got all day to kill," Pedrotti said. "I've got an idea."

"What's that?"

"I want to see Scooty."

Accorso thought about it for a moment then nodded. "Come to think about it, I would like to see him too."

They turned around, watching Pyke drive off in the squad car, followed by the two RMPs, the limousine, and the last of the mayor's cars, like a wagging tail, as they passed.

They climbed into their unmarked squad car and pulled off.

They went to Park Avenue in the West Bronx. The neighborhood was a mix of factories, houses, apartment buildings, and rattling through on its appointed schedule, the Harlem Line of the New York Central Railroad. Accorso parked the car on East 179th street and walked the block past the houses with older women sitting on foldable lounge chairs fanning themselves out on front lawns, kids running about in the barely trafficked streets, large red ball bouncing down in front of them. Ateer looked at the vibrant energy around him, girls busy with jump rope, boys playing stickball with a broomstick, and the occasional dog barking as they walked by a fenced in lawn.

Then suddenly all life ended.

Near the corner of the block, the building next to them was a simple, stark rough brick wall. Turning the corner, on the right side of the street was nothing save row upon row of factories. Busy with mechanical noises that could be heard from the outside, and women walking in and out of windowless buildings, it was an entirely different world from the one around the corner. To the left, across the street was a line of parked cars against a hurricane fence, blocking pedestrians from the railroad tracks after a gently sloping downgrade of grass and hardscrabble earth. The passing train would grumble by just this close to homes, no doubt at times disturbing the residents, causing them to pause from conversations. As for the noise of the trains affecting the factories, who cared?

Accorso led the way down the front of these lifeless buildings. Ateer marched behind him, wide eyed and wondering what was going on behind the many blank walls. He read the banners over the tops of the entrances to some of the sweatshops: hat makers, dress makers, every one of them on the block in the business of producing something, save one.

No banner overhead, no sign on the side of its gray painted door. Without having any doubt, Ateer knew that this would be the door that Accorso would entertain. His supervisor stopped before it, knocked three times and then jiggled the doorknob. After a moment a big, burly monster of a man with a bald head opened the door. His face was a theatrical mask of tragedy, mouth turned downward in a snarl. His broad, muscular shoulders, with pectorals that looked like freshly fluffed pillows, filled the threshold. He looked into Accorso's eyes and smiled.

Ateer's heart stopped its breakneck pace.

"Knuckles!" Accorso walked past the guard, patting him on his right breast, which sounded as firm as Deidre's buttock last night. The factory, of course, was not a factory at all, but rather an abandoned warehouse with its cracked concrete flooring, and iron girders spaced about holding up the joists of the dark ceiling. The ceiling, where skylights were opened to let in air but not light due to the filth that turned them opaque, was in darkness because the light sources, bulbs with conical shades hanging from long cords from the ceiling, made a distinct demarcation between the light below them and the darkness above.

And the enormous space below was filled with men dressed both casually and in suits. There were some tables, some chairs here and there, stools, a bank of phones against the wall, and the heavy smoke of cigarettes. Skipping about in the very air of the space was frantic energy as the men listened intently to several loudspeakers above somewhere in the upper, demonic dark layer of the warehouse.

Pouring from each speaker was different information, announcers calling out racing information from several tracks: Aqueduct, Belmont, Saratoga, and more. The excited men clenching racing forms were clustered in large groups where they could hear the information of their choice, late scratches, post-times, and even running descriptions of races in progress. From where he stood, Ateer could barely make out anything other than a shuffling of words. It sounded like a maddening cacophony of sound, the announcers talking over themselves, but certainly, if a person moved closer to a particular loudspeaker, it would no doubt drown out the rest and their particular information would become clearer.

On the left was a raised platform where eleven white shirted, black vest wearing clerks sat side by side, taking the action between the races, their faces obscured in half-darkness by green accountant visors over their brows. Before them on a lengthy table were black money trays with different denominations of cash separated neatly. Next to that was a fat pad of 'markers' to note the particulars of each person's wager. And every so often, when the tray slots filled with too much cash, an amount would be counted out, wrapped in currency bands, and dropped into a box at their feet. When this box filled, a runner would replace it with an empty one and disappear behind the clerks through a reinforced door. Between the clerks and the door, watching the entire operation from top to bottom were seven armed men in suits and ties. They paced about slowly like white blood cells in a boiling blood stream, searching for anything foreign or dangerous to converge upon.

As the three detectives stepped upon the raised platform and crossed the invisible line behind the clerks, the white blood cells floated their way, hands in their jackets, their eyes riveted on the hands of the intruders. Ateer stopped as Accorso and Pedrotti continued to approach the security force. Both converging groups slowed as two of the guards recognized Accorso and Pedrotti, breaking from their ranks, shouting, and embracing them.

Ateer calmed again by degrees. He knew where he stood. He had busted places like this many times. They were referred to as 'Nine-Eighty-Sixes' by the Public Morals Squad which was the Section that operators of these establishments violated: 986 of the Penal Code, which basically was a violation of the gambling laws and at best a misdemeanor. But Ateer had to admit that the 986's that he was accustomed to raiding were small fry compared to this massive operation. If he turned this place in, he could only imagine the commendations he would receive. There had to have been nearly three hundred men in the space, and there was ample room for many, many more. Lines formed in front of the row of clerks, twenty bettors long. Some men ran between races, some ran between tracks, trying to bet away what little they made in their soul-less jobs.

Accorso called out to him, and he walked over. Two of the security men, both mature with gray in and around the sideburns and the tops of their heads, smiled and shook Ateer's hand vigorously. These men were Accorso's and Pedrotti's training officers when they first became a detective. Cordial men, they spoke with the same amount of respect that they expected. Still the joviality and closeness between the four men was evident as they asked about families, children, fathers, and mothers.

Finally, Pedrotti asked, "Hey, where's Scooty?"

One of the men, Ateer remembering his name as Blake, said, "He's in his office. You wanna go back there?"

"Yeah, we wanna say hello."

"I know he'll jerk himself off, he'll be so happy to see you guys. You know where that 'brew's office is," Blake pointed at the heavy door behind him. Accorso patted Blake on the shoulder and set off to the back of the establishment, opening the heavy, unlocked door. This door usually stayed unlocked until something went wrong outside, and when it did, a heavy bar would come down across it from the inside, locking everyone in.

Ateer noticed this fact as he followed behind Accorso and Pedrotti. They led the way down a long, drab, picture-less corridor. Branching off on both sides were other offices where accountants labored over desks scribbling into ledgers. The office at the end of the hall was a large, lavish room with plush couches and chairs, blood red tapestries covering the dull, lifeless walls with an eye-opening splash of colors. The furnishings were of rich, dark wood, from the bookcases to the desks and bureaus.

Sitting behind the desk was a man dressed in a gray pinstripe suit and vest sans tie. He looked bored, holding up a brandy sniffer against his temple, deep in thought. His head was a long oval, his features covered with lines and wrinkles, crow's feet, laugh lines, and large ears with gray hair growing within them. The barely visible tufts of snow-white hair on both sides of his head bracketed a yarmulke at the top. He did not register their entrance immediately. Deep, dark eyes stared down at the desktop, oblivious, but only for a moment. Looking up tiredly he focused on the two men standing before him, both smiling broadly like little children. His aged and fatigued features brightened, his eyes flashed, and suddenly, what felt like a mortuary, burst with life.

"Scooty! You Jew bastard!" Pedrotti shouted, walking around the desk as if he meant the old man harm. However, Scooty made an effort to rise quickly from the chair and threw his arms around Pedrotti, burying his face into his neck. After a deep and abiding embrace, he held Pedrotti at arm's length. "Beat It!" He laughed between words. "How are you doing my little meshuggana spaghetti strand!"

"I'm doing good, Scooty."

He turned his mature features to Accorso this time, still smiling broadly. Like a toddler walking for the first time into the arms of an awaiting parent, Scooty walked with a little difficulty into the arms of Accorso. "How are you my *Eye*-talian boy. Stuffing any pasta and sausages into your pants pockets lately?"

"Naah, Pops," Accorso replied. Scooty looked him up and down. "You're getting older Fabulous."

"And you're getting younger you ugly motherfucker. How do you do it?"

"I try to fuck a teenage girl in the ass every night!" He laughed, made a fist, and pumped the air before him. They chuckled along with him.

"Now, who's this you got here?" He pointed a shriveled hand to Ateer who was standing several paces away to allow their reunion to occur unimpeded.

"This is a rookie to The Beast. Come meet Dylan Ateer." Accorso draped an arm across Scooty's shoulders and drew him close to Ateer.

"Pleased to meet you, Dylan," he said, shaking his hand.

Ateer returned the oddly firm handshake. "Please call me Mac," he replied, smiling cordially.

"Mac," Accorso continued, indicating the man in his arm with his other hand, "Please meet the only living genius smarter than Albert Einstein...Benjamin Levine, but we like to call him Scooty."

"Scooty, nice name," Ateer said, screwing up a smile even though he felt completely out of his depth.

"More like Count Frankenstein," Pedrotti laughed behind them.

Scooty turned around, wobbling like a penguin to face Pedrotti, "That's *Count* Dracula, and *Victor* Frankenstein, you stupid guinea!"

Pedrotti waved at him and began walking around his office.

"So, how's the wife," Scooty asked Accorso as he worked his way back behind his desk. Both men replied at the same time, "Being a bitch." Pedrotti had used the word 'fucking' in his description of his wife.

"I've always called you two a pair of drunken Schlemiels for getting married. The way you two whored around before getting married? I can't believe you could keep your little schmeckels in your pants long enough to walk around the block," he turned to Ateer, "Oh these two. They were unbelievable."

Ateer smiled, chuckled nervously. "Yeah? Before they became cops?"

Scooty's face went blank. He sat back and turned to Pedrotti who was looking at a glass cabinet. "How *new* is this putz?"

Pedrotti glanced back at him. "*Very* new."

"Hmmm," Scooty plucked a cigarette out of a crystal holder and put it between his lips, "you don't know these men at all, do you?" He flatly asked Ateer.

"I know them enough." Ateer nodded proudly.

Pointing to a corner of the room, he replied, "Boychick, go over there and bring a chair here."

Ateer turned to Accorso who nodded at him. In the corner of the room where Scooty pointed was a set of high-backed wooden chairs with lush red cushions. Ateer carefully carried it over to the front of Scooty's desk.

"Please, sit down. Sit."

Ateer did as he was told. Accorso walked off to a couch where Pedrotti had found a seat.

Scooty tilted his head to light his smoke, took a few puffs and then leaned over the desk towards Ateer. "Can I ask you a question, boychick?"

"Can I ask *you* a question, Scooty?" Pedrotti shouted from the couch against the wall to the left of the desk. "Where is your liquor cabinet?"

Turning to him, Scooty waved a hand angrily in the air. "I had that piece of dreck taken to your house, Beat It! You can pick it up when you get home, you goy bastard!" Everyone laughed but Ateer.

Scooty snatched up the receiver of the phone next to him and shouted into it in Yiddish. When done, he hung it up angrily and returned to Ateer. "Can I still ask you that question?"

"Yeah, sure," Ateer replied, staring into the dark eyes of the old man.

"Do you *know* these men?"

"I think I do."

Scooty stared at him in silence for a moment, then said, "What is Fab's daughter's name?"

Ateer blinked. He didn't even know that Accorso had a daughter! He frowned, stunned, shook his head. "I-I don't know."

"I know you don't know. You don't know anything about these men, because if you did, you'd know just how he felt about his daughter. He loves her as if she came from his loins...instead of *my* loins!" He slapped the palm of his hand against the desktop, causing a loud report like a gunshot, making Ateer jump.

"Scooty, she *is* my daughter," Accorso corrected.

"That's not what your wife told me,"he smirked. Returning his smiling features to Ateer, Scooty asked, "Why are you here?" His friendly grin made the serious and dark sounding words coming from him psychopathic and sinister. Ateer looked at him with a mixture of worry and concern. What was this old man really asking him?

The door opened behind Ateer, making him spin in the chair, his hand reaching for his shoulder rig. Two blonde-haired women eased though the door like languid smoke. Tall, and leggy, wearing short white pleated skirts, thigh high black stockings and buttoned sky-blue sweaters. They moved to the desk like waves of heat, both flanking Ateer, cocking their hips in his direction. Ateer sat bolt upright in his seat with a level of alarm, not exactly knowing what was to happen next.

Scooty pointed to the two detectives lounging on the couch. "Go and serve my guests you two shiksa nafkas!"

They sauntered casually over to Accorso and Pedrotti, listening to them. Ateer glanced, almost reluctantly, as the women bowed at the waists, sticking up their rear ends, allowing the hem of their dresses to rise teasingly over their posterior, showing off their narrow lace white panties, and garter straps going to the black lace tops of their stockings.

"Looks nice right?" Scooty said to Ateer, leaning over his desk towards him with a crooked and sly smile. His eyes twinkled.

Ateer turned to him, feeling uncomfortable. He slowly started to realize that this wasn't a social call, "Yes.,It does."

"They're bimbos. I have a whorehouse full of them three doors up the block on East 180th Street."

Ateer glued the uncomfortable grin onto his features.

Taking a long, final draw from his cigarette, he crushed it in a nearby ashtray and then blew smoke on it, appearing lost in thought. "I knew these two boys when they were teenagers. They used to come and do a little work for me here and there. It was hard to get a phone way back then. You had to practically know someone, plus, nobody in my line of work trusted the damn things. I mean, am I wrong?" He touched a hand to his chest and sat back. "I mean, if your friend can hear you, why not someone else? Am I wrong?"

Ateer shook his head. His radar tracked the women as they left the office.

Scooty continued, "They used to run paper for me. You know what that is?"

Ateer shook his head again.

"Messages. They used to take messages between my places of work for a nickel a message. I ran those little boys ragged. They should have grown up to be fat, greasy *Eye*-talians, but I ran every ounce of blubber off those two. And do you want to know something?"

Ateer cleared his throat, "What's that, Scooty?"

"They never complained. I'd work them from sunup to sunup and they never complained. Not even once. They are good boys." He tapped his sternum with a finger. "They are *my* boys!" He pointed to Accorso. "This one, his father blew himself up!" His finger swung to Pedrotti. "His father died of consumption. So, they became *my* boys. They're my only sons, you see, because my wife...that barren nafka! OH!" he paused to correct himself. "Let me speak more English," he paused again for emphasis, "that barren skinny assed, shiksa whore!"

Pedrotti and Accorso laughed heartily at their end of the office. Ateer turned to them, finding a little solace in their humor. He had to be honest with himself, sitting in front of Scooty was like sitting before a Devil's Toy. He patiently waited for it to go off.

"But she was," he whined to the two men. He returned to Ateer, his face sullen, "she *was*. She couldn't help putting that meat in her mouth. You know what I mean?"

"Uh," Ateer's mouth fell open.

"I'm talking about shvantzes!" He wagged a finger. "That little piece of thingy that swings between your legs."

"Oh."

Scooty waved a wrinkly hand in the air. "I can't fault her though,

Mac," he swung his arm off, pointing away to a place far beyond the walls of the room, "she's one of the whores from my whorehouse three doors up the block on East 180th Street."

More knee-slapping laughter from Accorso and Pedrotti, rocking back and forth in the couch. Ateer felt that Scooty's comedy was just a way to ease his tension, but it had a dishonest edge to it.

"But like all women, they are treacherous, deceitful, liars, and cheats. You can't trust anything that comes out of their mouths, remember that. They can't help it, you see. But that also makes them very predictable, and that is *very* good. You can anticipate everything about them easily. You can also trap them by dangling shiny things before them, and they'll follow you home and put your little thingy in their mouths. Do you understand?"

"I think so."

The two women returned with glasses and a decanter of bourbon on silver trays. They went to Accorso and Pedrotti, bending over and handing them the rock glasses, filling them with liquor. They also planted cigarettes between their lips and lit them. When done, the blondes stood off to the side at rigid attention, awaiting further orders. Scooty turned to them, "Katie, are you a dirty whore?" He asked the one closest to his desk. She turned to him, her comely features frowning. "No."

Scooty looked to Ateer, nodding. "She is," he laughed, "but that's the way they are. Deceitful. Liars. Always looking to do you harm." He shook a finger at Ateer. "I don't think you understand."

Ateer agreed with a nod, "I do," he said, but deep down he knew he was being set up for a fall.

"When those qualities are found in a man," Scooty continued, "it is VERY bad. He becomes UN-predictable. Disloyal. Dangerous. You can dangle shiny things before them, and they might not take it. Instead, they might want the chair you sit on. Or the house you live in. Or worse, to take everything from you and leave you with nothing."

He paused. Ateer sat stoically. All eyes, even those of the women, were on him.

"I'll ask you again...Mac. Why are you here?"

"I volunteered to join the Bomb Squad."

"Why?"

"It's the best damned squad in the NYPD, sir."

"Is that all?"

"Yes." Ateer grew defensive.

"You see, can tell when someone is lying. I can always get to the truth. Sometimes immediately, sometimes after a while. But I always find out. Like this///" he turned to the women. "Ariel, what are you?"

"I'm a dirty whore," she replied, her voice flat as if she was hypnotized behind her answer.

"And you, Alexa?"

"I'm also a dirty whore," same flat affect.

Pedrotti sat up in the couch, eyes wide with a broad grin. "They are?"

Scooty ignored him. He stood, held onto the edge of his desk, and used it to navigate around it. "Let me show you something," he said, holding out his hand. Ateer stood up and took it and the elderly man wrapped his arm around his. They walked slowly out of the office, down the hall, and into the betting area. As Scooty emerged, the guards drew close around him as if expecting orders. Ateer was expectant also. He was expecting his situation to go from bad to worse in an instant.

"Let me confess to you," Scooty said. "You see, I have a long-distance wire between the racetracks and a room back there with announcers who give us the information on races as soon as they happen." He pointed to the mass of men jumping up and down, waving papers, shouting, and throwing up torn markers into the air. "They pump money into my pockets, Mac. And you know, several doors down, I have whores that make Ariel and Alexa look like Knuckles right over there," he pointed. Then he took a small step away, looking up into Ateer's face, searching his eyes, still holding on to him, "and do you know what the men do in my whorehouse?"

"Have sex?"

Scooty made a face. "Do you really think that sex is all that important?"

"I suppose so."

"No, it isn't at all. It's just a nasty thing that you do to a woman through a hole in a sheet!" He punched Ateer lightly against the shoulder. "But do you know what is important?"

Ateer shook his head.

"They pump money into my pockets."

"I think I get it," Ateer said grimly, "but why is that important to me?"

"Because I've told you everything about me. You can decide what you want to do now. You're a cop. You can show your badge, empty this place, arrest my guards, clerks, and accountants, throw me behind bars. You can do all of this. So?"

"So?"

"What are you going to do?"

"I wouldn't do that."

"No?"

Ateer shook his head solemnly once more.

"My boys do not trust you. I can tell. They fear revealing themselves to you, and they have reason to be reluctant. Because you are being," he stopped, searching for the right word, "womanlike."

"Oh, I am?"

"No use denying it. Just like Ariel, she can deny what she is too, all night long, but would you believe her?"

"No."

"In this way, I don't believe you. But I want you to know, Mac, that they are good men. Very good men. They're like sons to me, and I watched them grow and they have never lied, hurt, cheated a man in their lives. They are deeply flawed individuals. They are human, just like you. But they also have a very sick love affair with The Beast."

"The beast?"

"The *beast*," Scooty smiled, "they assure that The Beast will change you, completely. Life will be completely different when it does. And your flaws and cracks and shames will come out, and then when you become weak and broken, how will you fix yourself?"

"I don't understand."

"I know you don't, because you haven't finished the path you are on," he reached up and rested a gentle hand on Ateer's shoulder. "Do me a service. Watch out for my boys. When you see their weaknesses, don't be a judge. Only God can judge."

He released Ateer's arm and shook his hands at the heavens. "Because boychick, your greatest fear, that of your own mortality, will look you in the eye. And when you crack, when your flaws are evident, the last thing you'll want is to have someone judge you."

Ateer looked at him, trying to understand his meaning, but finding him entirely cryptic. However, he could not shake the feeling that the old man could see right through him. Could he discern that he was a plant, a fraud, a snitch? And by some miracle Ateer knew Scooty excused him. Even when he accused him of lying, he brought him out of the office so that Accorso and Pedrotti could not learn of his determination of him. The old man was a gatekeeper, and he gave Ateer a pass.

He was in.

Scooty patted Ateer on the chest. "You stay here and let me get my boys out of here. I don't want you to walk in there and see what they are probably doing to Ariel and Alexa. New eyes should not behold the light so bright."

He walked to the door and one of his guards opened it for him.

He could report to Orlowski that he was one of Pyke's best men now.

Maybe he could have actionable information for Valentine.

Maybe.

FIVE
CHOCK FULL OF NITRO

"It has been said that idleness is the parent of mischief, which is very true, but mischief itself is merely an attempt to escape from the dreary vacuum of idleness."

GEORGE BORROW

The two men that walked out of the heavy door to Scooty's office had cherry red cheeks, necks, and foreheads. They didn't say anything about what had happened in the ten minutes it took for the old Jewish manager to go in and for them to come out. While he waited outside, Ateer wandered around the gambling floor, listening to the loudspeakers, watching the gamblers either fold wads of cash into their pockets or drop the little sheets of paper, their markers, on the floor and grind them underfoot.

Ateer and Pedrotti wished their ex-trainers the best and goodbye.

SUSPICIOUS LOOKING PACKAGES

They returned to the car and drove back into the city. Pedrotti had to do some clothes shopping and wanted to go to the shops below *the line*, known as 14th street. Accorso let him off on Bleecker Street, then headed to Brooklyn where he dropped Ateer off in front of his door on York Street.

Ateer went to the corner shop to buy a newspaper before going home and reclined across his couch to read it. His mode of information was normally the radio, but Ateer noticed that Accorso and Pedrotti lived on the newspaper. He learned that record breaking Lou Gehrig, the 'Iron Horse' of baseball died. He was 37. He heard many a Yankees game on the radio, but he wasn't a true fan. He never memorized line ups; he didn't collect cards. However, he still felt a sense of sincere loss over the fact that such a special man had died so young, of a very rare disease that had forced him to retire two years ago. A disease reached up and took him...but slowly. Drained him. He faced death and it dragged him off the earth.

Ateer had watched Pyke, Accorso, and even Mayor La Guardia face instant death. And for some reason, death by the beast didn't seem too scary. Death by slow demise seemed more horrible. It gave you time to reconcile your life that instant death did not. It gave you long nights of worry, painful days of contemplation. Instant death provided one with a flick of a switch and then non-existence.

No...that wasn't right. He had his eyes closed. His thoughts went back to the full details of the earlier events. He put himself in the place of La Guardia, walking towards certain death. A barrel with enough explosives to turn him into clods of jelly raining down on the people behind the police line.

And then it struck Ateer. No, the instant death was worse, much, much worse. Because, where a slow disease already announced that it would claim your life; you were allowed to live, you were supposed to live when you faced a bomb. You survived because you stopped moving towards it. And unlike a slow death, your life was compressed as you walked nearer and nearer to the device. Every step was like a month to someone dying a slow death. And for someone dying of life in general, waiting for old age to claim them, every step was like ten years. Life was compressed as if under the weight of great water, crushed in a state of panic that had to be swam up from, overcome, suffered through before the lungs gave out, or rather the nerve. You had to function under tremendous pressure, crushing pressure, and if you failed, the end came savagely and completely. It was called *terror*.

He saw the aftermath of it on La Guardia's face when he returned, jubilant, from the barrel. It was a mask that covered over a white-hot fear, his face glistening with sweat, his skin blanched, his eyes red, even though he put on a brave face, a broad grin, waving at the crowds behind the police line some distance away, who could not see the small dichotomies of his face that revealed his brush with death. Ateer was certain that La Guardia would never, ever do that shit again.

The thought of compressed life, concentrated into seconds of white-hot fear, it's squeezing generating the heat, enervated him. He stood, looked out the window, the sun was setting. The first 'trick' was almost over. He wondered what the second trick looked like, sounded like, who was there for it?

He showered, changed his suit, put on his hat and coat, and walked out of the apartment, taking the F train into Manhattan and to the precinct. He climbed up the stairs to the bullpen and found the desks forlorn and empty and frightfully silent. The ceiling lights were off, and he realized that the slanting light of the moon, which threw a silvery cast across the deep dark shadows of corners, walls, desks and chairs was not enough to do anything at his desk. He walked around the bullpen carefully so as not to trip over something hidden in a dark shadow and found an accountant's desk lamp on one of the desks on the farthest end of the bullpen. He unplugged it and carried it over to his desk, crawling under it and plugging it there in the raised sockets on the floor. Afterward he hung up his overcoat and hat and finally took a seat. He opened his drawer and pulled out papers, filling out his report forms of what he had experienced with the Pennsylvania station bomb. Not much, but it would go into the file generated by his superior with his report and many others, giving a clear picture of what happened that day that someone on a faraway date might need to read.

"What the fuck?"

The voice came from behind Ateer, startling him. He whipped about in his chair and found Accorso, a paper bag in one hand, his overcoat and hat in the hand and over the forearm of the other. "What the fuck are you doing here this hour of the night?"

"I wanted to see what the night trick was like."

Accorso hung up his coat and hat and took his seat across from him, looking at the lamp. "Where'd you get that from?"

Ateer pointed across the bullpen, "Over there."

Opening his bag, Accorso pulled out a sandwich.

"That's dinner?" Ateer asked.

"Yeah, my wife was being a real cunt tonight, so I walked out of the house."

"You guys had an argument?"

"Argument? I wish. She's an iceberg. Bitch is so cold that I have to wear my overcoat, hat, and scarf just to climb into bed next to her."

"Sorry to hear that."

Accorso bit into his sandwich.

"So," Ateer looked about, "where is everyone?"

While chewing, Accorso replied, "Probably out on calls. The night trick isn't like the day. If they go out on a call they usually don't come back to the precinct, but instead do whatever the fuck they want to do." Now, with the back of his hand against the side of his mouth, he whispered: "Some even have night jobs that if there's a slow night they're gone. But they do good work when called upon, so Pyke turns the other way."

Looking at him, Ateer's pencil hovering just above his paperwork. "So you just come here and spend the night?"

"Something like that."

"Do you do any work?"

"I do better than work."

"What's that?"

"Let me finish my sandwich, and I'll show you."

He had to admit, his interest was sorely piqued, but Ateer returned to his report, his pencil scratching on paper the only sound heard. After some time there came the sound of crunching paper as Accorso crumpled up his bag and wrapper and tossed them both into the trash can next to the desks. "Let's go," he said. "Get your coat."

Ateer dropped his paperwork into his drawer, snatched his coat and hat, and followed Accorso out of the precinct, taking the back exit into the motor pool, which was abuzz with patrolmen and detectives. Accorso led Ateer down the length of the lot to the mechanic's garage at the end where men worked on keeping the vehicles in good repair. A very long workbench was affixed to the garage wall with tools nicely laid out on it. All the way at the back half of the area were shelves and boxes, neatly stacked...and then there were the other things.

The other things.

Accorso walked past the workbenches to the very back of the garage. Ateer scanned the shelves where there were boxes, suitcases, briefcases, bags from cloth to paper, pipes and then the obvious things, mortar shells and hand grenades. Ateer had an idea where they were standing.

"These look like...bombs?"

"Yeah."

"Mockups?"

Accorso reached into his jacket and pulled out a pack of cigarettes. "Some are." He shook out a cigarette and stuck it between his lips, shook out another and offered it to Ateer. He looked at it, ready to decline, but there was something in him that not only wanted to prove to Accorso that he was 'Bomb Squad,' that he was one of them, but that he wanted to be like Accorso, the man himself, who himself was in the image of Lieutenant Pyke. He pinched out the cigarette and Accorso lit it for him.

"Some are," Accorso finally said. "Some are for training."

"Yeah?"

"Yeah. Inside they have all the component parts. Some were either reported from other police departments from around the country, or from what has been encountered right here in New York. And some are even the hobby of psychopaths in the precinct, such as Hayias and Beakey."

"Hobby?"

Accorso pulled out a green, leather suitcase and carried it over to the center of the workbench. "They like to build bombs. The scary thing is that they can build them better than the fucked-up bombers. If either of them was to go off the tracks, there will be a lot of dead Bomb Squads in their wake."

"Sounds like a morbid hobby." Ateer looked back to the shelves, "So how do I train on this thing?"

"See that light right there, in the right corner?"

Ateer returned to the suitcase. There was indeed a small circular opening covered with a red cell. "Yeah."

"That's the top of a red bulb. Inside this suitcase are all the component parts of a bomb that we've encountered in the years of doing this job. The only thing that is missing is explosives. Estimate it to be about ten sticks of dynamite, enough to level this garage and kill or maim anyone standing outside. If you complete the circuit, that red light will go off. That means you're flying through heaven past Jesus so fast that he'll say, 'what the fuck was that?'"

"So you want me to open it?"

"That's right," Accorso landed a heavy slap to his back, "and you can't leave until you do. But don't worry about that shit because it's the easiest training model that we have."

Ateer examined the suitcase with three clasps along the brass rimmed mouth of the opening, a leather handle, black leather trim, brass corners all riveted to the case. "What if the light goes off?"

"Stop what you are doing, back up, and it should reset. If not, you're dead and you can go home. Don't come back in. I don't wanna see you until the morning." He dropped his cigarette, crushed it with his toe and walked off, back to the precinct.

With his own cigarette hanging from the side of his mouth, the tendrils of smoke from it smarted his right eye, making him squint. Ateer looked at the sides of the rectangular suitcase. On its sides were more riveted leather handles. Without touching it he leaned on the workbench, looking around to the back of the suitcase. There it had three brass hinges riveted to the brass rimmed mouth of the case.

Accorso moved it off the workbench without care of closing the circuit, since Ateer knew it wasn't motion sensitive, by the way Accorso brought it down from the shelf. He took it off the workbench and set it down on the floor at his feet. He flicked his cigarette away and stared down at the clasps. He was absolutely certain if he went that way, it would turn on the light. He walked around the suitcase but could see no vulnerability. He lifted it, gingerly rested it back on the workbench, turning its end towards himself. The three hinges.

He went over to the tools on the bench and found a narrow, sharp pointed mechanical punch and hammer. He placed one side of the case against the vise anchored to the edge of the workbench to keep it from sliding from the blow, placed the point of the punch against the hinge pin and struck it with a hammer, pushing out the pin on the other side. He did the same with the two others. Then, with a pair of pliers he pulled the protruding ends of the pins out from the hinge barrels. He returned the tools and revisited the suitcase with a sense of pride. Lifting the top half of the case ever so slightly he peeped into the crack that he had made between the two case halves and before any light could get in from the roof lamps the red light on the case came on. He quickly closed the case; the light went out. So, what. He was dead. But then, if he put the hinge pins back in, and the light stayed off, Accorso would be none the wiser.

He softly hammered back in the tiny pins and smiled at his handiwork. Good as new. Now he flipped up the two outside clasps and flipped down the center one but did not open the suitcase. He glanced up at the light on the side and found it still off. And then he realized what was wrong. He was being tricked. Ateer walked the length of the workbench, scanning the tools, searching for the case that contained the Fluoroscope but did not see it. He went to the back of the garage, going through the shelves, finding nothing but mock-ups. He laughed to himself. No wonder this was the easiest bomb to open. He needed the proper equipment to defuse it which was why Accorso had told him not to come in and bother him. The joke was to have him either stay out here all night, or to go home feeling the loser. Funny, very funny.

Now knowing the deception, Ateer walked to the precinct and upstairs to the bullpen, finding Accorso sitting behind his desk, the desk lamp turned his way for his use. Upon hearing Ateer's noisy approach he looked up from his paperwork and smiled. "How many times did you die?"

Ateer took off his coat and hat and sat down, "Once, before I learned the trick."

"What trick?"

"I needed a fluoroscope to take the next step to opening the bomb."

Accorso chuckled, pointed at him. "That's your first problem. You don't have any clue what the fuck you are doing. Remember that."

"How am I supposed to know what the fuck I'm doing? All I've been doing is going through tons of file folders, drinking moonshine, and riding around in cars watching you and Pyke work on bombs," Ateer replied in a disgruntled tone.

"Let me help you here, because I tripped you up several times with this training exercise. First, we don't *open* bombs. No one *opens* bombs around here. We make them *safe*. When we say that the bomb is *safe*, that means that the immediate threat is over. Then we take the device somewhere for a controlled detonation of the explosive if need be. So, by trying to open the case, you were already on the wrong footing."

"So, it was a bigger trick than I thought."

"It was worse than that. You tried to get into the briefcase from the back, through the hinges, didn't you?"

"I thought that would be the smartest way."

"That's because you think you are thinking like Bomb Squad and not like a bomb maker. That particular training suitcase is only wired to explode at the hinges. If you had opened it up directly you would have gotten in. It's a mind trick. That's a bomb maker that is trying to think like you, so they wire it the way that is not so obvious because Bomb Squad would not take the obvious path."

"Funny." Ateer smirked. "So how would you have handled it without a fluoroscope?"

"I would have dropped the fucker in motor oil."

"So that's the all-purpose solution, motor oil?"

"No. There is no guarantee that you'll disable the bomb and make it safe. You might gum up the clock, you might gum up any moving parts, but if it's all soldered connections and a waterproof timer, you're still in danger. But most of the time the bomb will become inert. It's the one time that it doesn't that should concern you."

"I see."

Accorso stood. "But that was your first training exercise. Why don't we take a break and head downtown."

"Where?"

"Below The Line."

"The line?"

"14th street. It's the demarcation. It's like the head of the cock. It the line that separates the fucked up and raggedy streets from the neat streets and avenues in nice little rows and columns. So, it's called 'The Line.'"

"I got it."

"So? You going home to jerk off, or we get a squad car and head below the line."

Ateer smiled feeling a sense of true excitement. He didn't care that it was late, he didn't care that they had their trick early in the morning. He was throwing caution into the wind. He was being like Accorso.

"Sure, let's go." Ateer jumped up and went for his coat and hat.

The bar was on the East side, not far from Tompkins Square Park. The neighborhood was a quiet one of brownstones and stores and cafes, bars and liquor stores. Ateer was under the strange impression that they were heading to either Whack-ass Willie's or a poetry club. Accorso moved like a shark in the dark, weaving through the pedestrians on the sidewalk, past dandies in their winter coats, ascots and sharp fedoras, women in their short, knee-high woolen skirts and blazers. Their hats as different from others, like flowers in the woods.

They went a cocktail lounge. A set of descending stairs led down into the basement of a brownstone. At the bottom landing was a brass plaque with black, recessed script lettering that read, PLEASE KNOCK. PLEASE WAIT. DON'T BE DRUNK AND STAND UP STRAIGHT.

Accorso rapped on the door with his knuckles and waited. Ateer looked up the flight of stairs to the streets and had an angle where he could see quite a bit up women's dresses that made the error of passing too close to the top landing. The door opened and a tuxedoed gentleman with a handlebar moustache invited them in. After closing the door behind them he moved almost as if gliding across the floor through an area filled with couches, small, short tables with a candle lit in the center. The space was murky and somber, a funeral in a coal mine. People spoke in low tones, their faces glowing either in the candlelight of the table or the dim glowing brass fixtures on the patterned wall. They ordered their drinks and a waitress in a short, skirted uniform left their low coffee table at their knees.

"Nice place," Ateer said, "what is it called?"

"I don't know." Accorso looked around, "I just call it: Please Knock."

"I like it."

"What's there not to like? It's dark, the waitresses are pretty, the drinks are strong."

"You and Pedrotti come here often?"

"I've never brought Beat It here."

Ateer thought about that. Accorso sat in the corner away from him, arms across the back and armrest and crossed his legs. "So, what do you think about the bomb squad so far?"

"I haven't experienced anything. I want to know what the beast is."

"You'll learn soon enough. Trust me."

Ateer turned his body to him. "Why did you take me to see Scooty?"

"Beat It thought we had to. He's cautious like that."

"He doesn't seem that way."

"There's a lot of things about Beat It that you don't know."

They stopped to watch the waitress bend low and leave behind their drinks on the low coffee table.

"There's a lot I don't know. I'm a tad bit confused."

"About what?" Accorso bent over and took up his drink.

"Scooty is a criminal. His trade is vice. The place is illegal, which brings you into collusion."

Accorso hunched his shoulders. "You're going to turn us all into Public Morals?"

"Maybe your supervisor."

"Pyke? Good luck."

"Well maybe *his* supervisor."

"To Durtayne? You sure you want to do that? I mean, jump the chain of command like that. Do you think that's career healthy?"

Ateer meant *well* over Pyke's command, but to utter it would give him away and he'd lose any advantage in being exposed to more of their 'operation.' Not that he was about to do anything about anything. He thought just by making mention of corruption, Accorso would spill about more, or at least his feeling about engaging in it. But he stayed as cool as a block of ice, not even sweating.

"Mackie, Beat It is doubtful about you. He thinks we should move slow," he laughed, "Shit, any slower and we'd be riding turtles."

"Slow about what?"

"Beat It and I are not your average, run of the mill, Bomb Squad detectives. We do our thing because we do our thing. When shit gets thick in one way or another, they're not gonna call Beakey. They are definitely not going to call Dempsey. They're gonna call me, which means you and that means you have the unenviable position of growing hair on your balls faster than normal. I didn't want you in my unit. I was told you were coming; I was handed your file, and I was told to shut up and swallow it. And I did. You're on our team, just like Big O was put on our team. So that means that you'll have to deal with us."

"And Big O."

Accorso smirked, "Oh yeah, Big O."

"Why do you call him Big O?"

"Because he's a Big Ol' Shit!"

Ateer looked down to keep from smiling. "What do you mean that I have to *deal* with you? Do you mean you two dealing with people like Scooty?"

"Exactly."

That's why he was here. "I can do that."

"You didn't sound that way a second ago. You were sounding like you were about to shit all over us."

"Yeah, I was just feeding you a line. I just wanted to know why you took me to see Scooty."

"Well, meeting him wasn't the only reason."

"What?"

"We wanted him to meet you. Scooty has a way of cutting through the bullshit. He'll look into you like a flashlight up your asshole. And that's what he did. Like anyone, if you look far enough up their asshole you're bound to find some shit."

Laughing nervously Ateer finished his drink and placed it on the table, "What did he find?"

"That you're lying and keeping something from us."

"And you believe him?"

"Implicitly."

"So, what's next then?"

"He also said that there was nothing conventional about you. The pressure will heat up, you'll realize where you stand, and you'll spin like a," he snapped his fingers, "top!" He held up his hand and the waitress sauntered over to take orders.

"So, I'll turn into you?"

Accorso reached into his jacket, pulled out a pack of cigarettes. He shook one out and offered it to Ateer. He snapped it up. After lighting his, Accorso tossed the book of matches to Ateer. "Yeah. Like Saul riding to Damascus."

"Conversion, huh?"

"There'll be a white light, voices from heaven, you'll shit your pants...all that shit. And then you'll have a glow about you, and you'll be a new man."

"Because of the Beast."

"Something like that."

The waitress returned.

"Mackie."

"What?"

"Public Morals is as corrupt as a whore when the sailors arrive. Why are you faking like you're so clean?"

"I'm not faking. I'm clean."

"You scrub down with a bar of shit and come out smelling like a rose?"

"There's no shit in Public Morals."

"They didn't trust you either."

Ateer stared at Accorso, stunned. He didn't know what to say. The slope was slippery and Accorso was pushing him towards some form of confession. He didn't know how to get out of it. He had to derail the train.

"What were you doing alone with Scooty's whores?" Ateer asked.

"If they didn't trust you, that means either you walked around with a stick up your ass preaching to them that God is good, or they thought you were a spy."

"A spy?"

"Yeah, a plant. Like we do."

"You don't know Public Morals. It's not corrupt."

"Okay, let's say that is so, then you are here from Public Morals, searching for vice, and you were transferred here to do the same."

"I asked to be transferred to this squad."

"That's possible. Or was the vice starting to draw you. I mean, a cop has tremendous power over criminals, believe it or not. Positively gravitational."

"I never abused my authority."

Accorso hunched his shoulders and tossed his cigarette butt into his empty glass of melting ice. They fell silent.

"I'm a whoremonger," Accorso finally said to him.

Ateer looked at him, somewhat shocked. Their father figure was a pimp, so it was no real revelation. However, he had no reply. He stayed silent.

"I've been sleeping with whores for about ten years now." Producing a Benzedrine inhaler, he screwed off its false body and pressed its domed end against a nostril and inhaled deeply.

"Your wife doesn't know."

"No. And she shouldn't. She's a good woman. It's just that I have my issues."

"Is this from meeting the beast?"

Accorso's eyes glazed, his eyes unfocused and then focused. He sat forward, his shiny eyes boring into Ateer's. "Let me give you an honest truth. And it's so ground shaking that it should change your life completely. But it won't. You'll admit to its force but prove weak to its power. You'll do nothing. You'll just live your life like you did yesterday, like you'll do tomorrow."

Falling silent, Accorso rested back into the couch corner.

"So...what is this revelation?"

He smiled, his face changing ten years younger. Accorso, was indeed handsome, smooth, lean features. His hair oiled but not obviously so. "You're gonna die."

"I know that."

"No...you're *gonna* die."

Taking a breath, Atter said, "I *know* that."

"And you ain't gonna do shit about it. You're not gonna tell that skirt that you like that you think she should be with you. You're not gonna demand a pay raise. You're not gonna quit this job and do whatever it is that you dream of doing. You're gonna ignore that fact, and do you know why?"

"Why?"

"Because you see it in the future. You see it when you're an old man, gray haired, dried up and liver spotted hands. Your fucking back bent, and your cock doesn't get hard anymore. You see it as so far in the future that you can ignore the fact."

"Maybe."

"Who cares if you agree with me or not. But there's a quickly approaching day where you'll realize that your life could be over in an instant. Tomorrow. At 10:00 a.m. Sure as shit. When that happens, that'll be your fucking light from Heaven. It'll scare so much fear and white-hot terror into you that you'll hear horses talking and dogs reading to you. Trust me."

Ateer, once again, was speechless. Then: "You think so?"

"I won't bring it up again."

Accorso raised his hand and ordered another round. "How old are you?" He said to the waitress.

"Sixteen," she replied.

"Why are your tits so big for a sixteen-year-old?"

The waitress looked down at her low-cut blouse. "They just grew like that."

"Kiss your parents for me."

Both blushing and confused she backed away and then walked off into the gloom.

"What happened with Deidre and the garbage?"

Accorso chuckled. "You really want to know?"

"Yeah."

"We found her sprawled in a nook in the alley, nothing sticking out but her legs. We asked her if she was alright. The girl didn't even know what her name was. That's just a reminder for you, you can't fuck with moonshine."

"You took her home?"

"Hell no. We chucked her ass on top of a pile of boxes and fucked the shit out of her."

"And then you took her home."

"We left her there."

"Isn't that kinda...rough?"

"Why? She's a flooze. You don't take them home. You don't pay for their rent or bills. You fuck 'em and wait until the chance comes around to fuck 'em again."

"Sounds kinda heartless, Fab. I didn't know you had that in you."

"You'll find out, Mackie, that I act on every impulse, and I regret nothing."

The waitress came back, swapping glassware.

"What's your name?" Accorso asked.

"Janene," she replied.

"Give us another round, buy one for yourself, and tell your boss you're about to get a good tip and sit here," he slid over from the center of the couch and patted it with his hand.

Janene looked at the two of them uncomfortably, then walked off.

Ateer turned to him. "What are you doing?"

"I'm gonna screw her in the backseat of the car if I can."

"I thought you only had sex with whores?"

"It's been a lifelong difficulty of mine figuring out which women are, and which women aren't. I go for them all, like a fisherman, and if the hook bites..." His voice trailed off into a sly grin.

Ateer was certain that Accorso was going to have her in the back seat of the squad car with his looks. What was he going to do while he rutted in the backseats, head home on the train? Maybe he should.

"I don't think I'll ever be like you, Fab," Ateer said flatly. He reached out for his glass and drained it. "I'm not like you. My mother made sure of that."

Accorso smiled so broadly that the edges of his mouth crept to his earlobes. "Your mother?"

"Yes. My mother was a strong woman."

"Your mother was a saint, huh?"

"Yes."

"And she made you from immaculate conception?"

"I had a father too."

"Saints don't have sex. And you have no guarantee that your father was your father. You know the old saying: 'Mother's baby, father's maybe.'"

"So, you think your mother was an adulteress?"

Janene returned, set down three drinks from her tray, eased her way past Accorso's knees and sat down between them with a warm smile.

Accorso leaned across her to face Ateer. "My mother was a woman…I wouldn't put it past her."

Ateer plopped into his seat behind his desk and stared at its top. He was slightly hungover and thought that a cup of coffee might swing him around, make him more alert. A shadow fell across his desk. He turned and looked up at detective Malcolm Carter towering over him, suit, tie, and his green accountant's lamp in his hand. He waved it before Ateer as if he was about to haul back and strike him with it. "I found this on your desk this morning," he said.

Acting absentmindedly, Ateer sighed, "Hey, I was here late last night, and I took it so that I could work, and I guess I just left without returning it. I'm very sorry."

"I stayed here past my trick to talk to you, or Accorso, whichever one of you took it," Carter breathed in, breathed out, calming himself. "Look, Ateer, I don't mind—I really don't—if you use it. Just return it, alright?"

"Sure, yeah. I'll do that."

"Alright, good. Thanks." Carter walked off, heading to his desk far away. Ateer stood and went to the break room where he poured himself a cup of coffee. Upon returning he found Accorso going through his drawers before sitting down. "How're you feeling?" he asked as Ateer took his seat across from him.

"I'm alright."

Accorso nodded, opened his paper, and buried his face behind it.

Ateer thought about the night, with Janene sitting between them. She allowed Accorso to paw all over her while she inhaled alcohol on his dime. And when the offer floated to her, she demurely declined and went back to work. Accorso hunched his shoulders, finished his drink, and drove Ateer home.

Ateer looked at the headline on the paper in front of him: "Nazis Say Russia Gave Them Pledge To Spare Rumania." Russia and Germany were harassing Rumania like two dogs fighting over a shoe. Now Russia promised a sign a non-aggression agreement with Rumania which would serve as a buffer between the two nations. That part of the world seemed to be on fire.

Movement in the corner of his right eye caught his attention. Just behind him was a uniformed officer leading a man in a suit without tie, hat held against his chest, light overcoat over his shoulders. The officer knocked against the opened door of Pyke's office and peeked in. "I've got someone here."

"I'll be right there."

The officer stepped away from the door. Pyke walked out. Accorso folded down his paper and stared at the three men in front of the office.

The officer said, "This guy wants to talk to you about something."

"What?" Pyke asked.

The officer turned to the man. Tall, lean, clean shaven and well groomed. "Sir," he began, "my name is Theodore Peterson. I'm an unemployed cook, and I lost a suitcase the other day in Penn Station. I was returning to the city from Greenport and set my bag down as I was asking a clerk at the information desk a question, and when I turned around, it was gone."

"That was your suitcase?" Pyke asked. "With the clock in it?"

"I'm very sorry, sir, if it caused any problems. I was looking in the newspaper yesterday and the article described my lost luggage to a 'T'. I had lost my job as a cook in Greenport, and I was here going on a job interview and was late. If I wasn't so late, I'd went looking for it, but I had to go."

The issues of the cook washed over Lieutenant Pyke with little effect. "That's alright. No harm done. That's what we do."

With that, the officer patted Peterson on the back and attempted to steer him around, away from Pyke, but he stepped away, still addressing the Lieutenant. "Look, sir. I was wondering if I could get my suitcase back. I'm staying at the Mills hotel for a few days, and I can use the stuff in it."

"Really, now?" Pyke asked.

"Yes, sir."

"Well, go with the officer here and he'll give you directions to the Office of the NYPD property clerk and you can find your luggage there."

"Thank you, sir," he extended a hand and Pyke shook it once.

"Have a good day, sir," he said to the relieved cook.

"You too."

The officer led Peterson off, back to the stairwell down to the front desk.

The phone rang. Accorso snatched it up. He pushed his paper aside, pulled his pad in front of him and began scribbling then hung up the phone. Beakey and Dempsey stood from their desks in anticipation. Pyke turned to regard Accorso drawing closer to his desk.

"Bomb found near Tompkins Park. We can handle it." Accorso tore the sheet off the pad.

SUSPICIOUS LOOKING PACKAGES

. . .

The bullpen was empty, the phones quiet. Far off, at the far-left corner of the corral sat Frascone, elbows on his desk, head held down reading a Pep Comics. Pedrotti was leaning back in his chair, legs extended under his desk, crossed at the ankles. He held up Accorso's newspaper in front of his face, reading silently. Accorso himself smoked a cigarette and lifted a cup of coffee from his desk to take a sip.

Ateer was typing up his report to go into the file, using his two forefingers to strike at the keys. Not having any real typing skills at all, he had become swift at pigeon pecking the keys, faster than one could pick up seeds.

Accorso cleared his throat. "What are you doing tomorrow night?"

"What?" Ateer took his attention away from the keyboard to look at him. "What's that?"

"My wife wants to cook a big dinner for you tomorrow, so that you can get to know the family."

"Your wife?"

"Yeah, this is what she does. She has to put her big bazoo in everybody's business. She wants to meet you, pick you apart, examine the remains then toss you to the side. She's a soul sucking vampire like that."

"You make it sound unsafe to go."

Accorso chuckled at the remark. "I'll make it safe," he paused. "That's what I do."

Ateer turned from his typewriter on his right, against the balustrade then back to face him. "Sure, why not?" Opening his top drawer, he took out his pack of cigarettes and lit one. "Do I have to bring anything?"

"Bring whatever you want."

"Around what time."

"Six."

Ateer filled his lungs with smoke and then breathed a long gale of smoke down, between his legs, under his desk. "Fab, I've got a question."

"About the dinner?"

"No, uh, I've heard you mention a couple of times to Pedrotti about rolling something. Is that something technical that must be done before going on a call?"

"Yeah," Accorso crushed his cigarette out into his ashtray, then leaned forward, his voice lowering to a whisper. "Beat It is very superstitious about starting his day. He has two ruby dice that his father gave him when he was a kid. And he rolls them every morning. If he rolls 'snake eyes' he lays low on calls. If not, he believes he has his father's protection."

"You believe that too?"

"Fuck no. But if he needs it to get through the day, it's alright with me. Shit. I take a swig of Goat Whiskey every morning before stepping out myself."

"I've never seen you taking a swig."

He held up his cup. "A dash'll do."

Heavy laughter yuk-yuk-ed out of Pyke's office. The voices of both the Lieutenant and Hayias boomed from inside.

"What do you think that's about?" Ateer asked.

"Shoe sizes? Hat sizes?"

The phone rang. Accorso snatched it up.

Ateer turned to his typewriter, banging away once more until, after scribbling on his pad, Accorso stood, drained his coffee cup. "Let's go."

Pedrotti and Frascone were already looking in his direction. "First unit, let's roll!"

338 Madison Avenue, near 42nd street, was prime location, the bustling theaters not far away, businesses packed tightly around it, disgorging hundreds upon thousands of tired, stressed out and impa-

tient men and women from cramped offices, and the river that flowed from the buildings rushed by, throwing patrons like spray into the doors of the Chock-Full-O-Nuts restaurant. The press of the lunchtime crowds had begun to thin, still, the laminate counter that ran the entire length of the store was packed with men and women enjoying freshly brewed coffee and sandwiches, one being the town favorite, the 'nutted cheese sandwich,' which was cream cheese on dark raisin bread with chopped nuts inside. Every bolted stool had a happy, paying customer, others were lined up at the cashier, getting cups to go. The rest were at the tables that lined the large windows, watching the stormy flow of suits, ties, dresses, and hats move back and forth in great waves. Women pointed at stylish dresses; men pointed at beautiful figures.

This was shaping up to be another beautiful day. The sun was out, the temperature for this time of the year right on the mark, warming into spring, the cold of the winter finally giving way. But there was still the chill, and who didn't love a warm cup of coffee in their hands when standing against that.

William Brennan, the manager of the restaurant leaned against the threshold of the swinging door that led to the kitchen in the back and stared upon the smiling, mostly happy faces. At best guess, more tourists than natives of the city. Mirrors lined the wall on the other side of the counter, behind his hostesses made busy as bees pouring refills of the black stimulant, wiped down vacated sections, or hustled past him carrying plates of sandwiches. All this was evidence of how busy they were.

Brennan walked down the length of the counter, looking at faces, measuring ages, sex, attractiveness. People interested him. He was always where he needed to be, which meant to his slow, sloppy, negligent workers, places where he didn't belong.

He checked the service counter behind his hostesses where coffee brewed, and round urns of glass were kept warm. He checked the donuts. He checked the sugar dispensers, he knelt low to the shelves under the serving counter, checking the clean plates, cups, napkins, and a large brown medicine bottle that sat innocently on the shelf. It was labeled but the words were turned mostly away from him. He picked it up, standing and turning the label, which moved like tickertape around the waist of the bottle, a letter at a time coming into view. It read: Nitroglycerin. Danger.

At first the words were meaningless to Brennan. What would nitroglycerin be doing on a shelf in his restaurant? He didn't put it there. It was then that his imagination helped him to put the pieces together. It was no doubt planted in the hopes of it being knocked off the shelf and exploding. There was a lot in the large bottle. The explosion would have been fantastic, sending millions of shards of glass from the mirrors to the windows flying in all directions, causing heavy casualties.

Brennan never saw nitroglycerin in action, but he was keenly aware that any jarring, shaking, or dropping of the bottle would spell trouble, big trouble. He gingerly rested the bottle on top of the service counter and then started, carefully and calmly, going from section to section at the patron counter and informing the customer that they had to close the store. Coffee and the meal were on him. As he emptied the counter, his assistant manager, Marvin Kelp, walked over to him.

"Is anything the matter?" Kelp asked.

"I want you to go to the tables and tell them..." he suddenly stopped to catch the arm of a hostess rushing past, heading in the direction of the bottle. He held her fast, addressing her. "Tell the girls that they're off for the day with pay. Tell them all to go home."

"Really?" She beamed.

"Yes, please." He pulled her back, and with a hand against her spine directed her in the other direction. Then to Kelp he said, "Tell the tables that we are closing early and that their drinks and food are on the house."

"But why are we—" Kelp, just a freckled faced teenager, began to ask but halted as Brennan held up a finger to silence him.

"Marvin, just get it done, and then meet me out in the front of the building. Get all of your things before you do."

Concerned, but not yet afraid, Kelp nodded and went off to perform his task.

Brennan walked through the threshold to the kitchen and through it to his office, telling the kitchen workers that they were off for the rest of the day in his transit. He shut the door to his office behind him and sat down at his desk, pulling his phone closer to him. He dialed for the police.

The Bomb Squad had rolled out. Accorso, usually driving a black Plymouth squad car and worked his way through the traffic downtown with Pedrotti and Ateer in the vehicle with him. Behind him, struggling against the torpid flow of traffic was Lieutenant Pyke and Hayias in the same type of vehicle, and in the van at the rear was Frascone.

The reason for the heavy building traffic was that vehicles were being diverted from Madison Avenue at 42nd Street, having them head no further north but instead causing traffic to move either to the east or west on 42nd Street. Accorso drove his vehicle up to the traffic officer swinging his arms around and blowing into a sharp sounding whistle managing the confusion of vehicles around him. Accorso beeped his horn. The traffic officer came around the front of his car and leaned down to look through the driver's side window.

"Bomb Squad?" he asked without Accorso opening his mouth. Instead, he flashed his badge.

"Follow me." The officer walked off, Accorso keeping up with him. They crossed 42nd street to its northern mouth where two green and white RMPs were parked across. The traffic officer whistled sharply three times at the two cars. The one on the right started its engine and pulled up, making space for Accorso to continue up Madison with Pyke and Frascone behind him.

Here, the sidewalks, the streets, the stores were all deserted. It was as if the city was struck empty of people, leaving proud pigeons strutting on the sidewalks, zipping, and flying off. They continued, driving through 43rd street, where more RMPs had blocked off the eastern and western mouths of the intersection a block away in both directions.

Then came the tangle of official vehicles that Accorso was in search for. RMPs and squad cars, vans and other support vehicles parked about, inside intersections, about the streets. Accorso weaved around the haphazardly parked cars searching building numbers until they came upon the black and white checkerboard building with the large windows. Accorso stopped in the middle of the street and climbed out and turned back to take his direction from Lieutenant Pyke, who was already on the move. He walked across the street, heading for the center of the intersection where three cars, parked grill to grill giving the appearance of an asterisk were parked. Standing between two of the parked cars was the nerve center of the operation. The highest-ranking officials present were barking orders to redirect traffic, clear out the first floors of stores and restaurants in the area, keeping he sidewalks empty.

Pyke plunged in, catching the attention of the men of the nerve center. "Where is it?" He asked.

A uniformed officer with the twin bars of a captain on the collars of his white shirt walked up to Pyke with his single bar. He extended his hand, "Captain Frank Riley, Midtown Squad."

"Lieutenant James Pike, Bomb Squad." They shook hands.

"What do we have, sir?"

Riley, a more mature man than Pyke, with graying hair and a paunch over his belt turned and walked towards the restaurant that occupied the corner of the block. He had an obvious wobble in his gait that he tried to hide by walking like a cowboy from a long ride. He spoke over his shoulder to Pyke. "Manager of the restaurant here said that he found a bottle of nitroglycerin on a shelf of his service counter. He put it there, on top of the counter in the back."

They stopped at the revolving doors. Pyke looked in, scanning the

SUSPICIOUS LOOKING PACKAGES

area. The shiny aluminum front with black, polished marble on top of that, the words Chock Full o' Nuts splashed across the front and wrapped around the top of the revolving doors. He turned around, looked at his patrol cars in the distance, stuck thumb and forefinger into his mouth and whistled loudly.

Across the distance, Accorso knew his call. He turned to his unit, "Beat it, Mac. With me, Big O. Get ready to do your magic."

Accorso, Pedrotti, and Ateer joined Pyke and Riley at the front doors.

"Get to your men," Pyke told Riley, "stand behind your cars and duck low...well below the windows."

"You think that thing'll go off?" he asked, turning to look back into the store.

"Nitroglycerin creates a shock wave that travels at thirty times the speed of sound. It comes at you like a white-hot gas from the mouth of hell at a temperature of 9,000 degrees Fahrenheit."

"That sounds bad."

"A blowtorch can only reach a top temperature of about 2,000 degrees Fahrenheit. Can you see a ball of flame coming at you with the force of a freight train." Then as if a faucet was turned on against his back, his features quickly drained of life and soul. Pyke's face blanched, his eyes darkened, his voice grew hollow. "I know I won't survive that. So do these men. Do you?"

Riley swallowed hard. "Understood," he said. He grabbed at the top of his hat and fled.

"What do we do—" Accorso said.

Pyke held up his hand, interrupting him. "Give him a second."

All four turned and watched as Riley shouted to his men. Everyone jumped into their cars, and in a minute, after the screeching of tires and the smell of hot asphalt, the intersection with all the cars in it, were gone.

"Okay," Pyke said, addressing his men, "Accorso and I are going in. Ateer, you and Frascone wait out here. If everything goes pear shaped...don't worry about it."

However, all Ateer could do now was worry. He kept a brave face, unlike Frascone, who was as excited as a man just before a beautiful woman goes down on him. Ateer was fine. Fine and do-dandy until Pyke calmly laid out the facts. If a freight train from hell came roaring out of Chock-Full-O-Nuts, he was most certain that he would die. His heart rate went into high gear—

pounding, pounding. Then, Pyke's admonition for him not to worry caused a slow calm to crawl over him. Replaced with a deep sense of loss. He had so much to live for. So much life. Was he ready to die now? To sacrifice his entire life for…?

He could not readily answer the question. Fear and capitulation came together within him, producing nothing. He felt a strange, blank, nothing as he watched Pyke and Accorso go through the revolving doors.

Accorso felt the same nothing, but it wasn't as strange to him. It was his operating theater. He followed Pyke like a son would a father, going along the counter's length. Their eyes falling to the large brown bottle of liquid sitting on the far end of the counter. Pyke stopped short, with Accorso stopping behind him.

"What is the first thing that you need to know about handling explosives?" Pyke asked him, over his shoulder.

Accorso thought about it. He was always in a fluid state when approaching a call. He molded his decisions with the path that was laid out for him.

"Stay here," Pyke walked on. He watched as Pyke walked to the end of the counter, picked up the bottle and returned to him, holding the brown bottle before his face. Accorso looked at it, then him.

"You need to know if it was handled before," Pyke answered his own question.

They walked out of the restaurant. Ateer, holding back an overpressure wave of fright in his members, watched as Pyke and Accorso walked out through the revolving doors. They were calm, as if just finishing a cup of coffee and a sandwich.

"Is it safe?" he asked them.

"Far from it." Pyke replied. To Big O he said, "You, go to Captain Riley and tell him that the restaurant is safe. We're taking the explosive with us." He handed the bottle to Accorso who gathered it up fearlessly. "Ateer, take the squad car back to the station house."

"And we're going?" Accorso asked.

"To the Technical Research Laboratory," Pyke replied.

Peter Hayias's dark brown eyes scanned over the bottle that rested on the wide table in the center of the laboratory. The younger technicians, Aiden Meyers and James Sullivan, dressed in white lab coats like Hayias was, stood on the other side of the table, faces low to the tabletop also scanning the bottle that was covered with white fingerprint dust. Pyke stood to the left of Hayias, arms crossed upon his chest. Accorso to the left of him, looking around him.

Ross Kelly came up behind his two younger technicians, looking over their shoulders. "What do you have there?"

Hayias stepped away, going to one of the many cabinets in the lab and after opening a drawer, produced an eyedropper. He came back to the bottle and unscrewed the top. "Kelly," he began aloud, "did you get any fingerprints from the bottle?"

"Only the ones that we were able to exclude," Kelly replied. Much older than Hayias, his balding, wrinkled basset hound face pulled into an exhausted scowl. "Pyke's, Accorso's and the manager, Brennan. I fear that the handling by these men have ruined those that were there before."

"Nothing actionable?"

"Nothing actionable."

Hayias dipped the end of the long eyedropper into the Nitroglycerin, turned around and with a flick of his wrist sent droplets of the liquid splashing to the floor between himself and Pyke. Accorso stepped away in both fear and shock, but Pyke, like Hayias, stood in anticipation. There was no reaction from the droplets.

"Well, it's definitely not Nitroglycerin," Hayias said, returning to the bottle and sticking in the eyedropper. After drawing a good amount into the body of the dropper, he went around the table and handed it to Meyers. "Aiden, go tell me what this is."

Meyers took the dropper, turned around to regard Ross, seeking approval. Ross nodded bitterly. "Go ahead!" He said in exasperation to the technician. Meyers was off like a shot and Sullivan was off with him.

"What are you doing, Pete?" Kelly asked, glancing back and forth between Hayias and Pyke, his features pleading for help.

Hayias stroked his chin with the side of his forefinger. "That bottle..." his voice trailed off.

"What about it?" Pyke asked.

Hayias walked back around the table, closer to the bottle and knelt low, his eyes at the same level of the bottle. "I've seen bottles like this before."

"Where?" Pyke asked.

"Some thugs," Hayias remembered, staring at the bottle as if it was communicating with him, "some thugs were leaning on a textile company, and we posed as workers, and I kept seeing these bottles. Textile companies use a great deal of chemicals, and they are in bottles just like this one. It's like a standard that they use to measure amounts purchased or something."

Pyke turned to Accorso, "Get on that. Find any textile companies in a one-mile radius of the Chock-Full-O-Nuts."

Accorso nodded and left quickly.

Hayias sniffed the mouth of the bottle, wincing against the biting, burning smell.

Kelly eased over to Pyke, staying outside of Hayias's perception, who was too busy with the bottle. "Lieutenant, isn't he Bomb Squad?"

"Yes, he is."

"Then why is he always here acting like he is the head of my lab?"

Pyke turned to him. "Did you know that that bottle was used in textiles?"

"No."

Nodding, Pyke said, "That's why."

Accorso blasted through the gate of the bullpen, peeling out of his hat and coat as if they were on fire, threw his jacket over his chair and started to roll up his sleeves. "Alright, Bomb Squad, get the phone books!"

Beakey and Dempsey gave orders to their units to fetch copies of the phone book while they went over to Accorso's desk. Pedrotti and Ateer stood with them, making a huddle around the detective.

"Get ready to earn your title as detective. We need to find all of the textile companies in the area of the Chock-Full-O-Nuts on Madison and 44th Street."

"What for?" Beakey asked.

"Our first solid lead. The bottle that had the so-called Nitroglycerin was used in the garment district. Someone get a map."

Pedrotti ran off.

"Let's get to the conference room," Accorso said, leading them out of the bullpen and into one of two conference/interrogation rooms on their floor. Pouring into the room behind them were Nichols, Dale, Hardy, and Copeland in shirts and ties and carrying heavy copies of the phone book. They dropped them loudly and emphatically on the edges of the broad table, probably in some effort to prove that the books were heavy, liberating dust from them.

Pedrotti ran in right after with a large map of the streets of Manhattan, rolled up into a tube. He threw it onto the center of the table, all hands seemed to roll it open, resting the phone books on the corners to keep it open. The Bomb Squad leaned over the table, staring down at the map.

"Chock-Full-O-Nuts is here," Pedrotti pointed to the corner of Madison and 44th. I need a piece of string."

Barney Copeland ran off.

"What are we looking for here?" Beakey asked. "Textile companies?"

"Yeah," Accorso replied.

"How many?" Dempsey asked.

"All of them."

"Does this have something to do with your nitro call earlier that Ateer told us about?"

"That's right. We're going to do some old-fashioned door knocking and interviewing." Accorso went to a wall shelf and took from it a pencil holder filled with pencils. He returned to the table and passed around the pencils. "Why is everyone looking at me? Crack open those phone books and start putting Xs on the map."

The room went busy. They flipped through the phone books under the heading textiles and all its subheadings, manufacturers, dyeing, cutting, processing, and so forth. Copeland returned with a spool of thread and he and Accorso measured off a mile of string against the scale on the lower corner of the map, and by tying a pencil at both ends, a rudimentary mathematical compass was made.

"Jesus, Fab," Beakey said, he tapped an area of the map just south of Broadway and 42nd street, "that is the Garment District."

"Meaning?"

"There's gotta be about a hundred or more textile companies in that ten-block radius alone. From big companies to small mom and pop shops."

"That just means a little more interviewing, that's all."

The Xs on the map began to accumulate, concentrated in the garment district. So many at times that they were already marked. Xs on top of Xs.

"Factory buildings," Dempsey sighed, realizing the enormity of the job. Hours later, with all the textile companies, distributors and sellers marked and circled in the telephone books, Accorso tore out the relevant pages and left the conference room. "Clean this up," he said in leaving.

Everyone exited the room. Dempsey, at the threshold, pointed to the men in his unit, Nicols and Dale. "Clean that up."

Accorso stopped over Dempsey's desk, divided the paperwork and slapped it down on his desk. "Dempsey, in the morning, you take these, and interview everyone on your list. Find out if they use textile bottles and who handles them in their company."

Dempsey picked up the pages and nodded.

"Beakey," Accorso turned to him. "Your unit is out of this one. You roll on all calls tomorrow and don't get yourself killed."

"Gotcha," he replied.

"Call it an evening, guys. Be ready for tomorrow."

Accorso walked back to his desk, tossing the phone book pages on it. Pedrotti came up behind him. "Are we coming over tonight?"

"Are you?" Accorso looked over his shoulder at him.

"Mind if I leave now and see you there?"

"Why so early?"

"You know how Sienna can be."

Accorso sat, shook his head. "Go ahead. See you tonight."

Pedrotti walked to his coat rack to snag his hat and overcoat. Accorso looked up at Ateer, "What? You want to go home early too?"

Ateer sat down at his desk. "I'm alright."

"Go home. I'll stay here with Beakey and his men until the night trick comes on."

Ateer stared at him, marshaling his thoughts whether he should leave or not.

"Go ahead," Accorso softly encouraged, "I'll see you tonight."

"Should I bring anything?"

"Just your appetite." Accorso took his folded newspaper at the corner of his desk and snapped it open.

Going to his hat and coat, Ateer left.

Pyke and Hayias climbed into the all black Plymouth squad car, both shutting their doors then going still.

"Conference?" Hayias asked with a smirk.

"Conference."

Hayias rolled down the window, Pyke did the same.

"What's up?" Reaching into his jacket he produced a pack of cigarettes. He shook one loose and offered it to Pyke. He picked one out, lit it with his own book of matches. He tossed the book at Hayias.

"You know I couldn't care less where you work out of," Pyke began. "But you can't keep on coming here to the lab and stepping on Kelly's toes. He's senior in the lab. *You're* supposed to be senior in the Bomb Squad. Have you ever even given any thought to the sergeant's position at the Squad?"

Hayias sat with his back to the passenger door, tossed his fedora into the back seats. "Not really."

"I have to give it to someone."

"Give it to Accorso or Beakey. They're next on the list. Accorso's got the skills, Beakey has the seniority. Choose one of those guys."

"You don't want the position?"

Hayias sighed, "Look Pikey, this is just another way of nailing me to the cross of the precinct. As just a regular detective, I can come and go as I please."

"And that means you want to be free enough to come here and get under Kelly's skin."

"He's a hack, Pikey. The guy shouldn't be a head of shit. He's not interested in the job, or bombs, or anything. If it's not obvious, he'll just breeze right by it."

"But he's the man in charge, Pete, not you."

"I make him look good. Like today. I find the answers and he gets all the commendations for being the head of his 'team.' He doesn't want me gone; he wants me subservient. He wants me to do the work, but whenever someone else is around, like you were today, he wants to look like the one in charge."

"Well, he complained to me."

"He's always complaining to you. That's what he does. He complains. I say, fuck him. If I walk that lab is going to go to hell."

"You know, I don't have any call over the lab. I'm the commanding officer of the Bomb Squad. Kelly is the man on top of the lab, and he can make it so that you can never return to it."

"I told you; he doesn't want to do that. That's the reason why he's always bitchin' to you. He wants you to rein me in without making me go away. Because once I'm gone, all those commendations that he is piling up will blow away, like this..." he flicked his cigarette out of the window.

"I can't interest you in the sergeant's position then?"

"Instead, can you get me that lab office that I'm in now?"

"I have no control over the lab. Why don't you just transfer in then?"

"Kelly wouldn't approve it. My way, I get the office, and I got only *you* over me."

"I'll see what I can do," Pyke leaned forward and started the engine. "You want a lift home?"

"No, I'm going back up to the lab and see what that chemical was in the bottle. The 'Bookends' should have their examination of it done by now."

"Bookends?"

"The techs, Sullivan and Meyers. They're like attached at the hip. I call 'em the Bookends."

"Alright. I'll see you in the morning. Unless you're going to your 'office'."

"No, I'm coming into the Bomb Squad tomorrow morning." Hayias cranked up the window, stepped outside of the car. Ducking his head back in, he said, "Thanks for being in my corner, Pikey."

"Aww, get out of here," Pyke waved at him. "Tomorrow night, would you like to go out drinking?"

"Sure."

"Talk to you about that tomorrow."

Hayias shut the car door and walked back towards the building. Pyke watched him walk through the dark parking lot and enter through the rear door, then he headed for the precinct.

. . .

Daria Accorso opened the door to their simple home in St. Albans, Queens, New York. She stared up at him with large, soulful eyes, skin like rich cream, a heart shaped face and long, jet black hair, pulled back into a fancy bun. Her lipstick red lips were small and full, appearing like rose petals. She was tall for a woman, but shorter than Ateer, with a wire thin frame and narrow shoulders. She could have been a movie star with her striking good looks. Ateer stood for a second to take her in, appearing nervous to be before her door, but actually quite gobsmacked.

"Please come in, come in, Mr. Ateer," she said, waving him in.

Crossing the threshold, he handed her a bottle of wine. "I picked up a bottle of Merlot for you."

"Oh, thank you. I'll open it right away." She closed the door behind him, rested the bottle on a nearby table, and went to his shoulders for his overcoat. "Let me get that for you." She helped him out of the coat and took his hat, then motioned to the living room. As Daria vanished deeper into the home, Ateer walked into the neatly furnished living room, and sat on the couch. There was an easy, homey feel to the decor of the space, with nothing out of place. Simple, padded wooden chairs, end tables bracketing the sofa, a coffee table, and a love seat.

Daria, dressed in a print blouse and short black skirt that hugged her shapely hips, surged back into the room carrying a glass of wine, handing it to him. "Fab is just upstairs getting ready. He should be down in a moment."

"No problem," Ateer said.

"I have to apologize for my daughter, Leora. She would have been here to introduce herself but she's sleeping over at a friend's house tonight. Maybe she'll be here the next time you come."

"Hopefully."

Daria went to a table against the curtained window where an array of picture frames rested. Taking one up she returned to Ateer, giving it to him. "This is her. She's our little pride and joy. She's only fourteen years old and she is as precocious as an adult. The things that come out of her mouth sometimes!" Daria gushed.

"She looks just like you," Ateer said, staring at the black and white photograph of the young lady.

"Well, they say that she favors me, but her personality is all her father's." She stared at the picture lovingly for a moment when Ateer handed it back to her. "She is growing up so fast in this day and age. They don't even get a chance to be children anymore."

"I know. We live in a fast-paced world."

"You can say that again," Daria walked back over to the table and gently rested down the picture frame. "I remember when there were no cars on the streets. They were all horse drawn carriages. And the feces on the street, it was like an obstacle course just to get across it."

They both laughed.

"Let me go check on dinner. I'll be right back," she said.

"Sure."

Ateer sipped from his glass as Daria vanished into the nearby dining room. He looked around at the paintings on the walls. Small, simple paintings of forests and lakes and a cabin in the woods. Then he heard footfalls on creaky stairs approach from the hallway. Presently, Accorso walked into the living room, dressed in a print shirt and denim slacks. In this otherworldly attire he looked like a completely different man. Years younger, with rosy cheeks on his lean features. His heavy brows perked up as he made his loud entrance, pointing at the wine glass in Ateer's hand.

"What has she got you drinking that shit for?" he asked with a smile. "Wouldn't you rather have a scotch on the rocks?"

"I can handle that."

He plucked the wine glass from Ateer's hand and walked off to the dining room and to the kitchen somewhere beyond. There was a brief discussion in the distance as Ateer tried to mind his own business, looking down at the pale wood parquet floor, which was polished to a bright, clean shine. The house had the smell of pine, and some sort of flowers although there was nothing green or flowery in the room. Ateer went to the sofa and took a seat at the end farthest from the love seat.

Accorso walked back into the living room, carrying a rocks glass in each hand, and handed one down to Ateer. "This should fit you better."

"Thank you, Fab," he said.

Accorso found a nearby chair and plopped into it. "So, what did you do for the rest of the day?"

"I bought a bottle of pop from the store and went home."

"You drink pop at home a lot?"

"No."

"Where'd you get that from? The Public Morals Squad? They got you staying away from establishments that might try to bribe you?"

"No. The P.M. Squad is pretty good with corruption. We watch each other like hawks."

"Yeah, you mentioned that." Accorso played with the glass in his hands. "Is that how it works?"

"Something like that. We even give some establishments the chance to try to bribe us, so that we can conduct sting operations. I'm a little hazy about how we identify certain establishments of violations of the law. I think it's through these sting operations, or complaints from ex-patrons, rival establishments, or neighbors. The rest I do know is quite simple. We get a notice of malfeasance, and then we roll in and arrest them."

"Sounds kinda murky, doesn't it?"

Ateer hunched his shoulders. "It worked for me. I did what I was told. You'll notice that."

"I see it in you already. And when you don't have orders, you go home."

"I guess I just don't need a lot to entertain me. A drink, the radio, a sandwich for dinner—I'm fine."

"So, locked away in your little apartment makes you immune to corruption." Accorso laughed.

"I wouldn't go that far."

Leaning forward in his chair in excited expectation, Accorso asked, "Have you ever been offered a bribe directly?"

Ateer shook his head, "No. Never had the pleasure."

"That's too bad—or maybe that's too good. It's hard to tell with corruption."

"So, what are you trying to figure out with this corruption discussion? If I'm susceptible?"

"Well, I know of some guys who have a certain...moral inflexibility. You know what I'm talking about, right?"

"Actually, I don't."

Daria sauntered into the room with a glass of wine and leaned up against the side of her husband's chair. "Dinner should be ready in a few minutes."

"Thank you, Mrs. Accorso," Ateer said.

"Oh, please, no need to be so formal in this house, call me Daria," she waved at him playfully.

"Okay then, please call me, Mac."

"Alright Mac."

They continued to smile at each other. Accorso simply stared at him blankly. Ateer felt uncomfortable because he was being examined so unabashedly. To take a pause Ateer sipped from his drink, looked up, smiled, and said, "So how long have you two been married?"

"Fourteen years," Accorso said. "We had a kind of arranged marriage."

"Really?"

"Yes," Daria said. "Many years ago, the Accorso family was looked up to in our neighborhood. They had a great deal of money and influence at one time. It was somewhat of a privilege to know them."

"You know. I told you; my father was part of the mob," Accorso said. "He was part of the Black Hand, Mackie."

"Yeah, you told me."

"Well, there was a certain quiet prestige in being one of the Black Hand in the Italian community. People looked up to my father, and my father had money, when other fathers didn't. The Piccios, Daria's parents, saw an opportunity to have their daughter married 'up' so they had us wed when I was eighteen and she was only fifteen."

"Fifteen?"

"Yes. We had a nice wedding and we moved into a small apartment and started our family." Daria explained with a lilt as if almost singing. She reached over with a hand and ran her fingers through her husband's straight, well-groomed hair affectionately.

Accorso batted her hand away. "Is it time for dinner?"

"Yes, yes." She straightened, drained her glass of wine, and trotted off.

"Dinner will be ready in a moment," Accorso assured, straightening his hair with a hand. "So, you were never married, Mackie?"

"Never. Just never found the right one."

"There's time," Accorso raised his glass, "unless you're in the Bomb Squad!"

"Dinner's ready!" Daria called from the dining room.

They stood and walked into the egg-shell colored room with a large oval dinner table covered by a white cloth. Plates, glasses, knives, and forks were arrayed neatly, and a silver candlestick holder was at its center. Accorso gestured to a seat at the side of the oval for Ateer, while he took the end and Daria took the other end. Daria took a few moments to transfer to and from the kitchen with platters of food: Chicken, pasta, broccoli, meatballs, and bread. When done, she sat down and they dined silently, moving platters around with a level of mechanical precision.

"So, tell us about you and your family, Mac." Daria said, pausing from her repast.

"Well, I'm a second-generation Irish American. My grandfather and grandmother, Patrick, and Rebecca MacAteer, came over on an ocean liner from Ireland but my grandfather never made it. Something went wrong in a poker game and either he won a lot or lost a lot and didn't have the money. Whatever the case, he was set upon by the rest of the card players and thrown overboard."

"That's shocking!" Daria gasped. "Did they ever find out who did it?"

"Nah. Nobody cared about stuff like that."

Accorso chuckled. "Yeah, drunken Irishmen were probably falling over the rails into the ocean every night."

"FAB!" Daria shouted, chiding her husband.

"No, it's alright." Ateer waved at her. "I'm learning, in the Bomb Squad, they play hard."

"I can see that." Daria calmed by degrees, her face still red. "So, your grandmother came over to the new world all by herself?"

"Yeah. She was the one that dropped the 'Mac' from her last name to make it more English."

"Did she find a nice Irishman to marry and take care of her?"

Sorry for dashing her dream of some romantic ending, Ateer screwed up his face, said, "Unfortunately, no. She held two jobs. She was a seamstress by day and a prostitute by night."

"No kidding," Daria gasped, eyes wide, completely involved with the story.

Ateer nodded. "She got pregnant and gave birth to my father Brendan Ateer in 1873. He never knew who his father was."

"Do you want another drink?" Accorso asked, stood and pointing at his empty rocks glass.

"Sure, thank you, Fab."

Accorso took up the glasses and left for the kitchen.

"What kind of man was your father?" Daria asked, her eyes glittering like jewels.

"I, uh, never knew my father. My mother told me that he worked on the docks unloading cargo. It was very tough work and you had to pay to work. He would scrape his money from one day's work and use it to pay for another. To make ends meet, he worked long, hard hours and what little he could bring home he gave to my mother. She worked as a maid for a fine household, but as she tells it, my father was a drinker. After my mother, got pregnant with me he got more and more depressed, and would spend more and more time under the influence. After I was born, he went into a true slump, even missing days at work, until one day he walked out of the home and never returned. My mother was fortunate enough to move in with the family that she was a maid for. She soon found that she was pregnant with my sister."

"And you lived with this family?"

"Yeah, they were very rich and very nice. They raised us with their children, and I had a chance to go to high school. That's where I met Fabrizzio."

Accorso walked into the dining room with the drinks and rested Ateer's down in front of him. "Yeah. I met him but we never really 'knew' each other." Accorso lowered into his seat. "We ran in the same circles, but we never connected."

"Oh really?" Daria was amazed.

"Yeah, I hung around with the Wops, mainly, while he was basically a 'Green-Nigger.'" Accorso smiled again, his face going cherubic.

"That's true. I hung around with the loosely Irish boys who grew up in Irish ghetto neighborhoods. I was from a well-to-do neighborhood and they didn't really know me. It made me mostly a loner," Ateer said, staring down at the table, his thoughts moving far away.

"Is that why you like to spend your time at home? Alone?" Accorso asked.

"Maybe. I was never big on being out with groups of people."

Daria reached over for the bottle of wine and refilled her glass. "What do you think about the Bomb Squad?"

"Very interesting. I mean, it's been kinda busy, and I haven't been given a great deal of training, but so far so good."

"The Bomb Squad being busy. I can't imagine."

Accorso interjected. "That's 'cause you're a housewife. Nobody is busy to you."

Daria smiled at Ateer nicely, completely ignoring her husband's comment. "If my husband trains you, you'll find it more unorthodox than anything. I'll be the first to tell you that his thinking is a little off."

"What?" Accorso asked, shocked.

"I kind of got a taste of that." Ateer agreed. He finished up his meatball, stirring it in his sauce with his fork before eating it. "Your parents arranged your marriage?"

"We don't need to swerve the car this way, do we?" Accorso asked tiredly.

Dabbing the corners of her mouth with her napkin, Daria began, "What can I say? I was a gorgeous little waif and the moment Fab laid eyes on me, he was smitten. When my father and mother noticed the infatuation in his eyes, they quickly went to his father...uh...uh," she struggled to remember the name.

"Maurizio," her husband filled in.

"Yeah! His father," she continued as if she never stopped, "he liked the idea because I was so beautiful. He knew that with his son walking around with a wife that looked like me, the sky was the limit. And, Fab was *in love!*" She inhaled, balled her fists between her breasts, lost in thought.

"Yeah, back then," Accorso replied bitterly.

His tone shook her from her near delirium. She looked at him and scowled. "Well, it was sad because he bought us this house and the furniture, and then he died. A very tragic accident."

"I told him about it," Accorso said to her.

For a moment her eyes went wide, stunned, then she shrugged it off and returned to Ateer. "But even though he died, we were never, ever broke. Never at a want for money. That's my husband for you," she smiled at him.

He scowled back at her. "Alright," he stood with drink in hand, dropping his napkin in his empty plate. "I think it's time for Daria to clean up the dining room with we go out back and talk shop."

"Oh, okay," Ateer said, taking up his rock glass and standing.

"Daria, it was an amazing meal. Thank you so much for it and the conversation."

"Thank you, Mac. Now you guys go and talk while I take care of the dishes," she stood, shooing them away from the table with both hands. Accorso walked into the kitchen for a second while Ateer backed away from the kitchen table, giving Daria room to work.

Soon, Accorso walked out of the kitchen and beckoned Ateer to follow him down the hall to the back of the home and the back door leading out to a small back yard where four Adirondack chairs waited in the dark.

"Have a seat, Mackie. Let me turn on some lights," Accorso said, handing a bottle of scotch to Ateer before walking off to a post not far from the chairs where a lantern hung from a peg. He took it down, opened it, lit its wick, and hung it back up, glowing. He did the same to another lantern in the other direction. Soon the entire backyard was filled with the contrasting yellow glow of the lanterns against the pitch-black shadows of the night.

Crickets began to chirp, and the air grew cooler, but still comfortable as Accorso sat in a chair next to Ateer and began sipping from his rock glass.

Ateer lit a cigarette, inhaling it luxuriantly. Accorso took out his Benzedrine inhaler and started breathing in its vapors.

"I didn't know you had a congestion problem, Fab," Ateer said.

"Fuck no. I snort on this for the high."

"The high?"

"It's a fucking head rush. It lights up your world, turns your skull into an open room and your brain into a ping-pong ball, bouncing off the walls. It keeps you awake and sharp, focused like a searchlight."

"That's why alcohol doesn't seem to bother you?"

"It does, but I can kinda give it a jolt, righting the ship so to speak."

"I see."

"How do you feel now?"

"I feel good."

"Nice and glowed up, right?"

"Something like that. I'm not drunk yet."

Accorso leaned over and handed the inhaler to him. "Take this."

Ateer took the small cylinder and looked it over. On the side it read BENZEDRINE, with instructions in small print.

"Fuck all that," Accorso said. "Exhale fully. Stick it in one nostril, close the other, and inhale like your life depended on it."

"That's it?"

"That's it."

Ateer thought about it for a moment then did as he was instructed. Instantly after inhaling deeply, his right nostril turned into an icy tunnel, his brain seemed to shrink and the top of his head lifted away, letting in an icy cold blast of air that caused him to swoon. His shoulders became weak, and he fell back on the chair, his eyes opening like saucers and the world started to cartwheel. He could feel Accorso taking the inhaler from his hand as it went limp to the ground.

Accorso watched him with a wide grin, holding back guffaws. "You alright?"

"Holy shit." Ateer sighed. "What a rush!"

"That's what it is, isn't it?"

"Jesus, is that what you feel like when you snort one of those?"

"When I did it the first time. Now, not so extreme. You know, the more you use it, the less it puts you on the ground."

Ateer stayed slumped in the chair, enjoying the dream-like sensation of the reality around him. His mind was swimming in a comfortable, cool pool of existence. He took a smooth sip of his scotch and it flowed into him like honey, warming his cheeks and stomach like a belly full of hot coals.

"This is amazing. Is this why you never go to sleep?" Ateer asked.

"It also curbs your appetite." Accorso grinned.

"Wow," Ateer was suddenly lost in thought. A state that crept up on him slowly, where he found himself watching it, like a rising sun on the horizon. He didn't realize if time was passing or not.

"Mac," Accorso said.

"Huh?"

"Mac. Your grandmother was a whore?"

Ateer turned to him, focusing, "Yeah."

"If you don't mind my asking...how do you feel about that shit?"

"What do you mean?"

"You just mentioned it, like in passing. You never said how you felt about it."

"She was a whore. That's what she had to do to survive, to raise a son, to keep a roof over her head. I'm not disgusted by her, although my mother certainly was."

"Oh yeah?" Accorso poured himself another drink. He rested it and the bottle on the ground and pulled out a pack of cigarettes. After lighting up, he tossed the pack over to Ateer.

Accorso said in a flat tone. "You do what you have to survive. I mean, look at us. We throw away our lives every day, and on the next morning we'll go back and do it again until our number's up. We fuck with bombs."

"You're comparing the two? Us and whores?"

"Only in the sense of working to survive, my friend."

Ateer lit his cigarette and tossed the pack back. "You said that you're a whoremonger—"

"Uh-uh," Accorso interrupted. "We're not going to talk about that here."

"Oh, sorry about that."

"But you did bring up something interesting. Whores walk out the door every day knowing that they're going to toss their virtue into the streets, time and again. We do the same with our lives," Accorso said, staring up at the starry night as if reading his thoughts from there. Ateer suddenly understood the effects of Benzedrine on the mind.

"But you've got to realize something."

"What's that?"

"They don't have us wops in the Bomb Squad because we are

invaluable. They have us in the Bomb Squad because we're expendable. We are like Roman gladiators. They allow us our excesses because once the games begin, we may not be back. Capiche?"

Ateer nodded dumbly.

"You see," Accorso continued. "A cop goes out on a beat, and he can just about judge the danger he's in. When he decides that it's time to be in a gunfight, he places himself in one. His opponent is defending himself with the same desire to kill and not to be killed. Two humans facing off, you know? The same with soldiers. But we don't fight humans. We fight the beast. An Infernal Machine has no mind, no heart. It's just death waiting for life to extinguish. You give a soldier a gun and you put a bomb in front of him and tell him to fight, he'll run the other way, because that bomb isn't afraid of him just because he's carrying a gun. And it won't be hurt by him either. So, he runs. That's logical. What we are asking from you is *illogical*. Our bosses want you to go up to the bomb and carry it away from people and defuse it. They want you to handle it as if it was nothing, which couldn't be further from the truth. You realize the predicament you're in when a bomb call comes in. Every time," Accorso looked at his feet, wiggled his shoes, "every time a call comes in, you'll realize it."

Ateer's head continued to nod although he was only dimly aware of it. He was aware that he was wrecked, but it was a pleasant destruction. He turned to Accorso. "Fab, I think I've overstayed my welcome. I'd better get going."

"Really?"

He stood, finished his drink, and tossed his cigarette butt into the rocks glass. "I've gotta make it home to Brooklyn somehow."

"Take a cab."

"I'll take the subway," he wobbled on unsteady legs momentarily. "Maybe I *will* try to take a cab."

Accorso led the way back into the home, called out for Daria to bring his coat and hat. She came running, handing Ateer his articles.

"It was so nice meeting you, Mac." Daria beamed, she raised herself on her tip toes and kissed him quickly on his cheek.

"Nice meeting you too, Daria."

"Please, don't be a stranger."

"I won't."

Accorso steered Ateer to the front door and led him outside.

"See you tomorrow," Accorso said.

"Tomorrow."

"Are you sure you can get home?"

Ateer nodded, blinked slowly. "I got it. I'll be alright. Sleep tight."

"Sleep tight, Mackie."

Accorso watched as Ateer left his front steps, walked out of his front yard, turned, and headed down the street. Accorso watched him until he melted into the night.

In the morning, Beakey came early to catch any calls, but the phone remained silent for that part of the morning. Dempsey walked in and gathered his unit as they filtered in and was out to knock on doors before the trick began. As the unit left, Pedrotti walked in, hanging up his hat and coat and glanced over at Accorso's desk for the newspaper. By not finding any he realized that his superior had not yet arrived and left for the break room.

Later, Accorso walked in with Ateer directly behind him. As they settled at their desks, and with Accorso tossing a section of his newspaper on Pedrotti's desk, a uniformed officer came to Pyke's office. With him was the cook from Greenport, Theodore Peterson. He was dressed in a well-tailored suit, again meticulously groomed, no doubt still going on job interviews. The officer peeked into Pyke's office and told him who he was escorting, and Pyke quickly emerged to address the cook.

"Is there something that I can help you with, Mr. Peterson?" He asked.

Peterson licked dry lips, wrung his hands in front of himself.

"Well, Lieutenant, I went to the property clerk's office just like you told me for my suitcase."

"That's good."

All eyes in the bullpen slowly turned to the exchange between the civilian and lieutenant.

Continuing, with a clear reluctance, Peterson said, "When I got it, it was ruined. It had oil in it, on it, all the clothes and papers inside were ruined. The utensils were salvageable, but the clock I had to throw out."

Pyke nodded, cocked his fists on his hips. "I'm sorry to hear that. "Thanks for telling us." He motioned to re-enter his office, but Peterson shouted after him, causing him to halt.

"But! Sir! Everything is ruined, so I was wondering if there is any way for the city to reimburse me for my loss." Peterson smiled broadly, although it was a great weight to hold up against his face because his eyes betrayed the strain.

Pyke, already stopped in his threshold, with his back to Peterson, turned around slowly to take a position in front of him once more. "Excuse me?"

"I feel that I shouldn't have to pay for things that the city ruined. I mean, there was only a clock in the bag," Peterson explained.

The hinges of his jaw broke apart, Pyke's mouth falling open, stunned surprise in his face. He turned to the faces staring back at him in the bullpen pointing at Peterson emphatically. "Can you believe this jamoke?" Chuckling as he returned to the cook, he said, "Nothing doin'. Go climb up your thumb."

Peterson blinked, stunned by the Lieutenant's response.

To the officer, Pyke said, "Get this moron outta here."

Accorso, Pedrotti, Ateer and the rest of the bullpen watched as Pyke returned to his office and the officer escorted Peterson back out of the building. The bullpen exploded in laughter as Peterson vanished forever and Pyke slowly closed his door.

"Can you believe that?" Ateer asked Accorso.

"This is New York...I've seen stranger."

Pyke's office door opened, and he walked out, coming up to the other side of the balustrade to speak to Accorso and Ateer across from his door. "I just thought that you two would like to know, Peter was right about the bottle belonging to a textile company. The fluid inside was found out to be Sodium Chlorate in an ammonia solution which is used in bleaching textiles and pulp."

"So, we're in the right ballpark going through these companies in the phone book?" Accorso asked.

"Yeah, beat the bushes and see what comes out."

"Alright."

Pyke turned and left for his office.

Accorso turned to Ateer. "You'd better go and get a Benzedrine inhaler. It's going to be a long day."

SIX
CHASE THE WIND

"*Come Fairies, take me out of this dull world, for I would ride with you upon the wind and dance upon the mountains like a flame!*"

WILLIAM BUTLER YEATS

Accorso was right, it *did* turn out to be a long day. The three detectives went from building to building in the Garment District, which was one of New York's true urban valleys. Factories of stone and granite wrapped tight up against each other as if welded together, differing faces, differing windows, differing doors but they all seemed to melt into one, solitary, unified rock face, like the craggy cliff faces rising from restless seas. The Garment District was little more than several crisscrossing valleys of buildings, gray and lifeless, sprouting up from the surging sea of humanity at its base.

Crawling with activity, the lifeless buildings seemed to absorb life during the morning, hundreds of people packing into the vacant mouths of the silent monuments only to be vomited out at noon, filling the gray streets, the seamstresses, laborers, managers, clerks, cutters, designers and others removing themselves from the working rat warrens and stretching their legs, breathing the stale but fresher air, and purchasing food from street vendors.

It was a massive ecosystem, breathing, excreting, reproducing, feeding. Ateer felt swept up in this maelstrom, a mote of dust in a windstorm, following behind Accorso and Pedrotti more than doing anything else. Methodically, when the workday began and the dark monsters of masonry flanking the streets inhaled deeply and the soulless laborers filled the buildings with life and the many machines that sewed, cut, pressed, dyed, and washed awoke from their evening's slumber and began to spin or thrash, Accorso, Pedrotti, and Ateer began to go from door to door. At first, Ateer found it interesting, walking into a laborer's shop, speaking with the owner of the establishment, everything cluttered and cramped, dusty and grimy. Women and men, mostly women, worked over tables, sewing machines, with steam irons and scores of other utilities, just as mechanical as levers and pulleys in a machine. Life seemed pale in these establishments, stacked one on top of the other, a monotonous loop of silent desperation repeating itself, over and over again, from floor to floor. Accorso seemed to be inured to the blankness of life here, joyless, burdensome, tiring. However, intrepidly, he continued from floor to floor, company to company, talking to everyone.

It was the routine for the morning. They would enter one of the buildings, humming with power, like a human generator, fueled by blood and sweat and the musky stink of labor, and begin with the first door on the right. Usually metal, steel reinforced and large. A man would answer, filled with questions, assuring the detectives that nothing illegal was going on in their factory, inviting them in to walk around. Accorso would advise them that they needed to talk to their employees. Accorso explained that all they were doing was making the people sweat. Being a cop for five years and a detective for another five, Ateer knew exactly how to sweat a perpetrator. Look them in the eye, talk evenly, use the word *'you'* a great deal and wait for them to either grow nervous or confused. If they grew confused, move on. But if they grew nervous...

Nothing, nothing was more nerve wracking for a perpetrator than to have detectives appear, asking around, winnowing out the innocent, creeping towards them, the groping hand of justice. It would be an ordeal. It was this slow moving, molasses-like approach that they were employing today. One person at a time, carefully, methodically, they interviewed everyone in the factory from the owner to the laborer and when done, they moved on to the next factory. There could be anywhere from one to three or four factories to a floor, around thirty to a nine-story building and around twelve or so buildings on one side of a block.

Accorso seemed to be ignorant of this fact. That what they were doing could take a week to accomplish. All he did was study his map, the sheets of phone book pages, and knock on door after door.

Pedrotti, on the other hand, did not care about his surroundings, the drabness of the world of the laborer, neither was he interested in the responses that he received from those he questioned. Pedrotti was focused on the female faces. The hundreds of faces, soft faces, attractive faces, young faces, all under some form of stress, and annoyed that they had to step away from their work to talk with him, but this did not dismay him. He began to play a numbers game in his head, giving each woman a numerical value towards her beauty. An old bag got a one, a young beauty, a ten. It was this game that numbed the monotony for him. It made the daunting chore survivable because it was not his focus for the day.

Four buildings in, they stopped for a lunch break. Joining in with the masses that were allowed to take lunch, they filtered down into the street and bobbed like corks on the water towards Broadway. Making a left on the wide thoroughfare, they funneled into a deli.

Unsliced cold-cut meat waited behind display cases on the left, with white shirted, white aproned, white hat-wearing people came up to the other side of the counter, staring into the faces of their new patrons like goldfish in a bowl. Accorso led them as if he knew where he was going, an invisible sherpa before him, and found a booth in the dining section of the restaurant. The space was filled with chatting people filling every booth, but it was the motion of two couples standing and leaving theirs that had caught Accorso's eye.

After they sat in the recently vacated booth, Accorso waved the waitress over and she rattled off the specials for the day. After they had finished ordering and after she had left, they relaxed and broke out cigarettes.

"Fuck, my feet are killing me," Pedrotti groaned.

"Mine too," Ateer said, kicking his shoes off underneath the table.

Accorso looked away, something else catching his attention.

"Why don't we take a break for the evening and start up this shit again in the morning." Pedrotti offered, puffing smoke heavily.

"I don't want Dempsey to go through his list before we do," Accorso replied, still looking off.

"He's probably taking a break himself."

"He'd better not be thinking that he can take a half day just because this job is a pain in the ass." Accorso turned back to Pedrotti.

"Why?"

"Because this is a solid lead."

"This shit is gonna turn up bupkis." Pedrotti sat back in the booth, his shoulders sagging.

"I'll tell you one thing," Ateer said, his head propped up by an elbow on the table and a hand against the side of his head. "The lab was right about that bottle that we found in Chock-Full-O-Nuts. They're all over those factories that we were in."

"Yeah, I noticed that too," Accorso said.

The food arrived. Maybe it was being on their feet all day, maybe it was because of the ratty, industrial environment that they had waded through, maybe it was just time, but they were starving, commenting on how this kinda job kills in the long run.

SUSPICIOUS LOOKING PACKAGES

"I can believe that," Accorso said between bites.

"How did the dinner party go, Mac?" Pedrotti said to him with a beaming grin.

"It was nice. I had a great time," Ateer said, "Fab's wife is a great cook and an amazing hostess."

"You guys didn't get into a Frisco last night?" Pedrotti turned his question over to Accorso.

"Not while the guest was over. God, the bitch was laying it on thick. Playing Miss Sweet Pea, I guess she was supposed to be the model wife."

Pedrotti swung back to Ateer. "Oh so you must be someone special for her to go through all of the trouble. Usually, when my wife and I go, there's always a fight."

"Really?" Ateer was stunned.

"You put our wives together is like putting a flame to gasoline. I'd rather face a Devil Toy than to be around them."

Accorso grumbled, "Oh yeah, and you'd think that she'd be able to keep the cork on the fucking bottle but no sooner did Mackie leave the house she blew up. How rude I was, how unloving I was, how I did this wrong and that wrong. She wouldn't shut the fuck up!"

"You had a tussle anyway?" Pedrotti asked.

"Unavoidable."

Everyone except Ateer laughed. Ateer, for his part, was lost in the recollection of the evening. Daria was charming, sweet, bright, obedient and a knockout. What man wouldn't want that as a wife? What was wrong with Accorso? Was he a cad and a liar?

Accorso pointed to Pedrotti with his fork. "I just got an idea."

"What's that?" He replied.

"Why don't we have you and Sienna over, *with* Mackie!" He pointed at Ateer as if he wasn't there. "This guy can keep the wives on their best behavior, and I can have you over without all of the rapid oxidation."

"Sounds like a great idea. Hey, this could be your chance to invite over Pyke and Hayias!"

"Oh, I wouldn't push that shit. If that bitch has a combustion event with my superiors around, I'll never be able to live it down. I think that just having you and Mackie over will be a good enough start."

"You and your wife sounded like you got along pretty well the night I was there," Ateer pointed out.

"Trust me, Mackie. What you saw was a puppet show."

Pedrotti patted Ateer's back, laughing. "They *don't* get along, Mac," he turned to Accorso, "So what are you going to do tonight?"

"Take a hot soak," he said. "My dogs are killing me."

"You don't want to pace around these open tombs either for the rest of the day."

Accorso looked at his watch. "Within the hour we are getting back to work. I can smell the stink on this clue."

Pedrotti sighed in exasperation.

"What are you going to do tonight Pedrotti?" Ateer asked.

"Oh, I don't know. I might not be able to walk after this."

"We all know why you don't want to go back in those factories," Accorso accused.

Perking up, Ateer sat forward in the booth, leaning in towards Accorso. "I don't know."

"Pedrotti was raised in an orphanage."

Ateer turned to Pedrotti who worked on cutting his piece of corned beef with increasing agitation.

"You were? What was that like?" Ateer asked with astonishment.

"You see," motioning to Pedrotti with his fork, Accorso said, "Beat It's mother and father died of Tuberculosis when it swept through their entire tenement building. His mother—"

"I can tell the story," Pedrotti interrupted with an edge of displeasure. Obviously, for Pedrotti, this was a sensitive subject. One that Ateer could readily see. He turned to Ateer, continuing, "We all went into a sanitarium where we were encouraged to rest, eat red meat and sleep outside—shit we were encouraged to sleep all of the time. When I got well enough to leave, I was told that I was an orphan. I was ten years old and put into an orphanage and shortly after that put to work at a machinist shop on a drill press, in a place that stank and groaned, and cried, just like these fucking textile factories upstairs. I worked on that drill press for nine years, hole after miserable hole and unlike most of my co-workers..." he held up his hands before Ateer's face, showing him both sides several times, "...I got to keep all of my fingers."

To Ateer, the temperature in both seemed to drop several degrees, sending chills up and down his spine and causing his cheeks to flush with blood. This was territory shut up in Pedrotti, and Accorso was aware of that, and yet he put him through it still. Pedrotti was reliving nightmares over and over inside the factories, and somehow, over, and over, he conquered them to move on with the investigation. There was something else that became evident to Ateer, and that in Accorso's mind, and then by extension, Pyke's mind, Bomb Squad came first. Before personal preferences, before fears, before hatred, before anything you can come up with, Bomb Squad superseded all of them.

"Then I applied to the NYPD and in time, I ended up at the Bomb Squad," Pedrotti said, continuing, "I'm not too keen on going back in there."

Ateer looked at Accorso if he would dismiss Pedrotti. He concentrated on the mashed potatoes of his plate, stirring them around angrily, mixing them with the gravy. There would be no charity from him today.

"You can do this," Ateer reached out and grabbed Pedrotti by the shoulder.

"He can do this," Accorso assured. "He's Bomb Squad."

Pedrotti nodded, drawing strength from the assurances of the two of them. "I can do it," he lit a cigarette, began puffing.

After glancing at his watch, Accorso said, "We've got ten minutes, and then everyone that's gone to lunch will be back."

"I'll be back." Crushing out his cigarette in the cabbage in his plate, Pedrotti stood and walked off.

Ateer watched him head out several paces, stop the waitress to talk to her. She pointed off somewhere in the restaurant, and he struck off in that direction.

"Maybe we should let him off for the rest of the day. We should be able to handle this," Ateer whispered to Accorso.

"Do you know what he rolled today?"

"I never see when he does it. What was it? Snake Eyes?"

"No, a hard six."

Ateer shook his head, "What's that?"

"Two threes," Pushing his plate away from him and sitting back, Accorso snorted Benzedrine.

"Okay what does that mean? I don't know what that means."

"It means, no slack today, and he knows it. That means if there is a bomb or a gun, or a madman, or a stack of mail or memorandum, or even a tall drink of water, *he* has to take it."

Blinking in a weak attempt to follow, Ateer thought of some macabre game being played between the two men and grew upset. Life was no game. "You have some kinda outcome for every roll of the dice. Is this something that you made up?"

"No, not me. Beat It brought this shit with him. He said to me, 'I'll do anything after any roll, but if I roll snake eyes, I don't want to be anywhere around this place.' *He* told me that."

"He didn't roll Snake Eyes today...." Ateer's voice trailed off.

"That means he's got to get his ass in that factory and start questioning people. It also means something else."

"What's that?"

Accorso slid out from the booth, reached into his jacket, and pulled out his money clip. "That he can no longer hide from you. You'll see more of him now that he's told you that about his family."

"*You* told me that about his family," Ateer corrected.

Accorso threw cash on the table. "Tell Beat It that I paid for his lunch."

Watching him as he walked out of the restaurant, Ateer reached for his wallet.

SUSPICIOUS LOOKING PACKAGES

. . .

On the sixty or seventh factory, this one a small one, Accorso confronted an elderly man, his face wrinkled, and hair white as flour. His eyes were clear, understanding fully the situation that was being presented to him. He absorbed every word that came from Accorso's introduction. Although shorter than the detective, he was sinewy, his hands like veiny bear claws. He was the product of working hard all of his life. Even his voice came out manly and hoarse.

"You want to interview my workers?" He asked.

"Yes, Mr. Rosenberg, we're looking for someone who might have taken one of your chemical bottles and labeled it Nitroglycerin and left it in a Chock-full-O-Nuts as a hoax."

"Really." Rosenberg rubbed his stubbled face with the side of his hand. "All of my chemicals are accounted for."

"Can I see your inventory while my men question your workers then?"

"Sure, sure," Rosenberg waved them in, "anything to help the police."

They walked into the space, packed to capacity with tables and stacks of fabrics. Long cords were draped across the ceiling and fabrics were hung there, like unfinished clothes drying on clotheslines, they dangled overhead, making the owner and detectives duck their heads to navigate through.

Rosenberg pointed off. "My workers are down there right now."

Accorso sighted down where Rosenberg pointed. Much steam and noise was raised from that side of the space, many tables piled high with fabric remainders making an irregular path.

"Check it out," he told Pedrotti and Ateer. They marched off.

"Stanley!" A woman shouted, her voice screeching as if being dragged across a chalkboard. "Stanley! What's going on here?"

"The police want to look at our chemicals, Lila," he said calmly, trying to talk her down from her emotional ledge. She was frazzled, her hair wild. Incredibly so since it was gathered up into a hairnet.

"What's this all about officer?" she demanded. Accorso looked down at her. She was shorter than her husband, but obviously had more firepower than all the bullets in his gun. "Sorry to bother you, ma'am, we are investigating a bomb hoax—"

"Here?" She interrupted. "A bomb in here?"

"*Lila!*" her husband shouted. "Take him to the chemicals," he then said calmly.

"Alright, already," she hissed back at him. "This way, Mr. Policeman."

Lila walked off, leading Accorso deeper into the jungle of hanging and stacked fabrics until she brought him to a wall of bookshelves filled with bottles.

"Wow, you've sure got a lot of chemicals here," Accorso muttered.

"Sir, you can see, there's no bomb in here."

"No ma'am, its nothing like that."

"Then why are you here?"

Accorso explained to her the event at the Chock-Full-O-Nuts only a day ago.

"Well, we don't handle any nitroglycerin in this factory."

Rosenberg said, "That's right, detective Accorso. You can see that there is nothing like that here."

"How about Sodium Chlorate in an ammonia solution?"

"Now *that* we have," Mr. Rosenberg said. "Lila, show him our supply."

Lila led the way down the wall of bookshelves and bottles, holding up her finger close to their labels as she walked past. Soon, her wandering finger stopped at a bottle label overhead, then went down to the level of her knees, bending her over. "See, we have it, right here," she pulled away a large brown bottle, exactly the same as the one that Pyke had handed him in the Chock-Full-O-Nuts.

"Standard bottle for this stuff?" Accorso asked.

"All of these bottles are standard," Rosenberg said.

"Waitaminute," Lila said, she bent over again, looking at the shelf. "There should be four of them. There's only three."

Three, Accorso thought. One missing.

He turned in the direction that he remembered Pedrotti and Ateer walking off in and shouted. *"Guys! This is the place!"*

Pedrotti and Ateer broke through a sheet of fabric hanging from a line and found themselves at the other end of the factory. A stretch of it was free from the clothes lines and large, press machines churned, clamping down on sheets of fabric and blasting them with a loud hiss of steam. There were three of the machines at work, two female and one male laborer standing before them at their controls. Pedrotti shouted "Hey" several times over the din to get their attention. One by one they stopped their machines as Pedrotti, and then Ateer, following Pedrotti's lead, held up their badges.

"Ladies and gentlemen, we are the police and we're investigating a bomb hoax at the Chock-Full-O-Nuts on Forty Forth and Madison. The perpetrators used a—"

Accorso's voice called out from the distance, *"Guys! This is the place!"*

Like a young jackrabbit sprung from its hole, the young man at the last steam press took off with a shot, bolting into the clothes on the line and vanishing.

Pedrotti, just as quick, darted off after him, moving so swiftly he left his fedora in the air.

The young man bulleted through a path well known to him, as Pedrotti had to find his way through, slowing him down greatly.

As the runner neared the exit to the factory, Accorso broke from behind a curtain of cloth and slammed into the young man's side, driving his body harshly against the concrete wall, plowing him up and then stepping back, knocking all the wind out of his lungs.

Sprawling to the floor at Accorso's feet and panting, the youth immediately began to confess. "It wasn't my idea! I thought it was a bad idea!"

Accorso stepped on his shoulder and forced him onto his stomach. Then he knelt and planted a knee at the center of his back to pin him. "Don't wanna hear it, kid."

"I didn't *do* anything, I swear it!" he pleaded.

Pedrotti stopped over them, as did Mr. Rosenberg and his wife. "Do you have to be so harsh with him?" Lila asked, watching as Accorso pulled back his arms and handcuffed him.

"He tried to run, ma'am," Accorso replied. He looked up at Pedrotti who grabbed an arm, and together they hauled the young man up onto his feet. He was dark haired, narrow, his features sunken, his clothing clean. Accorso put his forearm under the kid's chin and forced him back against the wall, choking him. "What do you mean it wasn't your idea?"

"You're hurting him!" Lila said, reaching out for Accorso's shoulder. Her husband grabbed her by the shoulders and pulled her back, "Johnny, what did you do?" Rosenberg said to him.

"I-I was just talking to Willie about taking a bottle and labeling it Nitro and leaving it somewhere, but I was just talking."

"Who is this Willie guy?" Pedrotti asked, turning to accept his hat, being handed to him by Ateer.

"Willie Beveridge, upstairs on the seventh floor. He told me to get a bottle from somewhere the Rosenbergs would never notice and a blank label."

Accorso turned to Pedrotti, "You and Mac go up there and get that numb-skull."

They nodded.

They took the freight elevator up three floors up and entered a larger factory than the Rosenberg's downstairs and was immediately met by the owner. Pedrotti explained why they were there and asked to see Willie. Without any argument the owner marched them over to a tall, burly young man, dark haired and well built. He turned around from laboring over a worktable when the owner called his name and reluctantly approached the detectives who immediately took his arms and handcuffed his hands behind his back.

"Willie Beveridge, you are under arrest for perpetrating a bomb scare in a Chock-Full-O-Nuts on Madison Avenue," Pedrotti explained to him as he shackled him and walked him to the exit of the factory. Everyone else, men, boys, girls, and women who also labored on worktables around them stopped to watch Beveridge being walked out by the two detectives.

"Look, it was just a joke," Beveridge defended as he walked into the freight elevator and was turned around. "It was just for laughs."

"You don't see us laughing, do you?" Ateer asked as authoritatively as he could muster. He wanted to laugh out loud himself.

"Look, we didn't mean any harm."

The elevator operator stopped the elevator on the fourth floor to pick up Accorso and Johnny and then rode it down to the ground floor with the two young men arguing between each other, each blaming the other for devising the prank. The detectives remained silent all the way down. While walking to the car, Ateer asked, "What about the other unit?"

"What about them?" Accorso said over his shoulder.

"How do we let them know we got these guys?"

"Well, if you want to go through all the factories on their list to find them, go ahead." Accorso stopped at the squad car and opened the passenger door. "The day's almost over. They'll be finished in an hour or two anyway." He pulled the passenger seat forward and guided Johnny into the vehicle head first.

"That's if they continued after lunch with this madness," Pedrotti grumbled, grabbed Willie by the arm, pulled him around and pushed him towards Accorso who aided him into the car.

"You know what I just thought?" Ateer said.

"What's that?" Accorso walked off, heading around the car to the driver's side.

"We've lost a seat. One of us has gotta take the subway back to the precinct."

Pedrotti slipped into the front seat, slamming the door shut.

"And he's a detective," Accorso said to the two perpetrators in the back seats, then slipped behind the steering wheel and closed his door. "See ya back in the bullpen!" he shouted, started the engine, and cut his way into traffic. Ateer watched them as the current of cars carried them off, leaving him alone.

Ateer walked towards the subway, lighting a cigarette.

There was applause awaiting him when he arrived, and Ateer could do little more than smile. Pyke clapped him on the back several times, congratulating him, then congratulated the entire Bomb Squad. He gave Accorso, Pedrotti, and Ateer the rest of the trick off, which had little more than three hours to go.

They gathered their things and left the precinct, Accorso requisitioning a squad-car, and everyone climbed in. No one had any idea where to go, except for Accorso, who silently drove them south of the line to Thompson and Bleecker streets, near Washington Square Park.

They strolled down the block feeling the sort of euphoria that one feels after the excellent performance of one's duties. They walked like demigods, about a foot off the ground, ready for anything. A stampeding horde of feral men could pour up the block at them and all they would do would be take off their jackets and hats and loosen their ties, ready for the fight.

"Where are you headed, Fab?" Ateer asked.

Accorso did not reply.

"I know where now." Pedrotti said with a smile.

"Where?" Accorso asked him over his shoulder.

"Just believe I know. Shit, of all the clubs down here there is only one that you would go to," then turning to Ateer, Pedrotti put a hand against the side of his mouth, whispering, "Another hooch-house."

"Hooch, like in Moonshine?"

Pedrotti nodded "Fucking guy has a map of them in his head."

"Just in case Whack-assed runs out of my shit," Accorso said.

A restaurant presented itself on the corner. Large windows, tables outside for al-fresco seating on the sidewalk, it curved around the block and was packed with patrons. Men and women, laughing, drinking, eating, and enjoying one of the few early spring days where the cold weather was attempting to break, but the struggle for spring was on, like a teetering hand wrestle, with days being brisk and then sultry.

Ateer stopped just inside of the door, searching for a vacant table, and finding none. Accorso and Pedrotti continued to march on, deeper into the restaurant and then turned into a door marked MENS. Before vanishing inside, Pedrotti waved him in angrily. They had to go to the bathroom...okay. They needed him with them? Why? With a level of disgust, he marched off to the bathroom, struck the door with the flat of his hand and stalked in.

They waited for him in the spacious bathroom with tall, porcelain urinals against one wall while metal stalls were lined up on the other, their doors yawning open except for the last one which a Negro bathroom porter in a white uniform and gloves sat on a stool. He eyed the men as they entered, his face blank as he acted like he didn't notice them.

Accorso went to the sinks and washed his hands in one. Pedrotti lit a cigarette.

"What are we doing in the bathroom?" Ateer wanted to know with a level of annoyance.

At the last stall near the door a man was finishing urinating. He flushed the toilet, zipped up his zipper, looked up at the three men briefly and then did a ninety degree turn and left. The moment that the man was gone, Accorso walked over to the porter with wet hands, to which the Negro handed him a dry, clean hand towel.

Accorso said to him, "You can rub mama's belly..."

With a deep, almost musical lilt, the porter replied with a smile "...butcha betta not rub any lower!"

Both laughed. The porter stood, and for the first time, Ateer realized that the stall door on the end next to which he sat, had a lock on it. With a key, he turned the lock and pushed open the narrow door to the toilet inside, but as they filed in, Ateer found that there was no commode waiting for them, but instead another door, large, heavy, and black.

The space beyond was large, its walls painted dark gray. Large, bright crystal chandeliers lit the high ceiling like fireworks. A long, marble bar had room for many customers on padded stools. Most of the seating was sofas, loveseats and few divans, and padded chairs spaced about in a semi-circle from the bar. Further inside the semi-circle of couches were a score of circular tables covered with white sheets, and at the very center of the semi-circle was a wedge-shaped stage.

Busy and loud on this dais was a quartet. A piano player and his piano, a drummer, a bass player, and a singer. They played smooth music, jazz, by the sound of it. Ateer listened to music on the radio at times. He'd rather listen to the news. But here, he was immediately caught up with the seductive sound and the equally alluring black woman in a short black dress, low cut in front, glinting with a rhinestone pattern of tongues of fire wrapping around her lean, hard body. The dress on her was so sheer that it was almost transparent. He could easily see her dark belly button and if not for a large slip of glittering flame there would be another enticing dark shape clearly visible slightly lower than that.

For a moment, Ateer was confused as to which he liked better, the music...or the dress.

"Hey, hey!" Pedrotti pushed his shoulder. "We're over here."

Ateer turned to find that Accorso and Pedrotti were making themselves comfortable at a sofa near the bar. He walked over to them, taking a seat and whispering, "Is this a hooch house?"

"What?!" Accorso, leaning across Pedrotti, shouted back.

Louder, "Is this a hooch house?!"

Accorso sat back up, elbowed Pedrotti, raised his hand for a waitress. Pedrotti leaned close enough to be heard when he spoke into Atter's ear. "Well, it's a fancy hooch house, called a speakeasy."

"I've heard of speakeasies."

"Have you ever been in one?"

Ateer thought about it as if he had to. The obvious answer was no, but he wanted Pedrotti to believe that there was a *chance* that he might have been in one at least one time in his life. "No."

"It's really just the same as Whack-Assed Willie's except that the shit costs more. It's more presentable for the *ladies*, which I wouldn't call 'em that."

"Ladies?"

"Floozies." He waved his hand about, indicating the many women in the club. They seemed to crowd around the men, starving them for air. "All of this fancy crap is to make them feel comfortable."

The waitress arrived. Accorso ordered their drinks for them.

"Floozies?"

Pedrotti rested back in the couch with a comfortable sigh. "Watch out for them buddy, they'll come here and drink your wallet dry."

"And then that's it?"

"That's it. They don't put out. They'll play around with you to make you think they will, but they are no Deidre. Once you get one sufficiently high, her girlfriends will come, scoop her up and take her home without even a goodbye, much less a kiss on the cheek."

"Shit."

"But what do you care?"

"What do you mean?"

"I mean, as straight-laced a motherfucker that you are an' all."

Accorso jumped in, once again leaning across Pedrotti. "I told him that we fucked Deidre," he said to Pedrotti, but was staring and smiling at Ateer.

"Oh, you did?" Pedrotti said.

"Yeah, so now you have to come clean," Accorso sat back up forcing Ateer to lean in. "You haveta tell him what you are."

"I don't think so."

Accorso hooked a thumb at Pedrotti's chest, "This guy only fucks his wife on Holy Days of Obligation."

"How many are they?"

"Six or seven days a year or something like that," Accorso laughed.

"My wife's body is a sacred vessel to the lord," Pedrotti replied.

"Then you should really cut off your cock, Beat It, because you're soiling her." Pedrotti focused on the waitress as she returned with a tray of rocks glasses. She bent low, showing off her pendulous pair of breasts barely held in by the cut of her blouse. She handed him his drink, moved down the couch, and handed Pedrotti and Ateer's theirs.

Ateer sniffed his. It smelled like alcohol.

"I know what you want," Accorso said to them loudly, "I got you Pop Skull," he said to Pedrotti, "and I got you some Happy Sally," he said to Ateer.

Ateer remembered the taste. It was pleasant after the first two. He turned it up to his lips, knocking half of it back, then rested the drink on the carpeted floor between his feet. That was when he noticed that there was an end table at the armrest with a small candle burning. He picked up his drink and rested it on the table. He reached into his jacket and pulled out a Benzedrine inhaler, his very own. Purchased when Accorso suggested that he do so before going into the textile district.

"Watch how you fuck with that, buddy," Accorso said. "It'll give you a stiff one all night long."

Pedrotti laughed. "You practically have to beat her over the head with it just to make it go soft again!"

Everyone chuckled.

Accorso finished his drink with the second swig and rested the glass on the end table at his side of the couch. "You guys really did an excellent job today," he said, "I didn't get a chance to say it earlier, but you two stuck it out and in the long run, the lead paid off. I didn't think it would happen, no more than you did, but you had faith, and look at what this might mean for all of us. Commendations."

"Here, here!" Pedrotti and Ateer held up their glasses, Accorso held up his empty one, to clink them together, for the toast, and then held it up to the waitress in the distance. She approached, smiling. "Would you like another one?" she asked.

"Listen Toots, we're big boys here, so just keep an eye on us and just keep 'em coming. We'll let you know if you're topping us off," Accorso said to her. "This is a celebration, you know?"

"Yes, sir," she smiled and sauntered off.

No sooner did she leave did two women approach. The three detectives sat back in the sofa, looking up at them as they paraded themselves before them like prancing mares, turning, and laughing, crouching to show off their shapely posteriors, pushing up their breasts in a sort of playful dance, but not to the music. It was the music of lust that they believed pounded in the skulls of the men on the couch.

They were older women. A blonde haired one looked platinum, but in fact, she was a straw blonde with growing strands of gray hair beginning to fill out the color. The brunette, on the other hand, had her hair cut short, curled at her ears. She was easily pushing her fifties, but she kept the equipment and the frontage in good repair. In fact, she was a delight to look at, with her long, shapely legs literally shooting out from under her short dress.

"Would you gentlemen like to buy two ladies a drink?" The blonde asked.

"Scram," Accorso growled.

They turned to him, their eyes widening.

"I said, *scram!*" he said louder, this time getting their attention. They strutted off, making pouty faces.

"Hey! Whaddaya have to do that for?" Ateer complained.

"Floozies," Pedrotti said. "This place is lousy with 'em. That's why we don't come here often."

The drinks arrived. They picked out their glasses and returned the spent ones to the tray offered to them.

"But," Accorso said to Ateer, "if you want to bring a nice-looking lady here and get her drunk on only a few drinks, then carry her home in your pocket, because she won't be able to stand or keep her legs together, then this is the place to take her."

"The drinks hit the rubes like a Mickey," Pedrotti promised.

"Whatsa Mickey?" Ateer asked.

"When a drink hits you like a right cross from Sugar Ray Robinson. Exactly like what happened to you when we took you to Whack-Assed."

"Yeah," Accorso said while watching a long-legged red head walk by their couch, "but you didn't get the shit fucked out of you at the end of the night." When gone, Accorso turned his attention to Ateer. "That's the purpose of a Mickey. It'll sneak up on her and *bite* her in the ass. When she wakes up naked in your bed, she'll have very little recollection of what went on the night before."

"Or on a pile of trash in the back of an alley," Pedrotti added.

Ateer blinked his eyes. "Did you know that Accorso is a whoremonger?" he said to Pedrotti.

"He is?"

"He told me."

Pedrotti turned to him, "You told him?"

"I damn well did," Accorso said proudly. He knocked back his drink as a punctuation.

The powerful voice of the singer on the stage rose like a roar, it's pitch increasing to a shrill cry. Everyone stopped talking in the room as the music pushed her voice to the limit, the notes attempting to break her, but her powerful lungs could not be conquered. The music fell away, allowing her to howl in triumph, before stopping altogether. The entire audience stood up in applause, filling the space with their powerful praise.

After attempting to drown her in her standing ovation, the praise slowly died out, with patrons returning to their seats.

"Holy shit, did you hear that?" Pedrotti said with a broad grin.

"Calm down buddy," Accorso patted him on the shoulder.

Pedrotti finished his glass. "I'll be right back." He stood and left. Ateer watched him leave until Accorso slid across the couch to him.

"My brother has a problem," he said with a sly grin.

"Really?"

"That skirt on the stage is making his whistle shoot off like a bottle rocket."

"Really?"

Accorso turned to look at Pedrotti as he skirted the center of the establishment and edged to the side of the stage. The band had taken a break and were talking when he caught the attention of the singer. She approached the edge of the stage with a broad smile, and they conversed.

Accorso's eyes fell to Ateer, "You did good today, Mac. Your first time being on the investigative side of the coin."

"This is true," Ateer said, not taking his eyes off Pedrotti who already had his arm around the Negro's waist and leading her to the crowded bar.

"I'm gonna start leaving textbooks on your desk in the morning for you to learn about explosives when we don't have a call."

"Sure."

The waitress returned with drinks. Accorso took them off the tray without looking up at her, but keeping his eyes on Ateer, "Alright, go ahead and ask me."

Ateer turned to him, "Ask you what?"

"I find it hard to believe that a Boy Scout like yourself wouldn't stand in judgment over us by now."

Ateer knew that this time was coming. The Confrontation. This was the line in the sand for Accorso. Ateer had to make the cut if he was going to go any further after tonight. "Why should I judge you, Fab?"

"I told you what we are, I showed you who our friends are. What more do you need before you have something negative to say? Or do?"

Ateer thought what to say that would sound convincing, however, the feeling, the true emotion inside of him flowed upwards from a deep well, surprising even him, "Yes, I do have something to say."

"Go ahead."

"Around lunchtime today I despised the Bomb Squad. Again, another assignment that seemed to make no apparent sense. Just wasting our time so that we can tell the higher ups that we do something other than be dumb enough to walk up to something that might explode. I thought I was through."

"You did?"

"I think so. I don't really know. But I was tired, and disgusted, until we marched two perpetrators that could have sworn, we would never find them. And the teamwork involved, and how it seems that we are on the cutting edge of something here."

"We are."

"You guys do something more than just risk your lives making bombs safe. You actually catch criminals."

"We do, sometimes."

"How can I judge you for your indiscretions when you do the service you do? Your private business is yours. I hope you don't think that I'm here, gathering information on you. Because I'm not," and, truer than he cared to admit, Ateer said, "I want to learn from you Fab. I want to be you."

Accorso looked at him flatly, staring in his eyes because, to put it simply, he thought he was a good judge of character. Nothing like Scooty of course, but decent. Now, Accorso felt that he was in the wrong. Scooty gave him a thumbs up, meaning that Ateer was 'safe.' Now Accorso found himself poking the sleeping dog, just out of spite. Suddenly he flushed with shame. Why torture him? Because he was Irish? That's what it felt like he was doing now. Torturing him because he wasn't Italian like the rest of Unit One.

He was the one sitting in judgment of another.

Accorso slid back to his side of the couch, took up his empty glass of Goat Whiskey and held it up for the attentive waitress who was in motion the moment she saw him reach for his glass. She brought over two other drinks, and Accorso turned to Ateer and raised his in toast. "To the Bomb Squad."

Ateer did the same, clinking glasses. "To the Bomb Squad."

They turned up their drinks. Pedrotti plopped in the couch between them, smiling from ear to ear.

"So?" Accorso asked him.

"Her name is Melody, and she sings here on occasion," he said. "I bought her a drink."

"Are you going to see her tonight?"

He shook his head. "No, she has a man," he pointed to a sharp suited man at the far end of the bar, standing in near shadow. "That white guy...right over there."

"The white guy?"

"Yeah," Pedrotti grumbled. "Where's my drink?"

"Well, there's a lot of other women in here, Beat It," Ateer pointed out, looking around.

"Fuck these bitches. I'm going out and getting some 'strange' tonight."

"Not me," Accorso said. "I'm going home."

"You are?"

"Yeah, I'm tired."

Pedrotti turned to Ateer. "how about you? You goin' home?"

"I think so," Ateer reached into his jacket for his wallet.

"Well, I'm gonna dust out!" Pedrotti stood, pulled out his wallet and handed Accorso some cash. "I'll see you at the bullpen in the morning."

"See you then." Accorso stood and waved the waitress over.

Ateer stood and handed him cash for his drinks, but Accorso pushed his hand away. "Want a lift home?"

Somewhat stunned, Ateer frowned at the rejection of his offer, then hunched his shoulders. "Sure."

The Telegraph Bureau was the nerve center of communications for the NYPD. It connected the necessary operations and control at Police Headquarters to the many Radio Motor Patrol cars, otherwise known as RMPs, in the field. The Operations Room, located at the north end of 240 Centre Street, top floor, was commanded by a single person, the Superintendent, managed the Telegraph Bureau.

From here messages were broadcasted to the RMPs over WPEG, a police radio station using a five-hundred-watt transmitter on the roof. In the event that transmissions could not be sent out from the main transmitter, two other four-hundred-watt transmitting stations were set up to continue the needed service. One located in Brooklyn's Seventy-First Precinct, WPEE; and one located at the Bronx's Fortieth Precinct, WPEF.

At any given day there were hundreds of RMPs coursing through the bloodstream of New York, like white blood cells, searching out malfeasance at the speed of light via their valuable radio connection to the Telegraph Bureau.

In the center of the Operations Room was a huge U-shaped desk called the "indicator table" upon which a detailed nine-by-twelve-foot map of the five boroughs was displayed. One patrolman was in the role of "dispatcher" who worked along with another in the role of "announcer."

RMPs were represented on the map by small, round brass disks which were black on one side and white on the other and were located on the map according to patrol territories. There were other disks with other colors that indicate many differing states of readiness of the vehicles, such as whether cars were out of service due to routine maintenance.

At around 2:30 in the morning, the busy switchboard fielded a call which was quickly routed to the dispatcher. The call turned his blood to ice. A woman's voice said, "Another bomb will be placed in the World's Fair today."

The dispatcher, a veteran of the force, was not one to be easily swayed or bothered, but the deaths of the two Bomb Squad detectives was not only still an unsolved, but a still a painful sore spot to the NYPD. It was obvious that the trails were growing cold in the capture of the felons involved and even the reward money was not bringing in any valuable tips. However, this call could be the same culprits, bolstered by the inability to catch them, flaunting their superiority over the NYPD by placing another bomb in the same location as their last successful bombing.

But this was the NYPD, and the long arm of the law did not have a limit to its reach, be it length or time. This time, this call, just like the other one that brought on the death of two proud men, was going to be the last call, or bomb, that these criminals would make.

With his heart pounding, the dispatcher sent a message to the superintendent, and then scanned the indicator table for any RMPs available for assignment. Locator disks that indicated free RMPs had their white sides turned up, with the vehicle identification code number printed on it. He identified the location of Flushing Meadows on the map, and then all white disks in the immediate area.

The superintendent appeared in the room, coming up to the dispatcher and whispered into his ear, "Commissioner Valentine has been notified, but he hasn't returned the call. I know what he's going to say: Catch these bastards."

"Yes, sir."

With a step back from him, the superintendent left his trusted subordinate to perform his duties unimpeded.

With a pad, the dispatcher wrote down the first five numbers that he came across, attached with the message received and the location that the RMPs should be dispatched to. He passed those five to a runner on a white slip while he wrote down the next five RMPs that he found available in the area.

The runner went to the announcer. Upon reading the dispatch, the announcer was so stunned he had to read it twice. Then, for the first time ever, he added to the dispatch before handing it to one of his radiomen a notation that read: All and any radio cars in the vicinity were to respond as backup. The messages went out: "Car Number 454. World's Fair bomb threat, Queens. Signal 30. Authority Telegraph Bureau: Time 2:41 a.m." Followed by the next number on the dispatcher's list.

The announcer suddenly realized that his notation was redundant when the runner appeared again, tapping him on the shoulder and handing him another slip of five vehicles in the area to respond. He was in total agreement. Overwhelm the Fair.

At 3:30 a.m. the busy switchboard, fielding scores of calls an hour received another threat: "A bomb will be placed in the World's Fair today." This operator jumped from her seat and waved over the runner, telling him to fetch the dispatcher.

"Was it a woman?" the dispatcher asked upon arrival.

The operator nodded nervously.

The dispatcher walked around to the Supervisor who was still standing near the indicator table. "Another call came in."

"Is it from the same person?"

"That's the assumption, a woman. With the same warning."

The superintendent looked around at the Operations Room, which was always busy, but was now cranked up, as if shifted into high gear, with men and women running about or busy at their stations. The stress was starting to expand where others were slowly being affected by the import of what was happening.

"Notify the telephony technician," the Superintendent ordered the dispatcher calmly. "Have them notify the phone company. If this call comes in again, I want it traced."

"Yes, sir."

The dispatcher hurriedly went to the telephony technician, their liaison between their operators and the phone company with the request.

Watching the dispatcher run off, the superintendent's eyes went to the indicator table. The women and men around it were busy flipping over disks to black and pushing them towards Flushing Meadows. He walked over to the operators and rested his hand down on the shoulder of one of the young women, demanding her attention.

"Give me a line to the Bomb Squad," he told her.

SUSPICIOUS LOOKING PACKAGES

. . .

At 4:30 a.m., as seven police stations providing a hundred patrolmen and detectives, and thirty RMPs converged on the World's Fair, another call came in. This one was traced back to a telephone booth at Times Square. Once again, with the pressure building, the dispatcher searched out white disks in the immediate area of Times Square and reached out, grabbing a female runner by the arm and pressed the sheet of pad paper sending the closest five RMPs to the phone booth.

The Supervisor's phone rang in his office. His secretary stood, calling him over.

With a level of annoyance, he asked, "Who is it, Anna?"

"Commissioner Valentine."

The superintendent ran into his office.

The black Buick Century was parked across the street from his brownstone. Ateer closed his front door and walked down the stone steps to the sidewalk and looked both ways at the crossing foot traffic. When he found a break in the pedestrians, he crossed onto the street doing the same with the vehicle traffic. He took his time, marshaling his thoughts. He felt that he was making a big decision, crossing some kind of moral Rubicon. He laid on his couch most of the night, listening to his radio and the news of the war overseas, a land of fire and death that seemed not to be capable of extinguishing itself. Its only purpose being the destruction of the entire world.

And amid such hostility, Ateer wrestled with his commission.

He was no longer Public Morals, and it wasn't his to police the police. Public Morals had their job to do, and Bomb Squad had theirs, and in the middle of both, Ateer had his task, and that was *not* to police Accorso and Pedrotti and their coping mechanisms. It was to gather information on the effectiveness of Pyke's command. That was it. And from what he saw last night, they were just that. Effective.

He slipped into the passenger seat of the car, closing the door with a solid slam.

"We heard from the blotter last night that you caught the Chock-Full-O-Nuts hoaxers." Orlowski started the car and pulled out into traffic.

"Yes, we did," Ateer replied proudly.

"Was Pyke in charge of the investigation?"

"He was in complete command of it from making the bomb safe to sending out the investigatory teams to the Garment District."

"He's capable?"

"I've found nothing to refute it."

"How are you fitting in in the squad?"

"So far so good."

"Valentine was asking me how your spirits was. Up or down. What do you want me to tell him?"

"Up, of course, Orlowski."

Orlowski turned to him. "You do seem like you are feeling good. Still riding the high from that collar yesterday?"

"Oh yes." Ateer smiled. He twisted his body so that he was facing the jowled, tired appearing detective. "The arrests came out of nowhere. It was like infertile ground, burned and salted and a waste of time. Then...*bam*!" Ateer drove his fist into his palm with a loud retort. "We had two offenders in handcuffs, marching them proudly out of the factory."

"Felt good, huh?"

"Real good." Ateer righted himself in his seat, reached into his pocket and pulled out the inhaler.

"What's that?" Orlowski asked.

"Just Benzedrine," Ateer held it up, "for my headaches."

"Oh, that shit works on headaches?"

"For me it does," Ateer grinned, unscrewed its cap and inhaled from it deeply.

His morning unfolded like a flower of vibrant colors. He sat back with a smile from ear to ear.

SUSPICIOUS LOOKING PACKAGES

"Are you alright, Ateer?"

"I'm fine, detective."

Ateer walked into the bullpen, and before he even walked through the swinging gate into it, he felt that something was wrong. The only men in the bullpen were Accorso and Pedrotti, and they were standing, talking to each other. When Ateer walked over to the coat rack to hang up his hat and jacket, Accorso marched over to him, sending his face into his, almost nose to nose, whispering harshly.

"We've found the motherfuckers!" he hissed.

"Who?"

Accorso walked off, stopped, turned around to face Ateer, "The World Fair Bombers!"

"You did?" Ateer's mouth fell open. Although he could not register the full import of the situation, he was keenly aware as to how this one crime affected the entire Bomb Squad. They were a wounded animal and not only were they angry, but equally desirous to return the favor to whomever delivered the blow.

"They've planted another bomb." Pedrotti stepped up. "We've got all of the Bomb Squad out at the World's Fair with half of the NYPD searching every pavilion there."

"Great," Ateer replied, breathlessly, not knowing what to say.

Pedrotti kicked at his chair angrily, sending it rolling.

Ateer looked back and forth between the two detectives. "Uhh, why are we still here then?"

"Pyke's orders," Accorso grumbled, now pacing back and forth.

Ateer looked at the break room, thought better of it and turned to his desk, but could not move. What would be the appropriate thing to do?

Pyke answered his distressing question by walking out of his office and wagging his finger to call Accorso over.

"They've got this bitch!" He said angrily.

"It's a woman?" Accorso's eyes swelled.

"Yeah. She's been calling the Telegraphy Bureau since 2:30 this morning."

"What do you mean by 'they've got' her?"

"They've been tracing her calls from 4:30, every hour on the hour, moving in a general direction from phone booths in Time Square, towards Greenwich Village. The RMPs have been missing her by minutes of her call."

"What do you want from us, sir?"

"Catch up to the RMPs at the head of this and join in the chase. They don't know what they are getting into. If there are any Devil Toys introduced, I want you there, Accorso. I want you to take care of it."

"It'll be made safe," Accorso assured. He marched to his coat rack, snatching his fedora. "Unit one, let's roll!"

Accorso drove the RMP like he was an immortal, swerving through traffic while listening to the police radio, giving out the intersecting streets where the next phone booth was located. Pyke was right, the calls were coming from booths moving closer and closer to Greenwich Village. As the green and white that they were in reached the corner of Carmine Street and the Avenue of Americas a line of RMPs with sirens wailing, turned onto the Avenue, and skidded to a stop in the last known position of the most recent call. On the other side of the street were the parks of Minetta Green. Small slices of the outdoors, with trees and black asphalt grass, wooden and concrete benches, and monkey bars for the children. The park and sidewalks were thinly populated, the people of New York no doubt at work for the most part. The RMPs ahead of them stopped traffic entering the wide intersection at Minetta Lane while the vehicles disgorged patrolmen and detectives who ran to everyone walking on the street near the phone booth sitting innocently in the middle of the block. Accorso pulled the RMP to a stop behind another one and they emptied out searching for the usual clique of men who were in charge. Finding it, Accorso took the lead in running up to them, hand already outstretched to get past the formalities, "Detective Accorso, Bomb Squad, what do we have?"

Uniformed officers stepped out of the way, two suits did the same, leaving an officer with Captain bars on the collar of his shirt reaching out to grasp his hand. "Captain Francis Wheeler, Charles Street Station, the call just came from this phone about five minutes ago."

"You're *that* close?" Accorso was astonished.

"Just that close."

"What's your description of her?"

"Black woman, hair shoulder long, plain white blouse, black skirt, black bag. What we've been doing is questioning anyone near the booth who might have seen her. We've gotten a lot of people—"

A voice in the distance shouted for the captain. He turned around and ran in the direction of the voice, with Accorso, Pedrotti, Ateer, officers and detectives running behind him. Ahead, was a cab parked against the curb. A uniform yanked opened the rear door and reached in and brought out a black woman by the arm, matching the description of the caller.

He turned her around and flung her across the hood of the vehicle, kicking her legs apart at the ankles, patting her down, knocking her bag to the ground.

"HOLD IT! HOLD IT!" Accorso shouted, waving his hands in the air. "Don't touch that bag!"

The taxi driver got out on his side of the vehicle and walked around the front, concerned about his taxi. The uniform officer froze, pinning the woman's arms behind her back with one hand.

Accorso stopped the captain just a few scant feet away from the car, "Clear the area, sir. There might be explosives in her bag."

"What?"

"This could be a trap. All she needs is a stick of dynamite, a boxfull of nails in her bag and a detonator of sorts and she'll fuck up a lot of people."

Captain Wheeler's face blanched. "She could do that?"

"I would. Drive around town, draw us in, and at the last moment, detonate a device."

Wheeler turned around, shouting, and waving his hands, "Back! Get everyone back!"

Pedrotti ran to the taxi driver, shooing him away. Accorso went to the Uniform. "Cuff her, and get her the fuck out of here, quick! And don't touch that bag again."

The officer nodded, slapping the cuffs on her. When done, he yanked back on them, pulling her from the hood of the cab and steered her around towards the cordon that was being made yards away. Spectators were rushing to the chaotic scene from all directions, and all available officers were forcing them back a safe distance for their safety.

Accorso and Ateer now found themselves standing over the purse.

Ateer was standing over the Devil Toy as if brought via sleepwalking. The stopped taxi next to them purred, its engine running, drowning out any sound of ticking. However noisy the engine was, it was not capable to masking the squishing sound in Ateer's ears, his blood, rushing back and forth through the arteries in his skull, now under tremendous pressure. He was frozen, as if his joints were slowly hardening, getting him here, but now stranding him at the edge of the precipice.

Accorso knelt on one knee over the large, leather shoulder bag. He looked up into Ateer's pale face, realizing that if he didn't somehow engage him, he would simply stand there, motionless, eyes wide. He was in his own land of make-believe, where grinning death wasn't panting at his feet.

"Mac!" Accorso shouted. Then, at a more normal tone, "What would you do now?"

Ateer, waking from his delirium, focused finally at the black leather bag at his feet. "Find out what's inside."

"How? We forgot the fluoroscope back at the precinct."

That was right! Ateer frowned in frustration as he took an involuntary step back. His entire ribcage trembled with the beat of his racing heart. "Open it?"

"That could be the trigger mechanism. That could be her plan all along. She gets arrested, we take her into custody, and amid arresting officers or even in the precinct, wherever it was opened, boom." Accorso held up his hand, "Give me your pocketknife."

"I don't have one," Ateer shook his head.

"Never," Accorso reached to his back pocket, "never roll on a call without, at the very least, a pocketknife." Accorso produced a knife from his back pocket, pulled out its blade. "Let's cheat death and go in through the bottom."

"Okay."

"Are you alright?"

"I'm fine."

"How do you feel, Mac?"

"I feel alright."

Accorso nodded, turned his attention to the bag. He pinched the seam at the bottom corner of the bag and stuck in the blade, easily cutting through several stitches. He worked the blade back and forth cutting more and more stitches, making the hole larger and larger until he could peek into it. He lowered his face to the opening.

On the other hand, Ateer stood, panting. Believing that he could control his panic by controlling his breathing he could calm down and do something effective. It didn't work. His knees started to grow weak, and he considered stepping to the side and resting against the cab to keep from falling, but that would have made him look too weak to recover from. His mind kept playing, repeatedly, the bomb exploding. The charge rising from the ground, going up his legs, turning his bones into powder. Like taking off a pair of slacks, sinew and flesh peeled away, flying upwards, his skull bursting like a stomped tomato. There would be nothing left of him if it went off. Nothing.

And Accorso kept working on it. He wanted to run off, but Accorso's presence made the entire ordeal tolerable. If he wasn't present, Ateer would have run off. Ran as fast as his little legs could carry him. If the entire situation wasn't so distressful he would have burst out laughing.

"I can't get enough light inside of this motherfucker," Accorso said, his face down against the bag as if he was speaking to someone inside of it. He pulled his head away and began working on the hole once more. Something landed on his shoulder sharply, making Ateer squeak, jumping out of his skin, shifting his heart into overdrive. He swooned, almost fainting but the blow to the shoulder turned out to be a hand which closed on his collarbone sharply. He looked to his side, Pedrotti standing there, his arm across his shoulders, upholding him. "Did you piss yourself?" he asked with a broad smile.

"Jesus Christ! You didn't have to do that, Beat It!" Ateer said between ragged breaths.

"It's around this time that rookies usually puke up their guts." Pedrotti danced a little going over to Accorso and looking down at him, lowering his head once again to the larger slit that he cut in the bag. "Okay, I see some shit."

"What do you see?" Pedrotti asked, bending over to look down, hands on his knees.

"Looks like the chippy's shit," he grumbled. He stuck a finger inside, poked around. "Lipstick, compact, comb, I don't know what the fuck this is, but it doesn't look explosive."

"Are you calling it?" Pedrotti asked.

Accorso righted the bag, opened its clasp, and stood. "It's safe."

Ateer could take it no more. He leaned a hand against the cab and exhaled as if he was holding his breath all along. Accorso lifted the bag and walked off to the cordon of officers and Lieutenant Wheeler.

"How did you like spending some time next to the beast?" Pedrotti said, walking up to Ateer and gripping his shoulder, releasing, and applying pressure to calm him down. "No. The beast is when they go off. You meet the beast, and your entire outlook will change. You will too."

"I was completely useless," Ateer sighed miserably.

"Well, this is where you are going to deal with your first test. Do you *want* to continue in the Bomb Squad or not?"

Ateer could feel his strength slowly returning by degrees. Pedrotti looked him up and down. "Why don't you head back to the car and take a seat. We'll be leaving in a minute or two. I want to go to the precinct and follow up on this woman for my report."

"What do you think's going on?"

"The fuck if I know." Pedrotti turned and looked off into the distance, the cordon was breaking up. RMPs were pulling off, patrolmen were walking off to their beats. The panic, the excitement, was siphoning off into the wind.

"Come on," Pedrotti walked off.

Ateer pushed himself away from the cab as the driver came around, shutting the rear door. He was about to depart also. Walking with a slight wobble, like a newborn fawn, Ateer headed toward their RMP. Once inside, he began to relax in the shadows of the car. Soon, both Accorso and Pedrotti slipped into the vehicle and closed the doors.

"Can you believe it," Accorso said over his shoulder. "The crazy bitch is babbling to herself."

"What was she doing in the cab?" Ateer asked.

"The officer said that it looked as if she was readying to move off to another intersection and another phone booth. She was just trying to figure it out."

"So where are they taking her?"

"To the Charles Street station, sixth precinct."

"Are we going there?"

"Yeah," Pedrotti said.

Accorso pulled away from the curb and stepped on the accelerator.

. . .

The call went out to the resources now allocated to the World's Fair roiling through it in search for the bomb. The perpetrator of the phone calls was now in police custody. There was enough evidence present to conclude that the bomb threat was a hoax. By 8:20 a.m. phone calls were coming into the Operations Room from the RMPs at Flushing Meadows, informing them that they were now available to be dispatched to any other locations in their patrol territories. Matrons flipped over the black disks on the indicator table around the World's Fair to white, sliding them across the map to where each RMP said they would report to standby.

The energy of nearly the entire body of the NYPD, which was churning like a mighty storm, abated rapidly, going cold.

With both, a measure of relief and disappointment, the supervisor called Commissioner Valentine.

Uptown, on the west side, in a brown brick building that served as the precinct for the west Village of Manhattan a short column of RMPs went through the garage exit doors and to booking where the black woman was handcuffed to a long, wooden bench. Both detectives and officers buzzed around her to look at the maniac that had the NYPD on attack. A soaring opportunity to settle a score turned out to be a massive anticlimax. Accorso went to the desk officer. "Is Captain Wheeler around?"

Accorso was directed to the captain's office, with Pedrotti and Ateer in tow.

Wheeler invited them into his large, modern office. He stood to shake hands, "Sorry guys, I only have one chair in here."

"Yeah, yeah, no problem," Accorso said. "How'd it go?"

Lowering into his chair, Wheeler said, "Well, we have a Ms. Christine Lewis, nineteen years old of 109-57 Union Hall Street, Jamaica Queens."

"Nineteen, huh?"

Wheeler shook his head, sighing, "The minute we got her to the station house a dozen or so patrolmen recognized her. She's been arrested before for the same old shit."

"Really?"

Wheeler reached over, picked up a file and slammed it on the desk before him. He opened the folder and began to scan. "I see at least two times where this fucking nutcase made repeated phone calls announcing that she was about to commit suicide all over the place."

"That's great. Nothing concrete. No real connection to the World's Fair Bombing?"

"Nothing. I'm packing this fruitcake off to Bellevue psychiatric." With a certain angry flair, he picked up a pen and scribbled his name quickly, then dropped the pen. "Sorry about all this bullshit."

"No problem. We get this kinda stuff all the time."

Accorso leaned over the desk, shook Wheeler's hand. "Stay safe."

"Stay safe, detectives," Wheeler said, returning to his paperwork.

SEVEN
PEACE BEFORE WARTIME

SEPTEMBER 24TH, 1941

Young patrolman Andrew Latz walked confidently down his beat on Park Avenue in the Bronx. The sun was high but even though bright, it was not hot. Either way, hot or cool, Latz had found much shelter under the row of trees that lined the sidewalk, making the eastern side of the avenue shadier than the western side, which was the fenced off embankment down the train tracks of the Harlem Line. This side of the avenue was completely devoid of shade. This time of the afternoon the sun had dropped over the houses on the other side of the tracks but not low enough to close the day. However, the long line of shadows was drawing longer and longer, soon to vanish as the afternoon gave way to evening.

Children ran up and down the block, tirelessly. Their near constant flow of energy burning in them so vibrantly that the only solace their tiny minds could find was to run, and run, and run. Like birds in flight, they wheeled and turned, first chasing one and then turning around to chase the other. Running past, they barely rounded the walking cop, nearly knocking him over in their shouting, headlong run. A woman walked a large Doberman which stopped and raised its leg to a tree. He doffed his hat to two passing young women and nodded to a passing man.

He worked on his skill of twirling his baton, yanking on its leather wrist strap to spin it out and into his hand. Latz appreciated his beat —quiet with hard working middle-class citizens that cared about their neighbor and watched out for one another. Hearing rapid footfalls behind him, he turned around finding two teenage boys run to a stop before him. Panting, they told him that they found something on the corner of Washington Avenue and Claremont Parkway. Hurry.

Suspecting some form of prank, Latz only trotted behind them up the avenue and then right, on Claremont Parkway, a wide avenue with a great deal of traffic and businesses. Running was also a laborious effort for him because of his heavy leather utility belt from which his pistol and handcuff purse hung rocking on his hips. The teenagers stayed several paces ahead of him, as if fearful of losing him in the modest run to the intersection. But Latz was certain that if he did lose the boys, he would not have missed the gathering of gawkers standing around something. No more than half a dozen people, but their interest was piquing the interest of other passerby who altered their courses to come and see what was so interesting.

Latz pushed his way between two people and found himself standing before an inexpensive cardboard box in the shape of a suitcase with a plastic handle. Was this the prank? He looked up at the other faces around him just as confused to what all the commotion was about.

"Does this belong to anyone?" he asked aloud. Everyone either stared back at him dumbly or shook their heads. Latz touched it with the toe of his shoe and gave it a light nudge to push it around, finding it heavier than he expected. His nudge was met with inappropriate weight resistance. Whatever was *in* the suitcase, could not be carried by the plastic handle that looped across its top. He then jammed his baton into its leather retaining clasp on his utility belt knelt low and lifted the box, which was strong enough to hold together, even though whatever was inside was quite heavy. The weight immediately made Latz suspicious. An unidentified package not far from a main thoroughfare like the concourse could cause quite a commotion if it was a bomb.

He returned the suitcase and then urged onlookers to back up, creating a wide berth between them and the device. Then he left for the nearest call box.

The squad car and the Ford E83W pulled to a stop on Fulton Avenue. The homes on the left side of the tree lined street overlooked the lush and green Claremont Park in the Bronx, filled with trees sighing in the wind, dappled shade, and numerous large clearings. Pyke climbed out of the vehicle on the passenger side. He stretched and yawned, the park having a disarming effect on him. He slipped out of his jacket and tossed it in the front seat with his hat and walked up the block.

Accorso, on the driver's side of the car, did the same and pulled up the seat so that Ateer could climb out of the back. He tossed in his jacket but left his fedora on his head.

Pedrotti, climbing out behind Pyke kept his jacket and hat, slamming the door shut, and following behind his superior. Frascone stayed behind the wheel of the van, watching.

Up ahead were the parked green and white RMPs and black squad cars of the various precincts in the area, and something new. Pyke stopped, registering the parked green Mack truck with the gold words *Police Emergency Service* painted on its sides. In the back of the high and empty truck was a series of chrome railings so that the Emergency Squad men could use them to pull themselves up and sit face to face in the open-air rear of the truck on two rows of padded seats, the front seats of the roofless cab, also open air, and sans windshield. Everything seemed to be attached to the sides of the truck from spare tires, and ladders to fire extinguishers and lanterns.

Pyke wondered why they were here. He stopped cold, Accorso

and Pedrotti walked up from behind to flank him and stared in wonder at the well-equipped and manned vehicle ahead.

"What are *they* doing here?" Accorso tilted his head towards Pyke and spoke through the corner of his mouth.

"I don't know, but I bet something's wrong." Pyke set out again, leaving the sidewalk and heading for the center of the asphalt street which the diagonally parked truck blocked, going around the front of the vehicle and finding the 'nerve center' of the police action. A uniformed officer without a hat walked up to Pyke extending his hand. "Lieutenant Harvey of the Emergency Squad."

Pyke shook his hand, "Lieutenant Pyke, Bomb Squad. What happened here?"

Harvey turned and walked towards the park. Pyke walked with him while Accorso, Pedrotti and Ateer followed.

"A patrolman found the suspicious package and called it in. The precinct called us."

"And not the Bomb Squad?"

"No, just us. We called the Bomb Squad, but the suitcase was in a highly populated area, so we decided to move it into the park and dunk it in a bucket of oil."

"You what?"

"We put the..."

Pyke stopped; his lean face exasperated. "You moved it?"

Harvey stopped, turned back to face Pyke. "Why? We felt it was safe since the patrolman picked it up to see what was in it."

"Did the idiot shake it too?"

"What?"

Pyke inhaled deeply to regain a measure of composure. "That was an extremely foolish thing for the patrolman and you to do. If there was a motion sensitive trip switch, he and you could have been killed or maimed. Now, what else? You dunked it in oil?"

"Yeah, we've heard of you doing it, so we carry a large bucket and a barrel of oil around in the truck now just for these occasions."

"You're kidding, right?"

"No, I'm serious. We took it out into a clearing in the park and dunked it. Why? What would you have done?"

"Leave it the fuck alone until the Bomb Squad arrived."

"You don't have to get nasty."

"I think I do, sir. The Emergency Squad isn't trained to handle bombs. We are. Next time, locate, identify, remove people from the area...and then call the Bomb Squad. We'll take it from there."

Harvey snarled, turned, and struck off to the sidewalk and then a path that wended through trees, rich foliage, and lush lawn to open into a clearing which was wide, but not wide enough for the horde of spectators that went around the lone bucket at its center. It was as if a sporting event was being held, with everyone from fathers to mothers holding the hands of their children, struggling over the shoulders of those ahead of them to see a barrel with supposedly a bomb floating inside of it.

Pyke halted again, his shoulders sagging as he looked at the crowds that had also built on the sides of the path. "What is this?"

"They came out of nowhere." Harvey hunched his shoulders. "I'm just as surprised as you are."

Pyke stalked off, passing through the ring of spectators to enter the clearing. They approached the pail and to Ateer every step seemed to go on forever. Pyke was visibly upset, which meant that this was a situation that might have spiraled even out of his control.

Pyke turned to Harvey who had no fear of standing so close to a suspicious package.

"You know that all of these people are not in a safe zone. I would hazard to guess that if there is a decent explosive in this bucket that many of those people will be killed. What did you do, play a magic flute all the way from wherever you found it?"

"What do you mean? We dunked it into oil so it should be out of whack now, right?"

"Not necessarily."

"What? You mean that thing can still go off?" Now Harvey's relaxed demeanor melted quickly like an ice cube in hell.

"Yes. Believe it or not, but some bombs can be protected against an oil bath. And since it's becoming common knowledge that this is our usual method of operation, the people who make these things go off are going to build to defeat it."

Although he put on a brave face, Harvey's features began to knot in terror.

"We're the Bomb Squad. We are trained for this," Pyke continued.

"Uh," Harvey raised a finger. "I get your point. Give me a minute to talk to my men and we'll see what we can do to back up this area."

"As far as you can, lieutenant," Pyke said. "Shrapnel can travel long distances."

"Sure," and with that Lieutenant Harvey turned and trotted away at first, then it turned into flight.

Accorso chuckled watching him run.

"That's not funny, Accorso," Pyke said to him. "But it *is* funny," he smirked.

Ateer was still not comfortable near a Devil Toy.

"Ateer," Pyke said. "Go and get the Picker from Frascone."

With relief, Ateer turned and trotted off, crossing the clearing, piercing the crowds that the uniformed officers cleared from the path, and then down the block to the Bomb Squad van. Upon seeing his approach, Frascone jumped from the vehicle, excited. "Is it a bomb?"

"Don't know yet. It's sitting in the bottom of a bucket of oil. They need the picker."

Frascone went to the back of the van, reached in, and came out with the long pole-like tool. Ateer trotted back to the clearing, handing the device over to Pyke.

"Sir," Ateer said with a great deal of reluctance.

Pyke turned his attention from the pail to him, "What?"

"I don't think the lieutenant was successful in moving the crowd back."

Looking around, Pyke was amazed at the number of people that had built around the clearing and he knew it wasn't his imagination, their numbers were growing. Also, Ateer was correct in stating that Harvey didn't do a thing because he didn't. He most likely, Pyke thought, found somewhere to hide. Ignoring Ateer's observation he stuck the picker's pincer end into the thick, black fluid and dug around inside but whatever he pulled on would not give the pincer action enough purchase to pull the heavy object out of the bucket.

"Fuck, I didn't want to get dirty," Pyke said, rolling up his sleeves.

"I'll do it," Accorso said, rolling up his sleeves faster. When done, he dropped to one knee and stuck an arm in. He pulled up on something that moved from his singular hold, so he followed one hand with the other, now taking the suitcase in both hands he lifted it up and sat it down next to the pail. "It's pretty heavy."

"I saw that," Pyke said. "I couldn't get the pincer to tighten up on it hard enough to pull it out," he handed the tool to Ateer who held it dripping at arm's length. Pyke knelt low and undid the clasps to the now soaked suitcase.

"Sir, the crowds still aren't at a safe distance away," Ateer pointed out once more, the tension in his voice clear.

Taking a patient pause, and realizing that this was a teaching moment, Pyke looked up at Ateer. "Mac...is it?"

"Yes, sir,"

"Look Mac, there is more than enough chance that this is not a bomb. I have been doing this for years, so I am confident of that fact. But just in case I am wrong, do you think that there will be much left us to really give a fuck if these people were within the blast radius?"

Ateer shook his head, shivering as if cold.

"And another thing," Pyke added. "Only one man to a bomb. Unless you're trying to train someone," he looked at Accorso and Pedrotti, "I mean it you two. I've heard enough reports of the two of you making a device safe. Do not take stupid chances, only one to a bomb."

He flipped open the suitcase and an assortment of electrical supplies rolled out onto the grass. Two power drills, drill bits, hammers, and screwdrivers. Ateer didn't know that he was cringing even long after he identified that what they were standing around was not a bomb. He relaxed by degrees, his breathing slowly returning to normal.

A deafening roar rose from the spectators, followed by thundering applause and cheers.

Ateer smiled. Life in the Bomb Squad.

Pedrotti walked into his apartment. It was dark, no lights were on. The only illumination came from the window, where the glow of the streetlamps outside reached up to their six-floor walk-up and caused the ceiling to glow. He passed his living room to enter the kitchen. The small table sat in the dark, but he could see her outline in the semi-dark on the other end.

She sat with two bottles of wine and a wine glass in her hand.

"What are you doing up, Sienna?" Pedrotti asked.

"What are you doing still out? It's two in the morning."

"Had a couple of drinks," he walked past her, heading for the bedroom.

"I made you a bed on the couch," she said, "you can sleep there this...morning."

Pedrotti stopped short, breathed out a long-steady breath, then turned around, heading back for the living room, "Look, I'm too tired to argue with you tonight."

"I'm not going to argue with you," Sienna stood, resting her glass down and lifted a pack of cigarettes.

Walking into the living room, Pedrotti went straight for the couch, draping his jacket over its armrest, tossing his hat onto the coffee table. Sienna's tall, strong figure stopped in the middle of the living room from the kitchen, wearing a diaphanous pink nightgown and smoking a cigarette. "I lit a cigarette because I don't want to smell sex on your body."

"Oh boy, here we go." Pedrotti sat down on the couch and undid his tie, kicked off his shoes. "I'm going to sleep now. I have got to get up early in the morning."

"I know what you do, Beat It," she said, anger seasoning her voice. "You and Fab are out there whoring around, sticking yourselves in filthy places, and then you bring all that smut home with you, and you expect to crawl into my bed?"

Pedrotti took off his shirt.

"I've taken enough of this shit. I'm getting tired."

"Okay, Sierra," Now in his undershirt, slacks, and socks, Pedrotti stretched out on the couch, punched his pillow to fluff it up, and turned his back to his wife, burying his face into the back of the couch.

Sierra stood like a monument, puffing her cigarette. "I'm going to cheat on you to see how you'd like it."

"I'm not cheating, Sierra."

"The hell you aren't. You're a whore, Beat It. A man who lays with whores is a whore. You and your disgusting friend, Fab. There is no excuse for men like you. None whatsoever."

Pedrotti listened to her statements as long as he could, but he was indeed very tired and fatigued, and sleep came upon him quickly.

July 25th: Roosevelt embargoes shipments of scrap iron and gasoline to Japan and freezes all Japanese assets in the United States.

During the past decades, the military leaders of Japan have been advancing their agenda. Their moves were methodical, attacking China, using the war in Europe to sign a defense pact with Germany and Italy and placed troops in French Indochina. Roosevelt warned them to go no further. The president stopped the sale of aviation fuel and scrap metal, and when that did not provide the desired result, struck them with a battery of economic sanctions and trade embargoes, and had their assets in the United States frozen to prevent the purchase of supplies needed to continue. As months of negotiations continued it was unbelievable that Japan would ever attack the United States.

The Pearl Harbor naval base was too far away and too difficult to get to to attack. The European Colonies were a much more convenient and numerous targets in the South Pacific, well within striking distance of Japan. There was the Dutch East Indies, Indochina, Singapore, and many, many more targets to be had.

So, Pearl Harbor was left relatively unprotected with almost the entire Pacific Fleet stationed around Pearl Island in Oahu's harbor and hundreds of airplanes packed like sardines on nearby airfields.

Accorso sat across from Ateer in the bullpen talking about the Charlie Chan radio show. It was Accorso's opinion that Chan was more skilled than Sherlock Holmes. Sherlock Holmes came from England, had a higher education, and his companion was a physician, an equally learned man as a sidekick, whereas Chan had none of these fallbacks and still could solve some of the most convoluted of crimes. Chan was a true detective, and he would be equally amazing if he worked as a detective in the NYPD.

"Just think," Accorso said, "If he was sitting across from me. The bombs he could defuse."

Ateer laughed, but it trailed off as they both watched Lieutenant Pyke appear in his doorway and then walk over to the balustrade next to their desks. He stood over them, his face set in stern lines like some silent monolith. Although he was right next to them, instead of staring down, he stared straight ahead, making both Accorso and Ateer turn firstly, to see what he was looking at. When finding nothing of interest they turned to him. It was Accorso that spoke first.

"Lieutenant?" he said.

"I'm sorry gentlemen." Pyke shook his head, rousing himself from his personal delirium. "I was thinking there. We just received a call that there is a bomb at the Con Ed Headquarters near 4 Irving Place."

"Con Ed again?" Accorso stood up in his chair and pulled his jacket from its back.

"Yeah. Accorso, take Ateer, take your unit and take care of it. From Hayias's report on the last Con Ed bomb, this one could be capable of going off." Pyke took a step back, watching as his detectives gathered their things and rushed out of the bullpen, dutifully following his orders. Once gone, he returned to his office and Hayias in a chair.

"You sent Accorso?" Hayias asked.

"Yeah," Pyke walked around his desk and took his seat behind it. He looked at Hayias, whose face was pale and sunken. "Are you alright?" he asked.

"Yeah, I'm fine," Hayias said dismissively, "Good choice, Accorso and Unit 1. This one could be ugly."

"You think?"

"You know," Hayias let his voice trail off, "You can always choose Accorso to be your Sergeant. No one would dispute that. He deserves it."

"I was thinking about that, but you know how he is."

"How is he?"

"He's just like you. Accorso isn't interested in a promotion either. The only one I have champing at the bit is Beakey."

"I feel like a drink."

Pyke hunched his shoulders. "Go on, I ain't stopping you."

"C'mon, let's go."

"Nah, not today. I'm going to wait for 'The Call.'"

Hayias knew what Pyke meant by The Call. The call that either everything went north, or everything went south. There would be no middle ground and it is indeed the hardest call to pick up. Pyke remembered the World's Fair Bombing when he got that call. Something that never felt like it would ever happen, happened. On such a nice, sunny day with no indication whatsoever. He didn't knock over a saltshaker, a black cat didn't cross his path, shit, he didn't even walk under a ladder, and yet, such a mighty loss.

"You go through shit like this every day," Hayias said, "and you wonder why I don't want to be a sergeant."

"You don't want to be a sergeant because you don't like being around the action. You like the science of the Infernal Machine, but you don't like to deal with it when it can crawl out and bite you."

"Bullshit!" Hayias laughed. "I can make any bomb safe that you can."

"Sure." Pyke stood, crossed his office to a set of file cabinets against the wall. He opened the bottom drawer, reached into the back, and pulled out a silver flask. Holding it up, he said, "Just for special occasions just like this one."

"What is it? Moonshine?"

"Yep, the finest Goat Whiskey this side of Prohibition." Pyke smiled. He unscrewed the cap and took a deep draw before handing it over to Hayias.

"You know I don't drink this shit." He sniffed the opening, then turned it up to his lips. Upon taking the flask back, Pyke took it around his desk and sat down, placing it in his top drawer.

"Pikey, honestly. Do you really think I've grown chicken when it comes to Devil Toys?" Hayias asked weakly.

"No. No, I didn't mean that. You love the science. I've never seen you sweat one bead since we've been doing this all these many years."

"I'm not talking about the past; I'm talking about now. Do you think that phone call shook me up?"

"You're talking about the July 4th call?"

"Yeah." Hayias reached into his jacket and pulled out a pack of smokes, hitting it against the back of his hand sharply several times to pack the tobacco against the filters.

Pyke cursed himself. He wobbled like an infant from one bad statement to the next bringing him directly to this question. The call that Hayias was mentioning was on July 4th, 1940, at Hayias's home. Months ago, detective Joseph J. Lynch had received a call at his home, asking for him to come out to the World's Fair, at the British Pavilion to help on a bomb call that they had received. He relayed the call to Peter Hayias. Hayias's wife, Clara, explained that her husband was already on his way to the station. Lynch had no problem, he just wanted to include him. Hours later, Lynch and detective Ferdinand A. Socha would be pronounced dead at the scene. Pyke knew that the call had an effect like that of a seismic shift in his friend's behavior. He saw the call as his personal invitation to the afterlife and he stood up. A man, in his book, was not one who could snub death. Although he did, he just came to the bold, hard reality that it was not time to die. It was not his time, or his invitation went out too early.

Whatever the case, Pyke saw a marked change in Hayias. He walked with him towards many an unknown device, fearlessly. But whereas Pyke's fearlessness was because he had years of discerning when something was a bomb and when it wasn't, or maybe even a sixth sense about it; Hayias, on the other hand, had a devil-may-care attitude. He didn't really examine the situation on arrival or ask the right questions of those who had encountered the suspicious package before him. He did whatever he deemed fit at the time, no doubt believing that if his time was up, it was up, and there was little more that he could do.

Now, had this belief developed cracks, weaknesses from stress?

He examined his friend a second time today, and yes, he was pale, his face almost imperceptibly thinner, but he had lost some weight. Hayias appeared worn down, for some reason. Possibly all the emotional refuse inside of him was made turbid in the deep waters of his soul, happened when the alert went out last week that the World's Fair Bomber might have stuck their head out and desired to pit wits once more with the NYPD. Everyone was on edge that day, excited, aroused powerfully that a cold case had suddenly burst to life. Could this piquing of emotions stir up this self-doubt in Hayias?

"No," Pyke wanted to keep it brief. That way there would be no analyzing of his statement, "not at all."

Hayias nodded, thinking. It seemed to Pyke that his statement was going to be analyzed anyway.

"I think I'm going to the Harbor-View Docks," Hayias finally said. "Get something to eat and drink. I don't know about you, but I can tell you one thing."

"What's that?"

"You can sit there and nurse that phone all you want to, but it means nothing because you can't control the outcome. Good or bad, it's gonna be what it's gonna be, and nothing you do in your teeny-weenie office is gonna change that." Hayias stood and went to the coat rack, taking his fedora. "Listen. Come on down to the Harbor-View Docks, have a few drinks, and then come back up here and I'm telling you, Accorso will do his job."

The phone rang. Pyke looked down at it. Hayias went to the threshold of the office and shouted into the bullpen, "Beakey! Pick that up!"

The phone stopped ringing. Hayias turned to Pyke still standing at his desk. "C'mon, Pikey."

He walked off. Pyke stared at the doorway for a moment more before going for his hat and catching up to him.

Ateer drove a Buick Special Touring Sedan as the lead car, working his way through traffic clogging Park Avenue South. They were struggling through the tail end of the rush of cars hastening to get to their places of employment. Behind his car was Big Bertha, driven by Accorso, with Pedrotti in the passenger seat, lumbering like a huge bear through the avenue. And behind the ponderous carrier was Frascone driving the E83W van with their equipment. They worked their way down to Union Square East, passing the lush green park and made a left on East 14th Street.

Before reaching the end of the next block, which was Irving Place, they met up with two squad cars parked nose to nose, blocking off the mouth of the street. A patrolman approached Ateer with a swagger in his stride. Ateer flashed his badge out of the open window and with a wave, the patrolman had the two squad cars blocking their path part like the Red Sea. As the Bomb Squad convoy moved by, they found Irving Place cleared of traffic and pedestrians.

Further down there was a second patrolman waving them on until they were right before him, where he raised his hand to halt the vehicles. The patrolman walked around to the driver's side window and pointed. "It's right there."

Shifting into park, Ateer got out of the car, took off his hat, and tossed it into the driver's seat.

"Okay, come with me." He left open the driver's side door of Big Bertha, as Accorso climbed down out of the cab.

"Where's the bomb?" Accorso barked.

The Patrolman pointed again up the street. "It's in a red sock, right down there."

"You my friend are too fucking close to it. If it goes off, you're gone."

"You're shitting me." The patrolman's face went pale.

"We'll be mopping you off the walls." Accorso assured.

"Okay, I'll go to the roadblock on 15th street."

"That's too close, follow me." Accorso led them back up the side of Big Bertha. Waiting for them there was Pedrotti who went straight to the patrolman.

"Are you the patrolman that found the bomb?" He asked the cop.

"Are we safe here?" The cop replied, looking around in tremendous concern.

"Not yet," Accorso said.

Pedrotti rested a caring hand on the patrolman's shoulder. "Alright buddy calm down, now are you the one who found the bomb?"

"Yes, yes. It was in a red sock." The patrolman said, his face flushed red, "I pulled it out of the sock and there it was, a pipe, capped on both ends..."

"You picked it up?"

"Yeah, I picked it up, I took it out of the sock, and it matched the description of the pipe bomb found at the Con Edison building about a month ago. I put it back in the sock and laid it down next to the gutter, and then ran to a nearby phone to call it in."

"Did you drop it, or put it down?" Pedrotti asked.

"I put it down very gently."

"Good man," Pedrotti patted his back and walked off.

Accorso addressed the Patrolman, pointing off to the roadblock in the distance. "Head up the block, make a right on Irving Place and get out of here. Don't go back in that direction." Accorso swung his arm around, pointing in the direction of the bomb.

"Yes, sir." The patrolman said, and then struck off up 14th street. Accorso turned to Ateer who was standing behind him. "If you have any questions, save them for later. Right now, stick by me and observe."

"Okay."

They headed for the rear of the van. "We're going to put on the protective gear today so that you can see how to operate in them. It's a personal decision if you want to wear it or not, although you're supposed to be always in it," Accorso explained. "I think that's just the city covering it's ass."

Ateer glanced at his watch, it was 10:30 a.m. The sun was already climbing in a clear, blue sky—a wonderfully mild day. "Why don't you wear it all the time?"

"They're bulky, restrictive and fucking hot. To protect you, the bomb suit puts a layer between you and the bomb. That layer also removes you from the bomb. Some of your senses are dulled because of it. Senses that might alert you to danger."

At the rear of the van, the pompadour coiffed Frascone was helping Pedrotti into his bomb gear, like a squire helping a knight with his armor. On the street was a length of steel tubing several feet long next to the steel mesh envelope which was constructed from the same heavy steel cable mesh skin of the carrier. Accorso tossed his hat into the back of the opened doors of the van and started to drag out the heavy bomb garb. He donned the chain mail shirt. Frascone helped him with the apron, bucket-like helmet, and oversized gloves, and in only a few moments he and Pedrotti were dressed for the drama. They appeared to be like two cushion covered Tin Men from the Wizard of Oz.

Accorso, once dressed, said something to Ateer but his voice was muffled by the helmet which covered the entire face except for two eye slits. Ateer could only shake his head to let him know that he didn't understand a word. Accorso pointed to Frascone and mumbled something before walking to the pole, hoisting it on his shoulder with Pedrotti behind him doing the same on the other end. The 'envelope' dangled from the pole between them.

Frascone, looking more like a kid in his twenties, than a full-fledged detective, tapped Ateer on his shoulder. "Fab wants me to tell you what they're doing."

"And what's that?" Ateer stepped out of the way of the two armored men as they headed to the carrier.

"They're going to put the pipe bomb in that basket-thing, called the 'envelope'" Frascone pointed to it as it moved on.

"Why?"

"It's in the same design of Big Bertha. Everything is made from the same heavy woven elevator cable. They weaved it like wickerwork."

"Why is that?"

"It allows the dangerous gasses to escape if the bomb explodes. It'll also disrupt any wave forms that come from the blast. The mesh is also tight enough to keep shrapnel from escaping. That way the beast is all bark and no bite."

"I see." Ateer nodded, watched as the two armored men passed the Carrier and were now approaching the Buick. "So, they can survive a blast once they get the damn thing in the envelope."

"That's the plan but realize that the envelope is nothing compared to Big Bertha. If the blast is strong enough, it'll turn the envelope into a bomb."

"Killing them." Ateer concluded.

"Tearing them to bits. That armor won't protect them." Frascone said, the excitement high in his voice. Ateer turned to look at the manic face of his companion and could tell that Frascone loved being at the periphery of the action. He had front row seats to catastrophe, getting his kicks on the fact that there was boiling danger ahead, and in a perverse way, Ateer knew that a small portion of him wanted to see an explosion. Ateer wondered if Frascone believed that he would walk away from the Beast unscathed if it did emerge, angry and fiery.

Accorso and Pedrotti were now lost from sight, moving around in front of the Buick, and vanishing behind its bulk.

"Shouldn't we go down there and look at what's going on?" Ateer asked.

"No, we stay behind the van. The blast can cause a secondary fragmentation."

Ateer frowned. "What's that?"

"That's where the fragmentation from the initial blast can cause more fragmentation, like a cue ball striking other balls, which roll off in different directions carrying the kinetic energy from the cue. Like a piece of that pipe striking a sheet of glass. But that shit's nothing. What's worse is if there is a fireball from the blast so large that it ignites the fuel line of the car nearest to it, and there starts your secondary explosions. A fireball big enough can start a chain reaction from car to cars on the block which will cause more secondary fragmentation."

"Shit. A bad day sounds like hell with the lid off." Ateer breathed.

"That's an understatement. If anything goes wrong, not only will they die, but we, acting like spectators, can end up just as dead, or maimed, or just plain fucked up so badly that you'd wish you were dead." Frascone nodded, peering around the back of the van briefly. "There's something to *not* wearing protective gear. It's a choice not to survive the blast or end up a horrible cripple."

"It doesn't seem like there's any safe place to watch this." Ateer observed.

"Actually, there isn't. The safest place is reading it in the fucking newspaper tomorrow morning. Hell, a pipe bomb has enormous power because the explosion is contained initially. Secondary explosions can even ignite this fucking van all the way over there." Frascone turned around and indicated with a motion of his head the police blockade at the end of the block. All these cops and bystanders a block away can still get maimed in such a confined space as this street. Just think of them as standing at the mouth of a cannon." Frascone looked up and around at the tall limestone, granite and brick buildings towering over them.

Ateer watched Frascone, amazed at not only how knowledgeable the young man was, but also his strange excitement surrounding sudden, despicable death. "How long have you been doing this, Basilio?"

"Please call me, Big O, Mac."

"Okay, Big O—how long have you been riding in the van?"

"I'm still considered a rookie. I think they've decided to train you over me for some reason, but I've been at this for three years."

Ateer turned to him. "They're training me over you?"

"Shh," Frascone raised a finger to his lips. "They're coming back with the Devil Toy."

In the distance, Accorso and Pedrotti came around the Buick and strode up the side of the parked bomb squad vehicles. Reaching the end of the Carrier, they carefully rested the envelope on the asphalt. One of the armored men raised a thick and heavy door from the back of the carrier and out projected the rectangular Bomb Tank. They lifted it from the carriage that extended it out from the interior of the Carrier and rested it gently on the ground next to the envelope.

"What are they doing now?" Ateer asked.

"They're gonna strap the pipe bomb down in the bottom of the tank so that when they fill it with motor oil, it won't float to the top."

"They're going to submerge it in motor oil?"

"Yeah, if there's an opening in it, the motor oil will gum up its sensitive parts."

"But it's double capped. It shouldn't have a problem being dipped in motor oil."

"Well, that's what we do my friend. That's what we do." Frascone smiled.

Ateer stepped out from around the van and moved into a position where he could have an unobstructed view of the two detectives ahead. They took the pipe bomb from the envelope and placed it into the tank. After securing the pipe bomb to the bottom of the tank Accorso and Pedrotti lifted the heavy rectangular box and rested it in its carriage. Upon closing the door, the carriage was slowly sucked up into the bowels of Big Bertha.

"It's over?" Ateer asked.

"Far from it." Frascone assured. "The Toy is in the Pocket. Now the real danger begins."

"What's that?"

"Stopping the Beast."

Accorso and Pedrotti came to the back of the van and started to undress from their bomb disposal armor while Frascone moved about them like a titmouse, stowing away their armor, the suspension pole and the envelope.

When he lifted off his helmet, his face sweaty and red, Accorso said to Ateer: "Any questions?"

"Where to now?"

Taking a moment to hand the helmet to Frascone and reaching in for his hat, Accorso said: "Brooklyn." And planted the hat firmly on his head.

They sat in the bar at The Harbor-View Docks, leaning over the polished wood bar, their beers before them. The lunch crowd was due to arrive in another half hour, which meant that they would be cutting their pause in the day short. Hayias finished his cigarette, crushed it out in the ashtray next to him, sipped from his beer.

"I know I keep beating a dead horse," he said, "but do you think I'll have a hard time moving my office to the lab?"

"Certainly," Pyke said. He stared down in the mouth of his mug, his thoughts far away.

"What are you going on about?"

"What?"

Hayias used his chin to point out the beer before Pyke. "If your eyes were straws, you'd be on you fifth beer by now."

Pyke shook his head, turned to face him. "Sorry about that."

"I'm telling you; everything is going to be fine today."

"You and I need to go out and do a run."

"Sure. Later."

"Any reason for later?"

Hayias smiled, drank from his mug, finishing it. "One of the lab techs will be bringing in the bomb at 4 Irving Place soon. I want to be there to take it apart."

"I should've known."

"That first pipe bomb was making a statement, Pikey." Hayias waved over the bartender who approached, pointed at the empty mug and after Hayias' nod, spirited it away. "His hatred of Con Ed is consuming."

"So?"

"If it's the same construction, you have reason to start to worry about the members of the Bomb Squad. This guy means business."

"How can you tell?"

"Because this is his second warning to Con-Ed."

"How do you know it's the same guy?"

"Because it's Con-Ed," Hayias watched as his next beer arrived, his eyes glittering in anticipation. "This guy has an issue with Con-Ed."

"And you're under the impression that it's going to get worse?"

"Why should this guy bother with the fake bombs. Think about it. He's proving to Con-Ed and to us that he can leave his little Infernal Devices anywhere he wants around them. He's proven that he can make them functional. And he no doubt has a gripe against Con Ed. Means, Motive, and Opportunity. Jackpot. This motherfucker is gonna turn up the heat, and the Bomb Squad is smack dab in the middle."

"You're serious about this, aren't you?"

"Deadly. And I hate to use that word, but..."

"What are you predicting? Worse than the World's Fair?"

"Much worse."

Pyke laughed, returned to his beer, turned it up and drank deeply.

"Mark my words, Pikey. This guy is dangerous."

"And that's why you're gonna run off now to the lab, to look at this notice being sent from your mysterious bomber?"

"Yeah."

"Let me ask you, how are you getting along with, Clara?"

"What? You think this is about her?"

"It isn't?"

"No. Why are you bringing her into it?"

"To be honest?" Pyke turned back to him; all humor gone from his features. He was growing angry. "All this shit about your mysterious bomber is a bit unnerving. I came here to drink a dark cloud from over my head and you're blowing it back."

"Sorry. I thought you were interested about my opinions."

Hayias's lack of response melted Pyke's ire. After a sigh, he said, "I should have gone with Accorso."

"You go with him a lot. What about Beakey."

"Beakey is a barracuda. He likes being in charge. People like that worry me."

"Is that it?"

"One of the many 'ifs' in my life, my friend."

Hayias sat still, his eyes boring into the side of Pyke's head. He sat there, being obvious in his stare. Pyke ignored it but was keenly aware of its presence. They sat, in a form of suspended animation, one waiting for the other to break.

"I know you, you son-of-a-bitch," Hayias said. "Something is wrong. What is it?"

"What do you mean?"

"You've been off for a couple of weeks now."

"Yeah?"

"Yeah."

"Shit. I was going to keep this on the Q.T., but—"

"Don't tell me," Hayias interrupted. "It's about Barbara."

Pyke looked at him. "What's wrong with you?"

"What?"

"I'm trying to tell you what it is."

"Alright. Alright," Hayias held up his hands to stop his friend from berating him. "Go ahead. I apologize."

After a sigh, "I was called in to see Valentine."

"The commissioner?"

"No...the saint. Of course, the fucking commissioner."

Now, Pyke had Hayias's full attention. "What about?"

"Ateer."

"What about him?"

"Valentine wants me to mentor him."

"Why?"

"That's what I want to know."

They fell silent. Hayias thought about the possibilities, then, "Correct me if I'm wrong, but didn't he come from the P.M. Squad?"

"That's right."

Hayias reached out and rested a hand on Pyke's shoulder, "I know you know about Accorso and Pedrotti. You even hang around with them on occasion, so you know the shit that they get into. Do you think it's a good idea to put the new guy in Unit one?"

"Valentine said to keep him close."

"Jesus, he's gonna experience some really dark shit being around those two."

"Why do you say that?"

"Look, I don't know specifically what they do, but *you* do. I've only heard scuttlebutt about them."

"Why do you think I know?"

"Holy fuck! You were in a car accident with Accorso just over a month ago."

"Firstly, what the two of them do on their own time is their business, as long as they get the job done."

"I agree."

"Secondly, they're doing nothing criminal. Maybe immoral, but nothing criminal."

"Didn't he take you to some kinda illegal bar?"

"What?"

"And the women?"

Pyke sighed. "Victim-less crimes my friend. Victim-less crimes."

"But crimes nonetheless."

Pyke finished his beer. Took Hayias's pack of cigarettes off the bar and lit one.

"This guy, Ateer, could be investigating the Bomb Squad. And you dropped him into the single dark spot in the squad."

"Look, Unit one is my best unit. They understand the politics of dealing with other agencies. Accorso is liked by everyone. I can't say the same about Beakey or Dempsey. Beakey is a teetotaler, Dempsey is a hot head."

"I'm the last person that you have to explain that Accorso is your favorite. He's got the same magic that you do when it comes to going on calls."

"Why do people always say that? I'm not a legend. Now Owen Eagan, he was the true legend."

"I know this story, the man that put the 'Bomb' in Bomb Squad. Listen Pikey, you are the one everyone calls now to take care of the tough stuff. Eagan is long gone. Live with it." Hayias reached over and grabbed Pyke by the shoulder, squeezing it. "Listen, you've got to get to the bottom of whatever Valentine is up to. And you'd better pray that whatever shit Accorso and Pedrotti dip this youngster in doesn't get back to him."

"Why? What is he going to do? Fire me?"

"I doubt that. But Valentine has been in this business for far longer than you." Hayias glanced at his watch. "The bomb will be on its way to the lab in a few minutes," he stood from the stool, reaching for his wallet.

"Take off, buddy. This is on me." Pyke leaned over his beer again.

"Go get the call," Hayias patted him on the back, "you'll see that everything is alright. This time."

Hayias walked off, leaving the establishment. Pyke watched him leave, then crushed his cigarette out. Hayias was right. He had to find out what Valentine was up to. Either that, or whatever hell was waiting for him would certainly claim him.

"Fuck."

Ateer turned the Buick onto the apron leading into the abandoned ash heap in Brooklyn. The Carrier lumbered up onto it next, turning ponderously and then barreling down the length of the flattened heap, rumbling past the parking Buick, wheezing, and puffing like a mechanical dinosaur. Pulling up behind the Buick was the E83W Van rocking to a stop. Frascone jumped out of the vehicle and waited for the detectives to emerge.

Ateer stepped out and watched from a distance, the car between himself and Big Bertha, as Accorso and Pedrotti marched back from the Carrier to the van. When close Accorso patted Pedrotti on the back. "Why don't you help Mac into the gear, and he'll help me dunk the motherfucker."

Pedrotti waved to Ateer. "Hey, over here."

Ateer went to the rear of the van and Pedrotti snatched his fedora from his head and tossed it into the back. Reaching in, he pulled out a shirt of heavy chain mail. "Put this on."

Ateer peeled out of his jacket and crawled up into the chain mail shirt, followed by the heavy apron.

"What are we going to do now?" Ateer asked Accorso.

"We're going to fill the tank with motor oil," Accorso said, lifting his bucket helmet and placing it carefully over his head.

Pedrotti took Ateer's bucket helmet and slipped it over his head. Immediately, due to the proximity of the metal plates in the front of the helmet, pressed against his face, Ateer felt as if he was being suffocated. He gasped his first few breaths until he was assured that he could breathe and grabbed it by both sides to adjust it so that his eyes were lined up with the eye slits, allowing him to see. The most uncomfortable aspect of the helmet was the heat of his breath being blown back into his face.

Accorso mumbled something to Ateer who hunched his shoulders uncomprehendingly. Pedrotti patted him on the back of his head, catching his attention. "He says: 'follow his lead.'"

Ateer nodded. He and Accorso headed out to the rear of 'Big Bertha' up ahead. They marched at a steady pace, the weight of the armor slowing them down. Accorso reached the rear of the carrier, folding down its ladder and climbed up onto the platform at the rear door. Using the rope to the pulley overhead he pulled down causing the heavy and thick blast door to rise due to the counterbalances inside. As the door came up the bomb tank extended upon its carriage, lolling out like a tongue from an opening square mouth. Up close, Ateer could see the inner construction of the carriage and railings that it ran upon as they extended from Bertha. Everything inside was constructed of wood, to minimize shrapnel damage from the inside.

Accorso pointed to a pair of handles on the end and Ateer took his cue to reach for them and lift the tank from the carriage. As soon as he cleared his end from the carriage, Accorso took the pair of handles at the other end and with great care, he and Ateer brought the rectangular box down from the platform so that Accorso could clear the ladder and gain some solid footing on the ground. Once ready, they lifted the box between them and marched to a grouping of barrels in the distance.

Ateer could feel his heart skipping beats. Could this metal box, whose walls were thick but not heavy, contain the blast if the bomb decided to go off? Being where it was with the waist long length of his apron, and a codpiece stopping just below his crotch, Ateer estimated that a sufficient enough blast would tear his unprotected legs from his body. This thought kept replaying in his mind as he and Accorso continued their trek to the barrels. No matter how quick Ateer tried to pick up the pace, they still seemed to be moving in painfully slow motion. He looked at Accorso ahead of him, walking with his hands holding the handles behind his back, and with him as a focal point they suddenly reached the barrels. Ateer took his cue as Accorso turned around, keeping at least one hand holding the handle, and lowered the tank down to their feet.

Lying innocently inside was the pipe bomb wrapped in its red sock, strapped to the bottom of the tank. It was a simple length of pipe, much shorter than his forearm. As he stared down, captivated at the grinning death lying patiently in the tank, Accorso took a hose from the barrel, placed it in the tank and began to work the lever of the hand pump at the top, quickly filling the tank with the black, viscous liquid. When done, he returned the hose to its place and marched back to the van. Ateer rushed several steps ahead of him, stopping and turning when he noticed that he was in much more of a hurry than his superior. His entire body was electric, tensed like a frightened cat, however he didn't want it to become apparent. He paused, allowing Accorso to catch up and then with him, side by side, returned to the relative safety of the van.

As soon as they stopped at the van doors in front of Pedrotti and Frascone, the two men were upon them, helping them to undress from the heavy armor and packing it in the rear of the van. When the helmet came away, Ateer's face was covered in a cold sweat, his sign of relief was palatable to everyone around. Slowly his nerves began to unwind and settle.

SUSPICIOUS LOOKING PACKAGES

"How was it?" Pedrotti smiled. "Scared your balls off, didn't it?"

"It was okay," Ateer said, summoning up hidden reserves of courage.

Accorso burst out laughing. So infectious was his guffaws, Pedrotti joined in, followed by Frascone a minute later, somewhat reluctant to laugh at the rookie.

"No, it was okay," Ateer repeated, trying to convince everyone that he was more intrepid than he appeared.

Accorso stopped laughing, reached into the van and came away with his and Ateer's fedoras. "I could hear your knees knocking together like the beak of a woodpecker on a tree all the way." He crossed over to Ateer and handed over his hat.

"I was *that* obvious?" Ateer asked, blushing.

"You mean, in the way that you ran back here from that bomb?" Pedrotti asked with a grin.

"And I thought I was walking calmly."

"You thought."

Accorso closed the doors of the van. "Big O, you know the story from here. You can go home now."

"See you later guys. You take care," Frascone said, moving off. Before getting behind the wheel of the van, he turned around and pointed to Ateer, "Mac and you did good."

"Thanks, Big O," Ateer replied.

Frascone waved goodbye. Soon the van's engine roared and the large vehicle lurched away and drove off, heading for the apron of the lot and then off onto the local roads back to the precinct.

Accorso lit a cigarette and handed the pack to Pedrotti.

"What are we waiting for now?" Ateer asked as Pedrotti handed him the pack of smokes. He waved it away, reaching for his own from his jacket pocket.

"For a bomb technician from the lab." Accorso said, stopping at the side of the Carrier, placing it between themselves and the Bomb Tank, leaning back against it. Pedrotti leaned on the truck beside him. Ateer stood before the two of them.

"He's going to come and take it away?" Ateer asked.

"Yep. They get the call about the bomb, wait about an hour, and meet us here."

"In Bertha?"

Pedrotti scoffed. "In a newspaper. They're taking the chance that the bomb is safe when they arrive."

"Taking the chance?"

"That's right, until we learn differently."

"Why?" Accorso asked, "You have somewhere to be?"

"No."

"You do," he asked Pedrotti, smiling broadly.

"No."

In an oddly playful mood, Accorso said to Ateer, "After rubbing shoulders with the beast, Beat It is always in the mood for some strange."

Pedrotti turned to him. "Bringing that up, are we?"

"Just be careful not to put your dick where his has been." Accorso said slyly to Ateer.

"Oh really?"

Accorso nodded with a grin.

"Watch where his dick has been too. His is usually right after mine." Pedrotti pointed out. "Let me tell you something, rookie. This guy is always trying to play holier than thou, but the truth is he does everything I do and then some. But he's trying to pull the wool over your eyes. At least I'm straight with you. If I like to drink heavily, smoke dope, and chase strange pussy, I'll let you know to your face. But watch this guy." Pedrotti pointed to Accorso.

"Really?" Accorso moved the comments to an argument. "I've already told him that I'm a whoremonger."

"Oh, I need to do that too?"

"You should if you're going to accuse me of playing holier than thou."

They fell silent, staring at each other and smoking.

SUSPICIOUS LOOKING PACKAGES

"And Lieutenant Pyke lets you behave in such a manner?" Ateer asked cautiously.

Pedrotti flicked his cigarette away. "What has Pyke have anything to do when we're off the trick?"

"Yeah, Pyke is no one's daddy," Accorso said. "What did I tell you the other night, Mac?" He paused, giving Ateer an opportunity to respond, and when he didn't Accorso said, "We are expendable guineas. You my friend are an expendable green-nigger. You need to realize this. What is the point of counseling us about our vices when the next day, something like that Devil Toy back there," Accorso jerked a thumb over his shoulder at the pipe bomb in the distance. "will send us to our maker. It kinda makes any counsel about what we are doing to cope with this shit pointless now, doesn't it?"

Ateer nodded thoughtfully.

"Seriously, if you think I'm bailing a pitchfork full of hay in your face, just walk around this Carrier, reach in that Bomb Tank and check on that pipe bomb. I betcha that little Devil Toy will crowd out every other thought in your hayseed head. I betcha," Accorso said.

"I agree." Ateer dropped his cigarette and stubbed it out with his toe.

"Take the stick out of your ass, Mac," Pedrotti said. "Do what you wanna do, die like you wanna die and leave a tattered and broken corpse when one of these things goes off in your face."

A vehicle pulling up onto the apron of the lot caught their attention. It traveled up the distance of the lot, its tires crunching on the gritty asphalt, and stopped several yards away from the rear of the Carrier. It sat there with its engine idling. The afternoon sun was well up in the cloudy skies and Ateer was beginning to wonder how long they would have to stand around and babysit, or more accurately, leave themselves exposed to, this Devil Toy until someone emerged from the vehicle and took it away.

"Who's that?" Ateer asked.

"I don't know," Pedrotti said.

"Did you say that one of the bomb techs are coming?"

"Yeah."

"Then why is he just sitting there?"

"Who knows?"

Accorso nodded, agreeing with the statement.

The door to the vehicle opened and a well-dressed man with tie and hat stood from the car. He took a moment to button his jacket and slip a newspaper under his arm before walking up to them. Ross Kelly approached with his sad, bored shuffle, and his long, tired features. If he could be anywhere else, he would be. It was obvious to Ateer that behind Kelly's large, square eyeglasses, through his irises, and down the path of his optic nerves, there was a sleeping brain uninterested in the task that was at hand.

"Gentlemen," he said, nodding slightly, his face bored. "How long have you been waiting?"

"About ten minutes," Accorso said, looking at his watch.

"Can I have it now?"

"It's only been ten minutes."

"That's fine. The pipe bomb is practically watertight. The last time, the motor oil didn't even penetrate to the inside of the bomb. But I'm willing to gamble that this one is also not designed to go off."

"Seriously?" Pedrotti said.

Without replying, Kelly turned to Accorso, staring into his eyes. Translation: I don't want to be here. Let's get this show on the road.

"Okay, let's go," Accorso said, lurching from his lean against the Carrier and leading the four men to the Bomb Tank. He went to the side of the tank and with a foot kicked it over, spilling the motor oil. Ateer jumped out of his skin as the tank crashed on its side, splashing its oily contents out onto the beaten, lifeless earth.

"Shit." Ateer sighed, clutching at this heart.

"If Kelly is right, it shouldn't go off," Accorso said.

"What if he's wrong?"

"Then we won't be around to care."

Ignoring the conversation, Kelly knelt low removed the pipe bomb from the tank and picked it up in its soggy sock with the newspaper, wrapping it carefully. When done he stood and addressed Accorso "Did this one come with a note?"

Accorso shook his head.

"Thank you, Gentlemen," he said, and walked off, returning to the car. They watched as Kelly climbed into the passenger side of the vehicle and it backed away, clearing the lot, and driving off.

"Isn't he afraid that that damn thing will go off in his lap?" Ateer asked, watching the car before it vanished into the streets.

"We should be so lucky." Pedrotti muttered.

"C'mon, Kelly's not that bad," Accorso said.

"The only one of those lab people I can deal with is Hayias because he was Bomb Squad."

"The Lab is Bomb Squad."

"The hell it is."

"Let's clean this shit up and get the fuck out of here," Accorso said, patting Pedrotti on the shoulder and marching off.

Pedrotti pointed to a coil of hose not far off. "Mac, there's a hose and water spigot over there. Go get it and hose down this motor oil. Just spread it around. It's not going anywhere."

Ateer nodded and walked off.

In the largest borough in New York, Brooklyn, tucked near the ramp of the Brooklyn Bridge, and hidden behind a large candy factory was the renovated and enlarged NYPD Technical Research Laboratory. A three story, light brown brick building, once the Brooklyn Police headquarters, now housing the Police Academy. The large building, busy with cadets and Training officers, was alive with activity, crawling like an ant mound.

Hayias marched up the stairs, keeping to the banister on the right as young cadets raced up and down the flights, rushing to their next classes. On the top floor, much quieter because it had no classrooms, was the Technical Research Laboratory. White sterile walls, black linoleum flooring, a library chock full of technical manuals and procedural books, other shelving filled with bottles of chemicals, small mechanisms, microscopes, a micro-photographic camera which could enlarge objects to 1,200 times, a tintometer, weight scales, a binocular microscope, a movie camera. Another room served as a dark room, the largest room with its center worktable was the workshop with every tool imaginable, both electric and manual, on the walls.

In the beginning, in 1934, Commissioner O'Ryan allocated three small rooms in the old headquarters, and the size of the lab was modest at best, modeled after the laboratory used by the Swedish Police. However, due to the number of solved cases by the laboratory and the NYPDs growing dependence on science and technology to solve crimes, Commissioner Valentine enlarged the laboratory even more in size and quality.

Larger pieces of equipment, such as Ultra-violet and X-ray machines were added and improved, and although every bit of space was utilized, more rooms in the upper floors were opened, now giving them room for offices and more work areas other than the central workshop.

Inside one of the shared offices were 'The Bookends,' Aiden Meyers and James Sullivan hard at work on something, standing over their desks and pondering whatever was on top of it. Hayias waved at them, but they took no notice. Heading to the work room, which was unofficially his 'office,' Hayias looked for Ross Kelly, but did not see him when he passed his spacious office.

Hayias walked into the workroom, closing its door behind him. He turned off the glaring neon light overhead. He strode ahead to the long workbench which was divided into four sections and turned on the goose-neck coil machinist table lamp on the second area. The first work section on the right had each piece of the last Con-Ed pipe bomb atop it, disassembled and its parts placed neatly, one next to the other, ready for further examination.

On the second section patiently waited an opened-up newspaper and a blackened sock, no doubt left behind by Ross Kelly before he vanished to parts unknown.

Leaving the newspaper on the bench he went to the desk and after going through the drawer, produced a set of rubber gloves. He pulled up a rolling chair, donning the gloves and sat before the new acquisition. After a pause he pushed aside the newspaper and removed the sock, exposing the pipe bomb found earlier today.

First taking a deep breath he began working with the length of pipe, approximately four and a half inches long and capped on both ends. Caps that were so tightly wound that it took a great effort on Hayias's part to crack one and unscrew it with two small pipe wrenches. As he suspected, upon turning it over and shaking out its contents the familiar flashlight bulb, battery, steel spring and the even more bizarre throat lozenge came tumbling out. As he also predicted, no trace of oil seeping into its internals, again confirming that the oil bath was useless against this design.

Scattered before him once more were the parts of a bomb that could not detonate. Another calling card? This time, without a note? Hayias was seriously puzzled. Was this a black mark against the bomber? Could it be one of two things? Either the bomber did not have the knowledge to create a working bomb or maybe he lacked the intestinal fortitude to make something lethal or destructive. Hayias: two. Bomber: zero.

After separating the components with a pencil into neat, orderly rows he moved to the workspace on the right where the previous bomb still sat in parts, neatly spaced, and separated. He took a step back and viewed everything from a distance he could clearly see that the exact components on the right were duplicated to precision on the left. It was indeed the same person. Both bombs had the same creator who was attempting to speak to him.

The door to the office opened behind him. Hayias did not care to turn around but instead cocked his fists on his hips and continued to wonder at the parts on the two side by side workstations.

"Whatcha got there?" Ross Kelly said from behind him, somewhat reluctant in not wanting to intrude upon the bomb genius.

"We've got a serial bomber. But something is wrong."

"What's that?"

"He either can't or doesn't wish to be destructive." Hayias turned around and faced Kelly.

Ross Kelly was an older man, in his late fifties, who had been in the bomb technician department for nearly twenty years, but he never showed any affinity for the work. Hayias considered him to be somewhat of a hack after years of being around things as incredible as bombs and not finding a love for them. Kelly seemed to sleepwalk through his days, as if he was hearing the songs of sirens instead of trying to divine the intentions and identity of someone planning to harm others.

Kelly's face was a mess of deep wrinkles, and eyes constantly at half mass, as if his dim wit could not illuminate them enough to force his eyelids to raise to their fullest. He had Hippocratic baldness, the top of his head polished to a bright shine, the sides covered in a wreath of hair.

"Then he's not a problem." Kelly walked up to the workstations and looked at both bombs, shaking his head. "Okay, these are definitely the handiwork of the same man."

Hayias went behind the office desk, moved the Royal typewriter into the center, and sat down before it. "Is it that obvious to you, Kelly?"

"Why do you ask?"

"Because it is indeed the obvious that you are stating, and one thing about you I that know: you never work hard enough even to state the obvious."

Kelly smirked. "Be a smart-ass. I've got years in this department, not you."

"And your lazy ass hasn't moved on to any further position since. What? You like staying a lieutenant? This is a place to easily get buried, but you aren't angry, you seek it. You want to just stay somewhere cushy and wait out your retirement. So please then, do me a favor and continue to do that and keep your blinding insights to yourself."

"Oh, so you have 'insights' of your own into this psycho now?" Kelly approached the edge of the desk.

Hayias loaded a sheet of paper into the typewriter. "Of course. I say he's a dangerous psychotic that is only warming up. Two ersatz bombs that if they had a timer and black powder, they could have been formidable Infernal Devices. He's holding himself in check, waiting for something. The question is what."

"Shit," which was the word that Kelly addressed Hayias with whenever he was losing patience with him. "You should realize that all of your stunning clairvoyance falls on deaf ears. Pyke, Valentine, LaGuardia, none of those cocksuckers give a shit about you and your insights. The only thing that they care about is if the Bomb Squad can get the Infernal Device to where it cannot cause harm to life or property. All your reports are meaningless. When you realize this, you'll stop judging me as if I don't want to do this job. I do this job! It's not my fault that it's a dead end."

"They read everything that I write, trust me. Ever since the World's Fair bombing they're not playing games with these things any longer. They're still licking their wounds and they're not going to let some lazy fuck like you screw shit up. That's why I'm here because you refuse to do your job."

"So that's why you continue to grace us with your presence? Because I'm not doing my job?"

"That's right."

"For your information, I *am* doing my job."

"And what's that?"

"Watching your sorry ass."

Hayias scoffed and typed his name and position on his report.

"Well, Mr. Big Shot, what are you typing in your report?" Kelly asked, going to the work desks. He put his hands on the edge of the desk and leaned over the parts. "What are you going to tell them? That we have a reluctant bomber?"

Hayias started pigeon pecking the keys. "Yes."

"If you are so keen on your insight into this guy, then why the lozenge? What's he got? A sore throat?"

"That I don't know."

"Well, maybe this guy is just a prankster."

Hayias continued bent over the Royal, his fingertips dropping upon keys.

"Look," Kelly said, turning to face Hayias, "Pyke likes you here in the lab, and he has a lot of pull with Valentine. I'm not one to rock the boat. Besides, we've closed a tremendous number of cases here, and you've been an integral part of that, which means you're an asset to me. I don't intend to rock the boat."

Hayias continued to type.

"Look Hayias, just so's you know. I'm in charge here. When shit hits the fan, they'll come looking for me. That's why I say, don't make *me* look bad. For your sake."

Stopping to breathe deep, "I'm not afraid of you and your women's glasses," Hayias replied.

"These aren't women's glasses," he stalked to the door.

"Keep telling yourself that, Kelly." Hayias called out behind him walking out of the office.

Hayias thought for a moment, shaking off his exposure to such negativity, rocked his shoulders to loosen the muscles there, shook his hands over the typewriter and leaned forward over the keys. He began typing what he thought was the gist of his taking apart the pipe bomb. Once again, all the components were there except for a timer and explosive. What should have been a timer, a watch, or a clock, was a throat lozenge. Whatever that meant. Hayias felt that the bomber was laughing at them, hate and derision in his heart for Con Edison. Whatever the case he was preparing to strike, like a cobra sliding though tall grass, he was ready to stop, coil and lunge. It would take only an emotional trigger to set him off. But what could that be?

What could be the thing that turned his toys to machines of death and destruction? Hayias wondered. He had no clue, and the parts on the workstations would give no further answers. He apologized for his failure in answering the question in the report but warned that something far worse was on the horizon. Something was roiling towards them, and he could not see it. But one thing he was certain of, there will be destruction in the future for New York City.

Lieutenant Pyke, once again in the office after 11:00 p.m, bent over the glow of his desk lamp in his dark office, reading reports, stopped when he heard a knock on the threshold. He looked up, but the person seeking admittance stayed out of sight. He knew who it was without any process of elimination.

"Stop playing around Pete," he said.

Hayias walked in, taking off his hat and hanging it on the coat rack.

"I have my report," he said.

Pyke held up his hand, reaching out for it, "Please give me an overview."

Hayias placed the folder in his hand, then plopped in the chair in front of the lieutenant's desk.

"What did you find?" Pyke said.

"Well, it's definitely the same bomber. The Con Ed Bomber has a vendetta of sorts against the conglomerate."

"Was it capable of exploding?"

"No. It was another intentionally crippled device."

"You say 'intentionally.' Maybe he doesn't have the ability to make a viable bomb?"

"Possibly. It could even be a learning curve."

"Gut feeling. What do you think the problem is?"

"He's waiting for something. He's looking for something to trigger him, and I think he knows exactly what it is that he's waiting for."

"But *you* don't know what that is."

"I'm sorry. I don't."

Pyke nodded, frowned. "I have a question that I need to ask you. Have you made *any* connection to the World's Fair Bombing? Could this be the same man?"

Hayias shook his head. "The World's Fair Bombing was dynamite. I would go out on a limb and say that black powder would be packed into the pipe bomb when he's ready to build a functional bomb. No similarity in the signatures whatsoever."

"Signatures again?"

"That's right. It's clear that it's the same guy that is making the Con Ed bombs. If it wasn't for the signatures, I couldn't be so sure."

Pyke reared back in his chair, interlaced his fingers on his stomach. "Very good job as usual, Pete. Keep it up. I'll take your report to Valentine." He grinned broadly.

Hayias noticed the sarcastic smile clearly. "What?"

"You didn't piss off Kelly, did you?"

Sitting forward, making his point, he asked, "Do you know what this guy did?"

"What?"

"Got the bomb and just left it in my office for me."

Pyke laughed. "Pete, it's not your office. It's a workroom."

"But he didn't open up the bomb. He just delegated the task and then practically calls me stupid and threatens me."

"He's feeling insecure."

"He should be. He's for shit."

"Look, you know how some people can be. Bureaucrats. They play the politics of the job. Kelly is not stupid. You make him look good. You've got a natural talent that he doesn't so he's going to keep stroking your ego. He's just going to keep you from getting too big for your britches."

"I want that office, Pikey."

"Kelly's a lieutenant. I can't go over his head. He can't go over mine."

"But you've got pull with Valentine."

"I told you about that. I'm not so certain about that anymore. Ateer is here for some reason. I don't feel that trust in Valentine that I had before."

Hayias thought of something witty to say, thought of something like his friend was assuming the worst, but the truth was that he wasn't that certain either. Valentine was up to something. Good or bad he was an unknown. At present, everything in the lab is balanced on a tightrope. Kelly wasn't about to make waves, neither was Pyke. And if he stayed silent, he could still do what he liked, which is work on bombs on a technical level. And he could do one other thing...find this new bomber.

"Pete, do you think we'll find this guy any time soon?"

Looking up from the floor, Hayias said, "No. Not at all."

"Why are you so sure?"

"Because he doesn't strike me as someone who would make mistakes. Only through mistakes can we hope to catch this guy."

"His mistake might be that he can't even make a bomb work."

"He can. And if he can, what he's doing is not a series of mistakes but rather calculated moves."

"To what end though?"

"That's the question."

With a sigh of resignation, Pyke stood, tucked the file folder under his arm and walked over to his coat rack to take his hat. "I'm going to see the big man now."

"Pikey," Hayias turned around in the chair, watching him.

"Yeah?"

"I have reason to suspect two things. One, I think our mystery bomber is going to continue making mock-ups for a little while longer, so there is no real danger now and two, an oil dunk can't disable the bomb regardless."

"Okay," Pyke replied, expectantly.

"So, I'm thinking, can you instruct your bomb squad detectives not to dunk the next bomb. I want to dust the outside for fingerprints.

I know it's a long shot because he doesn't leave fingerprints on any of the internal components, but it's worth a try."

Pyke nodded. "Understood. I can make that happen."

Hayias turned around and pointed to Pyke's desk. "Do you still have that Goat Whiskey in your drawer?"

"Yeah, sure, take as much as you like."

Pyke left the office.

Hayias stood and went behind his desk. "Pikey!" he called out.

In a moment, Pyke stuck his head back into the office, "What?"

"Good luck."

Pyke went directly to 240 Centre Street, the Gold Dome, and requested to see the Police Commissioner. He was called up into the lavish waiting room and waited patiently until the blonde female assistant stood and waved him to the door.

"Lieutenant Pyke, please follow me," she said.

Pyke stood, straightened his suit, held his hat at his thigh and followed her into the office, and to his ultimate surprise, finding it empty.

"Please take a seat. The commissioner will be in shortly," the assistant said.

Pyke nodded and sat in a chair in front of the desk, resting his hat on his lap. He looked around at the dark wood paneled room and the number of floor to ceiling bookshelves ringing it. He wondered if the commissioner read them all or if he'd inherited them from his predecessor. He thought about how vapid his own office was—blank and bare walls with nothing on them but pictures of his superiors: Valentine and LaGuardia.

Suddenly the door opened, and Commissioner Valentine rushed in, peeling out of his jacket, with his assistant running behind him, taking it from his shoulders and running to the coat rack in the room to hang it up.

Dressed in a white shirt and black suspenders, and tie. His olive shaped face domed with a receding hairline and sharp, piercing eyes. Valentine plopped into his high backed, cushioned chair and sat forward over his desk.

"Alright James, what's up?" He asked.

"Hayias came back with a confirmation that the first bomb at Con Edison was made by the same person as the one we picked up in the street at four Irving Place today."

"So, we have a serial bomber?"

"Appears that way."

"Was this one a dud?"

"Yeah. It was incapable of detonating."

"Well then, this guy is nothing but an idiot."

"Pete doesn't think so."

"Oh really? What do you think," Valentine probed slyly.

"I believe Pete is right. He believes that this guy is waiting for a trigger to set him off."

"A trigger?"

"Yeah, something, some event in his life or current event, or anything, whatever. The thing is, is that he's waiting for a signal from God to start setting off these bombs. Pete came up with this theory and I'm certain he's right. When this maniac gets started, he's going to wreak havoc."

"Why?"

"I hate to say it like this, but I have a bad feeling, Lew."

Valentine smiled, sat back, his chair creaking underneath his weight. "A bad feeling?"

Pyke played with the brim of his hat. "Well, I feel that he thinks he's some kind of retribution for what the conglomerate had done to him. I don't know what that could be but he's leaving behind active bombs for some reason. The question is, is what is he going to do when he doesn't get the attention he wants?"

"You're painting a very scary picture there, James. This doesn't sound good for our city." Valentine raised an eyebrow.

"I agree, but I'm only trying to shoot from the hip, boss. I plainly asked Pete if we could catch this guy and he told me that he didn't think so. He's too careful. And if that is the case, there's going to be a lot of mayhem before we put this guy behind bars."

Valentine stood from his seat angrily, grabbed at the top of his slacks, pulled them up and walked to his window overlooking the street below and its traffic. "Shit, I asked you if you can catch this bomber and you said that you were confident."

"That was before I spoke to Pete."

Valentine turned around and faced Pyke from a distance. "Do you think more men will help you get him before he gets this signal from God?"

"I don't think so, Lew. I have the best men, the best technicians, the best morale than anyone you can find at my disposal. Your best bet is the ammunition that I presently have. We'll catch this guy, because he have no other options. We are in a corner."

"Jesus, James, I'll cut you all the slack you need because people aren't dying yet, and no property has been destroyed. If that keeps up, you are in my good graces. But if property starts to crumble, if bodies start to pile up, then, as you can probably figure out, I'll have to take decisive action."

"Understood."

"Good. Get to work and catch this bastard before he does some real harm."

"I will."

Lieutenant Pyke stood, perched his hat on his head and briskly walked out of the commissioner's office.

Ateer stepped into the bullpen, smoking a cigarette, his hat cocked on his head to the side. He looked like some young gumshoe instead of a seasoned and well-presented detective. Accorso was sitting behind his desk, nose buried in a file folder. Pedrotti was in his chair, feet up on the desk, crossed at the ankles, reading a newspaper.

Ateer hung his hat on the coat rack.

"What are you reading?" he asked over his shoulder.

Closing the file, Accorso waved it in the air. "The latest report from Hayias. He says we have a serial bomber now."

Ateer went and took his seat at his desk. "What does that mean?"

"That means that this motherfucker is going to make our lives miserable until he's caught."

"Really?"

Accorso tossed the file across his desk onto Ateer's. "Check it out."

He opened the folder while Accorso walked over to Pedrotti.

"What did you roll today?" he asked.

"I haven't rolled yet," Pedrotti said without taking his eyes from the paper.

"What are you waiting for? The call?"

"That's when I usually do it."

"Go ahead, roll it now. I think today is going to be a rough day, and I want to know if you will be useless or not."

Pedrotti looked up at him, sighed angrily. Folding up the newspaper, he rested it on the table, snatched open his top drawer and pulled out a pair of ruby dice. He held them lower than the seat of his chair at the side, shook them noisily and then dashed them across the desktop. They rolled and bounced off the side of his stapler and came to an immediate stop when they bounded onto the newspaper as if suddenly stuck.

"Does that count, with the newspaper in the way?" Accorso asked, pointing.

"Everything counts."

They looked at the roll, a 2 on one die, a 1 on the other.

"Shit, that was close," Pedrotti sighed.

"Ace Deuce," grinning, Accorso said, "that means I can count on you today."

"Yes, you can," With a hand he swept the dice back into the top drawer. He picked up the newspaper, snapped it open and began to read once more.

Getting the message, Accorso went to Ateer, and stood over him.

Looking up, Ateer asked, "We're in trouble, right?"

Retaking his seat, Accorso groused, "We're always in trouble, Mac."

Sitting forward, Ateer tossed the file back on Accorso's desk. "It's only a one-page report. He doesn't have much to say."

Accorso rolled his chair back, putting it next to Pedrotti's and tossed the folder on his desk. He rolled back in front of Ateer, leaning back comfortably. "He says enough. It's going to be a long, hot summer in New York for us boys in the Bits-and-Pieces Squad."

With a measure of reluctance, Ateer asked, "Do you think it would be possible for me to get a photostatic copy of the report?"

"Why?"

Cracking a wan smile. "I want to make my own file folder on this serial bomber so that I can catch him."

"Mighty cocksure, huh?"

Ateer hunched his shoulders.

"Sure, you do that," Accorso nodded. "And make several copies for the rest of the bullpen."

Ateer took the file from Pedrotti, left the bullpen, and went to the photostatic copy room. A large room separated into two parts, a patron area and a technician area with several of the huge boxy shaped machines at its end. One of the technicians approached the desk that also served as a partition and accepted the file. Within moments there were a dozen copies.

The original went back to Accorso, the rest were distributed among the other detectives of the bullpen.

Going to the Yellow Pages, Accorso scanned though it with Pedrotti standing beside him. After distributing the report, Ateer also crowded Accorso's desk, looking down at the large, yellow book.

"What are you looking for?" he asked.

"Well, if this guy is a serial bomber, he's going to need supplies," Accorso said. "I say we go to each and every pipe dealer in the city and see if someone out there is buying a large quantity of piping."

"This guy only made two pipe bombs," Pedrotti pointed out, "that doesn't sound like he's bought up a large amount of piping to be remembered by a distributor."

"This serial bomber is probably preparing to go on a bombing spree. That means a lot of pipes. We may get lucky."

Pedrotti groaned tiredly, turned around and looked at Beakey and Dempsey sitting at their desks. The phone rang. Beakey snatched it up. Dempsey sat, reading a manual.

"That's going to be a pain." Pedrotti muttered. "That's going to include every construction company building something."

"We'll exclude companies. We'll just look for individuals who are buying pipe in large quantities."

"What if they're not in the city?" Ateer asked.

"Have some faith, willya?" Accorso tore a page from the Yellow Pages and handed the book to Pedrotti. "You go the other way, get someone and have them search for the other components of the bomb. Especially anyone buying a lot of black powder."

"My bet is that he's not buying it in bulk. The purchase of that shit has been regulated for decades." Pedrotti brought out. "He's probably cracking it out of bullets."

"Cracking?" Ateer asked.

"Separating the bullet from the casing and shaking out the powder inside. Tedious but a way around the black powder regulation." Accorso said.

"So? What do you want me to search for?" Pedrotti asked, flipping pages of the book in his hands.

Tearing his page in half, Accorso handed one over to Pedrotti. "You might be right about the black powder. Do half of the pipe dealers first. Then we'll see what we have, and we'll do the black powder tomorrow."

"Alright." Pedrotti walked back to his desk. "Big O! Get your goofy ass up and let's hit the bricks!"

. . .

"I've told you guys; the parts are too basic." The hardware salesman said, raising his hands into the air in exasperation. He was thin and tall, and when he raised his hands, Ateer thought he was trying to take out one of the neon lights overhead. "Anyone can make a five-inch length of pipe from a three- or four-foot-long tubing. You're asking me if someone came in here requesting five-inch pipe. I gotta say, no."

Accorso shook his head. "How about a lot of caps?"

"Caps? A lot of caps? That's like asking a shoe salesman if he sells a lot of shoelaces." The salesman waved a hand at him. "Really, I don't know what you guys are after, but there's no way you're going to find it here."

"Well, thanks. No need to get all sore," Accorso said, patting the countertop with his hand. "Just trying to do a public service."

"Great. I have no idea how you're going to track one man's purchases, because he's really doing nothing that stands out other than, it sounds like, just buying a few pieces of hardware. People do it every day." The salesman, now done with helping the two detectives, turned, and walked off, down the length of the counter to another patron. Accorso turned to Ateer with a scowl.

"This is a dead end if I've ever saw one. I wonder how Beat It is doing?" he asked.

Ateer hunched his shoulders. They marched outside into the afternoon air, which was windy and getting colder day by day. It was strange weather. It snowed last week, then it was bright and mild the next. Right now, cars eased down the street and pedestrians, intent on where they were going, surged around them like a river around rocks.

"Where to now, boss?" Ateer asked, readjusting his hat after a stiff wind threatened to blow it away.

"Don't we have any more hardware stores?"

Reaching into his jacket, Ateer pulled out the folded page from the Yellow Pages and checked where they were on the list. "Nope, that was number eighteen. The last one."

"Shit, I say we head to the Village and get into some trouble. This is becoming a fucking headache."

They headed down the block. Accorso pulled out a pack of cigarettes and stuck one between his lips before passing the pack to Ateer.

"This Bomber is buried deeper than a tick on a dog," Accorso groused. He took out a book of matches, lit his cigarette, and handed it over. "It's not going to be easy to separate this guy from the rank-and-file handyman."

"Maybe he'll slip up?"

"Or maybe we will. And if we slip up my friend, we're fucked."

After lighting his cigarette, Ateer passed the pack and book back to Accorso. "It's going to be one or the other, in the long run, huh?"

"That's the problem. Either he'll flinch first, or we will. And we both are playing for keeps. Making bombs are just as unstable as defusing them. He takes risks every time he puts one together and carries it with him to wherever he deposits it. That makes him just as careful as us."

"I gotcha. We have to be the best we can be."

"Correct."

They trotted down the subway stairwell to the token booth and platform.

Liam Sullivan, the owner of Whack-assed Willie's was a mature Irishman, lean with dark red hair. Even when speaking to patrons over the bar, his clear eyes scanned his place in search for both familiar and non-familiar faces. Pyke and Hayias sat on the other side of the bar from him, listening to his tall stories about the antics of his patrons and staff. Something seemed to always happen in his dive, and he was its recorder, a scribe preserving history for later generations.

Hayias, who was usually jovial, and could come back with a cop story for Liam every time, was uncharacteristically quiet. He spent the time grimacing at his drink more than listening to Liam's tall tales.

"Something wrong?" Liam asked him.

Hayias looked up. "I don't know. Maybe your moonshine is finally getting to me."

"Not my moonshine," Liam assured, "I only buy from the best toothless rednecks."

Pyke laughed. Hayias grinned.

"What's the matter? Headache?" Pyke asked.

Hayias shook his head. "Upset stomach. Honestly, Liam. It was bothering me before I came in. I was just joking about your stock."

"Hey," Liam lowered his head to look into Hayias' eyes, "I'll get Paula to go to the drug store down the block and get you some stomach medicine."

"No, you don't have to do that," Hayias waved the offer away. "I'll be alright."

"Paula!" Sullivan shouted, "get your narrow ass over here!"

The short, thin brunette girl came running to Sullivan's side.

"Take some money from the petty cash and buy us a bottle of stomach-medicine, fast."

She nodded and ran off.

"Can I have another, Liam?" Pyke held up his glass.

Sullivan swept up the glass and walked down the bar. Pyke turned to Hayias, whose face was slowly taking on a whiter complexion. "What did you eat for lunch today?"

"I didn't," Hayias sat up straighter on his stool, breathed in deeply. "I'm fine."

"I talked to Valentine last night about your report," Pyke said. He paused as Sullivan returned with his rock glass half full of amber liquid.

"What did he have to say?" Hayias took a careful sip of his drink.

"He's gonna let us run with whatever we feel works, until the bombs start to explode."

"That's understandable. So, what did you do? Give the case to Accorso?"

"I sure as hell did. See if he can generate a lead. I'm all out of ideas on how to catch this guy."

"Why don't we put a plainclothes in front of the headquarters of Con-Ed. I mean, somebody that wraps a Devil Toy in a bright red sock is begging to be noticed."

"I'm sure he cases a place out before he drops one of those things. He'll probably notice the plainclothes almost immediately."

"Not a good one."

"Do you want to go with that?"

Hayias hunched his shoulders. "If you want me to."

"Here she comes," Sullivan said, throwing a hand towel that he was using to dry a glass over his wrist before turning to the returning Paula. She handed him a brown paper bag, from which he quickly produced the bottle of stomach medicine and rested it on the bar in front of Hayias.

"Have at it," he said with a smile.

"Thanks, Liam," Hayias said, twisting open the top and taking a few swallows straight from the bottle.

Sullivan went into another story as they waited for the stomach medicine to take effect.

Suddenly Hayias said, "I've gotta use the john."

He sprung off his stool and was gone. Sullivan leaned against the bar in front of Pyke. "Where's the rest of your crew?"

"Probably working late. Either that, or running around in the street being crude, rude and socially unacceptable."

Sullivan laughed. "That Fab and Beat It, I've gotta keep an eye on them."

"Why is that?"

"Because if I don't, those crafty bastards are going to have all of my waitresses pregnant."

"They're that bad?"

"Fuck, the girls call them 'Rooster Reds.' They don't drink as much as some of my patrons, but they've nailed a few of my girls."

"That's not your job making your waitresses keep their legs shut, is it?"

"No...but, gawddamn!" Sullivan laughed mightily. "Their wives need to keep their balls in their purses or there's going to be a Bomb Squad of little ones running around in Willie's."

Pyke laughed.

Sullivan went serious. "You should check on Pete."

Pyke suddenly noticed that it was some time since Hayias had left for the bathroom. Even if he took a shit, it shouldn't have taken this long. "Yeah, I think you're right. I'll be right back."

Pyke went to the bathroom and tried the knob, making sure it was locked. "Pete!" He shouted against the door. There was no reply. He began knocking on the door insistently, "Hey Petey!"

The door unlocked. Pyke pushed it open. It was a small, narrow bathroom with one commode. Hayias was sitting on it, his pants, and boxers down around his ankles. He leaned to the side, his head and shoulder against the wall. His face was sheet white and sweating, his eyes closed.

"What's wrong Pete?"

Hayias grimaced, "I need help Pikey. My stomach is really burning and I'm shitting blood."

As the growing night engulfed the city, and the headlights of cars flickered on and streetlamps burned, Accorso and Ateer found themselves standing in front of the Village Vanguard. Its black fabric awning stretched out from the front door almost to the curb of the street. They passed through the double wooden doors and were swallowed up by the dark club. They could hear the jazz music pounding out of the comfortable and smoky interior where they were made to stop by a doorman and pay at the admission window before entering in. The club fee was seventy-five cents each, and when done, they entered in and found a table in the corner. A candle in a glass holder was set for illumination.

A small trio of black musicians played on the small stage. A piano, a bass, and a trumpet player belted out tunes that were just above the din of conversation from the shadowy figures around them. A young waitress came over and took their drink orders and efficiently returned with their beverages.

"Hey, hey," Accorso said. He pulled out a silver cigarette case and opened it to reveal two joints, carefully rolled and held beneath the clip. "I've got a couple left."

"You're going to smoke them all now?"

"Just one," now laughing. "You're becoming a quick pothead, Mackie."

"I'm not addicted or anything, I just liked that high I got. It's far different from straight alcohol." Ateer told the gospel truth. The high that he got from smoking that joint at the poetry bar haunted him for days. He'd been drunk before, but high was an entirely different animal. He didn't feel an addiction to weed, like some otherworldly craving, however he still wanted to experience its effects again. So much so that when Accorso pulled out the cigarette case, his heart skipped a beat.

"It is, isn't it?" He lit one of the joints, took a few puffs and handed it to Ateer.

"How is the family?" Ateer asked.

Hunching his shoulders, Accorso pulled out a Benzedrine inhaler and began snorting from it. "They're alright as long as they stay out of my fucking hair. To tell you the truth, I have nothing to do with my daughter anymore. She's just unruly and shit. I can't even talk to her without her running up to her room crying. Touchy little bitch."

"Wow." Ateer pointed at the inhaler. "That's pretty harsh?"

"Look Ateer, she's my little baby and all, but sometimes I want to strangle her with my bare hands."

"I see."

Ateer reached into his jacket and pulled out his inhaler. "I'm sorry to talk about my family like that, but I don't have any room for all of the emotional shit. You know what I'm saying?"

"I understand."

"My wife says she's imitating me, but I don't throw tantrums. Dary throws more tantrums than me. Well, maybe not tantrums, but she gets moody, which drives me out of the house faster than putting a lit stick of dynamite in my bed. I swear to god, she can, just by her attitude alone, drop the fucking temperature in our bedroom by ten degrees."

Ateer laughed, puffed on the joint when it came back to him, struggling to stifle the coughs that still plagued him with each inhalation. "I've never really had a girlfriend."

"Never?"

"Never had the time," Ateer made a face, "I mean, I had one in school, but after graduation we went our separate ways."

"How about being in the Public Morals squad. You didn't meet women in the clubs or the prostitutes in the brothels?"

"Yeah, I met them, but they weren't my cup of tea." Ateer waved down the waitress. "My mother was always negative about my grandmother, who was a prostitute. She painted a pretty disgusting picture of the entire profession. When my father went missing and my little sister was born, she kept drumming into her head the importance of a chaste, quiet life. I guess I picked up on that training and here you have me."

"Well, the truth of the matter is you're not missing out on anything when it comes to brats and wives. Try to get yourself a good woman that knows her place."

The waitress returned with their drinks. "Hey!" Accorso said up to her. "Are you married?"

"Yes, I am," she replied.

Accorso waved her off. "We'll skip that one."

"I don't need you to fix me up, Fab. I'm quite fine. I'm still a young man."

"You're the same age as I am, right?"

"Yeah, thirty-one." Ateer smiled as his thoughts began to swim. Both the marijuana and the liquor clashed like a pair of cymbals in the center of his skull. He noticed that he was slouching in his seat and sat up over his drink.

A familiar voice came from over Accorso's shoulder. "You both are fucking fossils."

They turned to see Vaughn Davidson snatch a chair from another table and slide into it at their table. "I see you guys are here digging the tunes."

"Yeah, we're here to listen to some music." Accorso said, correcting Davidson's hipster talk.

Davidson was already carrying a glass of liquor. "What's shaking, man? A hard day playing with bombs?"

"Maybe pipes."

"What's up with you, Mac?" Davidson said to Ateer. "Did you smash your brains already?"

"I'm doing pretty good." Ateer smiled. "Where's Naomi?"

"She didn't wanna swing tonight. She's got a loose wig."

Ateer turned to Accorso, shaking his head. He didn't get the reply.

"She's on her period." Accorso translated for him, then turned to Davidson. "Right?"

"Yeah, she's all hung up with a bad attitude. A real drag, you know?"

Accorso scoffed. "That's what we were just talking about. Women and their 'attitudes.'"

"Well, they can keep them." Davidson reached into his jacket and brought out his trusty cigarette case. "Anybody?"

"Shit yeah," Accorso said, sipping from his drink.

Davidson popped open the case and handed a joint to Accorso. "You want one?" He asked Ateer.

"Sure." Ateer held out his hand. In moments the three of them were puffing on weed.

"I ran into my connection today and he had a heavy stash. I

almost bought him out." Davidson spoke with an awkward grin on his square face.

"You've gotta tie us in with your connection, Vaughn," Accorso said, comfortably smoking his joint, slumped back in his seat, and listened to the music, with his eyes half closed. Exhaling smoothly and slowly he allowed the smoke to linger in his lungs as long as possible.

"Huh, I can just see that," Davidson said sarcastically. "You cats tend to forget that you're detectives. A dope dealer really wouldn't like making your acquaintance."

"We're not going to bust him or anything."

"Well, if he trusts you, you've got it. But he'll think you're putting the shine on him to get *his* connections. Or that you might roll him for his stash and money. Cops just aren't hip."

"We don't want to be hip. We just want to get our hands on some smoke."

"Who knows. I might be able to arrange that. So, you squares are having women problems too?"

"He is," Accorso pointed to Ateer with his chin.

"I am?" Ateer's eyes popped. "He's been bitching and moaning since he got here," he pointed back to Accorso.

"Well, having problems with women is not your gig," Vaughn replied, sounding suddenly like an expert in women.

"Then do tell, what is it?" Accorso smirked at Davidson.

"Hitler."

"Hitler?"

"Yeah, now that guy's a drag. He's a big assed bring down. He's doing some weird things in Europe, and I swear, we're gonna be over there soon enough to blow his gig."

"Not you, rich boy." Accorso stubbed out what was left of his joint and lifted his drink. "Your daddy has a ton of connections in Tammany Hall. He'll make certain to shield his little boy from the big bad Nazis."

"He's a dude that's afraid that he's gonna flip, and if he flips the whole world flips with him."

Accorso heard his words but didn't comprehend much. He looked to Ateer to see if he understood the sentence, but he just hunched his shoulders.

"What's with all this heavy talk every time we see you, Vaughn?" Accorso frowned. "Can't you see that Mac is in no shape for this kinda shit?"

Davidson laughed. "Mac has made a *thing* out of his skull."

This was true. Ateer felt that he was sinking into darkness, or more likely a greyness that colored the entire world around him. The Benzedrine was no doubt keeping him from going over the edge, but his hold on sobriety was tenuous to say the least. He could hear Davidson talk about the developments in Germany, in his spirited, slang-laced voice, and he could see the yellow-tinged face of Accorso over the flickering light of the candle, but he felt outside of the conversation, set aside from any logic. All logic, save one thought that ate through his processes. Maybe he did make 'a thing' out of his skull. He thought about Commissioner 'Honest Cop' Valentine. It had been a while since he checked in with him, although he gave Orlowski updates whenever he saw him. However, for some reason he felt that he had to talk to the commissioner tonight. They were no closer to finding the Con Ed Bomber and there seemed to be no connection between him and the World's Fair Bombing, which was foremost on the commissioner's mind.

He had to admit, Ateer *did* make a thing out of his skull because there was a tiny voice in the back of his head warning him that he was too impaired to go before the Honest Cop with any kind of report tonight. Yet, there was this nagging need to do so.

"I think I'm going to head home, gentlemen," he said to his companions.

"Oh really?" Accorso said.

"Yeah," he reached over for his fedora, planting it inelegantly on his head, then peeled several dollars from his wallet, leaving them on the table. "I think that should cover my end."

"Looks it to me," Davidson said. "Go home, Mac. You don't want to fall out in a club, then you're vulnerable and are easy pickings."

"I got a feeling." Ateer stood and walked around Accorso, patting him on the shoulder. "Don't stay out here too late."

"You get home in one piece," Accorso replied. "We need fresh meat for the grinder."

Ateer waved to Davidson and staggered from the club and into the cool of the night. He took a moment under the awning of the club to get his bearings and to decide what it was that he was about to do. He had one of two choices, to ride the subway or hail a cab. He decided to hail the first cab that rolled up to the awning.

She strode down the hospital corridor in high-heeled shoes, and a long, long dress which was only an illusion because her legs were so long. Then came a blue cotton blouse. Her blonde hair was done up in a complicated bun. She strode through the doctors and nurses as if she was their supervisor, not even registering one of them in her passing. As tall as a lighthouse on the shoulder of a sea outcropping of rocks, her eyes swung to the left and right, not in warning, but in search of someone. From a distance she found Pyke sitting in a row of chairs and immediately set off toward him.

Pyke stood and waited as the Amazon-like woman approached, staring him eye to eye. "Okay, James. What happened?"

"I don't know. He was complaining about stomachaches and then he was passing blood."

Clara Hayias blinked. "He was urinating blood?"

"No, the other way," Pyke corrected. "I went in to check up on him in the bathroom and he was looking really bad, passing blood."

"What made you bring him to Morrisania Hospital?"

"That's where *he* told the ambulance to go."

Clara took a step back, looked around at the activity around her. "Where's his doctor?"

"They took him into the ER and that was the last thing that I saw. That's when I went to the phone booths to call you."

Thinking, she nodded, looked at the directional signs painted on the walls and found the one that read Emergency, and followed its arrow down the hall. Pyke rushed behind her long, leggy strides as she plowed through a pair of double doors at the end of the corridor and entering a busy theater with doctors and nurses running about. Sections of the area were separated by white cotton curtains and a large nurse's station was in the center of the space. Clara walked up to one of the nurses on the phone, and leaned over her. "Excuse me," she said.

The nurse raised her finger to silence her. Clara waited a minute, looking around at the busy hive of activity surrounding them. A set of doors banged open in the distance and doctors and nurses ran in, surrounding a gurney, they rushed the body writhing and crying out in pain through the ER to a vacant area of the theater. A nurse took a curtain, pulling it around closing off any further sight of the activity.

"Excuse me," again Clara said to the nurse, "my husband has been—"

The nurse covered the receiving end of the phone with a hand and said, "I'll be with you in a moment."

Clara reached over the desk, snatched the phone from the nurse's hand and hung it up. "No, you're going to talk with me now."

The nurse stood up angrily. "You don't come in here and give orders. I'm going to call hospital security."

Pyke walked up to the desk and flashed his badge. "Excuse me ma'am, but this is important."

The mature nurse looked at the badge, looked at Pyke and then to Clara, said, "What can I help you with?"

"Peter Hayias was brought in..." her voice trailed off. She turned to Pyke. Her eyes were like a pin jabbing him in the rear end.

"He was brought in about an hour and a half ago complaining of stomach aches and bleeding from the anus," Pyke rattled off.

The nurse sat down, took a nearby clipboard from the desk, scanned it and then stood. "He's this way."

They followed her around the nurse's station to the sectioned off areas at the far end of the theater and pushed away a partition. Ahead, lying in a hospital bed, was Hayias with an oxygen mask over his face and an IV in his arm. His eyes were closed as if asleep. Two nurses administered to him and stepped aside as Clara walked over to her husband, stroked his face with a tender hand and whispered his name in his ear. His eyes slowly opened.

As Clara sat on the edge of the hospital bed, her back to them, Pyke took the nurse by the arm and pulled her back away from the couple. "Can you get his doctor?"

The nurse nodded and walked off. Pyke pulled the partition around them, giving them privacy and left the ER., going to the waiting room where he was to take a seat and wait. Upon turning into the room filled with chairs, he found his wife, Barbara and teen daughter, Amanda sitting with several other people waiting for news. Amanda saw him enter immediately and was up and in his arms in a heartbeat. "What's going on, Jimmy?"

Pyke took his concerned wife by the shoulders. "Something happened with Pete's stomach. They rushed him here."

"Is he going to be alright?"

"I don't know," he turned her around and went with her to the seats around their daughter. "He looked a little better than he did when he was in the bar."

"You were in a bar?"

"Yeah. We just had a couple of drinks."

Barbara nodded, understanding all too well.

"I want you to be here to comfort Clara while she's here," he told her.

"Yes, of course," Barbara nodded.

Pyke turned to his daughter and mussed up her well-made hair on top of her head. She shouted, striking his arm with a small fist, "Stop daddy!"

He turned to his wife. "When did she start to get so touchy about her looks?"

"Since she found a boy in school that she likes."

"She likes a boy in school?"

Barbara nodded. "Do you want to go and get something to eat?"

"I'm hungry." He turned to Amanda who was still seated in a chair, smoothing out the errant strands of hair. "Would you like something to eat?"

"Yes ,please," she replied.

"I'll be right back," Barbara said and sauntered off. Pyke watched her hips in parting, as they swayed and rocked on her and could not help but smile. When his wife was gone, he turned to his daughter.

"Alright Amanda, who is this boy in your school that you like?"

He gave the cabdriver the address of 240 Centre Street and nodded off in the back of the cab. He wasn't aware that his head had drooped to his chest, and neither was he aware when the cab pulled over in front of Police Headquarters, the cabdriver shouting at him to wake up. Ateer shook his head to clear it, paid the cabdriver and climbed out into the night. He let the chill of the night center and steady him on his feet. The booze and weed had made him wobbly, and his world slow and dragging. He walked up to the imposing stone building, commanding even in the dark of the night, illuminated starkly by streetlamps and lit windows. He walked inside and met up with a uniformed police officer standing by the threshold of the vaulting vestibule, like some stone sentinel in an ancient temple.

Ateer stopped to explain to the officer that he wanted to see the commissioner.

"People just don't walk in and *see* the commissioner," the officer pointed out.

For a moment it wasn't clear that the uniform would allow him in. The officer looked him up and down, noticing Ateer's bloodshot eyes and uncertain stance.

"Are you *sure* you want to see the commissioner?" the officer asked.

"Yes, I would."

The officer walked into the vestibule, their footfalls echoing about the ceilings and corners of the stone and marble chamber. At the other side of the vestibule, against the side of the stairs a receptionist sat behind an impressive, polished marble desk shaped like an octagon. She stood on their arrival.

"He wants to see Commissioner Valentine," the officer informed her.

"Do you have an appointment?" She asked.

"No, but if you say that Detective Dylan Ateer is here to see him, if he doesn't want to see me, he'll send me away."

The receptionist and the officer regarded him for a moment. His request being somewhat unorthodox and not standard procedure. However, the receptionist made a phone call and paused to wait after a brief interchange with the person on the other end. Ateer was certain that either the Commissioner had called it a night, or that he did not want to be bothered. Besides, as he waited, he took stock in what he was doing and the condition that he was in. The booze and Benzedrine gave him a false sense of urgency, whereas the weed warped his perception of his capabilities. It made him believe that he understood more than he did, reasoned better than he could, dared more than he should. The receptionist hung up the phone and instructed the officer to escort him to the Commissioner's office.

In moments they were before Rita, the commissioner's assistant, in the long, tan carpeted foyer just outside the office.

"Please have a seat, Mr. Ateer," she cooed, gesturing to one of the plush leather chairs. Ateer made his way as steady as he could to the seat, removing his hat and pulling on the edges of his jacket and the knot of his tie to tidy up his appearance. She returned to her desk.

Alarms went off in Ateer's head now. He realized that he

shouldn't be here, he should be home, sobering up. Now, due to booze courage, he had placed himself in a situation that would cost him his assignment, position, maybe even his job.

He was a fool, on a fool's errand. Reaching into his jacket, he pulled out his Benzedrine inhaler, taking a strong and steady whiff to tighten up his raggedy edges, to give him the appearance of sobriety. Seconds later, he realized that this too was in error. He had opened his head, literally blown away the droopy, loopy world around him for one with greater clarity, with a dizzying spin to it.

"He'll see you now," Alice said, going to the door of the office and opening it for him.

Ateer strode into Commissioner Valentine's presence and stopped in the center of the office, taking in the crowded bookshelves around him.

Valentine sat behind his wooden desk of the same rich dark wood as the walls and the bookshelves from floor to ceiling. He was dark and brooding, his fingers steepled before his face as he sat back in his chair.

"Have a seat, Ateer," Valentine ordered. With a visible level of reluctance, he took a seat on the soft, cushioned chair in front of the stern looking Commissioner. Valentine looked older, tired, yet his eyes didn't seem as if he lacked sleep as far as Ateer could see, just patience, already heated over this imposition.

"Is there something that you wanted to tell me?" he asked, his voice level and calm.

"Yes, I have the latest report of my investigation into the search of the Con Ed Bomber."

"And what is that?"

"It looks like the two bombs are from the same creator, making him a serial bomber."

"Yeah, I read that report. Pyke brings them to me."

Dammit, you knew that Ateer, he thought. "I see," he said, at a loss for any other words.

"How about the investigation? Is Pyke making any connections between this serial bomber and the World's Fair Bombing?"

"No. Nothing that I can see. We've been painstakingly going over pipe dealers and plumbing suppliers looking for a lead to the identity of the Bomber, but like the Con Ed files, it's like searching for a needle in a haystack."

"How is Pyke holding up? Does he seem on the ball?"

"He seems to have his best men on the case. From what I can see he appears to be going over every lead that can be followed, it's just that there's nothing there."

Valentine nodded. "Have you been drinking, Ateer?"

"Yes, sir."

"I've heard about the 'Hard Chargers' in the Bomb Squad. They live pretty much like there's no tomorrow. How are you holding up in such an environment?"

"I'm coping."

"It's probably one of the more dangerous jobs in the NYPD. I'm not saying that the average cop isn't risking his life out there, but there is a level of 'do or die' when it comes to facing off with a bomb."

"Yes, this is true. It's quite frightening."

"I can imagine. I put you there and, in a way, I should apologize to you for giving you such a risky assignment, but like I said, you will be rewarded when both are these characters are brought to justice. You understand? You can get a transfer to any department you wish."

"Thank you, sir."

"Good then. If you are finished, go home, and sleep off that drunk so that you can be fresh in the morning in your service to Pyke. I don't want to hear how I handed him a detective too drunk to do his job."

Ateer stood to his feet. "I'll do just that, sir."

"And in the future, you don't have to come to me to give me these reports. As you can see, Pyke and Kelly keep me informed. That's why I gave you Walter so that you can communicate your observations of what Lieutenant Pyke is doing regarding all of these reports that I'm getting from them. I'll let you know the next time that I want to see you. Understood?"

"Yes, sir."

"Good night, Detective."

Ateer, feeling much better after talking to Commissioner Valentine, and after his metabolism had a chance to process a little more of the chemicals surging though his bloodstream, walked out of 240 Centre Street and stopped in the middle of the sidewalk. He looked up at the burning half-moon in the night sky and smiled, thinking that he was no doubt higher than the moon itself. It was comical to him, causing him to chuckle as he struck off down the block towards the subway station entrance. His gait was slightly steadier than earlier and because of the Benzedrine, his senses were sharp in the gloom of the night, not missing the passing face of any pedestrian coming from the direction that he was heading in. Gaudily dressed women, darkly dapper men, shuffled past him in the splashes of streetlights. Approaching him on his right was an interracial couple. The woman he recognized immediately. It was Vaughn Davidson's poet friend Naomi Brooks. Her smooth, perfect features shone in the divided illumination of the streetlamps and the partial moon, her shoulder length hair crashing in luxuriant curls at her collarbones, her large eyes focusing on Ateer and stopping short, a hand going up to her red, thin lips in surprise.

"Hey, I know you!" she said, pointing.

Ateer, never missing being able to attach a name to a face, nodded to her. "Naomi, right?"

"Yeah, Naomi Brooks, the poet. And you are again?"

"I met you at a poetry reading. My name is Dylan, but my friends call me—"

"Mac!" she exclaimed, pointing at him again. "Mac, right?"

"That's right."

"Well, it's good to see you again, Mac. Going to a club?"

"No. I had some business to take care of around here. Why? Are you going to a club?"

"Yeah, another poetry reading. This place is much more liberal than the last place you saw me at." She patted the man next to her on the shoulder of his dark blazer. "This is a close friend of mine, Marcus Washington."

Marcus Washington was a lean, tall black man. His features handsome, with a generous mouth, broad nose, and processed hair, straight as corn silk and black and shiny like slick oil in the lights of the night. He extended a hand and shook Ateer's.

"Hello Mac," he said.

"Hey Marcus."

"You like poetry?"

"I've only heard very little."

"Would you like to come with us? We're heading for the Village."

Ateer looked around in the night, as if an excuse could be found standing nearby him. "Uhh, I'll have to pass for tonight. I've got a lot more stuff to do before I can call it a night."

"Oh, sorry to hear that," Naomi said. "You really would have liked it tonight. I have some new material."

"Well, maybe next time." Ateer doffed his hat, took a step back and to the side, moving slightly around them. "Like I said, I really gotta get going. It was nice seeing you though, Naomi. And it was nice meeting you too, Marcus."

"Same here," they said.

Ateer waved them off and continued down the sidewalk, heading for the subway once more. He wondered, were they dating? He thought that she was Vaughn Davidson's girl, but then again, even though they came into the poetry reading together the last time he met them, they didn't seem too 'chummy.' Maybe that was a groundless assumption on his part.

Nodding, Ateer allowed the night of the city, it's neon storefronts, pools of streetlights, and passing automobile headlights to swallow him up.

SUSPICIOUS LOOKING PACKAGES

. . .

"And so where were you?" Sienna Pedrotti asked the minute her husband walked into the living room. He walked around a lounge chair and fell into it.

"Another long day," he had removed his hat and stripped out of his jacket the moment he walked into the apartment. The hat he had left on the coat rack at the door, the jacket was across his arm.

"You look terrible. You must have done an entire day's work today," Sienna stood in pleated slacks, simple blouse, and a white apron over them.

"I do an entire day's work every day."

She laughed, walked off, into the kitchen.

Pedrotti rested his head back, closed his eyes. He was on his feet all day with Frascone. He couldn't tell which was worse, his throbbing feet or Frascone's questions, followed by his rambling. He opened an eye, unless he had to deal with Sienna's prattle, which was, in his opinion, far worse.

She walked back into the living room. "Well, dinner will not be ready for a while."

"That's alright, I want to go and take a shower."

"Why?" she cocked a fist on her hip, "to wash the stink of sex off you?"

"Oh, is that what this is going to turn into? Because I've already had a day full of someone talking into my ear incessantly."

"I talked to Father Lozano about your indiscretions. He wants to talk to you."

Pedrotti stood from the chair and marched into the back rooms. She followed behind him, "He thinks that you should come in and talk to him. Unburden your soul. Explain to him what a wreck of a husband you are."

Stomping into the bedroom, Pedrotti threw his jacket across the bed. He worked his shoulder rig off and threw it, and his pistol on top of his jacket, and then sat down on the edge of the bed, removing his shoes, "I don't feel like talking to a priest, Sienna. That's your thing."

"But it could do you a little good to realize that you're answerable to someone."

"Who? God?"

"Exactly."

Sighing, Pedrotti said, "Last week it was a therapist that you wanted me to see," he snapped his fingers trying to remember, "what's his name?"

"Durham," she said.

"That's right," he sat his shoes on the floor next to him, stuffed his socks in them then stood, peeling out of his shirt, exposing his hairy chest, which hid his weak chest. Pedrotti wasn't much into exercise. "Mr. Durham would have been a great idea for you. You can address your need to be so unfaithful."

After throwing his shirt across the bed, Pedrotti did the same with his slacks. "I'm not unfaithful, Sierra."

"Don't lie to me, Gio. A woman knows these things."

"What do you know?" He turned to her, wearing nothing but his boxers. "Please, tell me, what do you know."

"You want me to disbelieve my mother. She knows about these things, and she wouldn't mislead me. She says, if your husband has a tendency of coming home later and later, and going straight to the shower when he does, he's cheating."

"Your mother wasn't married to a cop."

"You're not a cop. You work on the Bomb Squad."

Pedrotti turned to look at her. Her clear, cherubic features, like that of a little girl with big eyes and rosy cheeks. He bent over the bed, holding himself up by his arms and dug into his jacket pocket to produce his gold shield. He held it up before her face. "What does this mean?"

She ignored the identification before her, reached over and picked his jacket from the bed. "You're not a *real* cop, Gio." Going over to the closet, Sienna hung up the jacket, and pulled a pack of cigarettes and a book of matches from one of the pockets. Leaning back on the threshold of the closet she lit a cigarette. "I'm trying to work on this marriage. I tried to get you to go to a counselor, but you just don't care, do you?"

Pedrotti frowned, snatching his shoulder rig and gun from the bed, and hung it from the knob of the closet. "I don't know where you're getting all these newfangled ideas from. People don't go to counselors or therapists or even priests with their problems. I just don't need them."

"You need someone." Sienna walked over to the other side of the bed where an ashtray sat on an end table. "I would tell you to talk to Fab, but he's just as disgusting as you."

"What are you talking about?"

"What's her name, Gio? Tell me."

"Who are you talking about?"

"The woman that you've been sleeping with."

"I'm not sleeping with a woman, Sienna."

"I've smelt her sickly-sweet perfume, seen the reddish tint of her lipstick on your lips, smelled her sex on your body when you come and lay in the bed in a drunken heap next to me without taking a shower."

Pedrotti held up his arms. "Come smell me then. Do I smell like a man who has been in the company of another woman?"

"Not tonight. What time is it?" She snatched up the clock from the end table. "It's seven o'clock. That's early for you."

Pedrotti waved a hand at her dismissively. He walked into the bathroom, reached over the claw-foot tub to turn the controls on, running water into it. Senna pursued him in. "You worked today and decided to come straight home. That doesn't make you a faithful husband, you realize that don't you?"

Pedrotti waved his hand under the faucet, judging its temperature. "I don't realize anything anymore."

"Well, I realize that we haven't had relations in three months now," she replied.

"Oh, Sienna," he sighed tiredly, turning the shower control and almost instantly the shower head above burst a fall of water into the tub. "Can we talk about this tomorrow?"

"You're running out of tomorrows, Gio."

He pulled his boxers down, stepped into the tub, and drew the shower curtain around, obscuring her view of him and cutting off the conversation. She stood, puffing smoke for a minute, listening as he began singing and humming Chattanooga Choo Choo.

"Mark my words, Gio. You're running out of tomorrows," she threatened. Sienna lifted the commode cover and tossed her cigarette in, flushing behind it. She snatched his boxers from the floor and threw them in the clothes hamper and left.

When he heard her close the bathroom door, Pedrotti stopped singing.

He grew dark, dead silent as he scrubbed his body with a cloth and bar of soap. He rubbed his skin harder than he realized, and it slowly dawned on him that he was scrubbing so hard as to rid himself of the stain of his wife.

He was finished with her. He just didn't know how to get rid of her, because he no longer cared about his indiscretions. He just wanted out.

He just wanted out.

Ateer had come up from the subway two blocks away from the police precinct. He felt pretty good for a man that risked his job overnight. Valentine was as patient with him as a Benedictine monk in a monastery. He should have been terminated. But considering the environment that he had tossed him into, Valentine must have been relieved that he was only drunk, and not arrested, or worse, killed by now. He was no fool and knew precisely how close he wanted Ateer to follow the men of the Bomb Squad. Very close. Ergo his patience beyond belief.

Uniformed officers and detectives buzzed around the entrance to the precinct, tour change coming up. Some distance away from the entrance he noticed Accorso with his back against the stone wall of the building, with Charles Beakey, both smoking cigarettes.

Beakey, average looking, mature, his hair combed back and lightly oiled. His hairline was beginning to recede and combing it back made it appear worse than it was. His suit was clean and well pressed, his features clean shaven, with thin brows. He looked like a schoolteacher or scholar. He also spoke like one, his diction being flawless.

"Mackie," Accorso said, "Have you had a chance to meet Charlie?"

"I've seen him in the bullpen," Ateer replied. He extended his hand to Beakey, "How are you?"

"Good," Beakey replied, returning the handshake. "How do you like it in the Bomb Squad?"

"It's good. It's different," Ateer smiled. Turning to Accorso he asked, "what are you guys doing out here other than smoking?"

"Whadda mean?" Accorso replied, frowning.

"You can smoke inside," Ateer pointed out.

Beakey chuckled.

Accorso said, "Yeah. Pyke walked in today. He's in a shitty mood."

"Why is that?"

"Hayias took ill last night. He's up in a hospital in the Bronx."

"No shit."

"Really. Pyke just walked up and told us point blank. Then he went into his office and that was the last that anyone had seen of him."

"He's in a bad mood," Beakey added, flicking his spent cigarette aside. "Everyone's trying to stay out of his way."

"I'm thinking about going up to see him," Accorso said. "Wanna go?"

Ateer hunched his shoulders. "I never really met the man. The Bomb squad can be somewhat compartmentalized if you ask me."

"You're just going with us. That's unless you're going to take calls while we're out," Accorso said, he turned to Beakey and smiled at the humor of Ateer doing so. Beakey smiled back.

"Sure, why not?" Ateer said.

"Well, I'm going in," Beakey pushed himself from the wall. "Be safe, Mac."

"You too," Ateer replied.

Beakey walked off, entering the precinct. Accorso continued to smoke his cigarette which was burning close to the butt. Ateer looked him up and down. He couldn't be certain, but he was more certain than not that Accorso was in the same suit, shirt, and tie that he wore yesterday.

"Are you alright?" Ateer asked him.

"Yeah," he dropped his cigarette next to his shoe and crushed it. "Why?"

"Aren't those the clothes that you were wearing yesterday?"

Accorso thought for a moment, as if he was cooking up a lie, but then said, "Yeah. I slept here at my desk last night. I took a shower here this morning, but I didn't have another suit in my locker, so..." he held up his arms, displaying himself.

"Why?"

"You've met Dary, right?"

Ateer smiled at the joke. "You had a fight?"

"Yeah. I stayed out late last night. Got home and tried to get into bed but the bitch started throwing plates and shit."

"She throws plates?"

"Plates, bottles, glasses, shoes...anything nearby when she gets her dander up. One day I expect her to throw a stick of dynamite."

"Really?"

"You know that old sayin': 'live by the sword, die by the sword'," he lurched away from the wall and headed inside. Ateer strode beside him.

"So? What did you and Vaughn do last night?"

Accorso snorted, "I ditched him as soon as you left. I had a place that I had to go to."

"A place?"

As they climbed the stairway to the second floor, Accorso stopped short. He stepped to the side, against the banister to allow other officers and detectives' room to get by them.

"I went to a cathouse."

"Really?"

Accorso nodded. "I had to see a few of my favorite girls."

"I see."

"I don't think you do, Mackie."

"I don't?"

Accorso patted his shoulder, then returned to the stairs, heading for the second floor. Ateer followed behind him. Accorso's libido had gotten the better of him. Ateer could understand that clearly. They passed through the gate of the bullpen, hanging up their hats, taking their seats behind their desks. Behind Accorso, Pedrotti rolled his chair backwards into Accorso's desk. "Hey, are you still going?"

"Yeah. Did Pyke ever come out of his office?"

Pedrotti looked at the office, whose door, normally open, was closed. "He went in there and never came out."

"Let's get out of here then," Accorso said, standing. "We'll come back around lunchtime and see if there's any calls in."

Pedrotti rolled his chair back to his desk. Ateer went for his hat.

They left for the Bronx.

They walked into the hospital ward. Not finding Hayias immediately among the first three beds they walked near, they continued to the end of the ward where his bed was the last against the wall.

Hayias looked drawn, his face sunken and pale. Although he was smiling, his grin looked painted on over a frown. He was sitting up, reading a newspaper, when he saw them arrive. Almost immediately he folded his paper and set it aside.

"Okay, who blew up what?" he asked with a grin.

"This kid," Pedrotti pointed to Ateer.

"I don't know him," Hayias frowned. "Who are you?"

"He's our new rookie," Accorso patted Ateer on the back. "He's been with us for about a now. But you would've known that if you didn't spend so much time at the lab."

"I have an office there," Hayias said.

Pedrotti laughed, "That's not what I heard."

"What's going on with you," Accorso asked, cutting through the small talk. "Why are you here?"

"I've got an ulcer. Too much of this job will give you one, I suppose." Hayias rubbed his belly. "Or all the moonshine I drink."

"You don't drink moonshine," Accorso sneered, "I've seen you at a gin-joint maybe once or twice."

"That's where I was at when this ulcer hit. Ask Pikey."

Pedrotti chuckled.

"What's so funny," Hayias asked him.

"You calling him, Pikey."

"Don't you try that shit," Accorso warned. "He'll give you your own unit."

"You shouldn't say that, Fab," Hayias turned to him, "You're good at what you do. *That's* why you have your own unit. If you weren't, you would be point on his best unit."

"We should be *your* unit, Pete."

"Bullshit. I'm not the man for the job. Show me a bomb and I'll deal with it. Take it apart even, but managing a unit? I couldn't handle the responsibility. Look at me. I've got an ulcer just disabling the fucking things."

"That's not true, Pete." Accorso looked around, found a chair near the bed of another patient, and snatched it away. He placed it at the foot of Hayias' bed and took a seat, crossing his legs at his knee. "So, how long are you going to have to stay here with the dead and dying?"

"They don't know." Hayias leaned forward, adjusted his pillow higher behind his back, then sat back, sighing comfortably. "They don't know anything."

SUSPICIOUS LOOKING PACKAGES

"Where's your wife?" Pedrotti stood at the head of Hayias' bed.

"She'll be here in about an hour. She usually brings my lunch. I hate the shit they serve here."

Ateer, feeling outside of the conversation, looked around at the many men in the six beds with their heads against the walls, the space between them creating an aisle down the center. Many of the men were sleep, two sat up reading books. The one whose bed was on the other end of the ward, against the wall, was sitting up on the side of his bed, his legs dangling down as if he was preparing to leave. Everything around them was solemn and white and strangely enough, without visitors other than themselves. He wondered about that.

"Have you found out anything new about the Con Ed bomber?" Hayias asked.

Accorso shook his head, "Nothing. We went to a bunch of hardware dealers specializing in pipes but turned up nothing."

"And it took us the entire day," Pedrotti pointed out. "I was so tired I went straight home to my wife."

Hayias laughed. "You must have been pretty beat to go home to your wife."

"Damn straight."

"Beat It never goes home to his wife," Accorso said.

"You should talk. You're wearing the same clothes that you wore yesterday," Pedrotti pointed out.

Hayias and Pedrotti laughed. Ateer was too confused about what to do.

"Where did you have your ass at?" Pedrotti continued, "Maggie's Dollhouse?"

"No." Ateer sneered.

"Didn't she get raided?" Hayias asked.

Accorso turned to Ateer. "You know anything about that?"

"How should I know?" Ateer replied.

"Don't act like you don't have any buddies in the P.M. that you don't talk to."

"I don't."

Accorso looked at Hayias, cupped his hand around the side of his mouth so that Ateer could not see his lips, and mouthed silently: He does.

"How's Pikey doin'?" Hayias asked. He ran his fingers back through his hair, which was trying to stand on end, but his constant attention kept it tame.

"Don't know," Accorso replied. "He closed himself up into his office and has never come out."

"He walked in this morning looking like he lost his dog," Pedrotti said with a smile.

"You mean me?" Hayias looked over at him.

"Yeah, of course," Pedrotti replied. "Meaning no disrespect though."

"None taken."

"Can we smoke in here?" Accorso reached for his pack.

"No. But you can drink in here," Hayias said. "You got any of that Goat shit you drink?"

Accorso shook his head, "No. didn't get a chance to refill my flask."

"Got a question," Pedrotti said.

"What's that, Beat It?" Hayias replied.

"You said in your report that you expect the Con Ed bomber to escalate if he is triggered."

"I wholeheartedly expect that."

"So, can you give us a clue as to how we can catch him?"

Hayias shook his head. "That's the problem here, it won't be easy. He'll leave no clues. But did Pikey tell you guys not to dunk the next bomb you find?"

"Yeah," Accorso said. "He put it in a memo on everyone's desk, just to make it official. Isn't that kinda crazy? What if it's live?"

"It won't be."

"How do you know?"

"He's gonna toy around with us for a little while longer."

Pedrotti said, "I think you're looking at pie in the motherfucking sky if you think he's going to leave fingerprints on a pipe bomb. He knows that that's the only way we're going to catch him."

"He might slip up. If you don't check, you'll never know."

"To be honest with you, Pete," Pedrotti said, "I really don't want to walk around with a live pipe bomb if I can help it."

"It won't be live."

"I still don't see how you can say that." Accorso said.

"Because if it is, it won't be in front of Con Ed."

"Why?" Pedrotti asked.

"He's really angry at Con Ed, but I feel from his first note, by calling them crooks he's making the charge that they are thieves. If he was straight out angry, those bombs would have been real and caused damage to property and limb from the start. But leaving behind all of these mock-ups, it's as if he wants Con-Ed to make some sort of restitution to him."

"So," Accorso said, "It's just a gut feeling to you? There's no science behind it."

Hayias nodded. "Just a gut feeling. I don't think that the Bomb Squad is going to be anywhere around when he starts to build real ones. Because when he does, he'll just start blowing shit up."

"That's comforting," Ateer said.

Everyone turned to him as if he just appeared out of nowhere.

"That's the Bomb Squad," Hayias said to him.

The phone rang. It sounded louder than normal.

Pyke screwed the top onto his flask of Yak Yak Bourbon and snatched up the phone receiver. "Pyke," he stated.

"Lewis."

Pyke sat up in his chair, dropped the flask in the top drawer and closed it as if the commissioner could see him.

"Hey."

"How are you doing, Jim?" Valentine's voice sounded sincere.

"I'm fine."

"I heard your friend is in the hospital."

"Yeah, he went in early last night."

"How's he doing?"

"Well, I think. I didn't get a chance to talk to him. I waited outside in the waiting room until I got tired and went home to get a little sleep and then get here in the morning."

"You mean you haven't had a chance to talk to him?"

"No."

"Well, what the fuck are you doing in your office? Go see how our boy is doing."

"I'll go in a little while. Accorso and Beakey are out. If something hot comes in, I want to be here to take care of it."

"Why? Isn't Dempsey there?"

"Yeah."

"You don't trust him?"

"No. He's too much of a hot head. If he runs into trouble with whose got the bomb, he'll start arguing and then I'll have to hear about it."

"You're having trouble with that?"

"Not really, if you don't know how to handle the various departments. Sometimes making a bomb safe has a lot more to do with politics than mechanisms. Such as some Emergency Squad commanders. They think they're bomb squad since they've seen us dunk bombs in oil. If we can do it, anyone can do it."

"I can take care of that."

"No, that's alright. As long as I don't send Dempsey out to those calls, we should be alright."

"Well, I know how close you and Hayias are. Keep an eye on him."

"Since we're talking about him Lew, I was wondering if I can ask you, do you have any problem with Hayias having an office in the Technical Research Lab? I mean, he's there most of the time anyway and he's got good instincts when it comes to bombs."

"How does Kelly feel about a fifth wheel on his team?"

SUSPICIOUS LOOKING PACKAGES

Pyke paused. Valentine wasn't one to step on toes unnecessarily. "I don't think he likes it."

"You don't think? Or you know."

"He thinks Pete is stepping on toes."

"What do you think?"

"Pete's good for that spot."

"You think?"

"Yeah."

Valentine went quiet.

"Forget about it. There's a little give and take already going on between them. Let's let them keep that up," Pyke resigned from the discussion.

"No, no. Let me think about it. Just an office, right?"

"Just an office."

"I'll talk to Kelly and see how he feels."

"Sounds good."

"Well, don't stay in that office all day. Go check up on Pete and get back to me."

"Yeah, alright."

Valentine hung up the phone. Pyke set the receiver down and opened his top drawer, pulling out his flask.

Dempsey asked for the next call. Accorso and unit one had returned. The moment they sat down behind their desks Pyke said he was stepping out and would probably not be back during the morning trick. Accorso was in charge. Later, a call came in. A bomb was found in a subway. Dempsey wanted the call.

"Why?" Accorso asked him.

"I've been sitting on my hands all morning."

Accorso sat back in his chair. "Alright. See you later."

Dempsey clapped his hands, drawing everyone's attention. "Unit two! Let's roll!"

There was a quick flurry of activity on their side of the bullpen, but in moments unit two was gone.

"We're babysitting the bullpen?" Ateer asked.

"Yeah. Pyke's out. Whatever comes in is ours. Or if the shit hits the fan. You and I. I'll leave Beat it and Big O to be the last on call."

Ateer nodded.

Accorso said over his shoulder to Pedrotti, "What did you roll today?"

"A seven out," he replied, turned a page of the newspaper noisily.

"What's Maggie's Dollhouse?" Ateer asked Accorso.

Both men turned to look at him.

"It's a whorehouse," Accorso finally said flatly.

"Like you didn't know," Pedrotti grinned. "Whaddid you think it was? A bakeshop?"

Both men started laughing. Ateer grinned uncomfortably.

"Is that why your wife didn't let you stay home, Fab."

"Do you really wanna know these things, Mac?"

"I don't know."

Accorso looked at him. It was strange to Ateer. Accorso was maybe a few months older than him, but he was clearly the wiser one of the two. He stared at him with eyes that saw too much, far too much. He was looking completely through him, like Scooty did. A skill that he must have acquired from the older man.

"You are here in the Bomb Squad," Accorso said.

"That's right."

"Why the fuck do you want to be here?"

"Because the Bomb Squad is the best squad."

Accorso looked over his shoulder at Pedrotti. "Isn't this rich."

"It's a peach." Pedrotti replied.

"Come clean," Accorso said to Ateer. "Why are you here?"

"I think I've answered that question a million times."

"You mean you've lied about the question a million times."

Ateer sighed.

SUSPICIOUS LOOKING PACKAGES

Pedrotti rolled his chair back to his desk, snatched up his newspaper.

Accorso stood, took his pack of cigarettes from his desktop, and walked off.

"Why does everyone keep asking me that question?" Ateer asked Pedrotti. He didn't turn around to address it.

"Why?" he asked again.

Pedrotti did not reply.

"I talked to Valentine about getting you that office in the lab," Pyke said.

He sat in a chair that he found at the foot of Hayias' hospital bed.

"What did he say?" Hayias grinned.

"He said he'll talk to Kelly."

"Oh, you know what that means." Hayias made a face.

"Give Lew a chance. He'll pull something out of the hat."

"Sure."

The sound of high heeled shoes behind him caught Pyke's attention. He turned around, finding the tall, indomitable Clara Hayias marching up to her husband's bedside. She took his hand with one hand and felt his forehead for his temperature with the other, "How are you feeling?" she asked.

"I'm good, sweetheart."

"Thanks for coming," she said to Pyke.

"Somebody's gotta keep an eye on this guy," Pyke chuckled. "How are you holding up?"

"I'm good. Thanks."

"So, what does the doctors say?"

"He has ulcerative colitis."

"Fuck is that?" Pyke frowned.

"Chronic ulcers in the digestive tract," she turned to Hayias and stroked his hair tenderly.

"I've had it for a long time, Pikey," Hayias said to him.

"Why didn't you tell me about it?"

"Oh, you want me to have a shit discussion with you?"

"It's kinda personal," Clara said. "It was never this bad."

"It's bad now?"

"He had a bad episode."

"Is that what they're calling this?"

"That's what it is, Pikey," Hayias said. "Just a bad episode. A large ulcer opened…" his voice trailed off.

"So how long are you staying in here?"

Both husband and wife were silent. Neither wanted to offer or had the answer.

"What did the doctors say?"

"They don't know," Hayias said. "They can't get the ulcers under control."

"They'll get control of it," Clara said. "He's been through this before, Jim."

Pyke stared at them, stared at the clean, antiseptic world that he was surrounded in, stared at his hands.

"It'll be alright," Hayias said. "I'm tougher than I look."

Pyke looked at Clara, then back to Hayias, "Can I ask you a question?"

"Sure."

Pyke's eyes went to his wife, then back to him.

Hayias understood, "anything that you say to me, you can say to her."

Pyke nodded. "Could this be from the…" Pyke struggled on the word, "…moonshine?"

Hayias and Clara laughed heartily. Pyke looked at them, confused for a moment, then broke out into a smile.

"No, Pikey," Hayias said, "It's causes are unknown. The moonshine probably healed some of the ulcers. Nothing like straight alcohol on sores."

"Not likely, Peter," Clara said to him.

"Well, listen, I have to get back to work." Pyke groaned as he leaned forward and stood from the chair. "I can't stay here and jawbone with you all day. I have a squad to run."

"Don't get yourself all blown up while you're at it," Hayias said.

Pyke walked up to the bed and kissed Clara on the cheek, "You take care of him," he said, gripping her hand.

"I will. He's the only loser I've got," she said.

He reached over and rested a hand on Hayias shoulder. "Look, I'll be back tomorrow. My wife might be here today. I'll see you again."

"Sure."

Pyke walked off, heading down the ward and out into the hospital hall. He touched his hand to his jacket pocket, feeling the hardness of his flask. He had to take a stop at a gin-joint to fill it up before going back to work.

Ateer walked into the locker room, taking his rig and pistol out and strapping it on. He checked the inside of the jacket where a frayed hole was growing where his revolver and leather rig rubbed against it. He'd have to go clothing shopping soon for a new suit, or at least a jacket.

"Mac," Accorso said behind him.

Ateer turned around as Accorso went into his locker adjacent to his. "What are you doing tonight?" He asked.

"Nothing."

"Beat it and I are gonna rec a car and go somewhere."

"Where?"

"Maggie's."

Ateer was stunned.

"You said you wanted to know what it was about, right?" Accorso reached into his locker and came away with a silver flask. He reached into his jacket and produced another one, shaking it and finding it empty. "So, what do you wanna do?"

"I'll go."

Accorso put the empty flask into this locker and the full one in his jacket. "C'mon." He slammed his locker and walked off.

Ateer closed his and followed him.

After Pedrotti requisitioned a car, Accorso, not one to ride shotgun, drove them to the lower east side. The hovering full moon eased through the clouds casting a silvery glow on row after row of brownstones and their pleasant monotony. In the backseats, pressed against the small passenger side window, Ateer stared out at the night life, the many people, in hat or dress walked the streets. The chilly days, the blustering winds, all identifying the winter was soon gone.

Accorso roamed the streets, turning corners until he found a parking spot large enough for the squad car. Walking down the block, trailing the two detectives, Ateer wondered how good his decision was to go to Maggie's. He had never been to a cathouse before. He was clearly aware that sex went on inside, and that both Accorso and Pedrotti were admitted whoremongers. If that was what they were about to engage in, what would he do?

As if they were still searching for parking on the street, they continued turning corners on foot. This neighborhood was old, the root systems of the trees, where provision was made in the slate plates of the sidewalk for growth, were beginning to push up on the sections, making peaks and valleys in the walk. Ateer took care not to trip over a section in the streetlamp, moon glossed evening.

Up ahead, a pale painted five story building was tightly sandwiched between two darker colored brownstones which made it stand out slightly in the street. A black, wrought iron fence bracketed its front, pushing the sidewalk away from the front flight of stairs. Accorso went in through the gate, Pedrotti filing in after him, burning down a cigarette before flicking it aside. Ateer stopped at the mouth of the gate. The windows of the first floor of the building, underneath the steep stair before the front door, had bars, made of the same black, wrought iron material as the front fencing. The rest of the floors, each with no more than three windows, had rectangular flowerpots on their sills. Green tufts of plants and speckles of colorful flowers sprouting atop them.

Climbing the stair carefully, Ateer looked around at the people making their way on the sidewalk and wondered if they were aware of what this building was, or if they were catching the attention of the neighbors, labeling them men who frequent fallen women. He felt both vulnerable, and a level of shame as he moved up the stairs, stopping behind Pedrotti.

Accorso stood before the tall, arched front doorway, its doors painted a glossy black, and knocked vigorously.

As if another world existed on the other side from the quiet block of buildings outside, when the door opened a burst of light and music escaped, a maddening opposite. They filed into the building and entered a foyer which was a grand space. Two women, dressed in tight fitting, high cut lingerie and diaphanous robes with ostrich feathers along their fringes glided smoothly towards them. With soft hands, they pawed at the men, two women singled out Ateer, took his hat and jacket. As they pulled his jacket from his shoulders, revealing his shoulder rig and pistol under his arm, they were not shocked or taken aback, as if such sights were more than normal.

These were no doubt whores who have seen more than their fair share of the strange things in life. Ateer looked the two women administering to him up and down, made taller because of their high heels; long, laced black stockings, small wire thin underpants and small, black shelf bras pushing up their modest bosoms. Ateer's face flushed. Not that he was embarrassed himself, but for the women who traipsed around half dressed.

Ahead, there was commotion. The nymphs around him backed away, and Pedrotti stood aside, revealing Ateer to the madame of the house, who Accorso stood next to with an arm around her waist.

Slightly taller than Accorso, narrow and lean, she looked like a marionette of skinny limbs and narrow features. She wore a shiny pink gown, cinched at the waist, fabric straps which slipped from her shoulders. Her small busted bustier which held up very little in the way a breasts, left the upper part of her chest nothing more than ribs and collarbones under pale, white skin.

She had a youthful face, narrow cheeks with deep dimples, long nose, glittering eyes under heavy brows, and finally coiffed with short, dark curly hair.

Accorso brought her to him, wearing a smile equal to hers. "Mackie, meet Margaret Quinlan, the wonderful proprietor of this establishment."

She stuck out her hand to Ateer. "Hello, please call me Maggie."

"Hello, Maggie, please call me, Mackie." He shook her hand.

"Is this your first time in a place where you will be pampered and taken care of?" She cooed.

"Well, in fact, it is."

She moved in on Ateer, her lanky arm slipping over his shoulders. She waved Accorso and Pedrotti away. "You gentlemen know your way around. I'll take care of your friend here, personally."

Pedrotti patted Ateer on the back and walked off. Accorso saluted and vanished.

"Well, young man, you're in my little dollhouse," Margaret said with a broad smile across her thin lips. She smelled of flowers and although her face was painted, it was done delicately and not plastered on as he would expect from a 'fallen woman.' As smooth as a serpent, her arm wrapped around his and her head rested gingerly on his shoulder. "Many people believe that all places of pleasure are little more than throwing a woman over once or twice. But here, in my Dollhouse a man is not just sexed well, he is treated like a king."

With long, luxuriant strides which could only be done by a tall leggy woman such as her, she strolled him into a parlor of pale pink colors and draperies. A pale pink sofa with blood red cushions, red cushions and mirrors on the wall and pale pink stools around tall marble tables. Overhanging the entire lounge was a balcony of dark wood and light wood balustrades upon which a line of topless women wearing see through silks paraded.

In the lounge itself were several more women, stretched out upon a few of the couches, some at the tall tables. Women of all stripes and colors perked up, their heads swiveling like owls onto prey as he strode in.

On the other side of the large lounge, it was darker, more solemn area containing a long bar and more stools but in the deep colors of the balcony. She turned him toward the darkness of the bar, its ceiling painted with clouds. The walls were also painted, with lush landscapes between wood toned pilasters. Here were low tables and chairs grouped in fours and tall lampshade covered lamp stands.

Surprisingly, to Ateer, there were men seated behind tables, dressed in suits and ties, conversing with the women. Margaret stopped them at the demarcation between the two completely dichotomic rooms and whispered into his ear. "Sometimes a man doesn't need sex to be spoiled. Sometimes just decent conversation will suffice. Sometimes music, sometimes art. But every time it's something that can't be had anywhere else in the world, including home."

Margaret walked on, navigating through the tables and chairs to reach the bar with two women bartenders behind. They were dressed in short, frilly black and white Swedish maid costumes.

"Melissa," Margaret said to a passing barmaid, "make this handsome man a…" her voice stretched out the 'a' as she thought, "Tom Collins!" she said, pointing at him emphatically.

Melissa walked off. Margaret sat down on a stool and regarded Ateer with large soulful eyes that had a gem-like quality to them.

"What do you want, Mackie?" She breathed.

Ateer, still standing next to her, hunched his shoulders. "I really wish I knew. I came with my friends."

"Have a seat," she gestured to the stool.

Sliding up onto the stool, he rested against the bar top with an elbow, and turned to face her.

Margaret smiled. The drinks arrived. The barmaid rested one in front of Ateer and one in front of Margaret before leaving.

"Your friends are already having their needs met," she said.

"Having sex?"

A smooth easy smile came from her. "I really don't know what it is that they are into. They know the girls, they know the rooms, they know the floors. They, like all the men here, can move about at will."

"How are you paid?"

"By the time that you spend here. Some men stay all day. They write a check before they leave."

"Well, what I think I am asking you is; how much is this costing me?"

She laughed, as carefree as her smile. "You're a new customer. Everything," she leaned forward, whispering, "and I do mean everything," she sat back, "is on the house," she said at a normal tone.

"That's very gracious of you."

"I want to make you a repeat customer. If this is your last visit, I want it to be the best that you've ever had, so that it leaves an impression that you'll never forget."

"Sounds scary."

She laughed. "Now come on, Mackie. Are you afraid of a little...pleasure?"

"I never thought so, but for some reason I am worried."

"You? You're the one with the pistol. All I have is this dress. I don't even have underwear." She pulled the shoulder straps from her shoulders, allowing them to fall, leaving her bare from the top of her small breasts to the top of her head. "Are you afraid of the *men* in the bar?"

Ateer looked around at the men of various ages, some older, some quite young. Some with arms around a woman or two. Everyone though was in a state of merriment and laughter, drinking copiously.

Margaret reached out and took Ateer by the chin, turning his head back again to face hers. "Please, don't gawk here. It's impolite."

"Sorry."

Margaret took a long drink. "How would you like some drinks and company just for now? And I'll find out what it is you want."

SUSPICIOUS LOOKING PACKAGES

Ateer smiled. "Who are you going to get to keep me company while you try to figure out what it is that I want?"

"Well, for starters, how about me?" She reached out and took his hand, massaging it tenderly.

"Well, so far, you are...excellent company."

She opened his hand, fingered his palm, then rested it on her thigh. "Good."

"But what I would like to know is how are you going to find out what I want even when I don't know what it is that I want."

"Well, normally, a man wants what he can't get at home. If he has a nagging or irritable wife, he wants peace. If a man has too much control, he wants to lose it. If a man wants—shall we say—unusual sex, then that's what he comes here for. Men are pretty specific that way."

"So, I'm a man."

"And I can tell by the bulge in the center of your pants that you are," she raised an eyebrow. "Is it getting hard?"

Ateer blushed. "I don't think that's a conversation for a cultured woman such as yourself."

Margaret reeled back in laughter. "Cultured?"

Ateer's embarrassment turned into stunned confusion. "Well...I..."

She choked down her giggles and leaned forward, lips to Ateer's ear, "Kind sir, you do me well. I am but a common whore in a gilded cage. And if there is anything ladylike about me, it's due to the sum of my parts and little else." Margaret kissed his cheek and settled back on her stool. She picked up her drink, took a long draw, nearly turning it up.

"You don't wear a wedding ring, so you're not married and there are a million things that you no doubt want but are too ashamed to ask."

"Like what?"

"Oh, I don't know. Like I said, there are too many, and no doubt too many to mention. And like some men, you didn't come here hungry for sex, so I would guess that you are a virgin. Am I right?"

For some reason, her revelation caused his penis to stir, moving from a curled, flaccid, soft position in his slacks ever so slightly toward an erection, but it was reluctant, hesitant. He shifted his weight on his stool, turned his open legs away from her.

"Yes, you are correct."

"Why is that? Never found the time?"

"Well, I believe that sex should be between a husband and a wife only, to consummate their marriage."

"But you don't really believe that to you. You were taught that. You just follow it because you really respect the person that told it to you."

"Now how do you know that?"

Margaret snapped her fingers. Melissa returned. "Sweetheart, go and get me a deck of gaspers."

Melissa walked off. Margaret turned to Ateer again, smiling, "Because that's the old chestnut of sanctified church people. And a man involved with the church wouldn't be caught dead walking through the front door to my Dollhouse. There's a back entrance for them. You're not that. But you believe in it enough at least to spout it. So, it's not yours. Who's it from?"

"My mother."

"Oh, mothers. Very strong influence indeed."

"She raised me. I never knew my father."

"Oh, okay, I can see why you parrot her."

"Well, I believe in it, or I wouldn't be a virgin now, would I?"

"This is true, but if you *really* believed it, like I said, you wouldn't be in here."

Ateer thought about it. Thought about her soft voice, her smooth neck, the soft swell of her shoulders. "You're right about that."

"But you're not here for sex then. Not this time."

"Then what am I here for?"

"I would say company, but I think that would be wrong."

SUSPICIOUS LOOKING PACKAGES

"Why is that?"

"Because you have friends. You came here with them. You have all the company you need. You've come here for something else, and I think I know," she smiled slyly. Melissa returned with a pack of cigarettes and a lighter, handing them over to Margaret. She tore open the pack, shook one out and offered it to Ateer. He plucked one out and used the lighter to light his and hers. She pointed at him with two fingers, her cigarette between them. "You came with your friends. Whatever you are here for, it's about your friends. You want to know what it is that they are coming here for. That's why *you're* here."

"I don't think you're right now. You've jumped the tracks."

"No, no," she cooed. She winked slowly, closing one eye, then opening it. "You are either watching over them *or*...you're investigating them."

Ateer was completely stunned. She was so incredibly perspicacious that she became frightening to him. But no matter her insight, she knew something that no one should. He was investigating the Bomb Squad.

"I'll go even one further for you," she wagged a finger at him, "They've been here numerous times, and you know that. So, you obviously know why they are here and that they're in no danger, so there's no need to watch over them. Hence, you're here investigating them."

Ateer did not know how to reply so as not to reveal himself.

Margaret smiled. "Your silence condemns you."

Ateer knocked the ashes from his cigarette into a crystal ashtray on the bar, studying them breaking apart from the tip of his cigarette and falling. "Okay, so you see through me, Margaret—"

"Maggie."

"Maggie. But then, tell me what do I want?"

"You needn't be here to know what they are up to because they no doubt told you to bring you here. You know this is a whorehouse, so there's no mystery for you there."

"No, there isn't."

Margaret stared at him, looking into his eyes. "You're not here investigating anymore," she crushed out her cigarette. "I'm gonna go out on a limb here...you're waiting for something in you to make you just like them."

"What?"

"You admire them. Respect them, and in the end, you want to be them. That's what I see."

"So, is that what I want?"

She turned to him, surprised, eyes wide, mouth open, "Oh no, you are *here* because you want them to accept you, and you want to be like them. But what you *want*....well, what you *wanted*, was to hear me tell you that."

He smiled. She was right.

"Some men want peace. Some men want to lose control. Some men want sex. Some want conversation," she waved over Melissa, ordered two more rounds. As the barmaid walked off, she turned to Ateer.

"Tonight, you are here for the conversation," she smiled, "but who knows what you'll be here for," she lit another cigarette, "tomorrow night."

The rain was falling hard, making the streets shine with the wash of streetlamps and neon signs. People without umbrellas ran willy-nilly, crossing streets, running up and down sidewalks, jumping into doorway recesses and store entrances. As if he was ducking balls thrown from a pitcher, Pyke moved out of the way of the runners in the rain, giving them room to pass. He held his umbrella against the rain, marching harder through the cold wind. Thank God it wasn't cold enough for all this precipitation to come down as snow, he thought. He would rather rain than snow anytime. Snow just had the added aggravation of malingering long after it was pale, white, and beautiful. Even long after it turned gray and speckled black and ugly.

SUSPICIOUS LOOKING PACKAGES

He turned into the wood and glass doorway of the bar, pulling open the door and closing his umbrella, sweeping into the establishment. Pyke shook the rain from his jacket and plunged into the noisy and crowded space. Smartly lit to cast shadows in the proper corners and throw light on tabletops and doorways. Many people dined on decent American fare, reasonably priced. It was a cop bar, mostly filled with the people of the nearby precinct and law offices, and people from 240 Centre Street.

Oozing between patrons, Pyke worked his way to the bar, between two men and waved down the bartender. As the bartender drew near, he instantly noticed Pyke and stopped short. "He's at his usual table," he said to him.

Knowing exactly where to go. Adjacent to the crowded and noisy bar was the larger restaurant. The atmosphere here was more sedate, less brusque and raucous. It was a more genteel group, dining on the same fare as in the bar half, but here there were larger tables being served by attentive waiters and...

A clique of men in suits stood in a semi-circular formation about a table tucked in the corner in the back. The commissioner's protective detail gave him a wide berth, where they also made a small zone of empty tables around the commissioner's. Pyke walked up to the foremost escort who stepped aside without a word. Pyke went on in, past the empty tables to Valentine's, sitting down.

"That's one thing I have to credit you for," Valentine said, glancing at his watch, "you're always punctual."

"Thanks, Lew." Pyke took the napkin from the table and folded it on his lap.

"Thank you for coming."

Pyke looked around at the otherwise crowded restaurant outside of their border of protection. "Crowded tonight."

"Yes."

A waiter quickly came to the table and asked if Pyke had a drink order. He asked for scotch on the rocks.

"So, how are you doing?" Valentine asked.

"It was a good day."

Valentine reached for his drink next to him but did not lift it. "So, is Hayias still in the hospital?"

"Yeah."

"Do you know why?"

Pyke pointed to his belly. "Ulcers."

"Well, I guess that would be an occupational hazard in your line of work."

"I guess. I never had the problem."

"I'm surprised that I don't. The shit that I go through on a daily basis," he chuckled as if an afterthought, "but look at me comparing my paperwork with your pipe bombs. Ridiculous, huh?"

"I wouldn't say that, Lew. It is what it is."

The waiter returned with his drink and took their dinner order.

"Well, you know that even when I invite you out for dinner, it can be both social and professional."

"I expect that."

"I just find it a little too formal giving orders from my office all the time, and especially when it comes to men I consider friends."

"I understand."

Valentine took a sip from his rocks glass, "How is Ateer doing?"

"Good. I have no complaints, and his T.O. has given me no complaints."

"His training officer, is that detective first grade Accorso?"

"Yes, he's my best man."

"That's great to hear. Now…how's Accorso?"

"Doing fine as far as I can tell. I keep sending him out, and he keeps coming back in one piece, so I guess he's doing something right."

"Did I thank you for putting Ateer into the squad? He's a good man. He'll help you catch those bastards out there that are planting these Devil Toys around the city."

SUSPICIOUS LOOKING PACKAGES

"Yes, and I appreciate the thanks. He's a good guy."

"Listen, I know you know that this meeting is not about Ateer or Accorso, right?"

"I had a feeling, but there's no rushing the commish. Well, that's what I've been told."

"About a week ago, the Catskill Aqueduct had an event."

"Where's that, up to the north?"

"Yeah, Greenburgh, Westchester. I don't know where that is either. I just know it's up north, near the reservoir or reservoirs, up there."

"Okay, what kind of event?"

"The watershed police found a woman up there taking a detailed survey of the Aqueduct at the pumping station near Hartsdale. They put the elbow on her and in custody they found out that she gave them an assumed name, so they gave her the Third Degree for the rest of the night to the next day. Upon stripping her down to her freckles they found sixteen pages of engineering notes hidden in her clothing where they wouldn't be easily found. They started shitting sideways up there and soon they had the state troopers and the FBI involved, managing things. She finally spouted that she was a communist of Russian birth and gave them her true name and address—"

The waiter returned with others carrying plates of food. They quickly filled the table with fare and then were off once more, in a clatter of clinking, clanking plates and utensils.

Once out of earshot, Valentine continued: "They finally released her, but they've got eyes on her constantly."

"Why would the Russians want detailed data of our reservoir system unless they were thinking of doing something to it."

"That's exactly what the New York Board of Water Supply are thinking up there. They want the watershed police to increase the number of patrolmen guarding the New York watersheds by 36 percent."

"But don't they have sabotage scares all the time up there?"

"All the time, but they've been at best prank phone calls or toothless hicks sleeping in the woods, but never someone with engineering specs. In any event, it put the fear of god into them." Valentine rested his fork, washed down a morsel of food with a swallow of water, then wiped at the corners of his mouth with his napkin. "Look, to make this long story as short as possible, on Monday they will train these new officers at a training school at Neversink in Sullivan County for two weeks."

"That's good. They'll need it."

"Yeah, I thought you would think that." Valentine smiled. "They also want these fifty-eight new officers to be able to handle bombs and dynamite which would probably be the tool of choice if they're going after the reservoir structures."

"I think I'm following you all of a sudden." Pyke sat back, looked at Valentine tiredly.

"Good. You're going up there, the best of the best, to give them this invaluable training."

"For two weeks?"

"For two weeks. They've converted part of a huge lakehouse up there to be the school. They'll provide you with room and board for the two weeks plus that you'll be up there. Everything is taken care of. All you have to do is go up there and give them instructions."

"That's it?"

"That's it. Your best man, Accorso? He can run the bomb squad while you're gone and Hayias is laid up in the hospital."

Pyke thought about it. Accorso's abilities were, without question, able to handle managing the squad in his absence, Pyke had no problem with that. He was just turned around as to just how effective he would be training these new recruits for two weeks. He had to devise a course in five days and think of ways to involve and educate his students. Valentine mistook Pyke's pause.

"He can handle it, can't he?"

SUSPICIOUS LOOKING PACKAGES

Pyke waved off the comment. "Oh yeah. In his sleep." Pyke sat up straighter, "I was thinking about something else."

"What's that?"

"It's a lot of shit to cover, a lot of shit to develop, and a lot of shit to do to make them into even decent bomb squad material."

"I don't think that's possible, Jim. Don't try to make them bomb squad material. Teach them how not to make stupid mistakes that'll get them killed if they find something ticking on the wall of a dam."

"Like the Emergency Squad is trying to do?"

"Something like that."

"I see your point. If these guys start thinking like the clowns on the Emergency Squad…"

"They may take unnecessary risks." Valentine nodded. "That's why we need you up there to give them the tools that they'll need to deal with any bomb threats that they may encounter."

"Better than them doing things thinking they can do what we do just because they think it looks easy."

"I'll ask you again, do you want me to talk to the Emergency Squad Commanders?"

"No, no. It doesn't have to go up as high as you. I can take care of it."

"I mean, if you think these guys are going to set one of these things off and kill themselves and scores of people around them, then I want to know."

"I'm helping the ones that are having this problem to appreciate that fact. It's not all of them, and the ones that are, I will address. Don't worry about it."

Valentine turned serious, "Jim, I don't want to revisit this after a tragedy. Can I count on you to take care of it?"

"I'll take care of it."

"Good. So let your crack man know that you'll be leaving him in charge of the squad this Monday for two weeks."

"I will."

"Now, how is that wife of yours treating you?" Valentine asked, finishing his plate of food, and waving the waiter over to pick up the plate.

In the bullpen, Pedrotti and Accorso stood over his desk while Pedrotti shook a set of dice in his hand. With a toss he sent them dancing on his desktop, rolling, and bouncing until they stopped at 5 and 3.

"Easy Eight," Accorso said, patting him on the shoulder.

"Today's gonna be a good day." Pedrotti smiled, leaned forward to pick up his dice and held them before his eyes. Accorso returned to his desk, taking a seat. After tossing the dice into his desk drawer, Pedrotti rolled back to Accorso's desk.

"Did you talk to Maggie?" Pedrotti asked.

"Yeah, I had a little time with her. Our friend was busy capitalizing on all of her time last night."

"Who told you that?"

"*She* did."

"So? He fuck her?"

Accorso laughed, "You know better than me that if there were any fucking going on between him and her, it'll be *her* fucking the shit out of *him* and not the other way around."

"So?"

"No, she said he wasn't there for sex."

"What was he there for?"

"Just to spend some time with us off duty."

Pedrotti thought about the comment and the night for a second. "So, what do you think about him?"

"If he's a spy he should have turned us in for something by now."

"For what? That we buy weed from a dickhead like Vaughn and fuck strange women? Where is the crime in that?"

"What do you think he's here for?"

"I don't know."

They thought about it. "I'm still trying to figure out what you are here for," Accorso said, "you don't do any fucking work other than roll your dice."

"I vote we let the guy in. He's earned his wings enough to be taught how to survive in here. Let's make him Bomb Squad. That's why Pyke put him with us, isn't it?"

"Yeah," Accorso sighed, resigned to the decision, "we've shown him the dirt. Let's give him the skill."

"Let's do that," Pedrotti turned to look deeper into the bullpen, at Brock Dempsey's desk to see if he was listening. Dempsey was nose deep in a manual. For an instant Pedrotti wondered what manual he was reading. After being confident that he would not be overheard, Pedrotti turned back to Accorso. "Maybe Dempsey will get upset, blow his top, and have a stroke. Then you can give Mac Unit 2."

"Mac better first learn how to take care of 'Unit-his-ass', before worrying about taking charge of someone in the squad."

Movement and noise caught their attention. Both turned to the flight of stairs emptying out to the floor and found Lieutenant Pyke surging upstairs, and heading for his office briskly, his trench coat thrown over his arm, his hat in the other hand. Upon grabbing the doorknob to his office and pushing open the door, he turned to Accorso, right across from him. "Fab, get your ass in here."

Accorso turned to Pedrotti. "what the fuck did I do now?"

"Maybe Mac's report came in?" He chuckled.

"Yeah, thanks." Accorso pushed himself up out of his chair and left the bullpen, coming around the corral to Pyke's office and stepped in. Pyke was behind his desk, going through the drawers until he found his flask. "Close the door."

Accorso slowly closed the door and approached the desk, stopping behind the chair that usually sat in front of it.

Pyke unscrewed the cap and turned the flask up, taking a quick swig. He held it out to Accorso.

Not really needing a drink, but not wanting to offend his superior by turning him down, Accorso went to the desk, took the flask, and took a good sip.

"What's goin' on, boss?" He asked, handing back Pyke's flask.

"I'm leaving you in charge of the Bomb Squad for two weeks, starting Monday."

Accorso frowned, "Wha—?"

"I'm leaving to train some recruits on how to deal with explosives. So, while I'm gone, you're in charge."

"Is Valentine planning to have another Bomb Squad in each borough?"

"No. He wants me to go upstate, into Westchester or something or another, and stay in some kinda resort and train these guys to watch over dams and reservoirs. Ain't that rich?"

"They're blowing up dams?"

"They might." Pyke lowered into his chair, dropped his flask into his desk. "Keep watch over my squad, detective."

"I was just wondering. You know how much I'm a hands-on person. I don't know if I want to be stuck in this office while the newest recruit is backing up my boy. This sounds like a job for Beakey." Accorso pointed out.

"There's no ducking this ball, Fab. You can take your breaks when I get back."

"Breaks?"

"Yes. What do you think? I'm stupid on top of blind. You go running off and back and you look like you've swam a mile through lemon juice."

"Lemon juice?"

"Your eyes are so red that they look filled to the brim with blood. I don't crawl up your ass for shit like that because I do it too, but I can also do my job. You'd had better do my job to the best of your abilities or I'm coming back in a very bad mood."

"I get your point."

"You get the first call on the trick today. I want you on your Ps and Qs while I'm gone."

SUSPICIOUS LOOKING PACKAGES

"So? You're going to give me all the calls today?"

Pyke laughed, picked up a folder on his right and opened it before him. "Like you could. Get all your shit out of your system today and tomorrow so that on Monday you're on top of Beakey and Dempsey."

"Alright."

"Dismissed."

Accorso nodded, turned on his heels and marched out of the office. Returning to his desk, he found Ateer at his desk and upon taking a seat Pedrotti rolled back next to him. "So? What was that about?"

"What was what about?" Ateer asked, leaning over his desk toward them to hear.

"Next week, Pyke is leaving for two weeks and he's putting me in charge."

"No shit," Pedrotti said, flabbergasted.

Accorso nodded. "He's putting me in charge."

"Holy shit! Do you know what that means?"

"No, what?"

Pedrotti pointed to Accorso's chest. "That means *you're* going to be Pyke and," he pointed to his own chest, "I'm going to be Hayias!"

Accorso laughed.

"So? What am I going to be?" Ateer asked.

"You're gonna be the dumb donkey that stays in his seat until called for." Accorso smiled a broad, false smile.

Ateer sat frozen, not knowing how to take the comment.

"And you, you stupid guinea, what do you want to do today?" he said to Pedrotti.

"What do you mean?"

The phone rang.

Accorso pointed to the phone. "If we survive this call, what do you want to do for the rest of the day?"

"We're taking off?"

"Yeah," Accorso reached for the phone receiver, but it stopped ringing.

"Am I invited?" Ateer asked.

Accorso looked at him, screwed up his face. "What do you think? You're Unit One now. You go where we go."

Ateer smiled and settled back into his chair.

"*Accorso!*" Bellowed out of Pyke's office.

Accorso snatched up the receiver.

Lieutenant Ralph Conway, Emergency Squad out of the 110th was a tall, older gentleman, dressed in uniform and flanked by two of his men. As soon as Accorso parked the Plymouth, he came to the driver's side door and held out his hand as they made their introductions.

"I've got one for you," he said.

Accorso shook his hand, "Whaddaya got?"

They turned and walked off with Pedrotti and Ateer following.

"Do you think it's him?" Ateer whispered to Pedrotti who was busy trying to listen in on the conversation between Accorso and Conway.

"If it's in a red sock it is," he replied.

"We found it at the garage entrance." Conway led them down the block in the largely industrial section of the borough with large factory buildings without windows stretching across lengths of blocks. Ahead were the train tracks of the Long Island Railroad Port Washington branch running along with 45th street. The large reddish-brown building next to them was the New York and Queens Electric Light and Power Company, another utility. In the car ride over, the speculation ran rampant that this could be the Con Ed bomber branching out to other utility companies. Accorso reminded them that they were to fingerprint the pipe bomb so no dunking it in oil. No more was said about it until they pulled the car up to the factory building with Frascone in the van behind them.

SUSPICIOUS LOOKING PACKAGES

"Was the pipe bomb in a red sock?" Accorso asked Conway as they turned the corner. Before them, on this street were the crowds being pushed back by irritated and tired uniformed officers, squad cars parked up on the curb, and on the fenced in embankment down to the tracks themselves. Also present was the long, green, and gold Mack truck with the words Emergency Squad Police stenciled in gold along its sides.

It was a cool day. Cooler than the ones before, but it did not deter the people who seemed to accumulate around explosives like tin drawn by magnets. Accorso wondered what was the important thing that they were looking for which could cost them their lives. The officers did their best to create a wide enough perimeter should the bomb go off, but without knowing the explosive payload, there really was no way to judge a safe distance, unless you used the maximum safe distance for just about anything—which was to be *no* where around.

"Pipe bomb?" Conway replied. "It's a mysterious package. It has no address or markings of any kind, wrapped in brown paper and tied with twine."

Accorso turned around, glancing at Pedrotti and Ateer. "It doesn't sound like our boy."

"Your boy?" Conway asked just before plowing into the backs of the spectators ahead, his two men flanking him now taking positions in the front, cutting through the crowd like the prow of a ship through water, making a path through and past the officers holding back the mob.

As if striking and invisible wall, Conway, and his men would go no further. Conway pointed off into the distance. "It's a package right up there, next to the entrance to the garage dead ahead."

Accorso stood for a moment, thinking, staring off into the distance, then turned to Pedrotti. "Go check it out."

Pedrotti nodded and walked down towards the package. Accorso turned to Ateer, "Tell Big O to do his magic. We're coming to him." Ateer ran off. To Conway he said, "Whoever is in charge of the uni's on crowd control to get these people on buses to the next stop. Get them anywhere but around here." Conway nodded and walked off.

Ateer raced back to the van, finding Frascone behind the wheel, staring through the window. Upon seeing Ateer come near, he hopped out, panting. "Is it a bomb?"

"Dunno, but Accorso said to do your magic right now."

Without another word, Frascone jumped back into the van, "Get in!"

Ateer ran around the front of the vehicle and jumped into the passenger seat. Frascone already had a map unfolded before him, holding it against the steering wheel so that he could locate where they were with a finger first, and then move it around to the closest lot that he could find.

"Hold on," he said, crumpling the map and pushing it over his shoulder into the back. Ateer held onto the dashboard as Frascone started the van, shifted into reverse, and peeled out in reverse from the curb, and spun the van 90 degrees upon entering the intersection, the inertia making Ateer lean against the force of the turn. Upon straightening up Ateer was then forced into the seat as Frascone stepped on the gas, spinning rubber in the intersection, and blasting off down the street.

"Shit, Big O! You could've run into somebody!" Ateer shouted.

"I checked the side view mirror!" Frascone shouted back.

He skidded the van on a sharp right turn, cutting off a car attempting to turn onto the same street from the oncoming lane. The engine of the van revved as if struggling to tear itself from the hood of the vehicle as they roared down the street.

"Look on your right! Look on your right!" Frascone said, his eyes locked dead ahead.

"For what?! For *what*?!" Ateer shouted back, his heart corkscrewing out of his chest.

"The lot! There should be a lot opening—"

"*I see it!*"

"Is it big enough?"

SUSPICIOUS LOOKING PACKAGES

"What's big enough?"

Frascone slammed on the brakes, forcing Ateer to grab dashboard and fight from putting his head through the windshield. Taking another sharp, fast turn, the van felt as if it went skipping on the sides of its tires, committing the vehicle to the maneuver. People on the sidewalks stopped to see the small van roar past, grabbing another turn in a cacophony of squealing, as tires protested the abuse.

"So that it can be said that we did at least the minimum to protect the people if it goes off." Frascone was standing in his seat, leaning over the steering wheel, his face almost pressed against the windshield.

"How the fuck should I know?!" Ateer shouted back.

"Screw it. It's big enough!"

Up ahead at the next block, people were running for their lives. Frascone skidded the sturdy E83W to a shuddering halt, the stink of burning rubber thick inside the van. Creeping up on the next block, Frascone went slow enough to allow the fleeing people to surge past the van and head off to parts unknown. Up ahead, turning the corner, walking in the middle of the street, was Pedrotti, holding a package in both hands in front of him. Frascone stopped the van.

"Gimme a hand," he slipped out into the street.

Ateer did the same, running to the back of the van where Frascone was throwing open its doors and climbing in. In the middle of the small, cramped space inside the vehicle, filled with all manner of paraphernalia, from crowbars to hammers, hacksaws, poles and such sat dead center a dull colored barrel with Danger Bomb Container stenciled in black around it.

Frascone pushed the barrel out on a hand truck, allowing both to drop to the asphalt. Ateer, standing in front of it, reached out, keeping the barrel from falling off the truck upon landing. Frascone jumped down next to the barrel and grabbed hold of the latch on the upper rim and pushed it open, breaking the seal on top of the barrel. Ateer reached for it, and no sooner did he take the top off the containment container did Pedrotti come around to the back of the van with the box, about the width of a shoe box held out before him. He shouldered Ateer from his path and gently rested the box on top of the oil. Upon releasing it, it did a half roll over, and then sank under the black.

All three men paused, sighing. Frascone finally saying, "Shit, goddamn."

Ateer put the top back on the barrel, Frascone closed its latch. The three men then gathered around the barrel and loaded it into the back of the van and shut the doors.

"Where to, Big O?" Pedrotti asked.

"We found a spot," Frascone went around the van and climbed behind the wheel. This time he backed away much slower and did a gentle turn in the intersection. Ateer and Pedrotti crawled into the Plymouth with Accorso already behind the wheel. He shifted in reverse and backed up. "Did he find anything?" He asked Pedrotti.

"Yeah, we found a lot," Ateer answered.

They followed Frascone through the streets at a normal pace.

"Why don't we bring Big Bertha for jobs like these?" Ateer asked.

"Some streets aren't friendly to the size of our big girl," Pedrotti replied. "We know where the streets will allow her to get in and out. Other times we just take the van," Pedrotti said.

"It's a judgment call," Accorso said, taking a turn with the steering wheel. "If nothing blows up and kills hundreds of people no one really gives a flying fuck as to how we disarm the shit. But if we used the van and it exploded in the middle of a crowded block of people then Valentine and La Guardia will come down on us like a stack of bricks."

Pedrotti turned his head halfway towards the back to look at Ateer through the corner of his eye. "The good thing about that, Mac is that we'll probably be killed in the blast, so you won't really care what the fuck Valentine and La Guardia feel about how we dispose of these things."

Ateer nodded. He had to agree with that.

Up ahead, the van turned into a small lot composed of broken bricks and other masonry, trash, and tufts of grass. Accorso parked the car on the sidewalk, the Emergency Services truck pulled up behind them with two other police RMPs. Accorso went to the Emergency Services truck, meeting Lieutenant Conway halfway.

"Now what?" Conway asked.

"We let it sit in the barrel until we're pretty certain that it won't explode."

"How would you know?"

"Well, if it was ticking, which it wasn't, we'd listen to the side of the barrel with a stethoscope until it stopped. But in cases like this, we just use our best guess." And a fluoroscope, he thought to himself.

Ateer and Pedrotti climbed out of the car and helped Frascone get the barrel from the back of the van. Pedrotti and Ateer attended to the hand truck, wheeling it out and setting it down in the center of the lot. Frascone stayed in his van. Everyone else leaned against the squad car, smoking cigarettes, snorting Benzedrine, and sipping from flasks. Conway returned to his truck.

Pedrotti, staring out across the distance to the red barrel sitting alone in the middle of the rubble of the lot, said, "Do you think it's time to use the fluoroscope?"

Accorso flicked his cigarette away, "Yeah."

They walked off, Ateer dropped his cigarette and followed behind them.

Frascone watched them in the side view mirror, then walked through the van and opened the rear doors from the inside. Hopping out, he handed the box containing the Fluoroscope to Accorso.

Taking it by the handle, Accorso led Pedrotti and Ateer to the barrel. Conway and his men, seeing them head off in the direction of the barrel, stayed back, inside of their truck. Not that they were safe inside something little more than a roofless flatbed with benches along its inside.

Accorso stopped at the barrel. "Watch how this is done," he told Ateer.

He and Pedrotti unpacked the equipment. Pedrotti took the

emitter to one side of the barrel, Accorso using the hooded screen on the other. After staring through it for a few minutes he called Pedrotti, and they switched places.

"Can you make out anything?" Accorso asked him.

"Shit no. I can't make out a damn thing," Pedrotti waved Ateer over. "Come, take a look."

Ateer walked up and took the screen by the straight wooden handle protruding from the bottom of the triangle shaped device. The wide end of the triangle was the screen, and it was pointed at the barrel. The narrow end had an opening, padded, and shaped to the contours of a face around the eyes.

"Look through here." Pedrotti positioned Ateer in front of the barrel and put the padded eyecups before his eyes. Suddenly he was in pitch black darkness as he peered at a black screen ahead of him with the white outlines of the box and the white silhouette of something large inside that he could not make out. Whatever it was it comprised more than half of the box.

"What is it?" He asked.

"Hell, if I know." Pedrotti replied.

Everything suddenly went all black and Pedrotti took away the screen from before Ateer's eyes, the slanting sunlight of the afternoon causing his eyes to smart. Accorso came from the other side of the barrel with the Fluoroscope's emitter, "Let's wrap this shit up and open the damn thing," he said.

He and Pedrotti re-packed the equipment and returned to the van. Pedrotti, being the closest one to the package, gave Frascone a list of what he thought they would need to open it. Frascone, with his unique skill, reached in and came away with everything asked for without the slightest search.

Meanwhile Ateer looked around and noticed that people were gathering around the edges of the lot, their numbers building as if there was something interesting other than a barrel. The uniform police left to meet them and drove them further from the lot, across the street and onto the next block.

SUSPICIOUS LOOKING PACKAGES

"Ready?" Accorso asked.

Pedrotti nodded. "Ready?" He turned to Ateer. "Ready?"

Ateer looked at him, blinking. "What?"

"Are you ready?"

"For what?"

Accorso moved his head so that he could look around Pedrotti. "So that you can come and cut into this thing, jackass."

Surprised, Ateer nodded dumbly. "I'm ready."

The three of them walked to the barrel and removed its top. Pedrotti used the picker to grope at the submerged package and somehow snagged a length of the twine around it and pulled it up to where they could grab it and rest it on the broken brick and rubble earth at their feet. They crouched around the package. Accorso passed Ateer a small paring knife.

"Go for the twine first," he instructed.

Ateer was trembling. The only thing that kept him from running off to the police cordon in the distance was that Accorso and Pedrotti was right next to him, and they wouldn't risk their lives unless there was a good chance that the threat was manageable, or else they simply desired to be torn apart by the elemental forces of nature.

Ateer reached out for the twine his hands shaking, the knife quivering.

"Do you want to take a moment to steady yourself?" Pedrotti asked.

"No, no," Ateer replied, a rivulet of sweat running past the side of the corner of his eye even though it was not hot out.

After a deep inhalation, Ateer pinched the twine, next to the knot, and pulled it away from the package. He slid the knife underneath it, and with a twist, cut clean through the string.

"Okay," Accorso said, "using only the very tip of the knife, cut through the wrapping."

"Where? The top?" Ateer asked.

"Just at the corner."

Like drawing with a pencil, Ateer started at the corner and drew across the three edges of width, length, and height.

"Good, good," Accorso said softly.

Carefully he and Pedrotti peeled back the sheet of wrapping from the corner of the box like opening the petals of a flower, exposing the package.

"Now, using a little more of the tip of the knife, cut through the box at the three corners like you did the wrapping," Accorso instructed.

Both Accorso and Pedrotti held the box steady while, using a hacksaw like motion, Ateer sliced along the three edges of the box nearly to the other corners. When done, everyone looked at the package, taking a breather. Finally, Accorso said, "moment of truth."

Pedrotti and Ateer nodded. Pinching the corners Accorso and Pedrotti tore open the box down one side from the top corner to the bottom corner and folded back the ends. Oil poured like blood out of the interior of the box and then something about the size of a woman's compact moved under the oil, pouring out with it. Several other objects followed behind the first one, spilling down onto the debris of the ground. As the objects spread around their shoes, Pedrotti and Accorso picked up a few, and rubbed the slick, black oil from them. They stood, while Ateer remained crouching, staring up at them.

"Clams," Accorso muttered.

"What?" Ateer asked.

"It's a box of clams," he dropped the clam on top of the box.

Ateer stood, "who would leave a box of clams on the street like that?" He asked.

Pedrotti, still examining the clam in hand said, "And—even more importantly—where the fuck is the ice?"

Giuseppe Crivello was born in the coastal village of Santa Marinella on the western coastline of Italy in the region of Lazio. His father was a fisherman who plied his trade in the rough waves of the Tyrrhenian Sea. Giuseppe Crivello learned how to fish from his father, a rugged man, and a hard worker. Crivello was just as sinewy and lean as his father, a serious young man that was not given to antics with the younger boys of the municipality.

In school he met Veola Adduci, a dark-haired beauty, with crystal-like eyes, and they married within a year. Both were fifteen years old. In 1894, Crivello's father was lost at sea, taking with him the family fishing boat, the SFIDA. Without the boat, the business was crippled, and jobs were scarce. Taking the remainder of their savings and selling their modest home, Giuseppe took leave of Italy and boarded a steamship heading for America to pursue a new life in the developing land.

They arrived at Ellis Island in July of 1896 and settled in Italian Harlem in a tenement at Third Avenue and 119th street. Giuseppe took a job in the Meat Packing District as a laborer. Veola became a housekeeper to two homes on Park Avenue and later becomes pregnant and gave birth to Claudio Crivello, January 22nd, 1898. From his connections that he made in the Meat Packing District and being frugal about his savings, Giuseppe opened an Italian deli on East 115th street. When Claudio was old enough, he helped his father with the family business. At sixteen he met Camilla Sparacino, a regular patron at the deli and they were soon married, moving not far from Claudio's parents on Third and 116th street.

Claudio grew his father's business to a group of four delis, one in East Harlem, one on 96th and Columbus, one on 48th street between 8th and 9th avenues and the last one in Little Italy, on Baxter and Grand Street.

Giuseppe grew too feeble to work in any of the delis and moved into a lavish home in Fort Lee, New Jersey. Veola Crivello died in 1916 leaving Giuseppe alone in the large house where he lasted another four years before he expired. Camilla Crivello, a housewife, gave birth to Sienna Crivello on May 22nd, 1918. Camilla, having much free time doted on her daughter, dressing her up as her 'little doll' until she was seven. With Claudio working most of the time, she seldom spent time with him. Whereas her mother micro-managed her life to such an extent that Sienna was many times reluctant to decide, usually deferring to her mother to do things for her.

After the death of his father, Claudio moved the family into the Fort Lee home. Sienna was sent to school in the city, where she could spend time around her father to aid in their relationship, who would commute in and drive her to her classes. In 1932, as a freshman in high school, she met the handsome and dashing twenty-one-year-old Giovanni Pedrotti who was a solitary figure, silent and reserved. He too would come in the mornings bringing a group of high school aged kids from the orphanage to and from school. His standoffish behavior and rakish good looks drew Sienna, like a tin spoon to a magnet. Sienna, now free of her mother's controlling influence while at school, made one of the very few decisions on her own which was to be Pedrotti's girl. She followed him from school, playing hooky from her lessons on occasion, and spent much of her time shadowing him around the border of East Harlem and Harlem. Pedrotti's home was a room in Harlem, on Lenox Avenue and 126th street, near East Harlem, and Mount Morris Park on 124th.

In time Pedrotti noticed Sienna's duckling behavior and approached her. Every step that he took towards her caused her heart to pound and her little knees to knock. Pedrotti was taken by her youthful beauty and long auburn hair. On one day, when she should have been in economics class, she lost her virginity in Pedrotti's small bed, finally making herself his girl. She had finally planted her flag on his territory. She had blossomed into a woman, although her small breasts, never grew and her hips stayed narrow and girlish.

Five months later, of near constant intercourse, she missed her period. Sienna went to her parents, informing them that she was pregnant with a baby. Camilla was stunned. She could not and would not believe that her daughter would make such a rash and very important decision to have sex without confiding in her for direction first. She viewed her actions as a form of betrayal and wanted her out of the house. Her father, Claudio could see no wrong in his daughter and fumed over what he believed was her succumbing to some tenement Casanova preying on young girls. He compelled his daughter to take him to Pedrotti's room and confronted him. Melting before Claudio's fiery anger, Giovanni yielded to his order to marry his daughter.

They were married a month later, long before Claudio's daughter began to show, on April 19th, 1933. Two months after the wedding, Sienna lost the baby. Pedrotti could not make ends meet on a machine shop worker's salary, so he applied and was accepted into the NYPD.

Sienna would quickly admit her error in marrying her husband. She married the first man that she had sex with. Other than a carnal attraction, and her craving for copulation itself, she and Pedrotti had very little in common. Sienna dropped out of school to become a housewife. In time Sienna mended her relationship with her mother and father and her father found a newly renovated brownstone on Broome and Ludlow Street in the Lower East Side which he gave to his daughter. It had enough rooms for them to raise a family and it kept them in the city, where Pedrotti worked. Uprooted from her home and her school friends, Sienna closed up and became withdrawn, not that her husband cared or even noticed.

For reasons that they never discussed, Pedrotti moved into the Bomb Squad and met the wretched Fabrizzio Accorso who took her husband under his wing, and before long, the two were inseparable. Because of the bond between their husbands, Sienna fell into the orbit of Daria Accorso, who appeared to her to be the motherly type. Immediately she kowtowed to Daria's stronger personality, hiding in her shadow, taking her direction. As their sex lives began to taper off, the two women grew closer and closer and in time became armchair detectives, searching their husband's clothing, wallet, schedules until they came away with the only two solutions to their growing sexual frustrations, either their husbands were homosexual and having an affair, or they were both engaged in assignations with either desperate or fallen women.

Although they do not consider themselves equals, they became a sisterhood of pain and frustration.

Sienna walked down the street, looking at the pale faces in the October chill and wondered about the might-have-beens in her life. If she had just stayed at home with her mother, she would be outside the tomb of her marriage. She was made a widow long before her husband's death and too early for her time. She noticed how the eyes of men would follow her long after she had passed, and she found herself dressing for more and more attention. Just two weeks ago while she was sitting in a cafe in the East Village, an older woman, when passing her, lowered to whisper into her ear, "you're such a beautiful young woman. There is no need to dress like a hussy."

But was it her fault? Sienna had beautiful, well sculpted legs, and she showed them off by wearing pleated skirts on the short side, well above the knees, a true attention getter. Her breasts were firm and perky, even without a bra, so she never wore one and she kept her blouse unbuttoned low. She didn't have much of a cleavage, she never did, but she knew how by peering inside of her shirt, a person could see the smooth, creamy contours of her breasts. Nearly the entire breast, save for the nipple and half of the areola, which drove men mad.

She strode down the block, her high heels clicking on the concrete, her heavy coat pulled tightly around her, a simple head covering of a cloth flower and a velvet bow on one side and a piece of netting veil to cover her face. She felt like a different woman when she wore it, as if the veil altered her features instead of barely obscuring them.

She headed for Greenwich Village via Third Street, past many of the sidewalk produce vendors with their carts ladened down with fresh vegetables lined up in their carts against the parked cars, narrowing the sidewalk and making foot traffic difficult, constricting the casual flow into a more frenetic, excited current, like rocks exciting a stream. She shouldered past individuals shouldering past her, her purse clutched to her breast and turned onto Sixth Avenue, heading towards the restaurants and shops of West Fourth street. Here the avenue was wider as well as the sidewalks, giving her freedom from the more claustrophobic lanes between East and West Village.

On the corner of Sixth Avenue and Washington Place was a dark, quiet restaurant with large windows so that patrons could look out at the pedestrians and the street life of the wide avenue. Adding to the dark, mysterious nature of the restaurant was a black, traditional awning with a sign band that read: Table Pour Deux.

In the window on the right of the door, at a table, was Daria Accorso.

Walking into the restaurant, a Maître d approached her, and she pointed out the table at the window. He walked her over to the empty chair across from Daria and pulled it out for Sienna to take a seat, then handed her a one-page menu before walking off.

"How long have you been here?" Sienna asked.

"Oh, just ten minutes." Daria held up her hand and tugged away at the fingertips of her long white gloves, removing them, and folding them into her purse at her lap. "How are you today?"

"I'm okay." Sienna rested her purse on the floor, beside her chair. "I took a walk here instead of taking a cab. The brisk air helps me to think."

"What were you thinking about?"

"Nothing really."

"It's a very long walk from your place. If you meant to take it here, you had a lot on your mind."

Sienna smiled uncomfortably, "My mother called the other day, and she filled my head full of nonsense and after I had to deal with her, Gio comes in early from work, looking like he jumped out of a moving car to get home."

Daria's mouth fell open. "Was he in a fight?"

"No, he was out drinking, no doubt, with you know who."

"I don't even need to guess," Daria raised her hand to call over the waiter. "Can we have two martinis please?"

The waiter nodded and was off.

"When was this?"

"Last Wednesday."

"I don't remember even seeing Fab on Wednesday."

"Well, I talked to Father Lozano of our...of *my* church and he says that I need to bring my husband in and start counseling."

"Are you going to do it?"

"Gio's not. He doesn't even go to church with me. It was a stretch, but I had to try something, because I'm at the end of my rope."

"I can tell." On her body, Daria gestured to her sensible powder blue blouse buttoned up to the neck with a Mandarin collar. "You're missing a few buttons there."

Sienna looked down at her shirt and frowned, undoing another button. Her blouse now opened to her belly.

"Ouch," Daria said, "you *are* in a mood."

Laughing, Sienna redid the button, and one more, so as not to embarrass her friend. "I can't tell you what I'm in the mood for, Dary."

"I know what," Daria said with a sly grin, "You want some strong muscled man to drive you like a car!"

The waiter had returned, hearing her comment, and quickly started to blush around the neck and cheeks. He set down their drinks as the two women looked at each other with wide-eyed shock and chagrin, then burst into laughter as soon as the young man walked off.

"Oh my, god! I can't believe you said that." Sienna held a hand to her mouth, not touching her lips so as not to smear her blood red lipstick.

"Oh, I feel the same way!" She waved at her. "Sometimes I intentionally try to get Fab both angry and worked up so that he'd tear off my clothes and throw me around the house a few times like we used to do when we were first married." She looked down at the empty table, a delicate vase with a colorful flower in the middle, and salt and pepper shakers. "Now, we barely even talk to each other."

"Same here." Sierra sipped her drink. "I'm thinking of having an affair."

"You know better than that, Sie. It'll eat you up inside."

"It doesn't seem to be affecting my husband any."

"Your husband's a cur. So is mine. The job just made what they are inside come out. I guess that's just what happens when you put men like them under such strain. I mean, I've heard stories of men returning from World War I having problems when they came home with a lot of things. Sex included."

"Well, I'm growing tired of waiting for Gio to pleasure me," she looked towards the restaurant to make certain that the waiter was outside of earshot, "I'm going to start pleasuring myself."

"Oh, my god!" Daria was astonished. "Are you serious?"

"I find myself...touching myself...in the bath."

"Well," Daria leaned close, "I masturbate."

"You filthy little thing you!" Sienna laughed.

They both broke out in guffaws, and if it was some sort of signal, the waiter returned to the table. "Are you ready to order?"

Daria, barely able to contain her laughter, said, "Oh, I'm so sorry. We haven't even looked at our menus yet. Could you come back in five minutes?"

"Sure, ma'am."

She lifted her menu before her face, still giggling. They scanned their choices.

"I heard," Sienna said, "that it'll make you hysterical."

"I'm already hysterical from my damn husband. Look, the way I see it, it's either that, sex with him, or sex with another man. My husband has cut off sex with him, so, I'm down to number two."

"Well, I'm beginning to think that way too."

"Sex with a man?"

Sienna nodded, a huge smile on her face.

"Aren't you afraid of getting pregnant."

"I've thought of a way around that."

"How?"

"I have sex with Gio once in a while—"

"How often?"

"About once or twice a month."

Daria nodded. "I'm about the same."

"Well, I'll find a man that looks almost exactly like Gio and if I get pregnant, I'll tell Gio that it's his."

Giggling, Daria waved over the waiter, and they made their lunch order.

"You'd better make certain that you have sex with him before you start showing."

"I will. I can shrink and stretch the months. He'll never know. And do you know what the greatest joy on my part would be?"

"What's that?"

"That he'll be raising my lover's baby and never, ever know."

"That does sound appealing."

"I say we do it!"

"*No!*" Daria wagged a finger at her. "No, no, no. It'll never work. Sex with two men…all kinds of things will happen to you."

"Like what?"

Daria thought about it. "Women weren't made to have sex with more than one man. You see how insane whores are." Suddenly a thought burst in her mind, her face lit up. "Just like a fallen woman. *You'll* be a fallen woman!"

They giggled again, but Daria was serious.

"I'm glad you're kidding," she said.

Sienna thought about it, then said, "I'm thinking of throwing a dinner party next week."

"Oh yeah? Who are you inviting?"

"Well, I'm thinking you and Fab…Mac," she thought, "Peter is still in the hospital.Oh, have you been over there?"

"No. Not yet. How are they holding up?"

"Peter looks like he's losing weight. Clara seems to be holding up well."

"We should go there today."

"You want to?"

Sienna thought about that, sat back when the waiter lowered the plates of food on the table, then leaned forward. "I think we should. Clara is a dear."

"Clara is kinda...like a man."

"She's pretty strong."

"She's *very* strong."

"Oh, you are so bad, Dary!"

They focused on their meals. Without looking up, Daria asked, "So, you're thinking about a dinner party?"

"Yes! I was thinking you, Fab, Mac, and their Lieutenant...James."

"I'm so sorry, dear, but he's going to be gone next week for some kinda seminar."

Sienna made a face; she wanted a larger party. "Are you kidding me? Are our social circles so small that we only have a handful of friends?"

"Well, four of them are unavailable, but do you know what I'm thinking?"

"What's that?"

"Since her husband is gone for a while, Barbara might be pretty lonely in that house of theirs alone. Why not invite her and her daughter Amanda, and I'll bring Leora, and the girls can play together, the men will be together, and we'll have Barbara with us."

"That sounds pretty good."

"So that's eight people."

"Do you think we should at least extend an invitation to Clara? She's probably alone too."

"She's probably with her husband in the hospital. Are we going there after lunch?"

"Yes, let's do that."

They returned to their repast. Daria stopped, looked out the window at a passing couple arm in arm.

"Are you really going to find a man to sleep with?" she asked.

"I'm thinking about it," Sienna sat back, dabbed at the corners of her mouth with her napkin, "I just have to figure out where to find him."

"Hmmm," Daria said, pensively.

Like most of the clubs that liberally peppered the city, Club Tunnel started as a speakeasy during Prohibition. It was a hide-away basement joint hidden under a brownstone on the west side of 52nd street. Club Tunnel drew patrons like a black hole does all matter. No car or cab could cruise past it, and with such a powerful attraction it was surprising that it was never raided in the entire fourteen years that it was an outlaw spot. It even sold alcohol on Sundays, to be patently reprehensible. Because of its dark and illegitimate management, it drew not only people searching for sin, but also a motley array of new and existing performers who could not get a spot at any regular club or nightery, shady types making illicit deals, women looking for a safe place to meet men, and whores searching for the same. Many transactions of a financial or sexual nature were made under its roof.

After Prohibition the owners, Maxwell Greene and Sanford Edwards a struggling vaudeville act during the 1920s and 1930s—who sunk their meager earnings from their act into purchasing a storage area from the owner of the building and then had converted it into a club—now like a triumphant ruler returning to his city, purchased a space in the basement of a brownstone on 52nd street between Fifth and Sixth avenues, known also as 'The Street.' 52nd Street was invaded by legitimate clubs and bars in the late 1930s and its highest concentration of such were between Fifth and Sixth avenues. These establishments brought hot and stunning jazz musicians and Broadway acts to their stages, top and exciting singers, and sidesplitting comics along with A-list, actors, and actresses as patrons.

These spots brought an air of peril and debauchery to The Street, some even pushing the envelope by hiring black musicians and allowing black patrons to further the illusion of an environment of dissoluteness. Little did the entrepreneurs of The Street know that with the purchase of its basement spot, Green and Edwards brought over its patronage, true wrongdoers and cheats and an honest atmosphere of menace. Marching like ants from a mound to a cube of sugar, brawlers, con-men, thieves, whores, drug addicts and dealers darkened its black door.

Like in its Prohibition days, a special knock was needed to get in through its glossy black painted door. There were no neon signs or placards that indicated its existence, but there was also no effort to hide or keep the 'secret knock' private. People knocked on Club Tunnel's door openly and if whispered to cab drivers that they were seeking trouble, the driver would go directly to the club and show how to knock on the door on their dashboards.

At the door, known brigands and prostitutes were easily given admittance, whereas the door was closed to blacks. However sizzling black acts from some of the hottest clubs on 52nd street and Harlem were allowed entrance through the alley door in the back and could not leave the stage.

The Street at night was a glowing, flashing, glittering gem of neon beacons causing the eyes of the pedestrians on the sidewalk to spin like pinwheels. They moved and milled from posted schedule to posted schedule like well-dressed and groomed zombies attempting to find the act that would interest them the most. Whereas, on this chilly winter's night, Accorso marched through the crowds, a bloodhound unerringly following a trail to a flight of steps down behind the stairs of a brownstone, and a glossy black door. Ateer, following behind Pedrotti, wondered why they were turning into what looked like one of the only buildings on the block without some club or bar.

They caught the attention of some on the sidewalk above them as Accorso gave the door a series of knocks.

It opened quickly and a tall, lean bouncer invited them in.

The inside presented a long and dimly lit bar, lights shining on the bottles of alcohol behind the bartenders and a few spots at the bar. The tables were draped in gloom, lit only by a small candle in the center along with a vase and flower. Ahead, in the large space was an equally large stage well illuminated and glowing like a super watt bulb. At present it was empty, with nothing but two microphone stands with their microphones.

Accorso wended his way through the pond of tables and found one in the corner, halfway to the stage.

"Jesus Christ!" Ateer complained. "What is this? The fourth ring of hell?"

"What are you talking about," Accorso asked.

"Why is it so fucking dark in here."

"Because shit is happening all around you," Pedrotti said.

"You should know about this place, Mac," Accorso pointed out.

"Never seen or heard of it," Ateer replied.

"They've been paying off your supervisors religiously," Accorso said. "In a business like this, everyone makes out good."

They took off their coats and hats, hanging them on hooks on the nearby wall. A scantily clad waitress in a hip length black dress and high heels took their drink orders, and, as if dressed in dark camouflage, disappeared into the space.

"I can't believe how dark it is in here." Ateer looked around at he mostly filled establishment with more people flowing in by the minute. "We used to give fines for places that were dark like this."

"And why would you do that?" Accorso asked.

"Because felonious acts were being committed in the dark."

Accorso gestured at the visible sphere around them. "Well, welcome to the land of felony and violation."

"Unlike the rest of the clubs on The Street, this place is the eye of the storm baby," Pedrotti said like a proud father about his child.

"It's a good club," Accorso looked around, searching for something. Ateer wondered what since the entire place was shrouded in shadow. "Trust me, whatever you get here, from either the stage acts up front or the blowjobs out back, it's all top shelf, except for the liquor. They usually water it down. That's why it's so dark in here."

"That and more," Pedrotti nodded. "Pro Skirts work this place harder than the rest in this section of town. This is the Wild West for 52nd street. You've got thieves in the back alley selling stolen wares and con men at the bar selling the Brooklyn Bridge."

"Then, really, why do you come here?"

"Because it's fun."

"Picture *that*," Accorso said with a grin. The waitress returned with their drinks.

"A place rife with criminal activity is fun?"

"Well, while you were submerged in the P.M. Squad the rest of us in the world were going around having fun. Can you believe that?" Accorso reached into his jacket and produced his flask, pouring moonshine into his drink, then passed it over to Pedrotti who did the same.

"Want some?" Pedrotti held up the flask to Ateer.

Ateer could admit, he was submerged in the Public Morals Squad and the word 'fun' was a confusing concept for him. It was obvious to him and the men around him that he was only using the rules and regulations of the P.M. Squad to isolate himself from the P.M. Squad. There was a problem with the Bomb Squad…there *were no* rules and regulations that he had to follow. Also, to follow these two men where Valentine wanted him to go, he had to break some of the only rules and regulations that really mattered, those that are law.

But as of today, there were no longer any laws regulating Goat Whiskey. He took the flask and spiked his drink.

Accorso held out his hand for his flask, "I spike the drinks here because they—"

"Water it down," Ateer interrupted.

"Also, I bought a pretty good watch out back one night," Pedrotti played with the watch around his wrist.

Ateer started the laugh but struggled to hold it down.

"What's so funny?"

"What don't you guys do?"

Pedrotti hunched his shoulders.

"Anything we don't want to do, Mac." Accorso said. "Don't tell me that you don't feel your own mortality knocking on the door every time you walk into the bullpen?"

Yes, Ateer said to himself. "I feel anxious when a call comes in."

"Just like fucking Pavlov's dogs. The phone rings and you start to sweat under the armpits."

"Yeah, and..."

"And that's called anxiety. Get used to it, it'll eat the outside edges of your thinking until someone drops a book behind you and you jump out of your skin."

"Next time we're close to a Devil Toy," Pedrotti said, "and it alters your reality, you find ways of altering it back."

"Everyone does," Accorso said. "To repeat what I told you before: Everyone finds a way to deal with walking in a direction that everyone else is running away from. Be you a fireman, a cop on a bad beat, or a bomb squad detective, everyone deals with the stress in different ways. You're like a soldier in a pitched battle. You deal with extreme stress all day long, many times a day," he leaned across the table toward Ateer on his left, "until you realize that one day, one call, one bomb, one mistake and the laws of nature will dismantle you into so many tiny pieces that all the king's horses and all the king's men won't even bother to bury your ass."

"So, we burn off a little steam," Pedrotti said.

The empty chair at the table slid back and a beautiful blonde in a low-cut dress with sequined patterned flowers eased down into the seat. She was a simple beauty, a mid-western girl, her makeup covering the freckles across her nose. She smiled, showing off a pearly set of teeth within a pair of red lips and with a carefree toss, spilled a shock of hair across her face, over her right eye. "Gentlemen," she said in a sultry voice, "how would you like to buy a girl a drink?"

Accorso and Pedrotti looked at Ateer.

"Why are you looking at me?" Ateer was taken aback.

"Do you want to buy the girl a drink?" Accorso asked him.

"I don't know."

"It'll cost you twice the amount or a regular drink," Pedrotti pointed out.

"Why is that?"

"Because you're paying for her company. If she sits with us, she'll keep ordering drinks, and all of her drinks will be virgin. Before you know it, your tab is through the roof."

The woman sighed tiredly "Well, do you?"

Accorso waved her away. "Off you go."

She stood to her feet, angrily, like a shot, and sauntered off.

"Wow, that was harsh." Ateer was stunned.

"Don't be misled here," Accorso said, "this is not a place where you will find a lover or a friend. It's based on transactional rules. You come here to get something. If you know what it is, then you pay for it. If you don't, you'll end up paying through the nose for nothing." He pointed to Pedrotti's timepiece. "Like Beat It's watch. He came here, he saw the watch, he bought it. Like the girl, she came here, you want company, you pay for it."

"What did you call it? Transactional rules?"

"That's right. Know what you're paying for. That was a B-Girl. She'll do just enough to get her rent off you, or her groceries, or maybe even her hair done."

"What do you mean about 'just enough'?"

"B-girls are just under a prostitute. You can call them part-timers. During the day they do something respectable, like going to law or medical school, or are struggling actresses. At night they dress without panties or bras and will sit at a table and listen to your bullshit if you pay for their overpriced drinks. If you send her off, she or another one will come back in a few minutes and for a little more she'll give you a hand-job under the table, that's why the lights are so low, a little more and you can go out into the alley or into a stall in the men's room for a blowjob. If you're a real hard nut to crack," Accorso giggled, "-The Pro Skirts will swoop in from the bar over there and flatten some boxes in the alley or the basement and let you bang her until your hips grow weak, but you'll pay her price. Transactional rules."

"He's right," Pedrotti said, "if the B-girl comes back, you can ask her to bring over someone with cocaine, heroin, whatever, even a neat watch," Pedrotti held up his arm, showed it to him.

The B-girl returned, easing back into the chair. They turned to her. "Is there anything else that I can interest you gentlemen in?"

Accorso looked at Ateer. "Transactional rules, Mac. What do *you* want tonight?"

Ateer thought about it. What did he come here for? What did *they* come here for? "Just a drink," he sighed.

Accorso waved the girl off again. "You heard the man, run along."

With a level of calm she stood and said, "I'll get your waitress," and then was gone.

Accorso snorted, filled his glass with Goat Whiskey from his flask.

"So, you're just gonna sit here a drink from your flask?" Ateer asked.

"I guess so. What do you want me to do, get a hand-job to show you how it's done?"

Ateer had no reply.

"Easy on the guy," Pedrotti said. "He doesn't know why we are here."

Ateer looked at Pedrotti. What were they here for?

Accorso lit a cigarette.

"Why *are* we here, Fab?" Ateer asked.

"Because you're a stubborn, Irish, mick. You're holding onto your morals...for no apparent reason. Why?"

"I told you. My mother. Is that why you brought me here? You're trying to break me for some reason?"

"You'll probably break yourself. I'm here to listen to my favorite comedian, you've got a problem with that, Mac?"

"Who's your favorite comedian?"

Accorso looked at the stage. A band was building its instruments and sound equipment. He hunched his shoulders, "I dunno."

"Okay," Ateer nodded. His face flushed. "Why all this fucking pushing and shoving me, huh? Haven't I done enough. Haven't I passed all your stupid tests? When is it over, huh? When am I part of the team?"

No one answered.

"You want me out of the Bomb Squad because I'm Irish, is that it?"

No one answered. All attention at the table, save Ateer's was on the stage.

"What is it then, eh?"

"Mac, you're already part of the team, you just don't realize it," Accorso said. Accorso turned from staring at the stage to narrow his eyes on Ateer. "You're wrapped too tight, Mac. You're going to pop like a cork in Unit One, I guarantee it."

"You don't know that."

"Yes, I do. Look, you are Bomb Squad, alright. You're not being tested anymore. Not by us. We're just going to go on and do what we do. You can follow, but when you feel that you are nearing the end of your rope, quit."

"Why?"

"Because your fear of your own death will cause you to make a stupid mistake, and that mistake is going to cost lives. Maybe ours, maybe innocent people, all because you felt that you were tougher than you are."

"So what? By your standards, I become immoral, and it saves lives?"

"Could be. Do what your stone headed, Green-Nigger brain

wants, that's fine by me. Beat It and I did what we could. The rest is up to you. Now, if you don't mind, I want to enjoy the show. I have a few transactional rules to go through."

Ateer nodded. "Alright," he stood, reached into his wallet pulled out cash and dropped it on the table. "I'll see you two tomorrow."

"Take care, Mac." Pedrotti said.

"Off you go," Accorso said, knocked back the remainder of his rocks glass and turned to the stage were a young black girl climbed up behind the microphone and the band did a final tuning of their instruments.

She started singing as Ateer walked out of the club.

Pedrotti entered his brownstone and pounded up the stairs to the third floor, pulling off his coat, removing his hat. He walked into the master bedroom and hung his coat in the coat closet, tossed his hat on the top shelf. He walked into the dressing room and hung up his clothes, stripping down and strolled through the second bedroom into the bathroom to take his shower. When done, he wrapped himself up in a plush blue towel and headed downstairs to the dining room and the kitchen beyond. He opened the refrigerator door and stuck his head into it.

"Gio," Sienna said from the doorway.

Pedrotti came out of the refrigerator with two plates of cold cuts and went to the kitchen counter, "Sienna."

"I want you to invite your friends from work this Wednesday for dinner."

"Here?" Pedrotti began making a sandwich from the bread in the cabinets.

"I have dinner for you in the oven."

"I'll just make a turkey sandwich first. What's up with the dinner party? Why now?"

"I would like to get the girls together."

"Oh, it's for the girls?"

"You guys get to blow off steam all the time."

"Like you girls don't."

"Not like you guys. You hang out until all hours of the night, doing god-knows-what and come strolling in two, three, four in the morning without saying a word and at seven you get up and do it all again."

Pedrotti stopped making his sandwich, held up his butter knife with a dollop of mayonnaise at its end to make a point. "That's because we have jobs and make a living. You girls go off shopping and lunching and all that bullshit to blow off steam. And then god-only-knows what the fuck else you ladies do."

She walked past him to the oven, turning it on low. "What are you implying, Gio?"

"I'm not implying anything. I said what I said. You don't know about what I'm doing just like I don't know what you are doing, alright? We both can think the worst if we want, so don't come to me and make it sound like just because the sun is down, my absence is me up to no good."

"You *are* up to no good, Gio. I don't do what you do."

Pedrotti held up the sandwich, "I'm good for tonight. You can put dinner in the refrigerator."

She turned off the oven and ran after him. He headed into the dining room and sat down at the table. Sienna came around the table to face him from across it.

"You want to accuse me of something, Gio?"

"What? Whoring around, Sienna?"

"Do you think I'm whoring around just because *you* are?"

"Wow, it's getting hard to eat this sandwich," he stood. "I think I'm going to head to bed."

"Tell your friends, Gio!" She shouted behind him as he headed for the stairs. "We're having this party on Wednesday!"

"Sure, sure," he groaned, pounding up the stairs.

. . .

They were once again in the back of the auto-repair garage at the precinct. Mechanics were in the other three quarters of the garage making mechanics noises, the ring of metallic tools striking the concrete floor, the grunt of men engaged in physical labor, the slamming of hoods and car doors, the bouncing of fully inflated tires, and the laughter and curses of men involved in the work. Over the din of the background noise Accorso brought Ateer into their corner of the building and went into the back to the shelving. He came back with a black case that Ateer was familiar with. It was the Fluoroscope.

"I'll leave you the manual when we get back in," Accorso said, resting the case on the workbench, "I can go into all the gobbledygook that makes an X-ray and how X-rays penetrate matter, but what's more important are the parts of the damn thing and where the on switch is."

Accorso pulled the components of the device out of the box and lined them up on the worktable, one by one. Accorso went to a shelf and found a briefcase, and then a suitcase and then a box and placed them on the workbench side by side. Then he set up the fluoroscope with the emitter on one side of the suitcase and handed the fluoroscope itself, a bulky device, to Ateer.

Examining it, Ateer found the body of the device to be covered with a black leatherette covering and the viewing port, where the eyes went, was a one-piece eye shroud, with both eyecups enclosed by a face fitting hood edged with fur to completely close off all light to the eyes save for the light on the screen on the other end of the device.

Accorso pointed to the wide, square end. "In here is a piece of fluorescent screen made out of cardboard and covered with crystals of barium platino-cyanide which glows brightly when placed in the X-ray beam. The entire device itself makes it possible to see the screen in a well-lit room because it blocks off all light."

Ateer nodded even though most of the information went over his head. He would have to look at the manual later to catch up. Once everything was in position and the emitter was on, Ateer peered through the device and saw dark and light shapes. Accorso explained that denser objects would appear black, while thinner objects that allowed the x-rays to go through, were whiter. Accorso pointed out that the shapes he should be interested in were almost always dark.

By using the mock-ups, he showed Ateer the shapes to be on the lookout for: pocket watches, clocks, sticks of dynamite, and so forth. One by one he would bring some box, case or pipe down from the many shelves in the garage, and set them up for observation, then put them back. After a half an hour he packed up the equipment, handed Ateer the manual and they marched back to the precinct.

"Is this about the other night?" Ateer asked his back.

Accorso stopped at the rear entrance to the stationhouse and turned to him. "What are you talking about?"

"Are you proving to me now that I am part of the unit? By taking the time to train me?"

Accorso stepped away from the entrance so that officers and detectives moving in and out of the building could not hear them. He leaned his back up against the wall and pulled out a pack of cigarettes. "I train you when I feel it's right to train you. My rule is, *first*: see if you can stand walking up to a live device, and getting close and personal with it, and *then*: teach you how to deal with it once you're there. Do you have a problem with that?"

"No, of course I don't. I'm just wondering when you'll stop being so gracious if I don't cross over into debauchery with you guys."

Accorso laughed, held out the pack to Ateer who plucked out a cigarette, "Frankly, I don't give a fuck what you do, Mac. You can be asshole boy and are uncomfortable with being around us and women. That's your problem if you don't open your mouth. But don't think that Beat It and I are going to change our ways because you have your head in the church of your mother."

Accorso handed him a lighter. Ateer said, "I'm not trying to change you guys."

"Good, then we have no problem. So, since I'm the head honcho of unit 1, and in two days, head honcho of the Bomb Squad, I get to decide when and where I train you. When it comes to *that*, you can shut the fuck up."

"I understand." Ateer lit his cigarette and handed back the lighter.

"When you're off the clock, do whatever the fuck you please, Mac. But when we're here, in this world, I am god."

"Yes, lord."

"I'm serious, Mac. You do what I say and then everyone gets to go home to their families, understand?"

"I get it."

Accorso lurched from the wall, dropped his cigarette, and crushed it with the toe of his shoe. "I'm a hard charger, and I don't make any apologies for it. But I'll tell you now…if you ever come up to me crying that you can't take it here, or so sloppy drunk that you can't perform, then you've become public menace number one in my book. You're out of here."

"I won't fail you, Fab."

Accorso walked off, turning into the stationhouse. Ateer, still smoking, watched him leave.

Two cops walked past Ateer from standing in the doorway and one whispered to him, "Bomb Squad, tough shit, huh?"

"You can say that again," he replied to them in passing.

Ateer entered the bullpen under the watchful gaze of Accorso as he sipped from a mug of coffee and took his seat across from him. He didn't care to return his gaze, but instead rooted in his desk drawer for nothing. The sound of Pedrotti's chair rolling back to Accorso's desk made him look up.

Now sitting at the side of their desks, leaning back as if reclining on a beach, Pedrotti said, "Look motherfuckers, my pain-in-the-ass wife wants to have you," he pointed to Accorso, "and your wife and kid, and you," he pointed to Ateer, "and your girlfriend over to the house for dinner."

Accorso smiled. "Is your wife cooking?"

"Of course she's cooking."

"I think I'll pass then," he laughed, "no, I'm just kidding. When?"

"This Wednesday," he turned to Ateer, "you got a girlfriend, Mac?"

"No."

"Then bring yourself. Pick up a Pro Skirt on the way and we'll all do her in my rumpus room for dessert!" He made a wide eyed, gaping mouth face.

"I don't think his mom is gonna approve of that," Accorso mumbled.

"I'm not the choirboy that you think I am, Fab," Ateer replied.

"Oh, no? Can I bring a floozy over as a date for you?"

"You got one?"

"Shit, you don't think I can get one?"

This was indeed a hoop that he knew he would have to jump through sooner or later before Accorso was going to lighten up. It would no doubt be one of the whores from one of the many whorehouses around the city, and it wouldn't be solely for the purpose of coitus. He would just have a woman on his arm, or to talk to while he was there at the dinner party. What would be so bad about that? "Sure," he said, "I don't have a problem with that."

Astonished and with a grin, Accorso looked at Pedrotti, who returned his surprised stare, then turned to Ateer.

"No shit?" Pedrotti asked.

"Set it up. I'd like to meet a nice young lady."

Accorso raised his hand. "Say no more. I'll have her there at Pedrotti's place for you."

Pedrotti sat up and slapped Accorso against the shoulder with the back of his hand, "I know *exactly* who to bring. She's over the top without being slutty."

"Who?"

"Candy!"

Accorso thought about it. "You know, she'd be great, but we've gotta change her name."

"To what?"

"I'll figure it out and tell her. You're gonna love this girl, Mac. She's a firecracker and she has looks that kill! You'll have our wives eating their hearts out. It'll be a fun night with them teaming up against her."

"You want our wives to have agita at my dinner party?"

"Hell yeah. Why let them have a good time? Them bitches are only getting together for the evening to give us the same."

"You think?"

Accorso looked at him with a scowl. "Both of you will thank me for bringing Candy and having something to do during the party."

"You intend to do her?"

"I mean do, not *do*. She'll be Mac's date. We can't disrespect our brother like that. Besides, how many times have you been with her already?"

Pedrotti nodded. "Alright, that's the plan. You think you're up for this, Mac?"

Ateer nodded. "I'm excited in fact."

"Good. I'll let my ball and chain know about it and we'll see you all on Wednesday." Pedrotti turned his chair around and kicked away, the wheels at the legs of his chair carrying him back to his desk.

Excitedly, Accorso jumped up out of his chair and went to the coat rack.

"Where are you going?" Ateer asked him.

Accorso adjusted his shoulder rig and pistol, then snatched his jacket and coat from the rack, donning them. "You just don't go to a girl like Candy and tell her at the last minute to show up somewhere. You've gotta get her days in advance."

"You're going to see her now?"

"Yep," Accorso plopped his fedora on his head and walked off.

"Do you want me to come?"

"Oh, no. I want her to be a surprise when you walk into the dinner party."

Accorso left the bullpen. Ateer opened the manual on the desk and began to read until a shadow darkened the pages. He looked up to see Pedrotti standing over him.

"You made his day, Mac," he said.

"Really? Why?"

"He thinks you're a virgin more than some kinda strait laced bible thumper."

"Why would he think I was a virgin?"

"Because you're still scared of women."

"I'm not afraid of women."

Pedrotti sat on the edge of the desk. "Who was your last girlfriend. High school, right?"

"Honestly, I never had a high school sweetheart."

"I know."

"But that doesn't mean that I'm afraid of women."

"Trust me, after my dinner party, you'll say that with a lot more conviction."

Ateer closed the manual. "Let me ask you, who's paying for Candy?"

"Two things...well, maybe three. Candy is a close friend, and she likes us, so she'll come for nothing. Then we're gonna show her a good time, feed the shit out of her, and let her get as drunk and high as she wants. She'll hand out blowjobs like playing cards just to have this kinda fun for the night. You'll see."

"What if I don't want a blowjob?"

"Trust me, when you see this girl and she pulls your cock out, you'll stare at her wide eyed because you won't believe a woman so beautiful does such fun things! You want to see that face wrapped around your pop stick like a sugar frosted donut."

"Well, I don't know—"

Pedrotti stood up, rested a hand on Ateer's shoulder consolingly. "Look, I know a woman hasn't blown up your balloons yet, but listen to me, if she doesn't bite it off, trust me, you'll want another and another every day for the rest of your life."

"It's addictive?"

"Like heroin, but forty times as much. You won't be able to look at a woman without wanting to jump into her mouth. And if a professional like Candy gives you one, you might not want to go to regular women..." he lowered his voice, cupped a hand around the side of his mouth so that others in the bullpen could not see his lips move, "...or your wife for a blowjob again." He patted Ateer's shoulder. "I'm going out for a gasper, wanna come?"

"Uh, no." Ateer said, opening his manual. "I think I'm going to stick around and read this."

"Alright." Pedrotti walked off.

Ateer looked down at the manual for the General Electric Company, Model F, Suitcase Portable X-ray unit. He opened it to the first page and began to read.

That Monday, Ateer swept into the bullpen early, the manual for the Model F under his arm. He hung up his coat, jacket and hat and found Pedrotti sitting at his desk, feet cocked up and crossed at the ankles on his desktop, newspaper before his face. Ateer came up behind him. "Is he in?" he asked.

"Yeah, he's in Pyke's office," Pedrotti replied, not taking his eyes off his paper.

"What are you reading about so much in the paper, Beat It?"

"The war in Europe."

Ateer nodded. He listened to some things on the radio, but he was like most, or so he believed, that didn't want any part of the squabbling going on overseas. He felt that the governments in Europe were acting like kids in a schoolyard, with everyone siding with the bully of the yard to keep from getting pounded on. What was America supposed to do? Run in and be the biggest bully?

"I don't know about this freezing of Japan's assets. They are going hog wild in the pacific and all that we're fucking doing is freezing their assets," Pedrotti complained.

"What do you want us to do?"

"Go in there and straighten them nips out."

"Yeah, right," a booming voice said from behind Ateer. He turned around to see Dempsey standing behind him with his barrel chest and broad shoulders. "Beat It just wants us to ignore the fact that the *Eye*-talians are siding with Hitler."

Pedrotti turned the page of his newspaper.

"Mussolini and Hitler are two brothers in a bathtub," Dempsey continued. When he realized that he was being ignored by Pedrotti, he turned to Ateer, smiled, nodded, then returned to his desk.

"You think I can go in and talk with Fab?" He asked Pedrotti.

"Sure, go-ahead in. He's probably in there doing the crosswords."

Ateer went in. Accorso was in fact not doing the crosswords but instead reading reports. He looked up when Ateer walked in.

"Can I talk to you for a moment?"

"About what?" Accorso closed the folder he was reading from and sat up.

"The party in two days."

"Have a seat," Accorso gestured to the chair in front of the desk.

Ateer sat down.

"What about the party?"

"Did you get a chance to talk with Candy about being my date at the dinner party?"

"Of course. That's where I told you I was going to go. I wasn't going to wait until today to ask her to free up her evening."

"What did she say?"

"She almost pissed herself. It's kinda a boring life when you're living in a whorehouse, just waiting for a john to choose you out of all the women there. That's why, a lot of the bottom rung women sneak out and street walk just to make some quick cash."

"Bottom rung?"

"Uglier girls. Chicks that don't get chosen all night. After a couple of days, they realize that the competition is too much in the house, so they walk down the block and try to intercept johns before they get to the house. But if the Madam learns about that, she gets her thugs to go out there, rough them up, and haul their asses back in."

"Why would she do that?"

"First, her thugs know how to beat up a woman so as to leave no marks. Second, when they go out like that, they take all the cash for themselves and don't pay their cut to the house. I can understand that because she didn't work in the house so why should she pay for the house? But Madams don't think in terms of location. They think in terms of pussy. You use it, she gets a cut."

"Why don't they just go farther?"

"They do. Some even take the train."

Ateer frowned. "How do you know all of this, Fab?"

Accorso smiled. "You know people have hobbies, right? Some people collect stamps, some people go to fancy restaurants and eat fancy foods, some people even play an instrument. I like to think of myself as a whore connoisseur."

"Aren't you afraid of catching something?"

"No," he laughed.

"What about your wife?"

"What about her?" Accorso leaned forward, over the desk, smiling broadly. "Look, I've got the night all set for you. Great food, great drinks, great company. You're going to have a helluva time so stop worrying."

"I'm not worrying."

"Good."

They sat quietly.

"Is that all?" Accorso asked.

"What are we going to do today? Any calls?"

"Not unless we're the last ones here. I'm going to stay here just in case the big call comes in."

"Big call?"

"From people like Durtayne, O'Connell, or even Valentine or La Guardia. If they call in, I don't want Dempsey or Beakey to be here picking it up."

SUSPICIOUS LOOKING PACKAGES

"I see." Ateer stood. "I'd better let you get back to work."

"Yeah, you do that." He opened his folder and returned to reading.

Ateer walked out of the office and back to his desk, opening his manual. Calls did come in, and Beakey and Dempsey were quick to put their units on it. Ateer snorted Benzedrine and smoked cigarettes. The Big Call never came in although Dempsey and Beakey rotated around for the remainder of the day. At the end of the trick, Accorso was walking out of the office, donning his coat, and turning over the shift to Malcolm Carter who was just getting to his desk in the bullpen.

"What are you doing tonight?" Pedrotti asked Accorso as he breezed past his desk to his.

"Going home. I got home too late last night to tell Dary about your party," Accorso said, going through his desk drawers.

"Her and Sienna are joined at the hip. Trust me, she knows."

"I have to tell her about Candy too."

"You talked to Candy?"

"Last night," he pulled a flask out of the drawer and dropped one from his jacket in.

"So, is she coming?"

"Yeah, of course," he donned his coat and hat, "she was so excited about it she smacked her madam in the face."

Pedrotti made a face. "You need better jokes, Fab."

"That wasn't a joke. She did."

Accorso walked out, patting Ateer on the shoulder in passing.

"Well, he's got you set," Pedrotti said.

"Sounds like it," Ateer stood. "What are you doing tonight?"

"Nothing. You have something planned?"

"I do, but I don't think you can attend."

Ateer nodded.

. . .

When Accorso got home, he found Daria reclining across the couch, a glass of wine in her hand, the bottle of wine on the coffee table within reach. His daughter, Leora was in the love seat, her legs curled up underneath her night shift, reading a book. She turned to her father when he walked in and smiled.

"Hi dad," she said.

He stepped into the living room. "Hey, sweetheart. Isn't it kinda late for you to be up? You've got school in the morning."

"Mom said I could."

Accorso turned to Daria who was on her back, against the armrest of the couch, cushions piled up behind her, propping her up. She didn't acknowledge him when he walked into the room, and neither did she reply to his stare. Instead, she raised her drink to her lips and took a sip.

He returned to his daughter. "Get to bed. I'll be in your room in five minutes to tuck you in."

Leora slipped from the love seat and ran past her father, heading for the stairs. Accorso returned his cold stare to his wife who continued to ignore him. Smoothly, she slid her legs off the side of the couch, sitting up and placing her wine glass down on the coffee table.

"Do you know that we were invited to Beat It's for dinner?" he asked her.

She reached for her pack of cigarettes and matches on the table. "I helped her plan it."

"Well, when you get the chance, tell her we need seating for four."

She lit her cigarette, one eye closed, flicked her hand at the wrist to kill the flame of the match. "Who's coming?"

"A woman that I know that wants to meet Mac."

"If it's a woman that you know, she must be some kinda whore."

Accorso looked at her as if wounded. "No, she's a nice woman that we met."

"Met where?"

SUSPICIOUS LOOKING PACKAGES

"We did a bomb call in her apartment building and she started asking us a ton of questions and we got her phone number."

Daria turned her large, search-light eyes to him. That was the one thing that Accorso couldn't get out of his bloodstream when it came to his wife, her huge eyes could melt the iciest of hearts, even his own.

"Why did you need her phone number?"

"Because Mac was too chicken-shit to ask for it himself."

She nodded slowly, refilled her glass, and sat back, taking a sip.

"So let Sienna know, alright?"

"One of our husband's whores is coming up," she replied, laughing bitterly.

"I wish you would just drop it. It's not funny anymore."

She looked at him knowingly, then stretched out, once again, on the couch.

He headed upstairs, tossing his coat, hat, jacket, and shoulder rig on the bed before walking into his daughter's room. She was bundled up in her sheets and covers. He sat on the side of her bed, stroked her soft hair.

"Sleep tight, sweetheart. Do good in school tomorrow."

Leora didn't reply. She only stirred. Accorso tucked the sheets under her, bundling her up and kissed her forehead tenderly. Back in his bedroom he thought of ways of throwing his wife off the scent of his whoring. Before, she made passing comments about it, but lately it has been declaration of fact, and that bothered Accorso. He didn't want to lose his marriage, but neither did he want to stop his favorite hobby.

Last night, he went to the Crack of Dawn, Sheila 'Big Tit' Malone's whorehouse. He had asked to see Candy. Taking him by the hand she had taken him upstairs, disguising the fact that she was about to make a side deal. To keep Sheila clueless, he paid for an hour with the beautiful woman. All he wanted to do was explain to her his plan to bring her to Ateer. She was elated to go to the Pedrotti home for dinner and drinks. Candy, whose true name was Candace, explained to Accorso how secluded her life was being in this sweet-smelling, pastel silk and richly cushioned prison. She was surrounded by comfort and all the trappings of an easy life, but social things such as dinner parties or holiday feasts she never had the opportunity to attend. She could do with a movie now and then, but mostly it was work, and that meant spending days and nights in her bedroom. Just the thought of being considered as a guest in their homes was more than enough to make her day.

There was one important caveat, Accorso said, she had to roll Ateer over once or twice. Candy had no problem with that. Accorso slipped her some cash for herself since when he went downstairs, he would be paying Sheila for his time with her and Sheila would just give her a small cut, but she stopped him, grabbing at his arm as he jumped off her bed. His face was not flush enough to walk by Sheila, Candy noted. Before Accorso could question how or why, she had reached into his slacks, fished out his penis, and performed fellatio on him. After a knee buckling orgasm he staggered, pink faced, out of the house, kissing Sheila good night and leaving her a generous tip.

The good thing about coming home last night was that Daria was in bed asleep, and there was no need to take a shower to rid his body of the sweet, flowery smell of Candy's perfume. Although Candy's sexual performance still caused his members to tremble, flashing lightning up and down his spine.

But he had to do something. Daria appeared to be lingering with him, still caught in his orbit, but he feared she had already broken free. It was just that her flying away from him was so slow that she seemed to be standing still. However, something told him that she was lost to him, spinning away on a course that would take her to the deepest of space. Maybe if he had a few nights of sex with her she would get back in the pocket and stop dropping the hints. Women did not need sex like men did, so this as a solution could miss the mark, but it was a start. It was either that or money so that she could buy herself things to forget his dalliances.

He crawled into bed and turned off the light, waiting for Daria to come to bed. He knew what she would most likely do, and that was slowly reach into her underpants and stroke herself at her 'tiny spot.' However he would not know for certain because fatigue was faster, and sleep sucked him down before she got off the couch and came upstairs.

Detective Beakey stepped into Pyke's office and closed the door softly. Accorso looked up from the many memos of the day, uneasy. Beakey's stoic features and receding hairline made him look like a postal clerk. Accorso readied himself for his weird diction, it was flawless as if practiced in some special school.

"May I speak with you?" Beakey asked, standing at the door.

"Sure," Accorso motioned to the chair in front of his desk. Beakey came around and sat down, his features uptight, his jaws clenching as if he chewed on something stubborn.

"So," Accorso began, "whaddaya want?"

"I realized as I ran up and down this city chasing calls that you are in line for the sergeant's position and Pyke is just using this time to groom you for it. I don't stand a chance," he said.

"No, he's just putting me in charge because I have the most seniority, not because I'm deserving, neither that I want it."

"Are you going to tell me that if he asks you to take the position, you'd turn it down?"

"What if I told you that he's already talked to me about the position,"

"He did?"

Accorso nodded.

"And you turned him down?"

"Let's say he talked to me; I didn't get a chance to talk back."

"But he intends on giving you the position."

"He's thinking about it. He wanted to float it past me. I didn't bite."

"Question: why aren't you biting?"

Accorso thought about it. Never had he put his feelings about a promotion into words, or even thoughts. It was more instinctual, more visceral. "It's just not for me."

That wasn't the answer Beakey was looking for. He wanted something with dimensions, with edges that he could feel around for correctness, for veracity, all he got from Accorso was nebulousness. "That's it?"

"That's it."

Accorso watched Beakey deal with the answer. Finally, he hunched his shoulders and stood to leave.

"Beakey," Accorso said, halting him, "I'm Bomb Squad. I feel comfortable with walking up to a Devil Toy and dealing with it. I could never feel comfortable with sitting in a cage like this across the hall, pushing papers, going out when something crazy happens. I want to be on the front lines, Beakey. This," Accorso looked around at the walls of the office, "this is not for me."

Beakey had reached satisfiability.

"Take care, Fab," he left the office, leaving the door opened behind him.

END OF BOOK ONE

AUTHOR'S NOTES

*"...the wretched refuse of your teeming shore.
Send these, the homeless, tempest-tost to me...."*

EMMA LAZARUS "THE NEW COLOSSUS" (EXCERPT OF POEM AFFIXED TO THE BASE OF THE STATUE OF LIBERTY)

ORIGINS

New York was never a stranger to bombs.

The native American tribes of Manhattan were called the Manates. The Dutch found them to be difficult, dangerous, and contentious. Yet, they sold Manahatta, "The Hilly Island," for baubles and beads before leaving in 1626. From then on, the hilly island became a cultural magnet, an allure of sorts. Along with the Dutch came the native tribes that moved in, with and around the settlers, each bringing their cultural novelties with them. The Dutch were the very inception of the influx, the trickle before the flow.

Not long later, a little less than three centuries, Frédéric Auguste Bartholdi, the French sculptor breathed life into the Statue of Liberty and yet long before her dedication on October 28, 1886, where she was erected on Bedloe's Island (renamed Liberty Island in 1956), the doors to New York City were already open wide to immigrants. And these inviting 'doors' very quickly into floodgates. Distressing conditions overseas made living in certain areas of Europe intolerable for many, which over time caused an exodus to occur. The failure of necessary crops, land and job shortages, taxes and famine in many locales were more than enough motivation to emigrate. Individuals seeking personal freedoms or fleeing religious persecution also fled to American shores. Whichever was the case, an enormous migration of disparate ethnic groups swarmed the United States in pursuit of a new life with better opportunities and living conditions.

Despite the scores of entry points into the United States through several different Ports of Arrival, since individual states regulated their immigration into the United States, more than 70 percent of all immigrants entered the country through New York City. It was because of this enormous influx that the city was known as the "Golden Door."

In the late 1800s many immigrants arrived through the Castle Garden Depot near the tip of Manhattan, but it was quickly overwhelmed by the sheer number of immigrants, so in 1892 the federal government took over the entry process and an Immigration Processing Center opened on Ellis Island in New York harbor. By the latter parts of the 19th century the demographic of New York was composed of more than fifty nations, a literal city boiling with immigrants burgeoning at a rate of 20,000 a month.

Within these came a modest number of immigrants from differing locales in Italy, but as time marched on even their humble volume skyrocketed. In just fifteen years, 3,035,308 Italians had become part of the American population. Although most of this

AUTHOR'S NOTES

number were just immigrants like any other—in search of a better life in the New World—a small trickling of a criminal underclass entered in amongst them. Five thriving 'families' settled in New York, while a sixth one made northern New Jersey its home.

From the five in New York emerged a dark force of ex-cons and desperadoes that gave themselves dubious monikers to differentiate their tactics, their organized units, their leaders, and lieutenants. Names such as the Camorra, the Mafia, and the Black Hand that were quite familiar in the 'old country' began to make themselves known in Gotham. Back in the outlaw areas of Italy, at this time Sicily, dangerous men and organizations found the expanding opportunities in the New World desirable. In the old country they were known, had mechanisms in place to earn a dishonest living, either paying off the police or slipping from the slower ones—all these troubles and deals could be done away with in America where they could begin again with a clean slate.

To the objections of lawmakers and law enforcement, the most propitious element for these criminals was that the Immigration Laws in the New World were incredibly porous. It could even be said that it was lax to the dangers that were floating in by the scores in nearly every arriving ship bobbing in the harbor outside of Ellis Island.

The very beginning of the end for these criminal organizations came from a city street sweeper who at the time was found on the Manhattan Riverfront. The legendary Alexander S. "Clubber" Williams, walked by, stopped, and asked this fellow: "Why don't you join the police force?" Whatever Williams saw in this young man was probably an immutable skill and ability that some have for police work. What this young man had most of all, in spades, was not only youth—but vision.

This young man was Giuseppe "Joseph" Petrosino.

He was of medium height, stout, unassuming, far from a towering and charismatic figure of authority that one would believe would singlehandedly go after the growing cancer in the Italian community.

A community that found itself in a most dire predicament.

AUTHOR'S NOTES

The parasitic nature of this arriving criminal element attached itself to the law-abiding members of the Italian neighborhoods, largely the Sicilian businessmen, and began a timeworn scheme called the 'Protection Racket.'

Attacks such as kidnapping, assaults, and the destruction of property were on the menu for the profitable businessman once they started to receive letters from "Mano Nera," The Black Hand, sometimes smeared with blood, but consistently leveling threats against life and personal property. If some businesses did not pay up, they would find their stores or shops burned to the ground, windows shattered, or much worse—bombed completely out. Their modus operandi was simple: either the store owner, bank, or other business entity had to pay them a sum of money, or they would be faced with the destruction of their livelihood. The Black Hand would simply throw a stick of dynamite into the establishment and the resultant damage could, and most often did, cripple or destroy the business or bring loss of life.

Before long, large numbers of Italian businesses were being terrorized by bomb wielding criminals intent on either being subsidized by them or ruining them. The number of bombings in Italian neighborhoods continued to escalate at alarming rates. The public outcry forced the NYPD to act.

With Petrosino being assigned as Commanding Officer of the Italian Squad, starting at five or six detectives, he implored that he needed more. He begged for ten, over time he would command upwards to thirty or more men. His opponent? What was first thought of to be just a scattering of independent cells turned out to be 5,000 strong in New York, 30,000 members of the criminal element country wide. Petrosino hurled himself and his men against this hurricane of bomb throwing miscreants, even as the public uproar was beginning to demand "emergency measures against these criminals."

Lieutenant Petrosino would end up apprehending five men in 1908 just two years after the formation of the Italian squad,

AUTHOR'S NOTES

including the master bomb maker for the Black Hand. A year later his rabid chase for the Black Hand would find him across the Atlantic to Italy, where he would lose his life after being lured into Marina Square in Palermo. Although Petrosino would not topple the Black Hand in his day, he did set it upon a course that led it to its fateful end.

The Black Hand and other bomb-throwing evildoers were eventually vanquished, and the Italian squad went through several iterations over the years, changing its name many times as its mission altered. Its aims wove itself into the times around it. It became the Bomb and Radical Squad in 1920. In '31, the Radical Squad was excised from the Bomb Squad, taking enough men to reduce the now Bomb Squad once again to six men.

In '35, the Bomb Squad merged with the Forgery unit to become the Bomb and Forgery Squad. They analyzed hostile writings, thus bringing an end to a duplication of efforts.

Like a constantly changing chameleon, this squad changed with the environment, making it adaptable, resilient, versatile, and therefore a survivor.

And then on July 4th, 1940, it became something else.

ABOUT THE AUTHOR

Gregory Delaurentis was born in Brooklyn, New York and spent most of his life in the city, enjoying its highlights and history and because of this love, has written three previous fictional books, two about the NYPD and a third about a hotel/apartment in Gotham. He has an enduring love of the NYPD and has read several books about its form and function. After reading a compelling book about the Mad Bomber of New York, he wanted to retell the story, not through the bomber's eyes, but his impact on normal people and the city itself. This series of books are the culmination of over ten years of work, carefully laid out to enthrall the reader, detailing the complex environment surrounding the NYPD in the 1940s and 50s, the vice, the crime, the corruption, and its growing fears of the massive war growing in Europe followed by the demands of a madman.

f

ALSO BY GREGORY DELAURENTIS

SUSPICIOUS LOOKING PACKAGES SERIES

Suspicious Looking Packages: The Bomb Squad: A Crime Story

Book 2 Coming soon!

DARKNESS SERIES

Cover of Darkness

Edge of Darkness

STANDALONES

Home

www.ingramcontent.com/pod-product-compliance
Lightning Source LLC
Chambersburg PA
CBHW020529030426
42337CB00013B/787